A Tribute to Gleason Archer

A Tribute
to
Gleason Archer

edited by
Walter C. Kaiser, Jr.
and
Ronald F. Youngblood

MOODY PRESS
CHICAGO

Library of Congress Cataloging in Publication Data

A Tribute to Gleason Archer.

    Bibliography: p.
    Includes Index.
    1. Bible.   O.T.—Criticism, interpretation, etc.
2. Archer, Gleason Leonard, 1916-   . I. Archer,
Gleason Leonard, 1916-   . II. Kaiser, Walter C.
III. Youngblood, Ronald F.
BS1171.2.T75   1986   221.6   86-17967
ISBN 0-8024-8780-7

1 2 3 4 5 6 Printing / AF / Year 91 90 89 88 87 86

Printed in the United States of America

Contents

Part I

OLD TESTAMENT
CRITICAL METHODOLOGIES
ASSESSED

Part II

OLD TESTAMENT
HISTORICAL RESEARCH
APPRAISED

Part III

OLD TESTAMENT
EXEGETICAL CONCLUSIONS
APPLIED

Preface

Gleason Leonard Archer, Jr., is the epitome of the gentleman-scholar. One of us has had the privilege of being his student, and both of us have been honored to be his faculty colleagues. In every case the setting has been a theological seminary, for seminary education has all but monopolized the professional career of our good friend and mentor for the past thirty-five years.

Academic credentials, brilliant intellect, unparalleled linguistic skills, disciplined life-style, diligent work habits—Gleason possesses all of these and more beside. Unfortunately, they are the only aspects of his background and character that many people associate with him. We too could expatiate on them at well-deserved length and with suitable awe. But we would prefer to portray another side of the man by relating a few of the myriad impressions that come readily to mind whenever we think about him.

Who, for example, could ever forget his delightful seminary-senior spring banquet talk delivered over thirty years ago entitled "Give Romance a Chance in the Manse"? How about the time he shouted down the hall to a student bewildered by the intricacies of Gardiner's *Grammar*, "If you don't learn hieroglyphics, you'll never be able to preach from the book of Exodus"? Where can you find another man who will take the time to help you purchase a World War II silver German coin as a souvenir for your son who is recuperating from serious surgery? How do you take the measure of a consummate scholar who, during a two-week marathon series of important Bible-translation sessions, never once even thinks of trying to usurp the committee-chairman responsibilities of a former student fifteen years his junior?

Gleason, we and our coauthors are delighted to honor you with this modest volume. We do so in full recognition of your international stature as a scholar, teacher, preacher, apologist, defender of the faith, and much more. We also do so with love and esteem, grateful to have known you not only as a friend and colleague but also as a stalwart and devoted servant of Jesus Christ. We wish nothing but God's richest blessings on you, Sandy, and your family for many happy years to come.

Oh yes, one more thing: *We* should look so great if and when we become septuagenarians!

WALTER C. KAISER, JR.
RONALD F. YOUNGBLOOD

Abbreviations

AB	*Anchor Bible*
AbrN	*Abr-Nahrain*
AcOr	*Acta orientalia*
AHW	*Akkadisches Handwörterbuch,* W. von Soden
ANET	*Ancient Near Eastern Texts,* ed. J. B. Pritchard
ANESTP	*Ancient Near East Supplementary Texts and Pictures,* ed. J. B. Pritchard
AOAT	*Alter Orient und Altes Testament*
ARM	*Archives Royales de Mari*
ASV	*American Standard Version*
ATD	*Das Alte Testament Deutsch*
AUSS	*Andrews University Seminary Studies*
BAR	*Biblical Archaeology Review*
BA	*Biblical Archaeologist*
BASOR	*Bulletin of the American Schools of Oriental Research*
BDB	*A Hebrew and English Lexicon of the Old Testament,* F. Brown, S. R. Driver, and C. A. Briggs
BHS	*Biblia hebraica stuttgartensia*
BibOr	*Biblica et orientalia*
Bib	*Biblica*
CAD	*Chicago Assyrian Dictionary*
CBQ	*Catholic Biblical Quarterly*
BibSac	*Bibliotheca Sacra*
CAH	*Cambridge Ancient History*
GAG	*Grundriss der Akkadischen Grammatik,* W. von Soden

GKC	*Gesenius' Hebrew Grammar,* ed. E. Kautzsch, trans. A. E. Cowley
HUCA	*Hebrew Union College Annual*
ICC	*International Critical Commentary*
IDB	*Interpreter's Dictionary of the Bible,* ed. G. A. Buttrick et al.
IDBSup	*Interpreter's Dictionary of the Bible,* supplementary volume, ed. K. Crim
IEJ	*Israel Exploration Journal*
Int	*Interpretation*
ISBE (rev.)	*International Standard Bible Encyclopedia,* ed. G. W. Bromiley
JANESCU	*Journal of the Ancient Near Eastern Society of Columbia University*
JAOS	*Journal of the American Oriental Society*
JB	*Jerusalem Bible*
JBL	*Journal of Biblical Literature*
JETS	*Journal of the Evangelical Theological Society*
JNES	*Journal of Near Eastern Studies*
JPSV	*Jewish Publication Society Version*
JQR	*The Jewish Quarterly Review*
JTS	*The Journal of Theological Studies*
KB	*Hebräisches und aramäisches Lexicon zum Alten Testament,* L. Köhler and W. Baumgartner
KJV	*King James Version*
LXX	Septuagint
MT	Masoretic Text
NAB	*New American Bible*
NASB	*New American Standard Bible*
NEB	*New English Bible*
NIV	*New International Version*
NKJV	*New King James Version*
P Oxy	*Papyrus Oxyrhynchus*
PEQ	*Palestine Exploration Quarterly*
PTR	*Presbyterian Theological Review*
Or	*Orientalia*
RSV	*Revised Standard Version*
SBLDS	*Society of Biblical Literature Dissertation Series*
SOTI	*A Survey of Old Testament Introduction* (rev. ed.), Gleason L. Archer, Jr.

TB	*Tyndale Bulletin*
TDNT	*Theological Dictionary of the New Testament,* ed. G. W. Bromiley
TDOT	*Theological Dictionary of the Old Testament,* ed. G. T. Botterweck and H. Ringgren, trans. J. T. Willis, G. W. Bromiley, and D. A. Green
TEV	*Today's English Version*
ThR	*Theologische Rundschau*
TSFB	*Theological Students' Fellowship Bulletin*
TWOT	*Theological Wordbook of the Old Testament,* ed. R. L. Harris, Gleason L. Archer, Jr., and B. K. Waltke
UT	*Ugaritic Textbook,* Cyrus Gordon
Vg	Vulgate
VT	*Vetus Testamentum*
VTSup	*Vetus Testamentum,* supplements
WTJ	*Westminster Theological Journal*
ZAW	*Zeitschrift für die alttestamentliche Wissenschaft*
ZPEB	*Zondervan Pictorial Encyclopedia of the Bible,* ed. Merrill F. Tenney

Part I

Old Testament
Critical Methodologies
Assessed

BRUCE K. WALTKE (Ph. D., Harvard
University) is professor of Old Testa-
ment at Westminster Theological
Seminary, Philadelphia.

1

Oral Tradition

Bruce K. Waltke

Form criticism, tradition criticism, and canonical criticism are all based
on at least two principles: (1) that most of the literature of the Old Testament had a long oral prehistory before being written down, and (2) that
during its oral stage, the "literature" was often transposed into new settings with new meanings. Source critics think that much of the biblical
material was transmitted orally at local sanctuaries by tradents who preserved, reinterpreted, reformulated, and supplemented Israel's diverse traditions and theological heritage.

H. S. Nyberg stated the first conviction in a famous quote:

> Transmission in the East is seldom exclusively written; it is chiefly *oral*
> in character. The living speech plays in the East from ancient times to
> the present a greater role than the written presentation. Almost every
> written work in the Orient went through a longer or shorter oral trans-
> mission in its earliest history, and also even after it is written down the
> oral transmission remains the normal form in the preservation and use
> of the work.[1]

More popularly and less guardedly Gene M. Tucker expressed the consen-
sus of form critics on this point as follows: "All ancient . . . cultures had a
body of oral 'literature'—that is, folklore—long before they developed written records and literature."[2]

After tracing the development of scholarly opinion regarding oral tradition from Hermann Gunkel through the views of Scandinavian scholars such as H. S. Nyberg, Ivan Engnell, Harris Birkeland, Sigmund Mowinckel, and Eduard Nielsen,[3] Walter E. Rast expressed the second principle of source critics who attempt to reconstruct the history of a text even in its oral stage: "Such study shows that the messages of the Old Testament texts have experienced development over long periods of time. Different generations have taken them up, either in oral or written form, and transposed them into fresh settings and understandings."[4]

These convictions of form critics and their successors profoundly influence the way in which one regards the historical accuracy of the Bible and its meaning. Concerning the former, it stands to reason that if the "literature" in its oral stage was flexible and reworked like putty, it contains only a kernel of historical accuracy. As William F. Albright noted,

> In recent decades there has been a steady increase of the use of aetiology (the analysis of stories explaining ancient names or practices) to identify legendary accretions in orally transmitted material. The discovery and application of the method of form criticism, especially by H. Gunkel, M. Dibelius, and their followers, have given a great impetus to the utilization of the aetiological method, which has now reached a point where its leading exponents are inclined to deny the historicity of nearly all early stories of both the Old and the New Testaments.[5]

In spite of Albright's caveat that this view has gone too far, it still prevails. Tucker's words are representative:

> Sagas usually tell us more about the life and time of the period in which they were circulated and written down than they do about the events they mean to describe. A careful form critical and traditio-historical analysis . . . can help the historian to distinguish between the old and the new and the historically reliable and the unreliable in those sagas.[6]

Also, the notion that Israel's sacred heritage was handed down in a fluid and complicated prehistory raises a whole complex of problems about authorial meaning. For if tradents reworked and reformulated the "literature" to meet changing needs, it stands to reason that many meanings lie buried within it. The canonical critic's view that only the final meaning of a text in the Jewish canon matters relieves this problem to some extent. Nevertheless, one is still left with the uneasy conscience that the text's original meaning(s) to the people of God has/have been deliberately obfuscated by the final redactor.

The common teaching that the literature of the Bible has passed through a long and often complicated oral prehistory must be critically appraised for the sake of both true knowledge and sound doctrine. In this study I aim to debunk both of the principles outlined above. With pleasure I dedicate it to my friend, Gleason L. Archer, who has advanced sound knowledge and doctrine through his many publications and his teaching.

The first and major part of the study attempts to demonstrate that proper evidence (that is, evidence from the ancient Near East) leads to the conviction that the biblical literature had a short oral prehistory and was transmitted conservatively. In the second and much more brief section the goal is to show that even more inferential evidence (that is, evidence from shortly after the time of the Old Testament's completion at about 400 B.C. and/or evidence from neighboring non-Semitic-speaking peoples) does not suggest that oral traditions were transmitted in a fluid state. Finally, the question will be addressed as to whether the prepatriarchal narratives in Genesis, which contain stories of happenings before the invention of writing, depend on oral tradition. If it can be established that oral tradition played a minor role in the transmission of the text and not in the way envisioned by men such as Albrecht Alt and Gerhard von Rad and their schools, this will help both to restore more confidence in the Old Testament's reliability and to clarify its meaning.

ORAL TRADITION IN THE ANCIENT NEAR EAST

To decide whether the literature of the Old Testament was changed by tradents over a long period of oral transmission, it will be instructive to turn to the cultures of the ancient Near East, which undoubtedly influenced all of the Old Testament's literary genres: to Ebla in northern Syria (c. 2350 B.C.); then successively to Mesopotamia, whose coherent culture can be traced with confidence for over two millennia until it was dealt what proved to be a fatal blow by Alexander the Great (c. 330 B.C.); to the Hittites (1450 to 1250 B.C.); to Ugarit (c. 1400 B.C.); to the Egyptian culture, whose literatures stretch from about 2500 to 500 B.C.; and finally to the Northwest Semites. In this last connection the Hebrews will be considered, including the internal evidence of the Old Testament itself. In this wide-ranging survey a single question is asked: "Did the people under investigation preserve their cultural heritage through an oral tradition subject to alteration or through written texts precisely with a view that its heritage not be corrupted?" If the evidence for the former is negative, there is no reason to accept the first principles, along with the historical and exegetical difficulties entailed, on which form, tradition, and canonical critics construct their methods.

EBLA

According to Giovanni Pettinato, the texts unearthed from the royal archives of Ebla include the following types: economic and administrative texts (regarding the various branches of industry, such as metals, wood, and textiles), historical and historical-juridical texts, lexical texts ("scientific" lists of animals in general, fishes and birds in particular; lists of professions and personal names; of objects in stone, metal, and wood; various lexical texts; grammatical texts with verbal paradigms; and finally bilingual vocabularies in Sumerian and Eblaite), and true literary texts (myths, epic tales, hymns to divinities, incantations, rituals, and collections of proverbs).[7] This ancient city, which antedates the Hebrew patriarchs by three to five centuries and Moses by about a millennium, was highly literate and preserved its culture and heritage in writing. So far as they have been translated and published, the Ebla texts make no mention of oral tradition or tradents. But much still remains to be deciphered.

MESOPOTAMIA

In Mesopotamia there is much evidence that the Akkadian culture conservatively transmitted its heritage in writing. By comparing collections of Sumerian proverbs that achieved canonical status among the Akkadians as early as c. 1500 B.C. with later collections dated to the Neo-Babylonian period (c. 600 B.C.), it can be shown that they were transmitted in writing with relatively little modification.[8]

The great Akkadian creation epic *Enuma elish* was probably composed during the time of Hammurapi (c. 1700 B.C.), and its earliest extant copy, clearly not the original, is dated only one hundred years later.

The lawcodes of Lipit-Ishtar, Eshnunna, Hammurapi, and others antedate Moses by centuries. Moreover, they promised blessing to those who preserved the written laws and threatened judgment against those who altered them. The stele containing Lipit-Ishtar's lawcode reads: "May he who will not commit any evil deed with regard to it, who will not damage my handiwork, who will [not] erase its inscription, who will not write his own name upon it—be presented with life and breath of long days.''[9] The epilogue to Hammurapi's code is similar:

> If that man heeded my words which I wrote, on my stela,
> and did not rescind my law,
> has not distorted my words,
> did not alter my statutes,
> may Shamash make that man reign. . . .
>
> If that man did not heed my words . . .
> and disregarded my curses, . . .
> but has abolished the law which I enacted,
> has distorted my words,
> has altered my statutes, . . .
> may mighty Anum . . .
> deprive him of the glory of sovereignty . . .
> the disappearance of his name and memory from the land.[10]

According to Otto Weber, it was the rule among the Akkadians that only an agreement fixed in writing was juridically valid.[11]

Hymns from the early Sumerian period (c. 1900 B.C.) are also found in Mesopotamia. What arrests our attention about them here is that, though they were intended to be sung at cultic centers, they were written down. In fact their technical terms, probably related to their liturgical use, have not as yet been deciphered by Sumerologists, even as the same kind of notices in the biblical psalms cannot at present be deciphered by Hebraists.[12]

Letters were read from written texts, as evidenced by letters from Mari. These typically state: "Your tablet which you did send forth, I have heard."[13]

Representing the historical literary genre in Mesopotamia we have the famous Sumerian king lists and the later and equally famous Assyrian annals. Representatives of the religious genre include rituals, incantations, and descriptions of festivals. We may infer that events referred to in this literature that occurred before the invention of writing were transmitted by word of mouth, but we cannot reconstruct its nature. After writing evolved to communicate effectively, there is no indication that a fluid oral transmission alone was the principal means of preserving memory in Mesopotamia. In this literature there is no mention of either tradents or oral tradition. Eduard Nielsen, contending for oral tradition in the Near East, conceded: "The fact that religious and epic texts of major importance in the high cultures of the Ancient Near East were ordinarily put into written form has already been stressed in the case of Egyptian literature. The evidence points in a similar direction in the case of Mesopotamian literature."[14]

What evidence is there for oral tradition after the invention and evolution of writing? The best Nielsen can offer against G. Widengren's contention that texts were always written is one example, which may introduce a minor correction. A colophon in a hymn reads: "Written from the scholar's dictation, the old edition I have not seen."[15] In fact, however, Nielsen's one exception actually proves Widengren's rule. Commenting on this text, J. Laessoe observed: "It would seem to appear that oral tradition was only reluctantly relied upon, and in this particular case only because for some reason or other an original written document was not available."[16]

The situation reflected by this colophon differs *toto caelo* from that supposed by source critics who presuppose a long and often complex oral tradition. The scribe is a faithful copyist, not a tradent manipulating his heritage.

There is evidence, however, that redaction of older written sources into later ones did occur. As Donald J. Wiseman pointed out,

> Tigay has shown that redactors completed the remoulding of the earlier Sumerian poems into one "Gilgamesh" tradition (ca. 1800 B.C.), about the same time as the Hittites made a summary of 5 tablets of Gilgamesh into one; and about the same time as the Kassite period of Babylonia (1540-1250) when scribes began copying the Gilgamesh, and other epics, in a traditional way which was to hand them on virtually unchanged for more than a thousand years.[17]

Some texts show that the written tradition was to be accompanied with memorization for oral recital. Nielsen called attention to the following: (1) from the Irra myth: "The scribe who learns this text by heart escapes the enemy"; (2) from Ashurbanipal's prayer to Shamash: "Whosoever shall learn this text [by heart and] glorify the gods"; (3) from tablet 7 of *Enuma elish*: "The sage and the learned shall together ponder [them], father shall tell [of them] to son and teach [them to] him."[18] These texts, however, do not argue for a long and complicated oral prehistory before the material in view was written down. Rather they suggest that oral recitation accompanied the written texts. R. K. Harrison rightly commented:

Modern scholars have largely misunderstood the purpose and function of oral transmission in the ancient Near East. The firm tradition of the Mosaic period, as well as of ancient peoples other than the Hebrews, was that any events of importance were generally recorded in written form quite soon after they had taken place. . . . The principal purpose of oral transmission was the dissemination of the pertinent information. . . . It is entirely fallacious to assume . . . that an oral form of a narrative was the necessary and normal precursor of the written stage. There can be little doubt that in many cases both oral and written traditions existed side by side for lengthy periods.[19]

Bendt Alster explored the possibility that, because poetic lines turn up in the same form in several Sumerian poems, these may be traditional formulas of an oral tradition.[20] In fact, however, traditional formulas may point to oral composition, not to a long and flexible oral tradition, and there is no direct evidence about how such texts were composed. Ruth Finnegan argued against any fundamental, qualitative difference between oral and written literature: "We can only discuss a continuum rather than a distinction between oral and written literature."[21]

In sum, from Mesopotamia there is evidence of redaction from earlier written sources into later complexes followed by a conservative transmission of the literary achievement with an accompanying oral recital, but there is no evidence of a flexible oral tradition.

HITTITES

The Hittite literature and history are mostly known from the archives recovered from its capital at Hattusilis (modern Boğaz-köy). These archives yielded texts similar to those encountered elsewhere in the ancient Near East. Its international suzerainty treaties, which are remarkably parallel to the book of Deuteronomy, according to George Mendenhall,[22] Klaus Baltzer,[23] and Meredith Kline,[24] enjoyed canonical status. A treaty between Suppiluliumas and Mattiwaza contains this provision against change:

In the Mitanni land (a duplicate) has been deposited before Tessub. . . . At regular intervals shall they read it in the presence of the king. . . . Whoever will remove this tablet from before Tessub . . . and put in a hidden

place, if he breaks it or causes anyone else to change the wording of the
tablet—at the conclusion of this treaty we have called the gods to be assembled and the gods of the contracting parties to be present, to listen
and to serve as witnesses.[25]

In sum, the Hittites, like the other great peoples of the ancient Near East,
committed their important literature to sure writing instead of to an un-
sure oral tradition.

UGARIT

Richard E. Whitaker discovered that 82 percent of the language of the
Ugaritic poems is formulaic. This high frequency of formulae and formulaic structures led him to suppose that "we are dealing here with an orally
created poetry."[26] But once again it is necessary to note that he is talking
about oral composition, not about a long and complicated prehistory before its transposition to writing. The fact is that the peoples of ancient
Ugarit wrote down their hymns and myths celebrating their nature deities
and recited them at their sanctuaries. Nothing in them suggests that oral
recitation existed apart from written texts or that it had priority over the
written witnesses to their beliefs. It seems more plausible to suppose that
these potent, magical words were considered as unalterable and written
down either at the time of composition or shortly thereafter.

EGYPT

From Egypt have come numerous texts of many of the literary genres
represented in the Bible. These texts demonstrate that Egyptian scribes attempted to preserve their heritage in writing as accurately as possible. Albright wrote:

> The prolonged and intimate study of the many scores of thousands of
> pertinent documents from the ancient Near East proves that sacred and
> profane documents were copied with greater care than is true of scribal
> copying in Graeco-Roman times. Even documents which were never in-
> tended to be seen by other human eyes, such as mortuary texts, manu-
> scripts of the Book of the Dead, and magical texts, are copied so that we
> can nearly always read them without difficulty if the state of preservation
> permits.[27]

Kenneth A. Kitchen called attention to the colophon of a text dated c. 1400 B.C. in which a scribe boasted: "[This book] is completed from its beginning to its end, having been copied, revised, compared, and verified sign by sign."[28]

Is there any evidence of oral tradition among the Egyptians? B. van de Walle[29] laid an excellent foundation for understanding the development of textual criticism of Egyptian literary works. Askel Volten in his editions of the Teaching of *Any*[30] and *Insinger*[31] laid down the following basic principles concerning the main types of error to be encountered: (1) entirely graphic error, (2) auricular errors, (3) slips of memory, and (4) the usual unintentional slips due to carelessness. G. Burkard[32] took issue with Volten's thesis that by far the majority of errors were *Hoerfehler,* "mistakes of hearing," but argued rather that the most common type of mistake, apart from simple carelessness, arose from copying directly from a written text and that the next largest group of errors was caused by writing texts from memory. This procedure led to omission of verses, transpositions of maxims or lines, the substitution of synonyms, and on occasion the intermingling and confusion of maxims or pericopes. Such scribal errors do not provide a foundation for building a theory that the Egyptians transmitted their heritage in a pliable oral tradition. All three scholars describe these changes as errors in *the writing of the texts,* assuming that the scribe intended to preserve and transmit the written heritage in writing and that the material was memorized for personal edification and dissemination. By contrast the hypothetical tradents imagined by modern source critics do not accidentally change the text through faulty memory that accompanies the written tradition but intentionally alter it, sometimes drastically, to keep the traditions contemporary with changing historical conditions.

NORTHWEST SEMITIC

Apart from the Ugaritic texts, treated above, and the Old Testament itself, the literature from the Northwest Semitic cultures is poorly preserved, probably because of the perishable nature of materials other than clay and rock in a hostile climate. What evidence exists suggests widespread literacy in this part of the ancient Near East due to the invention of the alphabet based on the acrophonic principle at c. 1600 B.C. The Proto-Sinaitic inscriptions (c. 1475 B.C.) represent the written prayers of Semites enslaved by the Egyptians,[33] giving us strong reason to think that Abraham's descendants, though lowly slaves in Egypt, were literate.

The Old Testament witness about the manner of its transmission comports favorably with what has been found elsewhere in the ancient Near East, namely, that its sacred literature was transmitted in writing with oral dissemination. Its authors appeal to literary sources: "The Book of Songs" (3 Kings 8:53, LXX); "The Book of the Upright" (8:13); "The Book of the Wars of Yahweh" (Josh. 10:13; 2 Sam. 1:18); "The Diaries of the Kings" (Kings and Chronicles). The Hebrew Scriptures represent its laws as having been written down in books at the time of composition (Ex. 24:7; Deut. 31:9; Josh. 24:25-27; 1 Sam. 10:25) that must not be changed (Deut. 4:2; 12:32). The prophets refer to the law as a written document (Hos. 8:12). And to judge from Isaiah 8:16 and Jeremiah 36, the originally oral messages of the prophets were written down shortly after their delivery, exactly in the same way as happened in the case of the Quran (as we shall see shortly).

Even Moses' song was written down at the time of its original recitation (Deut. 31:19, 30). From this evidence may we not assume that the same was true of other songs mentioned in the Hebrew Scriptures (cf. Num. 21:17 and elsewhere)?

By comparing the Ugaritic poetry and the Amarna glosses (c. 1400 B.C.) as his *terminus a quo* for the earliest forms of Hebrew poetry and Amos and Micah as his *terminus ad quem* for the later standard forms, David A. Robertson concluded (with the qualification that each one contains standard forms) that Exodus 15 is unqualifiedly early and that Deuteronomy 32, Judges 5, 2 Samuel 22 (Ps. 18), Habbakuk 3, and Job are early.[34] Even if they were passed on through the generations by word of mouth, they were not drastically reformulated.

A man must write a bill of divorce (Deut. 24:3); kings had secretaries to assist them in their writing (2 Sam. 8:14). According to Judges 8:14, a young man wrote down for Gideon the names of the seventy-seven officials of Succoth. This text assumes the literacy of Israel's youth.

To be sure, the law was to be memorized and recited orally (Ex. 12:24-26; Deut. 6:6, 20-25; Josh. 1:8; Ps. 1:2), as were the proverbs (e.g. Prov. 22:18) and Israel's sacred history (cf. Ps. 44:1), but we must not pit this oral activity against a stable written tradition. The evidence from the surrounding countries strongly suggests that the two kinds of tradition complemented one another: the written to preserve Israel's religious treasure, the oral to disseminate it.

By comparing synoptic passages in the Bible, Helmer Ringgren demonstrated that variants crept into the text in the same ways as Volten and van de Walle uncovered in Egypt.[35] But he too speaks of them as "mistakes," assuming that copyists were attempting to preserve the tradition rather than that tradents were at work deliberately reformulating and re-presenting it. In sum, these changes introduced by copyists are both qualitatively and quantitatively different from that supposed by critics who base their theories on a protracted and complicated oral tradition.

Robert C. Culley thought that the formulaic language found in the Psalms pointed to their origin in a tradition of oral formulaic composition. He wisely left open the question, however, of whether any of the present psalms were originally oral compositions.[36] In any case his study pertains to oral composition, not to a pliable oral tradition, and as such has no more bearing on the issues raised in this essay than Whitaker's study on the Ugaritic poems.

ORAL TRADITION OUTSIDE THE ANCIENT NEAR EAST

Obviously analogies from the literature of non-Semitic speaking peoples and/or from a time later than the composition of the Old Testament do not carry as much weight in deciding the issue addressed as analogies from the ancient Near Eastern literatures or from the Old Testament itself. Nevertheless, a consideration of this data is instructive.

HOMER AND THE CLASSICS

According to Milman Parry, Homer composed poetic epics for easy oral recital in a preliterate society.[37] Once again, however, it is important to note that the topic here is oral composition in contrast to a complex oral transmission. Furthermore, according to Robert B. Coote, the material in Homer is altogether different in type and extent from that of the Bible,[38] and Parry's evidence for oral composition in Homer is not applicable in the case of the Bible. Coote wrote: "None of the characteristics . . . which make Parry's designation of repeated lines and phrases in Homer as oral formulas by analogy with the Yugoslav oral formula so compelling is to be found in the Hebrew tradition."[39]

Some classicists are inclined to visualize a period of oral transmission in pre-Homeric times.[40] It is beyond my competence to make a judgment here. The fact that pupils were expected to memorize Homer and Virgil in classical antiquity is parallel to the use of oral tradition in the ancient Near East.

THE JEWS AND THE TALMUD

The Mishna and Gemara were both composed and transmitted orally for some period of time. But it may be supposed that these interpretations of the written laws found in the Bible were regarded at first during their oral stage as qualitatively different from the Scriptures themselves. In fact, they were probably put into writing only after they achieved an authoritative status among the Jews.

THE HINDUS AND THE RIG-VEDA

The Rig-veda is the most striking example of a religious tradition passed on by word of mouth over centuries, from probably before 1200 B.C. to no earlier than about the fifth century B.C. The oral transmission of the later Vedas and the Brahmanas also embraced centuries. This manner of preserving religious literature in the environs of the Indus River stands in striking contrast to what is known of the civilizations along the Nile and Tigris-Euphrates rivers. But even this more remote evidence does not support the second principle of modern source critics that the text underwent complex reformulations. Projecting back from the modern Hindu practice where thousands of Brahmins still accurately learn the Rig-veda by heart (153,826 words!)[41] to the earlier centuries, it may be supposed that those reciting this tradition aimed not to change it. And, of course, what is disconcerting about modern source critics is not so much their theory of oral transmission as their presumption that an oral tradition in the case of the Bible entailed a complex development of the literature, calling into question both its historical reliability and the clarity of authorial intention.

THE ARABS AND THE QURAN

Arabic literatures provide us with a much closer analogy to the Hebrew Scriptures. South Arabic inscriptions, which are notoriously difficult to date, do show that even bedouin were literate. From a much later period Widengren demonstrated that Muhammad not only contributed directly or indirectly to putting the Quran into writing but even made some interpolations in the text.[42] Regarding the role of oral tradition in the composition of the Quran, Widengren wrote: "We are confronted with the fact that in the earliest Islamic period the first generation were the collectors of traditions."[43] The situation in Islam seems very similar to that of Christianity: Within the generation or two that witnessed Jesus Christ, written testimonies about Him were made.

Regarding pre-Islamic poetry, Bridget Connelly pointed to an article by Monroe arguing that on the basis of formulaic expressions these poems were composed for oral recitation.[44] Once again, oral composition is not directly relevant to the present study. However, Mary C. Bateson's investigation of five pre-Islamic Arabic odes rejected even this possibility.[45]

OLD ICELANDIC AND SERBO-CROATIAN

The best evidence for an oral tradition such as that proposed by modern source critics comes from Indo-European peoples of a much later time, especially from Old Icelandic (c. A.D. 1300). Here one finds a mighty priesthood trained in the oral transmission of their religious heritage. But the objections to founding a theory on this sort of evidence ought not to require demonstration. In fact, to make an appeal to it appears to be an act of desperation and actually weakens the case. Widengren asked:

> Is it not queer to observe that in order to prove the predominant role of oral tradition among such a Semitic people in antiquity as the Hebrews all real evidence from their closely related neighbors, the Arabs, has been left out of consideration . . . whereas evidence from all kinds of Indo-European peoples was adduced, so that even the old Icelanders were called upon to render their service in which case neither the "great interval of time" nor that of space seems to have exercised any discouraging effect?![46]

The field study of Parry and Albert Lord on a living oral tradition of Yugoslav narrative poetry showed that the poets did not memorize their traditional poems but freshly created them in each performance.[47] But the objections to applying their study to the Bible are obvious. First, the date is not comparable. Coote wrote: "The severest obstacle to the application of the theory to the OT is the lack of verse analogous in type and extent to that of Homer or Yugoslavia."[48] Second, the biblical literature was composed and received as the inspired Word of God, and therefore it would have been treasured as authoritative at the time of composition and less likely to be changed. Finally, the evidence is too far afield in time and culture to be convincing.

CONCLUSION

Having examined the literatures of the ancient Near East and other literatures as well, no evidence has been found in any Semitic cultures, including Islam, that tradents molded an oral tradition to meet changing situations over the centuries. John van Seters hit the nail on the head when he said, "Gunkel, Alt, von Rad, Noth, Westermann, and others . . . have not made a case for regarding the traditions of Genesis as . . . deriving from an oral base."[49]

THE SOURCE OF THE PATRIARCHAL NARRATIVES

On first reflection it may seem necessary to assume that the stories in Genesis about the patriarchs must have been handed down orally. William Sanford LaSor, David Allan Hubbard, and Frederic W. Bush assume that the patriarchal narratives (that is, family history) were handed down primarily by oral tradition. They see no objection to the hypothesis that the narratives were put into writing in Moses' time.[50] The case for oral tradition becomes most strong, however, for the stories in the first eleven chapters of Genesis, some of which must antedate by centuries the invention of writing. Though admitting that Israel's memory of the patriarchs was handed down by means of an uncertain oral tradition, Gleason Archer nevertheless pointed in the right direction in this statement: "The legacy of faith was handed down through the millennia from Adam to Moses in oral form, for the most part, but the final written form into which Moses cast it must have been especially superintended by the Holy Spirit in order to insure its divine trustworthiness."[51]

The only reliable information we have about the antediluvian and postdiluvian patriarchs is not from oral tradition but from the written records preserved in the canon. Furthermore, it is gratuitous to assume that the anonymous author of Genesis—and all biblical narrators are anonymous—depended on oral tradition for his information. The truth is, as Robert Alter pointed out so brilliantly, that every biblical narrator is omniscient.[52] They know the thoughts of God in heaven and characterize the earthly subjects not by adjectives, such as the "wily Jacob," but by telling us their most private thoughts and conversations. Such storytellers are not dependent on oral tradition. Did man originally learn either about the creation of the cosmos as recorded in Genesis 1, assigned by literary critics to P, or about the creation of man out of the earth in Genesis 2, assigned by the same critics to J, from oral tradition? In the final analysis the creation stories derive either from creative. imagination or from revelation. The Bible and Spirit affirm that we are dealing not with prose fiction but with true knowledge, and we have no reason to think that it was not revealed to the storyteller himself who inscripturated it in Holy Writ. The biblical authors are surrogates for God and as such are not dependent on oral tradition. That is not to deny that the successive patriarchs knew God's earlier promises to their fathers, and there is nothing objectionable in thinking that the author of Genesis, who prefers to remain anonymous, used them. It is inapposite, however, to think that he (or any other of the omniscient narrators of the Bible) was dependent on oral tradition. Undoubtedly the successive patriarchs knew antecedent revelation, but we do not know the extent or form of it.

It is difficult to verify or refute the claim that oral tradition lies behind the patriarchal narratives referring to events before the invention of writing. Whatever be the types and extent of sources that our omniscient narrator may have used and the manner in which he may have used them, the important point is that God's inspired spokesman told the sacred stories in his own way. For this reason there is no reason to doubt their historicity or to be uncertain about his meaning.[53]

NOTES

1. H. S. Nyberg, *Studien zum Hoseabuche* (Uppsala: Lundequistska, 1935), p. 7 (translation mine, italics his).
2. Gene M. Tucker, *Form Criticism of the Old Testament* (Philadelphia: Fortress, 1971), p. 17.
3. For a full survey of the work of Scandinavian scholars see Douglas A. Knight, *Rediscovering the Traditions of Israel*, SBLDS 9 (Missoula, Mont.: Scholars, 1973).
4. Walter E. Rast, *Tradition History and the Old Testament* (Philadelphia: Fortress, 1972), p. 18.
5. William F. Albright, *From Stone Age to Christianity* (Garden City, N.Y.: Doubleday, 1957), p. 70.
6. Tucker, *Form Criticism*, p. 20. For a survey of literature treating the relationship between historicity and oral tradition, see Jan Vansina, *Oral Tradition: A Study in Historical Methodology* (London: Routledge and Kegan Paul, 1965).
7. Giovanni Pettinato, *The Archives of Ebla: An Empire Inscribed on Clay* (Garden City, N.Y.: Doubleday, 1981), pp. 42-48.
8. Bruce K. Waltke, "The Book of Proverbs and Ancient Wisdom Literature," *BibSac* 136 (1979):221-38.
9. *ANET,* p. 161.
10. Ibid., pp. 178-79.
11. Otto Weber, *Die Literatur der Babylonier und Assyrer* (Leipzig: J. C. Hinrichs, 1970), p. 249.
12. Samuel N. Kramer, *The Sumerians* (Chicago: U. of Chicago, 1963), p. 207.
13. Cf. *ARM,* 1. 6:5; 9:5; and others.
14. Eduard Nielsen, *Oral Tradition: A Modern Problem in Old Testament Introduction* (London: SCM, 1954), p. 28.
15. Ibid., pp. 28-29.
16. Jorgen Laessoe, *Literary and Oral Tradition in Ancient Mesopotamia* (1953), p. 205.
17. Donald J. Wiseman, "Israel's Literary Neighbours in the 13th Century B.C.," *Journal of Northwest Semitic Languages* 5 (1977):82.
18. Nielsen, *Oral Tradition*, pp. 19-20.

19. R. K. Harrison, *Introduction to the Old Testament* (Grand Rapids: Eerdmans, 1969), pp. 209-10.

20. Bendt Alster, *Dumuzi's Dream: Aspects of Oral Poetry in a Sumerian Myth* (Copenhagen: Akademisk Forlag).

21. Ruth Finnegan, *Oral Literature in Africa* (Oxford: Clarendon, 1970), p. 61, cited by R. C. Culley, "Oral Tradition and the OT: Some Recent Discussion," *Oral Tradition and Old Testament Studies, Semeia* 5 (1976). The title of this issue of *Semeia* may cause confusion by confounding oral composition with oral tradition. Evidence for the first is not evidence for the second as that term has been traditionally understood in Old Testament studies.

22. George E. Mendenhall, *Law and Covenant in Israel and the Ancient Near East* (Pittsburgh: Biblical Colloquium, 1955).

23. Klaus Baltzer, *The Covenant Formulary* (Oxford: Blackwell, 1971).

24. Meredith Kline, *Treaty of the Great King* (Grand Rapids: Eerdmans, 1963).

25. *ANET*, p. 205.

26. Richard E. Whitaker, "A Formulaic Analysis of Ugaritic Poetry." Ph.D. dissertation, Harvard University, 1969.

27. Albright, *Stone Age*, p. 79.

28. Kenneth A. Kitchen, *Ancient Orient and Old Testament* (Chicago: InterVarsity, 1966), p. 140.

29. Boudoun van de Walle, *La transmission des textes litteraires egyptiens* (Brussels: Fondation egyptologique reine Elisabeth, 1948), p. 12.

30. Askel P. F. Volten, *Studien zum Weisheitsbuch des Ani* (Copenhagen: Levin and Munksgaard, 1937).

31. Askel P. F. Volten, *Das demotische Weisheitsbuch: Studien und Berarbeitung* [An. Aeg. 2] (Copenhagen, 1941).

32. G. Burkard, *Textkritische Untersuchungen zu aegyptischen Weisheitslehre des Alten und Mittleren Reiches* [Aeg. Abh. 34] (Wiesbaden, 1977).

33. William F. Albright, *The Proto-Sinaitic Inscriptions* (Cambridge, Mass.: Harvard U., 1969).

34. David A. Robertson, *Linguistic Evidence in Dating Early Hebrew Poetry* (Missoula, Mont.: SBL, 1972), p. 154. For the problems involved in dating documents see my *Intermediate Hebrew Grammar* (Winona Lake, Ind.: Eisenbrauns, forthcoming), par. 2.8.

35. Helmer Ringgren, "Oral and Written Transmission in the Old Testament," *Studia Theologica* 3 (1950-51):34-59.

36. Robert C. Culley, *Oral Formulaic Language in the Biblical Psalms* (Toronto: U. of Toronto, 1976).

37. M. Parry, "Studies in the Epic Technique of Oral Verse-Making. I: Homer and Homeric Style," *Harvard Studies in Classical Philology* 41 (1930):43-147.

38. Robert B. Coote, "The Application of the Oral Theory to Biblical Hebrew Literature," *Semeia* 5 (1976):52.

39. Ibid., pp. 56-57.

40. Albert B. Lord, *The Singer of Tales* (Cambridge, Mass.: Harvard U., 1960).

41. F. Max Müller, "Literature before Letters," in *Last Essays* (1st series), pp. 123, 130, cited by Nielsen, *Oral Tradition*, p. 24.

42. Geo. Widengren, *Literary and Psychological Aspects of the Hebrew Prophets* (Uppsala: Universitets Arsskriff, 1948):10, 49.

43. G. Widengren, "Oral Tradition and Written Literature Among the Hebrews in Light of Arabic Evidence, with Special Regard to Prose Narratives," in *AcOr* 23 (1959):201-62.

44. Bridget Connelly, "Oral Poetics: The Arab Case" (paper prepared for the Oral Literature Seminar, Modern Language Association, 1974), cited by Culley, *Oral Formulaic*, p. 6.

45. Mary C. Bateson, *Structural Continuity in Poetry: A. Linguistic Study in Five Pre-Islamic Arabic Odes* (The Hague and Paris: Mouton, 1970) cited by Culley, *Oral Formulaic*, p. 6.

46. Widengren, "Oral Tradition," p. 225.

47. Lord, *Singer*. For a survey of field studies on oral poetry and oral prose in India, Africa, Mongolia, etc., see Culley, *Oral Formulaic*, esp. pp. 3-4, 9-12.

48. Coote, "Application," p. 52.

49. John van Seters, *Abraham in History and Tradition* (New Haven, Conn.: Yale U., 1975), p. 148.

50. William Sanford LaSor, David Allan Hubbard, and Frederic W. Bush, *Old Testament Survey: The Message, Form and Background of the Old Testament* (Grand Rapids: Eerdmans, 1982), pp. 108-9.

51. Gleason L. Archer, Jr., *SOTI* (Chicago: Moody, 1964), p. 21 n. 4.

52. Robert Alter, *The Art of Biblical Narrative* (New York: Basic Books, 1981), p. 128.

53. Lest I be misunderstood, let me state that my objection to form criticism pertains not to the objective identification of literary genres and forms—this practice is an indispensable exegetical tool—but to the subjective practice of tracing the history of a tradition.

LARRY L. WALKER (Ph. D., The Dropsie College for Hebrew and Cognate
Learning) is professor of Old Testament and Hebrew at Mid-America
Baptist Theological Seminary, Mem-
phis, Tennessee.

2

Notes on Higher Criticism and the Dating of Biblical Hebrew

Larry L. Walker

Coming into full bloom at the end of the nineteenth century, higher criticism claimed to be "scientific" in methodology. That claim assumed knowledge of the Hebrew language adequate enough to use it in a scientific way to argue for the theories of the critics who were hostile to the traditional understanding of the origin and nature of Old Testament literature.

Much has been learned about biblical Hebrew since the heyday of higher criticism, and a new assessment is required of the old methodology of the critics in their use of language. New light on the history of Hebrew and its background makes it possible to evaluate old linguistic arguments of classical higher criticism.

LATE WORDS

A common accusation of the critics involved so-called late words that betray late authorship. Such was the case with the language of Daniel and parts of the Pentateuch. Aramaisms (to be discussed later) were generally assumed to reflect late intrusions into biblical Hebrew, and poetic diction was also often taken to reflect late diction. That assumption meant in many cases the divorce of the literature from its traditional author (cf. Moses and Daniel).

Of course the very principle of "late" words has been much abused. The danger should be self-evident. As Robert Dick Wilson observed, "No one can maintain that because a word occurs only in a [demonstrably] late document the word itself is late; for in this case, if a late document was the only survival of a once numerous body of literature, every word in it would be late; which is absurd."[1]

If the Bible had been written in Akkadian, we would be in a better position to date its language because we possess hundreds of thousands of documents in Akkadian spanning over two and one-half millennia. The situation with Hebrew is not as fortunate. Significant discoveries like those at Ugarit, however, provide much light on the history of the Canaanite or Hebrew language from as far back as Moses.

At times, late words were so designated because they were found only in late documents in the Bible. However, it should be noted that the documents were labeled late because they contained late words. The obvious circular reasoning involved requires a more scientific approach. The excavation, exposure, and elucidation of many texts in Hebrew and cognate languages have profoundly altered and improved our understanding of the language of the Old Testament since classical higher critics did their work at the end of the last century.

The argument from silence must be carefully noted in this issue of "late" words. Because a word is found only in extrabiblical documents of late vintage does not prove that the word was unknown earlier. It can only be said that as far as scholars are aware, that word was not used earlier. In fact, some words at one time considered "late" by critics have now been found in earlier documents.

The two forms of the first person singular independent pronoun 'ănōkî and 'ănî were treated as follows according to higher criticism: The longer form was preferred by J and E and was nearly always used by D, whereas the shorter form was almost exclusively used in P and other "late" writers.[2] That clearly implies that the shorter form is the "late" form. But the appearance of both forms intermixed in the Ugaritic texts (fourteenth century B.C.) puts both forms back into the Mosaic era.

Ecclesiastes has been dated late on the basis of its Hebrew. Samuel R. Driver claimed that the "political condition which it presupposes, and the language, make it decidedly probable that it is not earlier than the latter years of the Persian rule, which ended B.C. 333 . . . and it is quite possible that it is later."[3] As early as 1855 Christian David Ginsburg claimed that very few in Germany attempted to defend Solomonic authorship. The only issue by then was whether the composition was to be assigned to the earlier or latter part of the Persian dominance.[4] For the majority of the critics of the last century the language of Ecclesiastes presented a parade example of late Hebrew, divorcing the composition from its traditional Solomonic authorship.

In more recent years Otto Eissfeldt wrote of Ecclesiastes that "its language also reveals words and expressions which may with at least some probability be regarded as Graecisms."[5] He dated it in the postexilic period and claimed that among all the books of the Old Testament it is most affected by Aramaisms.[6] The unusual nature of the Hebrew of Ecclesiastes has caused several scholars to find in it Aramaic influences.[7] The late kind of Hebrew allegedly used in Ecclesiastes led to the abandonment of Solomonic authorship by such conservative scholars as Ernst W. Hengstenberg, Franz Delitzsch, and Edward J. Young. The discovery of a second-century-B.C. fragment of Ecclesiastes among the Dead Sea scrolls plus continuing studies of its language have caused scholars to take a second look at the dating of this unusual book. Gleason Archer[8] addressed this subject at length in 1969, leaning heavily on the observations made in 1952 by Mitchell Dahood.[9] Archer's influence seems to be reflected in two recent commentaries on Ecclesiastes.[10]

Some examples of "late" words in Ecclesiastes have now been found at Ebla:[11] *nāsî'*,[12] "leader," spelled *nase*, and "gold," *ketem*, spelled *kutim*.[13]

The parallel terms *mkk/dlp* in Ecclesiastes 10:18 were identified as late and probably under Aramaic influence, but now the same parallelism has been found in Ugaritic.[14]

The term *kišrôn*, "skill, success," found several times in Ecclesiastes (also in Ps. 68:7; Esther 8:5) was considered a clear example of Aramaic, but the phonetic shifts involved from the Ugaritic *ktr* suggest that it would have appeared as *ktr* in Aramaic instead of *kšr*. Inasmuch as Ugaritic *t* becomes *š* in Phoenician, it could have gone from Phoenician into Aramaic.[15]

The book of Psalms was viewed by critics as containing late words that betrayed late composition. Ferdinand Hitzig was convinced that "from the third book on all psalms must be assigned to the period of the Maccabees."[16] Of Psalm 119 Moses Buttenwieser wrote that "it is a product of literary decadence . . . written around the second half of the third century, when the Hebrew language had entered on a stage of rapid decadence."[17] Samuel R. Driver[18] wrote of the language of the Psalms that "Aramaisms and non-classical idioms are likewise marks of a late age," and later his son G. R. Driver wrote that "the diction of Hebrew poetry owes much of its distinctive colouring to the Aramaic language."[19]

The discovery of the Ugaritic texts and the striking analogies between them and the Psalms brought about a new perspective on the poetry of the Hebrew Bible. Instead of reflecting Aramaic (and therefore late) influence, the Psalms are found to be precisely in the tradition of Canaanite poetic style.

In addition to the problem of the argument from silence that characterized some of the critics, bad reasoning from data that was available led others astray. S. R. Driver's analysis of the language of Ecclesiastes included making a list of some thirty words common to the Hebrew and Aramaic of the Targums and Talmud that were also found in the Old Testament in "late" books (Ezra/Nehemiah, Esther, Chronicles). He concluded that this was evidence for labeling a word "late."[20] But Wilson[21] pointed out that the so-called late words collected by Driver are not limited to these "late" books. Also Wilson's collation of data revealed that later Jews, who wrote the Targums and Talmud, made extensive use of the very words found in the Scriptures that they translated and expanded. They did this without regard to the date of the book translated or expanded and regardless of the date at which the translation or exposition was made. This was natural and spontaneous, and this linguistic data cannot be used to read back late dates into the source Scriptures.

LATE MORPHOLOGY

Critics identified not only certain words as late but also certain forms. Many critics were convinced that such nominal endings as *-ût, -ôn, -ān* were conclusive evidence that the forms reflected late and Aramaic influence. Even Delitzsch accepted such as evidence that Solomon did not write Ecclesiastes. However, Wilson[22] discussed the *-ût* ending as common in Akkadian for abstract forms and therefore to be expected in a book with such a philosophical nature as Ecclesiastes. This formation does not reflect linguistic decay as earlier critics suggested. Wilson gave many examples of words ending in *-ût* from extrabiblical sources between 2000 and 625 b.c., and of course the number would be many times greater today with our increase of texts available for comparison. He also revealed that this formation is attested in every Old Testament book except the Song of Solomon, Ruth, and Lamentations. Moreover, he found these forms in passages that critics insisted are early. He did similarly with words ending in *-ôn* and *-ān*.[23]

The *-ût* ending has also been discussed by W. J. Martin,[24] who listed words of this formation and pointed out that this is not a neologism[25] in

Daniel but already had been used in Numbers 24:7, 1 Samuel 20:31, Jeremiah 10:7, 49:34, 52:31, and elsewhere.

This formation is already attested in the Akkadian of the code of Hammurapi and earlier. Stanislav Segert[26] compared the Akkadian noun formation *abbūtu*, "fatherhood," with Phoenician *'bt*, and the same formation is suggested for Phoenician *r't*, "will," on the basis of Hebrew *rē'ût*.

The formation is found in Ecclesiastes 10:13 in the word for "madness" *(hôlēlût)* and the word for "folly" *(kislût)*. It should be noted that this word for "madness" in this same book was also vocalized with a final *-ôt* instead of *-ût* in 1:17, 2:12, 7:25, and 9:3. Such a termination of abstraction has been attested in Phoenician/Punic *FELIOTH (p'lywt*, "product").[27] Because this formation is often used to indicate the abstract concept of a root, it is not unusual to have it in a book like Ecclesiastes.

Despite such facts, Robert Gordis still refers to the "plethora of Aramaic words, forms and constructions"[28] in Ecclesiastes, and from these he deduces a late date for the book. In fact, he still uses this same example of abstract nouns ending in *-ût* and describes it specifically as a late morphological development induced by Aramaic.[29] Because of such reasons and other alleged "late" signs, Ecclesiastes was assigned a late date by traditional critics, and more recently an Aramaic source has been suggested.[30] Christian D. Ginsburg concluded that the book was written in "Rabbinical Hebrew . . . and originated at least in the latter end of the Persian government"[31] (350-340 B.C.). In fact, he believed that if it could be shown that the Old Testament canon was not closed till after that time, the language of the book would fully justify assigning it a later period. Modern critics repeat the same line of argumentation, either using linguistic observations or ignoring them.[32] A widely used introduction to the Old Testament stated of Ecclesiastes that "the Hebrew marks it as one of the latest books of the Old Testament . . . written at the beginning of the Greek Period; hence *circa* 300 B.C. is the earliest possible date, but half a century later is more probable."[33] Claus Westermann wrote that "the book belongs to the latest writings of the Old Testament. It originated in the second century B.C."[34] Otto Kaiser argues for a date in the third century B.C. and claims, "In no other book of the Old Testament is the language so far along the road from classical Mishnaic Hebrew as Qoheleth."[35] It should be noted that Ecclesiastes is attested in the manuscripts from Qumran, which are dated very close to the original, according to Kaiser's date. Also it should be noted that Kaiser, writing in 1975, was still arguing from alleged Aramaic formations, such as the abstract *-ût* termination.

Numerous other grammatical forms were targeted by critics as reflecting "late" language. Repeatedly these forms have shown up in early non-biblical sources, disproving their alleged lateness. As knowledge of the history of Hebrew grows, scholars are in a better—but always precarious—position to describe what is an early or late form. The critics of the last century often argued from silence or engaged in circular reasoning.

ARAMAISMS

The influence of Aramaic is so widespread throughout biblical Hebrew that it deserves special attention. There is no doubt about the ever-increasing influence of Aramaic on later Hebrew of the biblical period. There is much doubt about using Aramaic to prove a late date for certain words or grammatical features found in parts of the Hebrew text traditionally considered "early." Although the influence of Aramaic on Hebrew was significant, the dating of this influence becomes complicated.

First of all, Aramaic is attested as far back as the patriarchal period, and of course there were predecessors before that. Aramaic did not begin *de novo* in the time of the patriarchs.

Laban was an Aramean who lived in Aram Naharaim and spoke Aramaic, as reflected in the stone "heap of witness" (Gen. 31:47) that was given an Aramaic title by Laban but a Hebrew title by Jacob. Aram[36] as the name of a region appears throughout the second millennium B.C. Very early nomadic groups called Sutu and Ahlamu presumably spoke some dialect closely akin to Aramaic. Tiglath-Pileser I (c. 1100 B.C.) records his encounter with the Ahlamu-Arameans who came from the desert areas.[37] By about 1100 B.C. Arameans had expanded throughout the area of Aram and penetrated into northern Transjordan, resulting in continuing conflicts later with the Israelites during the time of David.[38] Their widespread commercial activities along the major trade routes of the Middle East, along with their inherent wanderlust, put them at the "fore of Middle Eastern commerce from the ninth century B.C. onwards."[39] The widespread use of Aramaic continues to be attested in numerous documents from this time on until it became the *lingua franca* of the Persian period, spreading over an area from Asia Minor and the Caucasus to India, Afghanistan, northern Arabia, and Egypt. Even earlier, Aramaic had played an important role in the realm of administration and diplomacy in the Babylonian and even the earlier Assyrian empire.[40]

In view of such widespread use of Aramaic during the Old Testament period, it is surprising that more Aramaic influence on biblical Hebrew is not encountered.

Higher critics have always been quick to identify Aramaic words and forms within the Hebrew text of Scripture to be indicators of late date for that particular passage. Critics have done this with the books of Ecclesiastes and Song of Solomon[41] and even the book of Jonah,[42] and of course many other passages of Scripture.

One example from Jonah that reveals the complicated situation regarding the dating of Aramaic words is "sailor, mariner" (Jonah 1:5; it should be noted that this word is also in Ezek. 27:9, 27, 29). Because the word was Aramaic, it was assumed "late." Early lexicographers related the word to *melaḥ*, "salt," but now it is recognized as a loanword from Akkadian *malāḫu*, "sailor," which in turn is a loanword from Sumerian *MÁ.LAḪ* and certainly is not late.[43] Akkadian loanwords in Aramaic are not uncommon, as one might expect.[44] Possibly some Akkadian words entered Aramaic via Amorite, but we lack adequate texts in Amorite to enable us to isolate loanwords within it. Also it must be kept in mind that Akkadian itself was influenced by Aramaic and Amorite.[45]

Earlier lexicographers and critics were prone to identify a word as Aramaic if attested only in Aramaic/Syriac sources. Of course this is a kind of argument from silence if treated superficially. Just because a word has appeared only (up to now) in Aramaic/Syriac certainly does not prove the word is not Canaanite. Edward Y. Kutscher[46] gave the example of *'ātâ*, "come," which is not standard biblical Hebrew (for expressing this concept) but is standard Aramaic. The presence of such a word within biblical Hebrew would therefore suggest it is an Aramaic loanword,[47] and for many critics this meant it was "late." However, the word is now attested in the Canaanite texts of Ugarit, where it is commonly used in these archaic poetic texts. It seems doubtful that an Aramaic loanword is present in such early Canaanite texts. More likely the word is an ancient term preserved in both biblical Hebrew and Aramaic. Possibly it was an ancient "Aramaic" or pre-Aramaic term used by such predecessors of the Arameans as the Sutu or Ahlamu peoples. At any rate, such words cannot be used to argue for a late date.

An area that needs further study concerns Canaanite loanwords in Aramaic. It is certainly possible that some alleged Aramaic words are really Phoenician or Canaanite (Ugaritic) loanwords in Aramaic. The floating of words from one language to another is a phenomenon readily admitted but not so easily traced. Paucity of source materials has up to now hampered scholarly analysis of such words. With the increase of knowledge of the history of Aramaic and Canaanite scholars are in a better position to distinguish true Canaanite vocabulary from Aramaic. But the lack of knowledge of such "border" languages as Amorite frustrates detailed analysis.

Several avenues to penetrating this problem remain to be fully explored. One approach that needs to be updated and published was observed long ago by Wilson with his characteristic perception. For his readers he referred to the old work on Aramaisms in the Old Testament by E. Kautzsch,[48] which listed 350 words as being certainly, probably, or possibly of Aramaic origin. Of these, fifty were found in the Pentateuch. Wilson[49] reasoned that if these were Aramaic, the Targums (Aramaic versions) should be expected to render them by some form of the same root. His analysis, however, revealed that over one-half of these so-called Aramaic words were translated by other words in the Aramaic translations. This analysis needs to be updated in the light of new discoveries and insights.

Space does not permit a discussion of alleged Aramaic grammatical forms in Hebrew, but one example will reveal the caution to be exercised here. The masculine plural -în ending is characteristic of Aramaic in contrast to the Hebrew -îm ending. However, it should be observed that this is the regular masculine plural ending in Moabite, and it is also found in the song of Deborah (Judg. 5:10) and elsewhere in Hebrew. W. Gesenius listed over a dozen different words using this ending. One word, millîn, "words," itself occurs over a dozen times.[50] He claimed it was "found almost exclusively in the later books of the OT (apart from the poetical use in some of the older and even the oldest portions)."[51] Hans Bauer and Pontus Leander also admitted the one occurrence in old Hebrew (Judg. 5:10) but claimed it was mostly "late," under the influence of Aramaic.[52] Mishnaic Hebrew nouns exhibit the plural -în almost as often as -îm.[53] Segert gave an example of this ending in the Canaanite text from Arslan Tash (seventh century B.C.).[54] This phenomenon could be dialectal within Hebrew, perhaps due to Aramaic influence on northern Israelite Hebrew.[55] If this is the answer, these forms have no bearing on "late" dating of the Old Testament portions involved.

LOANWORDS

Although Aramaic words within the Hebrew text were isolated for special note from the earliest period of critical study, other loanwords were mostly undetected. Before the decipherment of such ancient languages from the Bible lands as Egyptian, Akkadian, Sumerian, Persian, Hittite, and Hurrian, it would have been impossible to detect loanwords in Hebrew from these languages.[56]

According to Maximilian Ellenbogen[57] the largest number of loanwords comes from Akkadian (50 percent), followed by Egyptian (22 percent). It is not surprising to find Akkadian influence represented in all periods of Hebrew. As early as the Amarna period (fourteenth century) Akkadian had become the *lingua franca* of the Near East.

The presence of Egyptian loanwords in the Pentateuch was used by conservative scholars—sometimes with too much zeal—to support its Mosaic authorship.[58] We would not expect late writers in Palestine to use so naturally various Egyptian terms found sprinkled throughout the Pentateuch. Wilson was alert to the apologetic value of loanwords in Hebrew (and also in Aramaic) and wrote a lengthy article on the subject.[59] He questioned whether "these particular and correct kinds of foreign words could have been deliberately and knowingly inserted into the Pentateuch by writers . . . living as late as the 8th century B.C. (when the critics agree that J and E were written), or as late as the 6th or 4th century (where they place H and P)."[60] It would indeed be remarkable that these late writers and editors of the Pentateuch (according to classical higher-critical theory) were able to sprinkle the appropriate foreign words in the appropriate setting to create an illusion of historical and cultural authenticity. Wilson probably went too far when he concluded that the age and provenance of each part of the Old Testament containing foreign words could be determined approximately by the number and origin of foreign words found in it.[61] He expected Akkadian words in the accounts of the creation and flood, Egyptian words in the Mosaic material, and Persian words in the latest period. Although the situation is more complicated than he realized, he was trying to be "scientific" in his approach to the literature and openly admitted that *humanum est errare.*[62]

As knowledge of the linguistic background of ancient Israel increases, it will be possible to identify and better evaluate the significance of loanwords within biblical Hebrew. At one time in the history of Hebrew lexicography[63] it would have been as unthinkable to be able to identify Hittite, Hurrian, or Philistine words as it now is to identify Scythian, Urartean,[64] or Mannean[65] words.

The distinction between Hittite and Hurrian loanwords has been slow and difficult.[66] Hittites (or some "pre-Hittite" group) had contacts with the patriarchs Abraham (Gen. 23, 25) and Isaac (Gen. 27), and Abraham's purchase of the cave in Machpelah from Ephron the Hittite may reflect certain subtle distinctions in Hittite law concerning the sale of property.[67] Hittite suzerainty treaties have been compared by scholars with the literary form of the book of Deuteronomy. Hittite wives are found in Solomon's harem, and the husband of Bathsheba was Uriah the Hittite. The Carians in the Judahite royal court in the ninth century B.C. were part of the elite palace guard and appear to have Hittite connections (2 Kings 11:4, 19).[68] Despite such personal contacts between Hebrews and Hittites, relatively few Hittite loanwords have been isolated in biblical Hebrew. One scholar compiled a list of twenty-two such words,[69] but the more certain ones are considerably less.

In the Bible, Hurrians are referred to as Horites or Hivites[70] and include Hamor of Shechem (Gen. 34), the Gibeonites (Josh. 9:7; 11:19), and probably the Jebusites who ruled pre-Israelite Jerusalem. Hurrian personal names from the Amarna tablets[71] reveal that Jerusalem was ruled by a Hurrian dynast named "Servant of Hepa" (Hepa was a leading goddess of the Hurrian pantheon and consort of Teshub). In the light of this linguistic data it is noteworthy that the Hebrew Bible records that David purchased the site for the future Temple from Araunah or Ornan (the translations vary). The Hebrew consonants are 'rwnh/'wrnh (2 Sam. 24:16) or 'rnn (1 Chron. 21:18) and undoubtedly preserve a Hurrian term, possibly a title in view of a bilingual Hurrian-Akkadian tablet from Ugarit that has ewri- = bēlu, "lord," and ewir-ne = šarru, "king."

The Hebrew Bible's faithful preservation and presentation of such linguistic data on an ethnic group can only be appreciated in the light of the growing knowledge of such a dialect with Canaan. For the higher critics to have claimed that noninspired writers produced such accurate records, including such esoteric ethnic accuracies, is incredulous. The more that is learned about the linguistic background of the Hebrew text, the more its authenticity is observed.

On the subject of Philistine loanwords within Hebrew, only a few suggested examples can be found. Apparently the Philistines dropped their own language and quickly adopted Canaanite shortly after their arrival in the area. Early references to the Philistines in the patriarchal narratives[72] (Gen. 21:32, 34; 27:18) are usually dismissed as anachronistic, but it is probably more accurate to view these passages as references to the predecessors of the later well-known Philistines of the time of David. The reference to the Caphtorim in Deuteronomy 2:23 probably refers to some similar early group from Crete. The Hebrew term for "helmet" (k/qôba') usually listed as Philistine may ultimately derive from Hittite *kupaḫḫi*, and Hebrew *seren*, "lord," often compared to Greek *tyrannos*, may be related to Hittite *tarwanas*, a title born by Neo-Hittite kings in late Luvian (Hittite hieroglyphic) inscriptions of the eleventh to seventh centuries B.C.[73] Philistine personal names may be on the verge of being definitely identified. Goliath is viewed as coming from a Luvian base,[74] and the *-at* ending of Ahuzzath (Gen. 26:26) is compared to the same ending on Goliath. The name Phicol (Gen. 21:22, 32; 26:26) is hardly Semitic, but it can only be guessed what it is. John Bright[75] thought it was Hurrian, but it could be a title. The name Abimelech used of the ruler at Gerar who had contact with both Abraham and Isaac could also possibly be a title, despite its obvious Semitic appearance. Nothing discovered outside the Bible contradicts the linguistic data preserved about the Philistines, brief as it is. For example, the brief illumination that exists for *seren*, the technical term for the Philistine rulers, is perfectly in accord with its special usage in the Hebrew Bible.

The continuing discovery and illumination of the contemporary and background languages of biblical Hebrew does not support the theories of higher critics who viewed the biblical literature of the Hebrews as a mishmash of documents written by a variety of late authors over a vast period of time.

POETRY

For various reasons Hebrew poetry was often assigned late dates. In some cases it was due to alleged Aramaic influences. S. R. Driver and his son both used the presence of Aramaisms in poetry as evidence of a late date for it.[76] Discussing why many psalms traditionally ascribed to David cannot be his, the elder Driver wrote that "some of these have pronounced Aramaisms, the occurrence of which in an early poem of Judah is entirely without analogy, or other marks of lateness."[77]

One of these "other marks of lateness" Driver mentioned was the *-kî* pronominal second-feminine-singular suffix.[78] Gesenius simply identified this form as "rare" or "incorrect."[79] Why Driver compared it only to Aramaic is not clear, since Akkadian also has this suffix. Dahood suggested that it may be a Canaanite archaism,[80] and that is the vocalization assigned by Cyrus Gordon[81] to this Ugaritic form. As early as 1922 Bauer-Leander[82] had deduced from comparative Semitic linguistics that it was the original form. All of this points in the direction of another preserved archaism within biblical Hebrew and does not need to be explained as Aramaic influence. It certainly is not an indicator of a late date as some critics have claimed; rather, it points in the opposite direction.

From our perspective today we can see how premature such judgments were. Dahood observed of these alleged Aramaisms in Hebrew poetry: "Nor can Aramaisms any longer be used indiscriminately as proof of a late date. The gradual chronological extension of the Aramaic corpus of inscriptions renders more hazardous a post-exilic dating of Psalms that contain typically Aramaic roots."[83] Dahood also raised the question of why the LXX translators had such difficulty translating some of the very psalms that, according to critics, were almost contemporary with them.[84] Furthermore, the alleged late date for many psalms does not agree with the large number of fragments of the Psalms found among the Dead Sea scrolls, some of which date close to the time of alleged composition. Despite all this, R. M. Hanson,[85] writing as late as 1968, still assigned third- and even second-century-B.C. dates to some psalms.

Probably another archaism is preserved in the perfect tense sufformative -tî for the second feminine singular instead of the usual -t formation. The more original form, as might be expected, is preserved before suffixes.[86] That is the vocalization assigned to this sufformative in Ugaritic by Gordon,[87] and Klaus Beyer does the same for "Althebräische."[88] However, Kutscher[89] labeled such forms "mirage" forms received by the influence of Aramaic. By this he meant the form was in archaic Hebrew but not in "Biblical Hebrew." Later it was revived by the influence of Aramaic. Thus is created a "mirage," or appearance, of an early form. I doubt this. He followed this line of reasoning because such forms are found in obviously (for him) late books such as Ecclesiastes. Incidentally, it should be observed that the independent pronoun for the second feminine singular is normally 'at but appears in the Kethib as 'ty sporadically in Judges and Kings in stories reflecting an Israelite (not Judahite) dialect. Kutscher[90] noted this and also attributed it to Aramaic influence, but it should be noted that Akkadian has attī.

Another form found in poetry and often targeted as evidence of "lateness" is the relative š- for 'ǎšer. Gesenius[91] wrote: "In the later books . . . especially Ecclesiastes and the late Psalms, also Lamentations, Jonah, Chronicles, Ezra, and always in Canticles š- is used" [instead of 'ǎšer]. George F. Moore wrote: "The relative š- is frequent in late Biblical Hebrew." However, he does go on to say: "But it is unsafe to infer that it was of late origin."[92] Burney[93] took this š- in Judges (5:7; 6:17; 7:12; 8:26) to reflect a dialect of "North Palestine," and he compared it to Phoenician 'š-, which has the prosthetic *aleph*. Zelig S. Harris[94] also related *š*-to "North Palestinian Hebrew." Of its occurrence in 2 Kings 6:11, J. A. Montgomery claimed that "this good N. Israelite particle is appropriate in the citation of a Syrian."[95] Kutscher observed its use in the story of Gideon and once in the Israelite (northern) section of the book of Kings (2 Kings 6:11) and concluded: "Therefore there is reason to believe that its use was common in the vernacular of Northern Palestine."[96]

Possibly this grammatical feature *š*- is related to Phoenician (*')š*, which appears in late Punic forms as *š'/š'/š*. Robert G. Boling[97] referred to its use in Judges as "archaic."

Space does not permit discussion of numerous other features of Hebrew poetry now viewed as archaic.[98] Many of the very features once considered sure signs of lateness are now viewed as remnants of typically old Canaanite poetic forms.[99]

CONCLUSION

Some of the argumentation used by critics for late dating of biblical Hebrew was based on the argument from silence. Their alleged "late" words were attested up to that time only in late extrabiblical sources, but this by no means proved that they were not used earlier. With the increase of more ancient sources to study (e.g., Ugaritic) the scene has changed. Some of those words that had been preserved only in later sources (e.g., Mishnaic Hebrew) are now showing up in ancient sources.[100] Albright believed that the Old Testament preserved no more than one-fifth of the Northwest Semitic words used between 1400 and 400 B.C.[101] It is certain that the ancient stock of Canaanite words far exceeded what is preserved in the Hebrew Bible.

Another error of the new, so-called scientific approach to the Bible by nineteenth-century critics was the assumption that what appear as Aramaic words and grammatical forms can be used as evidence of a late date. I have already discussed at length the unwarranted nature of this criticism.

Some of the old classical higher critical methodology was based on ignorance of the language, and some of it was based on theological presuppositions concerning the content or teaching of Scripture possible at any given time in antiquity. Unilinear evolutionary philosophy controlled much of the higher critical approach to the Hebrew Bible during the last half of the last century, and this had a great influence on the attitude toward the language and text of Scripture.

NOTES

1. Robert Dick Wilson, *A Scientific Investigation of the Old Testament*, rev. E. J. Young (Chicago: Moody, 1959), p. 106.

2. Cf. Samuel R. Driver, *An Introduction to the Literature of the Old Testament* (1897; reprint, New York: Meridian, 1956), pp. 135, 155-56. A comparative table of usage is presented in H. L. Strack, *Einleitung in das Alte Testament* (Munich: Beck, 1895), pp. 42-51.

3. Driver, *Introduction*, p. 476.

4. C. D. Ginsburg, *Coheleth* (New York: Ktav, [1861] 1970), p. 228.

5. Otto Eissfeldt, *The Old Testament, an Introduction* (New York: Harper, 1965), p. 498.

6. Ibid., p. 496.

7. Cf. F. C. Burkitt, "Is Ecclesiastes a Translation?" *JTS* 22 (1921):23ff.; F. Zimmerman, "The Aramaic Provenance of Koheleth," *JQR* 36 (1945):17ff.; "The Question of Hebrew in Qoheleth," *JQR* 40 (1949):79-102. See also C. C. Torrey, "The Question of the Original Language of Qoheleth," *JQR* 39 (1948):151ff.

8. Gleason L. Archer, Jr., "The Linguistic Evidence for the Dating of Ecclesiastes," *JETS* 12 (1969):167-81.

9. Mitchell Dahood, "Canaanite-Phoenician Influence in Qoheleth," *Bib* 33 (1952):30-52; 191-221; cf. also "The Language of Qoheleth," *CBQ* 14 (1952):227-32. Dahood continued his thesis that Qoheleth reflects early Phoenician or North Israelite language in "Qoheleth and Northwest Semitic Philology," *Bib* 43 (1962):349-65.

10. Louis Goldberg, *Ecclesiastes* (Grand Rapids: Zondervan, 1983), p. 21; and Walter C. Kaiser, Jr., *Ecclesiastes* (Chicago: Moody, 1979), p. 28.

11. These examples from Ebla are mentioned by Kenneth A. Kitchen, *The Bible in Its World* (Exeter: Paternoster, 1977), p. 50.

12. Considered late by Driver, *Introduction*, p. 134.

13. Cf. Giovanni Pettinato in *Or* 44 (1975):372 n. 98.

14. *UT* §68:17. See also H. L. Ginsberg in *JAOS* 70 (1950):158-59.

15. Cf. Archer, "Linguistic Evidence for Dating Ecclesiastes," p. 178.

16. Mentioned by Robert Dick Wilson, "Evidence in Hebrew Diction for the Dates of Documents," *PTR* 25 (1927):357, who documents late dates assigned Psalms by Reuss, Cheyne, Robertson Smith, Bleek-Wellhausen, and even Perowne and Delitzsch.

17. M. Buttenwieser, *The Psalms* (New York: Ktav, [1938] 1969), p. 872.

18. Driver, *Introduction*, p. 383.

19. G. R. Driver, "Hebrew Poetic Diction," in *Copenhagen Congress Volume* (Leiden: Brill, 1953), p. 26.

20. S. R. Driver, *Introduction*, p. 473.

21. Wilson, "Evidence in Hebrew Diction," pp. 353ff.

22. Wilson, *Scientific Investigation*, pp. 88ff.

23. Ibid., pp. 118-22; See also "Aramaisms in the OT," *PTR* 23 (1925):244-45.

24. W. J. Martin, "The Hebrew of Daniel," in *Notes on Some Problems in the Book of Daniel* (London: Tyndale, 1965), p. 28.

25. S. R. Driver, *Introduction*, p. 506, listed this noun formation as first in a list of words, idioms, and formations characteristic of the kind of Hebrew used in an age subsequent to Nehemiah.

26. Stanislav Segert, *A Grammar of Phoenician and Punic* (München: Beck, 1976), p. 88.

27. Ibid., p. 87.

28. Robert Gordis, *Koheleth: The Man and His World*, 3d ed. (New York: Schocken, 1968), p. 59.

29. Ibid., p. 60 n. 9.

30. For example, F. C. Burkitt in 1921, F. Zimmerman in 1945, C. C. Torrey in 1948, H. L. Ginsberg in 1950. For bibliography see Gordis, *Koheleth*, p. 374.

31. Christian David Ginsburg, *The Book of Ecclesiastes* (1861; reprint, New York: Ktav, 1970), p. 255.

32. Eissfeldt, *The Old Testament*, p. 496, wrote: "However the linguistic question may be decided . . . it remains clear that Koheleth originated only in the post-exilic period. It is difficult to determine the date more exactly."

33. W. O. E. Oesterley and T. H. Robinson, *Introduction to the Books of the Old Testament* (1934; reprint, New York: Meridian, 1958), p. 215.

34. Claus Westermann, *Handbook to the Old Testament* (Minneapolis: Augsburg, 1967), p. 246.

35. Otto Kaiser, *Introduction to the Old Testament* (Minneapolis: Augsburg, 1975), p. 401.

36. Aram is attested as a place-name as early as the twenty-third century B.C. and in a variety of sources shortly thereafter. Cf. A. Malamat, "The Aramaeans," in *Peoples of Old Testament Times*, ed. Donald J. Wiseman (Oxford: Clarendon, 1973), pp. 134-37.

37. Tiglath-Pileser gave the name "Aramean" to Semitic nomads troubling his borders. *ISBE* (rev.), s.v. "Aramaic," by William Sanford LaSor, 1:229-30.

38. Merrill F. Unger, *Israel and the Arameans of Damascus* (Grand Rapids: Zondervan, 1957).

39. Malamat, "The Aramaeans," p. 148.

40. For the many Aramaic loanwords in neo-Assyrian and neo-Babylonian see W. von Soden in *Or* 35 (1966):1-20; *Or* 37 (1968):261ff. Cf. also S. Paul, "Daniel 6:8: An Aramaic Reflex of Assyrian Legal Terminology," *Bib* 65 (1984):106-10.

41. For Aramaic words selected to reflect the late date of Ecclesiastes and Song of Solomon cf. DeWette-Schrader, *Einleitung*, pp. 543, 561. Cf. also Cornill, *Introduction to the Canonical Books of the Old Testament*, p. 449 (cited in Wilson, "Aramaisms in the OT," pp. 251, 243).

42. For Jonah see S. R. Driver, *Introduction*, p. 322, who referred to "Aramaisms, or other marks of a later age." Eissfeldt, writing at a later period, repeated this same line of argument (*The Old Testament*, p. 405).

43. Max Wagner, *Die lexicalischen und grammatikalischen Aramaismen in alttestamentlichen Hebraisch* (Berlin: Alfred Topelmann, 1966), pp. 76-77. For the Sumerian see Rene Labat, *Manuel D'Epigraphie Akkadienne* (Paris: Paul Geuthner, 1976), p. 93. *MÁ* is Sumerian for Akkadian *eleppu*, "boat," and *LAH* is Sumerian for Akkadian *šalālu*, "to guide." But in this case Sumerian *MÁ.LAH* was borrowed directly into Akkadian as *malāhu*, "boatman, sailor."

44. For an extensive and in-depth discussion of this issue cf. Stephen Kaufman, *The Akkadian Influences on Aramaic* (Chicago: U. of Chicago, 1974).

45. Ibid., p. 25.

46. Edward Yechezkel Kutscher, *The History of the Hebrew Language* (Jerusalem: Magnes, 1982), p. 72.

47. Wagner, *Lexicalischen*, p. 31, lists *'ātâ* as an Aramaic loanword but has not a single word of comment in it.

48. E. Kautzsch, *Die Aramaismen im Alten Testament* (1902).

49. Wilson, *Scientific Investigation*, p. 125.

50. *GKC* §87e.

51. Ibid.

52. Hans Bauer and Pontus Leander, *Historische Grammatik der Hebräischen Sprache des Alten Testaments* (1922; reprint, Hildesheim: Georg Olms, 1962) §63t.

53. M. H. Segal, *A Grammar of Mishnaic Hebrew* (Oxford: Clarendon, 1980), p. 126.

54. Segert, *Grammar*, p. 111.

55. C. F. Burney, *Notes on the Hebrew Text of the Book of Kings* (1903; reprint, New York: Ktav, 1970), p. 172, regarded this dialectal in Judg. 5:10. Another example of a suspected dialectal form reflecting northern Israelite is the prefix *š*- (see below).

56. For a convenient collection of various loanwords in Hebrew see Maximilian Ellenbogen, *Foreign Words in the Old Testament: Their Origin and Etymology* (London: Luzak, 1962).

57. Ibid., p. vii.

58. A. S. Yahuda, *The Language of the Pentateuch in Its Relation to Egyptian* (Oxford: U. Press, 1933). See also *The Accuracy of the Bible* (London: Heinemann, 1934).

59. Robert Dick Wilson, "Foreign Words in the Old Testament as an Evidence of Historicity," *PTR* 26 (1928):216ff.

60. Ibid., p. 177.

61. Ibid., pp. 236ff. Space does not permit a discussion of foreign personal names distributed through the Hebrew Bible as a sign of authenticity and a tool of apologetics. The growing ancient Near Eastern onomasticon is a treasure trove in this area. Even the evolution of Hebrew names—certain patterns of names in vogue at certain times and places—reflects an authenticity of our records totally alien to the old higher critical theories of the origin of this literature.

62. Wilson, "Foreign Words," p. 241.

63. For a recent survey of the history of Hebrew lexicography see Creighton Marlowe, "The Development of Hebrew Lexicography." Dissertation, Mid-America Baptist Theological Seminary, 1985.

64. Progress is being made in the study of Urartian. Cf. G. Melikishvili, *Die urartaische Sprache* (Rome: Biblical Institute, 1971).

65. Referred to as Minni in Jer. 51:27. Cf. the chapter "Urartians and Manneans" in Edwin Yamauchi, *Foes from the Northern Frontier* (Grand Rapids: Baker, 1982), pp. 29-47.

66. Ellenbogen, *Foreign Words*, p. 180, listed four Hittite words and no Hurrian words. Grammars and lexicons on Hurrian and Hittite are listed in *A Basic Bibliography for the Study of the Semitic Languages*, ed. J. H. Hospers (Leiden: Brill, 1973), pp. 110-11 (Hurrian) and 87-89 (Hittite).

67. So M. R. Lehmann in *BASOR* 129 (1953):15-18. But this is rejected by H. Hoffner, *TB* 20 (1969):27-55.

68. Cf. Kitchen, "The Philistines," p. 77.

69. C. Rabin, "Hittite Words in Hebrew," in *Or* 32 (1963):113-39.

70. *IDB*, s.v. "Hurrians," by E. A. Speiser, 3:664-65.

71. *ZPEB*, s.v. "Hurrians," by H. A. Hoffner, Jr., pp. 228-29.

72. For a discussion of the "patriarchal Philistines" cf. Kitchen, "Philistines," p. 56.

73. Ibid., p. 67. Hittite *kupaḫḫi* has been compared to Greek *kymbachos* and *seren* to Ugaritic *s/srn* in Ludwig Koehler-Walter Baumgartner, *Hebräisches und Aramäische Lexikon Zum Alten Testament*, dritte auflage, neubearbeitet von Walter Baumgartner und Johann Jakob Stamm, 3d ed. (Leiden: Brill, 1983), pp. 727, 1011.

74. Ibid., p. 67. Also note Albright's statement: "That the Philistines spoke a Luvian dialect is now virtually certain; see *CAH*² II (1966) ch. 33, p. 30." Mentioned by him in his prolegomena to C. F. Burney, *The Book of Judges* (1920; reprint, New York: Ktav, 1970), p. 15.

75. John Bright, *A History of Israel* (Philadelphia: Westminster, 1959), pp. 73-74.

76. Cf. nn. 18, 19.

77. S. R. Driver, *Introduction*, p. 374.

78. Examples of this may be found in Jer. 11:15; Pss. 103:3; 116:19; 135:9.

79. *GKC* §91e.

80. Mitchell Dahood, *Psalms*, AB, 3 vols. (Garden City, N.Y.: Doubleday, 1966-1970), 3:25.

81. *UT* §6.7.

82. Bauer and Leander, *Historische Grammatik* §255k.

83. Dahood, *Psalms*, 3:xxxvii.

84. Ibid., p. xxxiv.

85. R. M. Hanson, *The Psalms in Modern Speech* (Philadelphia, 1968), p. xxvii.

86. *GKC* §59a-c.

87. *UT* §9.7.

88. Klaus Beyer, *Althebräische Grammatik* (Gottingen: Vandenhoeck and Ruprecht, 1969), p. 58; similarly Wolfgang Richter, *Grundlagen einer althebräischen Grammatik* (St. Ottilien: EOS, 1978), p. 110.

89. Kutscher, *History*, pp. 38-39.

90. Ibid., pp. 30-31.

91. *GKC* §36.

92. G. F. Moore, *Judges*, ICC (Edinburgh: T. and T. Clark, 1895), p. 144.

93. Burney, *Notes*, p. 208.

94. Zellig S. Harris, *Development of the Canaanite Dialects* (1939; reprint, Millwood: Kraus, 1978), p. 69.

95. J. A. Montgomery, *The Books of Kings*, ICC (Edinburgh: T. and T. Clark, 1951), p. 383.

96. Kutscher, *History*, p. 32.

97. Robert G. Boling, *Judges*, AB (Garden City, N.Y.: Doubleday, 1975); see also T. J. Meek, *JBL* 79 (1960):334, p. 109.

98. See D. A. Robertson, *Linguistic Evidence in Dating Early Hebrew Poetry*, SBLDS 3 (Missoula, Mont.: U. of Montana, 1972).

99. See the numerous writings of Dahood and his students.

100. See B. A. Levine, "Ancient Survivals in Mishnaic Hebrew." Dissertation, Ann Arbor: University Microfilms, 1964. Dahood listed some Ugaritic words not found in the Bible but surfacing in later Hebrew (*Psalms*, 3:xxiv).

101. W. F. Albright in *Peake's Commentary on the Bible*, new ed. (Edinburgh, 1962), p. 62. Cited by Ullendorf, *Is Biblical Hebrew a Language?* (Wiesbaden: Otto Harrassowitz, 1977), p. 4, who also described his personal correspondence with Albright concerning how such a figure was deduced from available evidence.

JOHN H. STEK (Doctorandus, Free
University, Amsterdam) is associate
professor of Old Testament at Calvin
Theological Seminary.

3

The Bee and the Mountain Goat: A Literary Reading of Judges 4

John H. Stek

The present study of Judges 4 is a close reading of the text with special sensitivity to the artistry of the narrative.[1] Its purpose is to advance good interpretation. Such an attempt should need no apology, yet it represents a new development in biblical studies.[2] Since the rise of critical scholarship in the seventeenth and eighteenth centuries, historical interests have dominated the scene. Biblical narratives have been minutely examined for whatever historical data they might yield. Even conservative scholars have studied them primarily for historical information. For both wings of biblical scholarship the study of artistry in biblical narrative has been essentially irrelevant. It could be left to the aesthetes because it contributed nothing to the desired knowledge. Substance is what counted; form is only a matter of taste (for both author and reader). An additional factor, it seems (though it is difficult to document), has been the modern assumption that the ancient Israelite narrators were hardly (yet!) capable of literary sophistication; the intent of their texts was presumed to be transparent, on the surface, and one-dimensional.

A spate of recent studies of Old Testament narrative has begun to show how mistaken this assumption was and how wrong-headed was the notion that form and content could be so neatly separated.[3] They have also shown how impoverished the modern reading of these narratives has been, not only because scholars have kept themselves insensitive to aesthetic effects but also because they have not been tuned to the subtleties and richness of the texts. Ignoring the artistry, they have too often misread and misconstrued the narratives.

But even now there remains a strong residual resistance. No doubt much of this is because biblical scholars by and large have not been trained in the literary arts. The ancient languages and documents and religions and cultures they know, and they are well read in the history and archaeology of the ancient Near East. They are practiced in textual criticism, and they have been exposed to all the various critical methods: source criticism, form criticism, tradition criticism, redaction criticism, historical criticism. But the art of narrative has not been in their curriculum. Hence most biblical scholars are at a loss concerning how to assess the literary aspect even when it is pointed out. And because literary analysis of this sort can hardly be reduced to a science, they remain suspicious of it. Furthermore, many evangelical biblical scholars seem anxious that a focus on the art of a narrative will weaken its value as report. Whatever the cause, L. Alonzo-Schökel is surely right when he complains that a literary study of the Bible raises "hermeneutical problems" for many interpreters of Scripture.[4]

However, in the final analysis any method must establish its validity by the results it produces. And in biblical studies the test is not whether literary analysis contributes to aesthetic appreciation (though that may be a significant by-product) but whether it advances understanding. Does it sharpen the ear and eye to the author's intentions? Does it enable the reader to catch all the nuances and details of the author's story? The only apology for the present study is my conviction that such an analysis of Judges 4 is persuasive.[5] It is left to the readers to judge the results.

I begin with an analysis of narrative structure[6] and then work through the account with special attention to other literary devices.[7] The final section will draw conclusions regarding the theme.

I

The bounds of this pericope are transparent. Introduction (4:1-3) and conclusion (vv. 23-24; 5:31b) employ the stereotype formulae[8] characteristic of the central cycle of narratives (3:7—16:31). Use of these formulae sets clear bounds to the prose account of the event (4:4-22). It also indicates that both the prose and the poetic accounts (5:1-31a) have been put to the service of the controlling theme of this central section of the book. Because the discussion here is limited to the prose account, only incidental references to the poem of chapter 5 will be made.

The stereotype frame of the account is itself significantly structured. It perfectly balances three primary verbal clauses (introduction) with three like verbal clauses (conclusion), all with initial *waw* plus preformative verbs. The pattern is thematically concentric, with reinforcing verbal links:

> A. And the Israelites again did evil in the eyes of Yahweh[9] (episode initiating): v. 1.
>
> B. And Yahweh sold them into the *hands* of *Jabin king of Canaan*: v. 2.
>
> C. And *the Israelites* cried to Yahweh: v. 3.
>
> C' And God[10] subdued . . . Jabin king of Canaan before *the Israelites*: v. 23.
>
> B' And the *hand* of the Israelites bore down ever harder on *Jabin king of Canaan*: v. 24.
>
> A' And the land enjoyed peace forty years (episode closure): 5:31*b*.

Thus concentric symmetry underscores reversal of situation. It also focuses attention on the narrated event as the decisive turning point, consistent with what is stated in verses 23-24, where the subduing of Jabin is ascribed to "that day" when Sisera and his mighty force were destroyed, though a continuing struggle ensued before Jabin was wholly "cut off."[11]

The basic structure of the main body of the narrative is also fairly clear.[12] Verse 11 marks a break in the action, as indicated by a circumstantial clause (plus continuative verbal clause) that introduces a new character and prepares the reader for the sequence of actions that follows. Then at verse 18 the scene has shifted to Jael's tent, where it remains until the denouement in verse 22. An initial reading leaves some uncertainty as to the function of verse 11, the precise point of juncture between the second and third sections (whether v. 17 closes the second or initiates the third), and whether the final section is structured as one or as two episodes.[13] But that the narrative is composed of three action sequences is obvious enough.

Verses 4-5 are prologue. They introduce the character who sets the action in motion, indicate her role in the community (as prophetess and judge), and locate her in the land. But the author has tightly bound this prologue with the first narrative sequence by means of a twofold *inclusio*. He begins verse 4 (in Hebrew) by abruptly naming Deborah and ends verse 10 (in Hebrew) by naming her again. Within this *inclusio* lies the second. The final clause of the prologue begins (in Hebrew) with "And they went up" *(waw* plus preformative verb), and the final clause of verse 10 begins (in Hebrew) with the same verb and form, "And she went up" *(waw* plus preformative verb). The actions indicated involve reversal of movement: "And they went up to her, the Israelites"; "And she went up with them, Deborah." Moreover, an inner connection binds these actions firmly together in plot development. In verse 5 the Israelites "went up" to Deborah for judgment; in verse 10 Deborah "went up" with Barak at the head of the Israelites to effect God's judgment.

Between this prologue and closure seven distinct developments fill out the episode, and a close reading discloses a second concentric structure:

> A. Deborah summons Barak to Kadesh: v. 6*a*.
>> B. Deborah transmits Yahweh's commission to Barak: v. 6*b*.
>>> C. Deborah transmits Yahweh's promise of victory: v. 7.
>>>> D. Barak, hesitant, negotiates: v. 8.
>>> C' Deborah commits herself to accompany Barak as an earnest of Yahweh's promise but qualifies the promise: v. 9*a*.
>> B' Deborah goes with Barak to carry out Yahweh's commission: v. 9*b*.
> A' Barak summons the tribes to Kadesh: v. 10*a*.

This structure highlights Barak's irresolution, his dependence on Deborah, and its consequences. The action advances (cf. A with A,́ B with B,́ and C with C), but suspense is also awakened: How will a venture led by such an agent succeed? Is Deborah the "woman" who will be covered with glory?

The second action sequence (vv. 11-17) balances the first in many interesting and significant ways. Like the first it begins (v. 11) with a circumstantial clause that ends with a continuative verbal clause ("and the Israelites went up to her," v. 5; "and he pitched his tent," v. 11). Functionally it also sets a new character on stage, establishes his relationship to Israel, and geographically locates him relative to the unfolding action. This parallelism with verses 4-5 heightens the substantive contrasts between them. Deborah as prophetess and judge is situated in the heart of Israel, and the Israelites go up to her for judgment. Heber, whose family has been allied with Israel since the days of Moses (Num. 10:29-30), separates himself from his clan in the far south (Judg. 1:16) and moves to the far north. He is a man of the fringes, but he is in position to be directly involved in the narrative's events.

The abruptness of this break (v. 11) in the narrative flow and its apparent discontinuity with what follows has perplexed interpreters. Yet its linkage with verse 12 is much closer than has been recognized (as will be shown later), and it serves to awaken expectations as to the role of this erstwhile ally of Israel in the present crisis. It also prepares for the aftermath of the decisive battle (v. 17). And, as is true of verses 4-5, it is firmly bound to the following sequence by *inclusio:* In Hebrew, verse 12 begins with "Heber the Kenite," and he is named again at the end of verse 17.[14] Following Heber's introduction, the action progresses through eight distinct developments. Here, too, a concentric structure is evident but with one significant asymmetrical element:

> A. Sisera is informed (by Heber): v. 12.
>> B. Sisera summons his army from Harosheth Haggoyim to the Kishon River: v. 13.
>> *Deborah sends Barak into battle: v. 14*a*.
>>> C. Barak descends from Mount Tabor to do battle: v. 14*b*.
>>>> D. Yahweh overwhelms the enemy: v. 15*a*.
>>> C' Sisera descends from his chariot to escape the battle: v. 15*b*.
>> B' Barak pursues the fleeing enemy to Harosheth Haggoyim and destroys Sisera's army: v. 16.
> A' Sisera flees to Heber's encampment: v. 17.

The structure effectively supports the development of plot and theme. It heightens the reader's perception of reversal of the power status of Sisera, the commander of King Jabin's forces, and of Barak, the commander of Yahweh's army. It also highlights (by asymmetry) the role of Deborah as Yahweh's spokesperson and (by centering) the role of Yahweh Himself as the great victor. This latter, Yahweh's decisive action, stands in sharp contrast to the center of the first episode, where Barak's irresolution as Yahweh's commissioned field commander is exposed, and it deftly points up how groundless was Barak's uncertainty.

Further comparison of the structures of these two episodes brings to light other correspondences and contrasts between them. These can best be shown by setting the action sequences side by side:

Episode I	Episode II
Prologue: Deborah, prophetess and judge, holds court in the heartland of Israel, and the Israelites go to her for judgment.	Prologue: Heber, erstwhile ally of Israel, separates himself from his clan and moves from far south to far north to be near his new ally.
A. Deborah sends for Barak.	A. Heber sends word to Sisera.
B. Deborah commissions Barak.	B. Sisera summons his army.
C. Deborah transmits Yahweh's promise of victory	C. Deborah sends Barak into battle with assurances of victory (in language that recalls the promise).
D. Barak negotiates.	D. Barak goes to battle.
E. Deborah commits herself to accompany Barak as an earnest of Yahweh's promise.	E. Yahweh overwhelms the enemy.
F. Deborah goes with Barak to carry out Yahweh's commission.	F. Sisera descends from his chariot to escape the battle.
G. Barak assembles his force on Mount Tabor.	G. Barak pursues the fleeing enemy to its base at Harosheth Haggoyim.
H. Deborah goes up to Mount Tabor with Barak.	H. Sisera flees to Jael's tent.

It seems evident from such comparison that the author has foregrounded Deborah, Yahweh's spokesperson, as Sisera's real (human) nemesis. But he has also (by introducing Jael) awakened uncertainty and therefore suspense concerning which "woman" will receive the glory for Sisera's fall.

The final episode (vv. 18-22) unfolds at Jael's tent. The narrative structure is again marked by symmetry. It begins with Jael "going out to meet" Sisera. She invites him in and motivates him with assurances of safety; he enters her tent, and she conceals him. It ends with Jael "going out to meet" Barak. She directs him to enter and motivates him with expectations of final triumph; he enters her tent, and Sisera is disclosed, dead by Jael's hand.[15] Once again symmetry heightens contrast.

Between these two sequences and accounting for the contrasts are two intervening sequences of speech and response, with shockingly different outcomes. In the first (v. 19) Sisera requests a drink of water to relieve a physical need; Jael responds, and Sisera ends up refreshed, reassured, and safely concealed. In the second (vv. 20-21) Sisera directs Jael to stand guard to secure him against his pursuer(s); Jael responds in a surprisingly new way, and Sisera ends up not sleeping but dead.

As in the first two episodes, the critical turning point occurs precisely in the middle (v. 20), when Sisera commits his safety wholly into Jael's hands. He directs her to stand guard at the door of the tent. To any pursuer who inquires, she is to declare that there is "no man here," a declaration by which Sisera unwittingly (and ironically) offers an all-too-true self-assessment and foreshadows his demise that quickly follows.

The three centers—Barak's speech, which betrays his irresolution; Yahweh's vanquishing of the enemy; and Sisera's speech, in which he unknowingly speaks the truth about himself—together characterize the two opposing field commanders and focus narrative attention on Yahweh's decisive action. That in the first episode Deborah and in the last Jael dominate the action surrounding the centers structurally reinforces a major theme in the narrative and evenly distributes the honor for victory between these two redoubtable women.[16]

When structure so effectively serves plot and thematic development, balancing action with corresponding or contrasting action, heightening parallels and nurturing irony, artistry both pleases and contributes to lucidity with economy. And it adds another dimension. It teases the reader into slowing his pace, into pausing now and then to take note of the several developments in their interrelatedness, also into savoring the pleasure of discovering that the author has presented not a flat photograph but a hologram to be viewed from various angles. It is fruitless to speculate as to the level of conscious deliberation it required of the narrator to design the structures discernible. These may have sprung simply from a practiced skill in effective narration and an intense sensitivity to the multifaceted and delicately nuanced meanings he wished to convey. But when the reader by some effort uncovers them, they help to bring the author's intent into sharper focus.

II

We are now ready to read through the account, noting additional literary devices employed by the author to convey his message.

The author's stereotype introduction (vv. 1-3) sets the event in the context of his overarching theme, introduced in 2:6—3:6 and consistently carried through in the central cycle of narratives (3:7—16:31). His story is one of Israel's persistent unfaithfulness to Yahweh in the form of stubborn apostasy that chose for the gods of the indigenous peoples of Canaan in blatant violation of the covenant. But it is also a story of Yahweh's stern discipline of Israel and His merciful deliverances when His people cry to Him in the crises that His punishment generates. It is, in fact, the latter to which the author devotes most of his narrative attention. And that is true also in the present pericope.

The introduction shows careful syntactic coordination and subordination. Three primary verbal clauses report the major developments: "And the Israelites again did evil in the eyes of Yahweh' , "And Yahweh sold them into the hand of Jabin king of Canaan who reigned in Hazor"; "And the Israelites cried to Yahweh." All other information is given in subordinate, circumstantial clauses.

The first of the main clauses echoes 2:11, where the "evil" is specified as "worshiping the Baals." The second echoes 2:14 (see also 3:8; 10:7), employing a metaphor borrowed from economic life. Because Yahweh "sells" Israel "for nothing" (as it is put in Isa. 52:3; see also Ps. 44:12), the emphasis falls on the act of giving over to someone else's control. Still, it probably evokes the practice of selling persons into slavery (see Gen. 37:27, 28, 36; Ex. 21:7, 8, 16; Deut. 15:12; 21:14; 24:7; 28:68; 32:30). With the recipient identified as "Jabin king of Canaan who reigned in Hazor"[17] (see also vv. 17, 23, 24), the "selling" is depicted as a transaction between two suzerains. The oppressor's location in the north completes the round of Israel's vulnerable frontiers, the four quarters from which her security could be threatened (Cushan-Rishathaim had invaded the south, 3:8-9; Moab moved in from the east, 3:12-13; the Philistines pressed from the west, 3:31). The third main clause has no direct counterpart in the introduction to the book, but it employs the conventional language of appeal for help[18] when in distress (cf. 2:15).

The first circumstantial clause, "and Ehud was dead," marks the time relative to Ehud's leadership (3:12-30) rather than to that of Shamgar (3:31). For this there was no doubt reason: Of Shamgar the author notes only a striking victory over the Philistines by which he "saved Israel." He ascribes to Shamgar no period of leadership and mentions no period of peace that the victory effected. In any event, the note that Israel apostatized again after Ehud's death comports with the generalization in 2:19, where it is stated that "When the judge died, they again corrupted themselves, more than their fathers, going after other gods."

The two circumstantial clauses attached to the second main clause introduce Sisera[19] as Jabin's field commander and locate his headquarters at

Harosheth Haggoyim. He is met, then, as a suzerain's designated representative[20] whose status and role in the narrative parallels that of Barak. Hence, when these two face each other at the Kishon, the fortunes of two kingdoms are at stake. Sisera's base cannot now be located with any certainty, though it is usually thought to lie somewhere along the Kishon River, where its chariot forces could readily control the plain of Esdraelon and the major highways that traversed it.[21]

To the third main clause are added two further circumstantial clauses. They provide the motivation for Israel's desperate cry for help. The first foregrounds the fearsome main battle force of Jabin's[22] army, the nine hundred[23] chariots of iron,[24] which Israel's volunteer foot soldiers greatly feared; the second indicates the severity and length of the oppression such a force enabled the king of Canaan to impose.

With the stage set, the author plunges abruptly into his story by naming Deborah. It would be well, then, to pause here to examine the names of all those who subsequently play a role in the account in order to note their meanings, of which the original readers would have been well aware and which the author could exploit, if he chose, to support the development of his plot.[25] Deborah means "bee," famed for both its sting[26] and its honey.[27] She is identified as "wife of Lappidoth," whose name refers to the flame of torches (7:16, 20; 15:4, 5; and elsewhere) or to flashes of lightning (Ex. 20:18; Nah. 2:4). The latter is the more likely to be evoked here because of the close relationship between Deborah, wife of Lappidoth, and Barak, whose name (*bārāq*) clearly means "lightning" (Ex. 19:16;[28] Job 38:25; Pss. 77:18; 97:4; 135:7; and elsewhere). But *bārāq* is also used to refer to or characterize Yahweh's sword (Deut. 32:41), His arrows (2 Sam. 22:15; Pss. 18:14; 144:6; Zech. 9:14), and His spear (Hab. 3:11). In one striking passage it is said of the chariots of Yahweh's army that He sends against Nineveh that "their appearance is as *lappîdîm* (lightning); they dart about like *běrāqîm* (lightning)" (Nah. 2:5, Heb.). Barak is further identified as "son of Abinoam," that is, of "My (divine) Father is Delightfulness"—the root *n'm* indicates that which is beautiful/pleasant/delightful because it bestows benefits (see Prov. 2:10; 3:17; 16:24; 22:18; 24:4; Pss. 16:6, 11; 133:1; and note especially Ps. 27:4-6, and also 90:17, where *nō'am* is usually rendered "favor" [of Yahweh]).[29]

The name Heber comes from a verbal root that, with a personal subject, usually means to unite with, be joined with, be in league with another (or others).[30] Its cognate noun refers to a companion, associate, partner, friend, ally (Pss. 45:7; 119:63; Prov. 28:24; Eccles. 4:10; Song of Sol. 1:7;

8:13; Isa. 1:23; Ezek. 37:16, 19).[31] Hence the name suggests "associate" or "ally." But the verb is also used (together with its corresponding noun form) in the sense of binding by means of casting a spell over someone (Deut. 18:11; cf. Isa. 47:9, 12) or charming a snake (Ps. 58:5). As a Kenite, Heber is identified as a smith/metalworker, for that is what the name suggests.[32] Jael's name means "mountain goat" (1 Sam. 24:2; Job 39:1; Ps. 104:18), and she is "wife of Heber the Kenite."

So the Israelite company of players in this drama is made up of Bee, wife of Lightning; Lightning, son of My (divine) Father is Delightfulness (source of favor/benefits); Ally the Smith; and Mountain Goat, wife of Ally the Smith. Though Deborah is not Barak's wife, their close association here and the synonymity of *lappîdôt* and *bĕrāqîm* suggests a narrative relationship between them that parallels that between Heber and Jael.

With the meanings of these names in mind, consider the story.

Deborah is identified immediately as a prophetess (before naming her husband).[33] This marks her as a spokesperson for Yahweh and signalizes her role in the events to follow.[34] It also presents these as Yahweh-initiated events. Her announced status as judge (v. 4), to whom "the Israelites go up for judgment" (v. 5), identifies her as the source of justice where the wronged in Israel can secure redress and the oppressed relief. In context, it awakens expectations that she will also deliver the oppressed tribes from Jabin's harsh rule.

Appropriate to her role as judge, she holds court in Israel's heartland ("between Ramah and Bethel, in the hill country of Ephraim"). But why does the writer pinpoint her position as "under the date palm[35] of Deborah"? That the date palm had certain sacred associations in the ancient Near East seems evident from its extensive use in glyptic art and in temple decorations (1 Kings 6; Ezek. 40-41).[36] But there may be an additional motive. It appears likely that what the Old Testament refers to as "honey" included the sweet syrup of the date.[37] If the author is playing on the meaning of names, he here shows us Deborah (Bee) holding court under a "honey" tree, where she dispenses the sweetness of justice (cf. Isa. 5:20; Amos 5:7; 6:12).[38]

While reading this prologue, the reader will have been arrested by a striking verbal link with the introduction. There, in a circumstantial clause, he was told: "And he (Sisera) resided (*yôšēb* [sat in command], participle) at Harosheth Haggoyim." Here, in a like circumstantial clause, he reads: "And she (Deborah) resided (*yôšebet* [held court], participle) under the Date Palm." Thus he has already received a hint that a fateful collision is in the offing between the one who sits in command at Harosheth Hag-goyim and she who sits in judgment in the hill country of Ephraim.

Action begins with Deborah's summoning the warrior Barak,[39] which her recognized status as spokesperson for Yahweh and as judge gives her the authority to do. She calls him from Kadesh Naphtali,[40] a few miles northwest of Hazor. There, quite belying his name (lightning), Barak has up till now remained passive[41] while the king of Canaan rebuilt his power and for many years imposed harsh rule over the northern tribes.

Wasting no words on Barak's reaction to Deborah's summons, on his journey to her, or on his manner of greeting her when he arrives, the author keeps focus on Deborah by reporting immediately the commission from Yahweh that she has for him ("And she sent, and she summoned Barak . . . and she said to him . . ."). Her opening words—"Has not Yahweh the God of Israel commanded?"—could be taken as a rebuke for Barak's failure hitherto to act on behalf of his fellow Israelites, either in accordance with some earlier directive or with Yahweh's standing orders (and promises) concerning the conquest of the land. And that is how some have taken them. More likely, they represent an asseverative: "Yahweh . . . has certainly commanded."[42] The idiom is emphatic.

It introduces the very words of Yahweh, which Deborah transmits as Yahweh's spokesperson. Here Israel's Great King speaks through the mouth of Deborah and charges His servant Barak (lightning) to "Go (*lēk*) and deploy (*māšaktā*) on Mount Tabor." The rendering "deploy" is uncertain,[43] though it may be supported by 20:37.[44] If correct, it suggests that Barak personally had a force at his command[45] that he was to augment with "ten thousand men from Naphtali and Zebulun."[46] Mount Tabor, an isolated peak at the northeast end of the plain of Esdraelon, is designated as Barak's base of attack. The Israelite reader would know its strategic advantages, that its steep, wooded sides provided absolute security against chariot attack and that its high summit (more than a thousand feet above the plain) gave a commanding view all around.

Immediately following Yahweh's commission comes Yahweh's promise: "And I will draw (*māšaktî*) to you, to the Kishon River, Sisera, the commander of Jabin's army, and his chariots and his troops." (Ultimately they are Jabin's, but Sisera commands them.) As Barak is to *māšak* his forces on Mount Tabor, so Yahweh will *māšak* the enemy army to the plain below, along the Kishon. The verb is the same, thus paralleling Barak's and Yahweh's actions and highlighting the fact that ultimately it is Yahweh who brings both armies into the field. Yet there is a difference. Yahweh is not Jabin, to send Sisera afield, or Sisera, to deploy his army; but He is the sovereign Lord. And the idiom is different: *māšak 'el*. He will "draw" Sisera "to" a fateful meeting with His servant Barak, and to the Kishon River, which will—but that awaits the event; for now, it only suggests a specific location for the upcoming battle and awakens curiosity as to the part the river may play in the outcome. The battle will be no mere skirmish. Sisera's chariots will be there in full force; that is foregrounded. But so will be his infantry. Sisera will be "drawn" into committing his whole army.

Now comes the climax of Yahweh's promise: "I will give him into your hand." That is Sisera, of course, but not apart from the army he commands and by which he has enforced Jabin's rule.

One might object that this early disclosure of the outcome reduces climactic tension, that it robs the story of suspense. But that would be to misconstrue the story. It is not an account of a battle but of a divine deliverance and of how those called to be servants of Yahweh respond to Him (specifically to His commands and promises).

Once the commission has been delivered and the promise spoken, Deborah—and Yahweh—fall silent. And Barak speaks for the first, and only, time. He responds to Deborah, not to Yahweh. He has heard Deborah, not Yahweh. Deborah has said. . . . Let Deborah act on her words. Only then will Barak undertake this impossible venture. Deborah has commanded, "Go!" Barak answers, "If you will go with me, I will go. If you will not go with me, I will not go." Deborah's (and Yahweh's) command to "go" is repeated in Barak's reply like a mocking echo.[47] According to Job 38:35, when God sends His bolts of lightning (*běrāqîm*), they "go" (*hālak*), but Barak (*bārāq*) will not "go" unless. . . .[48]

It is clear that Barak has not been eagerly awaiting a word from Yahweh to go forth as Yahweh's "lightning" sword against the oppressor of Israel. His quiescence all these years betrays him, and now also his dullness to hear the voice of Yahweh, and his hesitancy, and his negotiating for reassurances and support. He will not act simply upon Yahweh's command and promise. Perhaps he wished to have a messenger of Yahweh by his side in this bold undertaking to provide directions for the battle. But there was more to it than that. He had no confidence in Yahweh's word. He needed an earnest of Yahweh's promise, and he needed the courage and faith of this woman to be the staff on which his little courage and little faith could lean.

Quickly and resolutely Deborah responds: "I will surely go with you." She who had said to Barak in Yahweh's name, "Go," unhesitatingly commits herself to "go." She believes Yahweh's promise. So now the decisive commitment to "go" and the effective leadership in the "going" is Deborah's, not Barak's.

Barak's hesitancy, his lack of faith, and his dependence on Deborah affects the outcome and alters the promise. There will accrue to Barak no glory along the "way" he is "going" (participle). The language is ambiguous, no doubt studiedly so. Barak is about to go on a "way" (the Hebrew participle often expresses impending action). But he is also already "going"[49] a "way." That is, he is comporting himself in a certain manner. In the "way" he is now "going," and is about to "go," glory (fame/honor) will elude him. "For into the hands of a woman Yahweh will sell[50] Sisera."

The promise of victory is not withdrawn, but a woman will bring the awesome Sisera down. This time "into the hand of" is brought forward from the end (cf. v. 7) to the initial position to underscore the altered prospect.[51] And Deborah's word cuts two ways. To Barak's lack of faith it proclaims that Yahweh is able to "sell" Sisera even into the hands of a woman (just as He had "sold" Israel into the hands of Jabin and Sisera with their nine hundred chariots of iron, v. 2). Why should Barak (Lightning, son of My Father is Delightfulness) have doubted? It also announces that because Barak doubted, though victory will be his, the glory will go to a woman.

This exchange arouses suspense and focuses it. Victory for Barak, but what of the Kishon, and what of this unnamed woman?[52] As of now there is but one woman on stage, a woman who aggressively advances the action: "And Deborah arose and went with Barak to Kadesh" to carry out Yahweh's commission.

From Kadesh Deborah had called Barak; now back to Kadesh Deborah and Barak return. And there at Kadesh "Barak called out (*wayyiz'aq*) Zebulun and Naphtali," in accordance with Deborah's instructions (v. 6). The author could not resist a chiasm ("Naphtali and Zebulun," v. 6; "Zebulun and Naphtali," v. 10), or is it by chiasm that he emphasizes fulfillment of the first stage of Yahweh's instructions?

"And there went up at his feet 10,000 men." The actions of this verse correspond to the instructions in verse 6 ("Go and deploy on Mount Tabor, and take with you 10,000 men"), but they are carried out in reverse order (as they only could be). This correspondence and the nicely designed chiasm makes ellipsis possible: The "going up" refers to the mountain from which Barak is to launch his attack. The expression "at his feet" *(běragláyw)* means contextually "under his command," but it subtly reminds the reader that Barak marches at the head of foot soldiers in contrast to Sisera's chariot force.[53]

"And she went up with him, Deborah," to Mount Tabor, where she is found next (v. 14). As noted earlier, she (the "judge") now goes up with Barak and the tribes to effect a judgment on the oppressor of Israel (cf. v. 5). With "Deborah" the episode began and with "Deborah" it ends.

Now that Deborah, Barak, and the tribes are assembled on Mount Tabor, Yahweh's command (v. 6) has been carried out. The moment has come for the narrator to relate the fulfillment of the promise: "And I will draw to you, to the Kishon River, Sisera." Abruptly he injects a circumstantial clause introducing Heber the Kenite.[54] All the while the reader has wondered how Yahweh will manage to bring Sisera and his army on the scene. The author now tells us. But the reader must listen carefully, because he is offered only hints, as if to match the hiddenness and mystery of Yahweh's providential action. But the hints are there in the name, the relationship identified, the action mentioned, and the juxtaposition with verse 12. "Now Ally the Smith had separated himself from the Kenites (smiths), the descendants of Hobab, Moses' father-in-law, and pitched his tent by the Oak in Zaanannim, which is near Kadesh. And Sisera was told. . . ."

Heber belonged to a clan associated with Israel from the days of Moses and allied with Judah since the conquest (1:16). He has, however, separated from them and moved north, most certainly to ply his trade. And who would need a smith more than the king who was assembling a force of nine hundred chariots of iron? So Ally the Smith had made a new alliance. The clues are all present but in the manner of a riddle to tease the mind and awaken expectation of resolution. And it comes, at the very end of the episode: "For there was peace (an alliance) between Jabin king of Hazor and the house of Heber the Kenite" (v. 17).

Ally the Smith was tenting near Kadesh, so he knew of Barak's preparations far from Sisera's base at Harosheth Haggoyim. "And Sisera was told. . . ."

But why the notation "by the Oak in Zaanannim"?[55] Was it merely shade that Heber desired? Such trees were often the sites of cult places because there, it was thought, one might have communication with and enjoy the protection of the divine realm.[56] Perhaps that was Heber's main concern. The author does not say so expressly, but he hints as much, and the "Oak in Zaanannim" is obviously being played off against "the palm tree of Deborah" (v. 5).

"Barak son of Abinoam has gone up to Mount Tabor." That is the word sent to Sisera. From that he knows that his power is being challenged. "And Sisera called out (*wayyiz'aq*)" his forces. His response is to do exactly what Barak had done. A lengthening chain of parallel actions leads on to the fateful confrontation: Sisera sat in command (*yāšab*), and Deborah held court (*yāšab*); Yahweh, who sold (*mākar*) Israel into the hands of Jabin, will sell (*mākar*) Sisera into the hands of a woman; Barak is to deploy (*māšak*) on Mount Tabor, and Yahweh will draw (*māšak*) Sisera to him; all Israel went up (*'ālâ*) to Deborah, and Deborah went up (*'ālâ*) with Barak; Barak calls out (*zā'aq*) the tribes, and Sisera calls out (*zā'aq*) his army.

He calls out all the forces he commands: "his chariots, the 900 chariots of iron, and all the troops who are with him" (the battle will truly be decisive). He calls them "from Harosheth Haggoyim to the Kishon River"; Yahweh has "drawn" the enemy to the place He had chosen.

Now the hour of decision has come. Deborah the prophetess speaks to Barak. He has had his say (v. 8), his one speech in which he disclosed the irresolute spirit within him. He initiates no inquiry; he simply awaits directions from Deborah (the bee). Now it comes: "Up, for this is the day," the day of the Lord's triumphant action, "the day in which Yahweh has given Sisera into your hand." The tense of "has given" is usually indicative of completed action but was often employed to announce beforehand Yahweh's sure act.[57] "Sisera into your hand" is an echo of the original promise of victory (v. 6). But the qualification still stands: "Into the hand of a woman will Yahweh sell Sisera" (v. 9). So the puzzle remains.

Then comes an assuring word. "Has not Yahweh gone out before you?" Again the asseverative (cf. "Has not Yahweh commanded?" v. 6). Yahweh has certainly gone forth to the battle. You, Barak, need only follow the Great Warrior ("Yahweh is a warrior," Ex. 15:3).[58]

The reader does not yet know it, but this is Deborah's last word. Expectations have been awakened that she will be in on the denouement. Here as Yahweh's spokesperson, whose presence at Kadesh and on Mount Tabor was an earnest of Yahweh's commission and promise, she launches the attack that will bring glory to a woman. But when next a woman appears in the narrative, after the battle, it is Jael, wife of Heber the Kenite (Ally the Smith).

"And Barak descended from Mount Tabor." The language is sparse, but it evokes a scene of high drama, of fearful power unleashed. Yahweh has already sallied forth to the battle. Now, at the command of His adjutant, Yahweh's chosen field commander, Barak, descends from the top of Tabor. Yahweh's flashing sword/spear/arrow, His flashing chariot, descends from on high to engage the mighty host on the plain. And with him 10,000 from the tribes of Israel.

"And Yahweh overwhelmed Sisera . . . before Barak." That is all that is told, nothing more. But anything more would have distracted from the awesomeness of this divine act. The language chosen stirs the imagination to recreate its essential features. *"Wayyāhām Yahweh,"* says the author. The verb occurs thirteen times in the Old Testament, in all but three with Yahweh as subject. Of these, eight speak of Yahweh the Warrior overwhelming His enemies,[59] and in six of these He does so by attacking out of the thunderstorm,[60] He

> who makes the clouds His chariot,
>   who goes on the wings of the wind,
> who makes winds His agents,
>   flashes of lightning His servants (Ps. 104:3b-4).[61]

But most suggestive of all for the scene the writer evokes are the words of Psalms 18:14[62] and 144:6. In Psalm 18 David celebrates with graphic conventional imagery the onslaught of the heavenly Warrior against the powerful enemies of His servant:

> Yahweh thundered from heaven,
>   the voice of the Most High resounded.
> He shot His arrows and scattered them [the enemy],
>   great bolts of lightning and overwhelmed them
>   (*běrāqîm rāb wayyěhummēm*) (vv. 13-14).

Psalm 144 contains many echoes of Psalm 18, among them:

> Part your heavens, O Yahweh, and come down;
>   touch the mountains, so that they smoke.
> Flash lightning (*běrôq bārāq*) and scatter them;
>   shoot your arrows and overwhelm them
>   (*ûtěhummēm*) (vv. 5-6).

The picture is clear. Yahweh goes forth in storm cloud before Barak; then down from Mount Tabor comes Barak, Yahweh's "lightning" weapon. "And Yahweh overwhelmed Sisera . . . before Barak." The reader does not need the poetic account (see 5:20-21) to know that the heavenly Warrior has struck from heaven out of a thunderstorm to confound and mire and sweep away the great ranks of chariots and infantry. They were massed, he had been told, though only now he understands why, along the Kishon.

Sisera is overwhelmed "and all his chariots and all his encampment [army]." Once again (cf. vv. 3, 7, 12) the chariots are foregrounded as the main power base of the enemy. Yahweh overwhelmed them "by the sword" (*lĕpî ḥereb*). The idiom with *hāmam* is unusual,[63] but so is "before Barak" (*lipnê bārāq*), which follows. But by means of it the author has achieved a telling double wordplay with which to conclude this central,[64] decisive line. There is *lĕpî* and *lipnê*. But more striking and more plot central are *rekeb* (chariot), *ḥereb* (sword), and *bārāq* (Barak).

"And Sisera descended." So had Barak (v. 14). The chain of parallel acts is extended: Sisera *yāšab*/Deborah *yāšab*; Yahweh *mākar*/Yahweh *mākar*; Barak *māšak*/Yahweh *māšak*; Israelites *'ālâ*/Deborah *'ālâ*; Barak *zā'aq*/Sisera *zā'aq*; Barak descends (*yārad*)/Sisera "descends (*yārad*) from his chariot" to flee the battle. Structural balance,[65] similarity of the clauses both in syntax and length (nineteen syllables; seventeen syllables), and sameness in both initial verb and final pronominal suffix all contribute to highlight the parallelism, the contrast, and the irony:

> And descended (*wayyēred*) Barak from Mount Tabor, and 10,000 men after him (*'aḥărāyw*).

> And descended (*wayyēred*) Sisera from his chariot and fled on his feet (*bĕraglāyw*).

"On his feet" (*bĕraglāyw*) is idiomatically and logically superfluous but is employed here (see also v. 17) for ironic effect. After Yahweh and His Lightning have struck, Sisera's iron chariot cannot even provide a means of escape. Sisera has been reduced to the absurd, and our narrator knew how to depict it. But *bĕraglāyw* is also an echo. It recalls a phrase heard first in v. 10: "And 10,000 went up [Mount Tabor] at his feet (*bĕraglāyw*)." Barak ascends with 10,000 *bĕraglāyw*; Sisera descends to flee (alone) *bĕraglāyw*. The ironical contrast is intended, and to achieve it the author once more employs the technique of verbal repetition, thus extending his chain of parallels yet another link.

The mighty commander of chariots flees the battle like one of the lowly foot soldiers who are beating a hasty retreat toward Harosheth Haggoyim. But is Sisera among them? It is one of the narrator's finest touches that here he does not give us even a hint. He leaves us to believe, as did Barak, that Sisera fled with his troops. Only after he has brought pursuing Barak to the enemy's base does he inform us, and then it is to surprise us with Sisera's solitary flight to Heber's encampment.

He closes the episode with a pair of nicely balanced sentences showing us the two principals leaving the battlefield in contrasting pursuits and opposite directions:

> And Barak pursued after the chariots and after the army to Harosheth Haggoyim; and all of Sisera's army fell by the sword, not one was left (v. 16).

> And Sisera fled on his feet to the tent of Jael, the wife of Heber the Kenite; for there was an alliance between Jabin king of Hazor and the house of Heber the Kenite [Ally the Smith] (v. 17).

The victor and the vanquished are both pounding the earth with winged feet away from the site of battle. But the tables have turned: Barak presses on to catch Sisera before he can recover or find refuge; Sisera hurries to escape, so as not to "fall into the hands of"[66] Barak. Irony abounds. Barak with his 10,000 goes in hot pursuit of Sisera's chariots and army; Sisera on foot takes flight alone. Barak pursues to Harosheth Haggoyim; Sisera flees to Kadesh. Barak, triumphant, arrives at the enemy's base, mopping up the remnants of the Canaanite army; Sisera, defeated, arrives at the tent of a woman, far from the fury of combat and safe from the avenging sword.[67] Still, Barak misses his quarry. And what of Sisera?

The great battle is over, but the story is not finished; it cannot be finished. The author has raised expectations that must not be left suspended. Yahweh's promise to Barak had been, "I will give Sisera into your hand." And that promise had been subsequently qualified: "Yahweh will sell Sisera into the hand of a woman." The promise remains unfulfilled, and it is not yet known how it is that the glory will not be Barak's or who the "woman" is of whom Deborah had spoken. Is it dauntless Deborah, who was still with Barak on Mount Tabor and who had sent him descending the mountain into the battle? Or is it Jael, the wife of Jabin's ally Heber, to whose tent Sisera has fled for safety?

The last two sentences with which the battle scene closes report simultaneous actions: Barak pursuing, Sisera fleeing. These might have been given in reverse order. But the author had his reasons for the order he chose. He had a structural reason, as was observed earlier. And he had achieved a moment of fine suspense. But more than that, his chosen order allows him a smooth transition to the final act in the drama. Denouement takes place not at Harosheth Haggoyim but at Jael's tent, and that is where the narrator has brought us at the end of his battle account.

"And Jael went out to meet Sisera." No details are given about Sisera's flight, the course taken, the difficulties encountered, the time required, the fear that drove the fugitive on and the fatigue that slowed his pace, the hopes and expectations he entertained, or the plans he devised along the way for gaining Heber's protection. Because the outcome is affected by none of these they are passed over. When Sisera reaches Heber's encampment, his fate lies in hands other than his own.

Whereas Deborah had summoned Barak to come to her, Sisera arrives at Heber's camp on his own volition. But on his arrival Jael takes the initiative. She goes out to meet[68] her husband's ally, addresses the field commander with proper respect, and offers him hospitality and refuge: "Turn aside, my lord, turn aside to me; do not be afraid." As Deborah had instructed (imperative) Barak to "go," so now Jael invites (imperative) Sisera to "turn aside" from his going. Her motives remain hidden. Neither Sisera nor the reader have cause to suspect them. And yet there is Deborah's word about a "woman." There is also the fact that Jael intrudes in a matter that concerns Sisera and her husband Heber. Yes, she intrudes. Sisera is passing by on his way (no doubt to Heber's tent), and she intercepts him with her "turn aside . . . turn aside to me."[69] Alliteration calls attention to her word: "Jael went out to meet *Sisera,* and she said to him *sûrâ,* my lord, *sûrâ* to me."

Why, also, this "Do not fear?" Jael knows that out of fear Sisera is fleeing, that he will "turn aside" only if he has found a place where he need no longer fear. That is what she offers him. Implicit in her "Do not fear" is a promise belying Deborah's (initial) promise to Barak: You will not be given into any man's hand. The irony can hardly be missed.[70] But what of Deborah's revised promise? And what of this newly promising woman? The reader wonders.

"And he turned aside to her tent." The great general, who but recently commanded nine hundred chariots of iron and thousands of infantry, is diverted from his course by the invitation of a woman. As Deborah, wife of Lappidoth, had directed the course of Barak, now Jael directs the course of Sisera. Deborah sent forth Barak to public exploits; Jael receives Sisera into her private quarters: "And she covered him with a robe."[71] The erstwhile scourge of Israel, chariot-mounted and fearsome, lies prostrate on the ground shielded from the avenging Barak by a robe, a tent, and a woman.

From the ground he speaks; it is an appeal: "Please give me a little water. I'm thirsty." Like Samson, he is only a man and suffers an ordinary human need. Is his need also life-threatening, as it was with Samson after he had exerted himself in battle (15:18)? In any event, his total dependence on Jael is presented concretely.

In response, she acts the perfect hostess. Without a word "she opened a skin of milk and gave him a drink." Or, as the poem puts it:

> He asked for water, and she gave him milk;
> in a bowl fit for nobles, she brought him milk curds (5:25).

Mountain Goat brought him milk, the better, more nourishing drink, which was set before honored guests.[72]

Here the play on the meaning of Jael's name cannot be missed. It causes the reader to ponder the meaning of Deborah (Bee), the "judge" who has provided Israel the sweetness (honey) of judgment. And if the reader has missed it, it prods him to contemplate "Barak" (Lightning) and "Heber the Kenite" (Ally the Smith). If he has already suspected the author's play on these names, that suspicion is now fully confirmed.

"And she covered him (again)." Having refreshed and reassured Sisera, she returns him to his state of concealment but now in repose.

Again he speaks. No longer the suppliant, he now seeks to take charge of his situation. Jael has opened a skin of milk to revive him. He reads it as evidence of her trustworthiness. His wish had been her command. So now the general commands: "Stand by the opening of the tent." Once more he has a subordinate to take orders, though only this lone woman. He posts her at the door of the tent as a sentry. Irony grows toward full flood. It crests in his follow-up instructions, great Sisera's last words: "If any one comes by and asks, 'Is any man here?' you are to say, 'There is not.'" Unwittingly, Sisera provides a true self-assessment and a sinister foreshadowing of the fate that is about to overtake him. Moreover, by his own decision and act Sisera has committed his safety into Jael's hands, has given himself into the hand of a woman.

The author has reached the crucial midpoint of his final episode. The reader knows (yet) only that the crisis fast approaches. How will Jael respond now? Will she allow Sisera to take charge? Can she outdo her earlier exceeding of his request? Is this the fateful moment?

There comes an explosion of verbal clauses, and the answer becomes clear. "And Jael wife of Heber [Ally?] took a tent peg, and she took up a mallet in her hand, and she went to him stealthily,[73] and she drove the peg

into his temple,[74] and it penetrated[75] into the ground."[76] To which is brief-
ly added (four words in Hebrew),[77] "Now he was fast asleep, because he was
weary, and so he died."

The reader now sees that Yahweh has been at work to "sell Sisera into
the hand of a woman" just as He had effectively "drawn" Sisera and all his
army to the Kishon. The reader also sees clearly now the author's insight
into how Yahweh had accomplished both. He drew Sisera to the plain
along the Kishon by sending Barak and his men to Mount Tabor. He knew
that when the commander of chariots saw his power challenged, he would
prudently assemble his forces where he was confident he had the advantage. When his army was routed, he made another prudent judgment.
Abandoning his army, he made for the tent of his ally, where he thought
he would surely find safety only to fall into Jael's hands. Yahweh had accomplished His purpose through Sisera's own free acts. Moreover, ironically, the shadowy figure of Heber plays a decisive role in both developments. This renegade Kenite, who had shifted alliances to help build
Jabin's armaments, had betrayed Barak's moves to the field commander.
He had thus been instrumental in bringing Sisera to the Kishon. But it
was also his proven loyalty to Jabin's cause that recommended him to Sisera when disaster struck as the one to whom he could look for protection.
Thus Yahweh used and frustrated this unholy alliance also to achieve His
ends.

Suddenly it is over. Sisera is dead, and Jael wife of Heber is revealed as
the "woman." She had duped Sisera completely. To this moment she had
played the wife of Ally the Smith, associate of King Jabin, flawlessly. But
she too has been "under cover." Now with shocking suddenness she shows
herself to have been Jael wife of Charmer (the author says carefully "wife of
Heber," not as before "wife of Heber the Kenite"). She had charmed the
mighty warrior into a harmless sleeper and then dispatched him like a
snake.

She had no sword, only the implements with which women secured a
tent. A wooden tent peg was her arrow and a wooden mallet the bow with
which she shot it to its mark. Having taken *(wattiqqaḥ)* the peg, she drove
(wattitqaʻ) it into his temple *(bĕraqqātô)*—she, not *bārāq* (Barak). And the
commander of chariots of iron ends up pinned to the ground by a wooden
tent peg, driven home by a woman's hand.

Here, again, Yahweh's secret working quietly surfaces. Though Heber
the Kenite has shifted loyalties, Jael has not. Her heart is still with Israel.
When she sees Sisera approaching alone and on foot, she can guess the

outcome of the battle and that Israel's great enemy had eluded Barak. So she springs into action. With a courage and ingenuity that matches Ehud's, she invites the feared warrior into her own tent, puts him at ease, and then dispatches him. Her bold, fierce loyalty that steels her to act alone, contrary to her husband's commitments, without a word from Yahweh, and armed only with domestic implements, puts Barak to shame. And it is that loyalty that Yahweh uses to checkmate Heber's perfidy and remove the scourge from Israel.

The suddenness of this turn of events and the shocking violence of Jael's deed trigger a series of breath-catching mental images. As they shutter past the mind's eye, there is the half-expectation that the veteran warrior will suddenly spring from the ground and foil the dauntless woman stealing upon him. One forgets that he had said, "Say, 'There is no man here.'"

But nothing happens. The prone figure remains motionless under his covering. The robe that conceals him also conceals her. But is her approach utterly soundless? The only movement is Jael's, climaxed by her swift, fatal blow. And still there is no motion under the robe. The author explains: "Now he was fast asleep, because he was weary, and [thus] he died." From motionless sleep Sisera passed motionless into death, "sold into the hands of a woman" like a piece of chattel.

So the end has come.

But dead Sisera is still concealed from the eyes of the world by a robe, a tent, and a woman. And there was a strong hint in the qualified promise that the glory for Sisera's defeat would go to a woman. There must therefore be a revelation, an uncovering, and it must somehow involve Barak, for whom the qualified promise was a rebuke. So, though Sisera is dead, the story cannot end even yet.

Nor does it. "And [while Sisera lies there still], behold, Barak [comes into view], pursuing Sisera." Irony pervades all in the denouement. Victorious Barak is still pursuing his elusive quarry. But now he is pursuing a dead foe, a lifeless body pinned to the ground by Jael's tent peg.

How is it that Barak comes here alone? By what route did he come? Who told him of Sisera's direction and the goal of his flight? Or was it a shrewd guess that Sisera might seek the protection of his ally the ironsmith? All this is irrelevant to the story that is being told, and the author says nothing of it. It is enough that Barak is here, that though the enemy is destroyed and Barak's own men are (presumably) busy gathering the spoils,[78] he is still pursuing the one who (originally) was to be "given into his hand."

"And Jael went out to meet him." The chain of parallels receives yet another link: *yāšab/yāšab; mākar/mākar; māšak/māšak; 'ālâ/'ālâ; zā'aq-/zā'aq; yārad/yārad; bĕraglāyw/bĕraglāyw;* Jael "goes out to meet" Sisera/ Jael "goes out to meet" Barak.

"And she said to him, 'Come.'" She did not say, "Turn aside, my lord, turn aside to me," but spoke an abrupt, commanding "Come" (*lēk*), the very word used by Deborah when she transmitted Yahweh's command, "Go"[79] (v. 6). So again Barak is directed by a woman with an identical imperative. And a ninth link is added to the chain of parallels.

"And I will show you the man you are seeking." Jael knows that Barak is "pursuing," that he is "seeking the man" who was to be "given into his hand" but who had pronounced himself a "no man" and had become a "no man." Sisera she motivated with "Do not fear *(yārē')*"; Barak she motivates with "I will show" *(rā'â)*. She will show him the man he wants so desperately to get "into his hand."

Jael controls events now as in her meeting with Sisera. Sisera had spoken not a word until he entered Jael's tent and had been covered. Barak also speaks no word; he merely follows directions and enters Jael's tent to see. At last he has overtaken his quarry; at last his enemy will be "given into his hand."

"And, behold" is the tenth and final link in the chain of parallels. Shortly ago it was "And, behold, Barak"; now it is "And, behold, Sisera."

The moment of final disclosure has arrived; Jael uncovers Sisera, "fallen, dead, with the tent peg in his temple *(bĕraqqātô)*." Barak's *(bārāq)* quarry, the great charioteer and commander he had once feared, the vanquished foe he had so single-mindedly and strenuously pursued to get "into his hand," lies before him, with Jael's tent peg *bĕraqqātô*. It is the final irony, and it surpasses them all.

And Barak remains dumb. The story is ended.

Yahweh has fulfilled His word and delivered His people. Through Deborah, wife of Lightning, who held court under the Date Palm of Deborah, He has sent Lightning, son of My (divine) Father is Delightfulness, to strike a decisive blow on the battlefield; and through Jael, wife of Ally the Smith (but also wife of Charmer), whose tent was near the Oak in Zaanannim, He has executed Israel's oppressor. Through Bee and Mountain Goat, two faithful and fearless women, He has destroyed mighty Sisera and restored peace to the Promised Land that "flows with milk and honey."

There remains but to round out the literary framework within which the story is set. Like the introduction (vv. 1-3), it is stereotypical. Yet it provides in general terms some significant information. "God subdued that day Jabin king of Canaan before the Israelites." The decisive blow had been struck, but a power as old and resilient as this kingdom did not disintegrate in a day. "And the hand of the Israelites pressed down ever harder on Jabin king of Canaan until they had cut off Jabin king of Canaan." Never again would this coalition of Canaanites revive to threaten Israel. "And the land enjoyed peace forty years" (5:31b).

III

By almost any reckoning, Judges 4 is a little masterpiece of narrative. In this it does not stand alone in the Old Testament, of course, not even in Judges itself. But, as it has been seen, careful attention to its art evokes new appreciation for the narrative skill of the author of a story that by a more superficial reading tends to attract little special attention. No one would call it charming or beautiful; it is too lean and muscular for that, befitting its plot and theme. It is better characterized as efficient and effective. Its style is tight and economical. No superfluous details or narrative detours distract from plot development. Structure, syntax, repetition (the parallel chain), alliteration, wordplay, and narrative sequence all contribute coherently to message communication. Even select geographic locations are carefully made part of the story to illumine character roles and elucidate events. At strategic points the author employs conventional phrases that are richly evocative in order to interpret and to add vividness. Contrast, suspense, and irony—especially irony—are utilized to great effect. Most striking of all is the manner in which the suggestive semantic value of names has been put to subtle use to hint at connections and deeper levels of meaning. The narrator was an artist in full control of his medium.

But he was more than an artist, more than a teller of tales. The story as he told it was made to serve the theological theme of his larger narrative. One of the striking features of contemporary Old Testament scholarship is the boldness with which it layers historical hypothesis upon historical hypothesis in order to reconstruct hypothetically in some detail the history of Israel and of the biblical documents and then make these (often conflicting) reconstructions the basis and burden of biblical exposition. For Judges, two good examples are the recent commentaries by J. A. Soggin and R. G. Boling.[80] One result is the tendency to isolate the several accounts of the various judges from their larger literary context and to study them independently. Even those who, like D. F. Murray, find good literary grounds for questioning proposals of editorial changes within the separate narrative units are inclined to exclude the larger context from consideration when discussing the matter of theme. The end result is to treat the various accounts as independent stories. That the author drew on a body of separate traditions can hardly be doubted, but that he has done more than preserve a collection of stories seems beyond dispute. Rather, he chose certain traditions that served his thematic purpose and retold them in a manner conducive to that purpose. Hence context must be given due weight in determining the theme of Judges 4.[81]

No thorough discussion of the overarching theme of Judges can be undertaken here. A brief indication of its salient elements will have to suffice. It is generally recognized, and rightly so, that Judges was intended to serve as a continuation of the national epic narrated in the Pentateuch and Joshua. It fills in the gap between the account of the conquest under Joshua and the emergence of the monarchy, for which the ministry of Samuel came to be viewed as prologue (the story told in 1 and 2 Samuel). What should have been a time of consolidation turned out rather to be an era of progressive degeneration and disintegration (consolidation did not come until the reign of David, who completed the wars of Joshua). As a result, nothing went forward. So the writer had not so much a history to recount as an age to characterize.

And that is the focus of his theme, as he tells us expressly in 2:6—3:6. After the death of Joshua, the Israelites did evil in the eyes of Yahweh by turning to the gods of Canaan. No longer acknowledging Yahweh and all He had done for them, they violated the covenant and thus aroused the wrath of their heavenly suzerain. In His anger He turned loose the surrounding peoples on them and withheld His own power to defend them. But He did not altogether abandon them. When they belatedly cried to Him for deliverance, He sent them deliverers (the "judges") to throw off the oppressors and give His people relief. Even so, when the judges died, the people returned to their old ways, to sink even deeper into apostasy. At stake was the future of the kingdom of God on earth and the destiny of Israel. If it were not for Yahweh's stern measures and persistent mercies in the face of Israel's stubborn infidelity, the kingdom of God would have vanished from the earth, and Israel would have been submerged under the nations.

In the central cycle of narratives in which this theme is provided concrete exposition, the story of Judges 4 follows the account of Othniel (3:7-11) and Ehud (vv. 12-30) and precedes those of Gideon-Abimelek (chaps. 6-9), Jephthah (10:6-12:7), and Samson (chaps. 13-16). Given the fact that progressive degeneration is one element in the author's announced theme, that Othniel is depicted as a model judge and Samson as the most degenerate, that in the case of Jephthah Israel is dependent on an outcast freebooter, and that Gideon is an even more reluctant deliverer than Barak, the reader possesses one clue to the theme of the Deborah-Barak-Jael story.[82] Barak's quiescence in the face of Canaanite oppression (belying his name and in contrast with the vigorous initiatives of Othniel and Ehud) and his dependence on Deborah even after being commissioned by Yahweh expose Israel's failure to remember Yahweh and all He had done for her (2:10). Not remembering left her fearful and passive before the resurgent power of the ancient Canaanite kingdom of Hazor. Before chariots of iron Israel quailed, though the sword of Yahweh (Barak, Lightning) was among them.[83] Such was her abject submissiveness that at least one of her erstwhile allies (Heber) changed sides and threw in his lot with the Canaanites.

In this crisis and in response to Israel's cry to Him for help, Yahweh raised up two courageous and faithful women to effect His judgment on the oppressor and to subdue once for all the Canaanite threat. Through one He brought His reluctant sword (Barak) into play, and through the other He cut down the great warrior who had marshaled and commanded King Jabin's power.

The victory was wholly Yahweh's, who maneuvered Sisera and his army into a trap and then overwhelmed them before Barak, leaving to that one only to mop up the broken ranks of chariots and foot soldiers. Great Sisera, whom all Israel feared, He "sold" into the hands of a woman, meanwhile also frustrating the unholy alliance between Heber and Jabin. No honor accrued to Barak and his troops. Glory came only to two women who embodied the loyalty and dauntless courage that ought to have characterized the warriors in the army of Yahweh. Again Yahweh was gracious to His faithless people. But He effected deliverance in such a way as to shame Israel's doubts in their heavenly King. Even mighty Sisera is a "no man" to be subdued by a woman when Yahweh executes judgment. If through Bee and Mountain Goat Yahweh can throw off the yoke imposed by Sisera and his nine hundred chariots of iron and restore peace to the land of milk and honey, then Israel, if faithful, can withstand the world. And even when she is unfaithful, Yahweh does not forget His covenant or abandon His purpose.

The story rebukes and promises.

In canonical context, it relates an episode in the history of the Yahweh-Israel relationship that foreshadows Yahweh's mercies to His people through His servant David and ultimately through David's great son.

NOTES

1. The artistry of this passage has been studied before. L. Alonzo-Schökel offered an analysis ("Erzählkunst im Buche der Richter," *Bib* 42 [1961]:143-72; see esp. pp. 158-67). He was followed eighteen years later by D. F. Murray ("Narrative Structure and Technique in the Deborah-Barak Story, Judges IV 4-22," *VTSup* 30 [1979]:153-89), who undertook a more thorough investigation. More recently has come a brief treatment by B. Lindars ("Deborah's Song: Women in the Old Testament," *Bulletin of the John Rylands Library* 65 [1983]:158-75) in conjunction with his discussion of the literary craftsmanship of chap. 5. Others have offered incidental observations on artistic elements in this pericope while pursuing more traditional critical investigations. The present study makes use of these works but takes issue with some of their conclusions and calls attention to features unnoticed or undeveloped by them.

2. *IDBSup*, s.v. "Literature, the Bible as," by D. Robertson, pp. 547-51.

3. A good selective bibliography can now be found in Adele Berlin, *Poetics and Interpretation of Biblical Narrative*, ed. D. M. Gunn (Sheffield: Almond, 1983), pp. 159-70.

4. L. Alonzo-Schökel, "Hermeneutical Problems of a Literary Study of the Bible," *VTSup* 28 (1974):1-15.

5. The method and goal of structuralism is here rejected as philosophically wrong-headed and methodologically so abstract as to frustrate rather than promote good interpretation of specific texts. For lucid introductions to structuralism see Robertson, "Literature"; the articles in *Int* 28 (1974), an issue devoted to structuralism; Robert M. Polzin, *Biblical Structuralism: Method and Subjectivity in the Study of Ancient Texts* (Philadelphia: Fortress, 1977), esp. pp. 1-43; Philip Pettit, *The Concept of Structuralism: A Critical Analysis* (Berkeley/Los Angeles: U. of Calif., 1977). No attempt will be made here to develop some general theory of narrative. Nor is any general theory of narrative (e.g., genre identification, such as comedy, tragedy, etc.) employed as a basis for analysis. The only assumptions at work are such elementary ones as (1) that a piece of biblical narrative must be studied in the context of the literary tradition to which it belongs (for Judg. 4 that means the narrative literature of the Old Testament, because we have no other contemporary literature of this particular tradition), (2) that the pericope must be taken as a whole within the larger literary work of which it is a part (the synchronic method, which assumes the meaningfulness of the text as it has been transmitted, whatever the process of its composition may have been), (3) that the author exercised total control over his material so that he has excluded all that was extraneous to his purpose, and (4) that the author was in full control of his linguistic medium, aware

of the subtle powers of language and structure to express, suggest, nuance, highlight, depict, color, and thus to present a multifaceted interpretation of the event narrated. All this means that the author's intent can only be understood (the goal of exegesis proper) through close attention to all aspects of his composition, that the text itself must be our teacher, and that it contains nothing superfluous, accidental, or coincidental unless analysis should establish the likelihood of such. In my judgment, many literary studies of Old Testament narratives have missed the mark either because their starting points were from a general literary theory concerning narrative or because they were directed to the development of some such theory. In either case, the specific intent of a specific author with a specific text tends to be overlooked or skewed in the interpretation.

6. See S. Bar-Efrat, "Some Observations on the Analysis of Structure in Biblical Narrative," *VT* 30 (1980):154-73, for a helpful discussion of structure analysis.

7. This follows the general pattern of Murray, "Narrative Structure," and is chosen because it reflects a sound methodological sequence.

8. These are fully introduced in the paradigmatic account of the first judge (Othniel, 3:7-11) but are adumbrated already in the second part of the general introduction to the book (2:6—3:6).

9. All translations of the Hebrew are my own.

10. For the sequence "Yahweh . . . God" elsewhere in the central cycle see 13:8-9; 15:18-19.

11. It is thus evident that the accompanying poem is not arbitrarily placed between B ånd A. Earlier it would have intruded, later it would have fallen outside the structure so that its function within the central cycle would have been rendered ambiguous.

12. Alonzo-Schökel, "Erzählkunst," pp. 158-66, compares the action to a two-act drama with each act having two scenes: Act I: vv. 6-10 (scene 1), vv. 12-17 (scene 2); Act II: vv. 18-21 (scene 1), v. 11 (scene 2). Strangely, he treats vv. 1-5 as prologue, taking no account of the stereotype frame that links vv. 1-3 with vv. 23-24, 5:31*b*. He finds the placement of v. 11 strange, wonders why it does not stand with v. 17, and offers two suggestions: (1) to fill up a pause between the two episodes, or (2) literarily to set a tent between the two armies. It ought to be observed that the imbalance between Acts I and II makes this structural analysis highly questionable. Murray views the structure as made up of four episodes: vv. 4-10; 11-16; 17-21; 22 ("Narrative Structure," pp. 156-66).

13. More fully discussed below.

14. As was indicated in n. 12, whereas Alonzo-Schökel links v. 17 with vv. 11-16, Murray links it with vv. 18-21. He bases his conclusion on three considerations: (1) v. 17 contains a scene shift (to Jael's tent, where the next episode takes place), (2) circumstantial clauses (such as v. 17*a*) often serve to initiate episodes in Hebrew narrative (and do so here: vv. 4, 11—to which Murray adds v. 22*a*), and (3) parallel structure of the four (according to Murray's analysis) episodes, each of which begins with a circumstantial clause. These considerations are weighty, but not wholly convincing. They depend too much, in my judgment, on purely formal considerations that are of questionable value. It is to be noted (1) that v. 10 ends the first episode with a scene shift that prepares for the following episode (cf. vv. 10*b* and 12), (2) that circumstantial clauses are also used as episode closures (cf. v. 16), and (3) that the isolation of v. 22 as a separate episode does violence to the unity of vv. 18-22 (as will be shown later). The parallel structure of vv. 16*a* and 17*a* argues rather for a double circumstantial closure indicating concurrent actions on the part of Barak and Sisera subsequent to the battle, the outcome of

which is reported in v. 15. After the debacle on the battlefield, during which Sisera dismounts and takes to his heels, Barak pursues the fleeing chariots and troops while Sisera is fleeing afoot toward Kadesh. The episode closes, therefore, with this ironical reversal of movements on the part of the army commanders and a narrative return to Heber's tent, with a full disclosure of the (hitherto hinted) relationship between Heber and Sisera.

15. Alonzo-Schökel posits a break at v. 22 as between two scenes of an Act; Murray sets off v. 22 as a fourth episode coordinate with vv. 17-21. I have argued above (in agreement with Alonzo-Schökel) that v. 17 completes the second episode, so that Murray's schematic argument for reading the circumstantial clause at v. 22a as episode-initiating fails. It must, moreover, be acknowledged that *hinnēh* plus circumstantial clause can also stand in an inner-episodal position. Here that seems clearly to be the case. The action all takes place at Jael's tent, she dominates it throughout, and it marches by even stages to the denouement: Jael invites Sisera into her tent, she puts him physically and psychologically at ease, she kills him with her mallet and tent peg, she discloses to Barak his fallen foe. Barak, however, must be brought on the scene, which is achieved by the circumstantial *hinnēh* clause.

16. Murray's observation that after v. 7 "the story-line develops basically around the actions of the men" ("Narrative Structure," p. 168) is not borne out by this analysis. In fact, in the first episode Deborah wholly dominates the scene (Barak acts only as directed and supported by her) and in the third Jael. In the second episode Sisera reacts (he is being "drawn" into a trap, see discussion below), but the initiative for the battle itself comes from Deborah and the victory from Yahweh.

17. The supposed historical problems raised by this identification have occasioned extensive discussions. Because Joshua is said to have defeated Jabin king of Hazor and destroyed his royal city (Josh. 11:1-10), many scholars suppose the text here represents a fusion of traditions. The problem is aggravated by the fact that the title "king of Canaan" occurs nowhere else and that Hazor seems not to have been revived as a Canaanite royal city after its destruction by fire in the thirteenth century B.C. (see Yigael Yadin, *Hazor: The Schweich Lectures, 1970* [London: Oxford U., 1972]; also his article "Hazor" in *IDBSup*). See the commentaries and the further literature to which they refer. This is not the place to assess all the proposed solutions that have been offered, but it is appropriate to raise the question of whether the problem might not be largely of the critics' own making. Historical scholarship, like physical nature, abhors a vacuum, so it rushes to bridge gaps in the sources of our knowledge by means of ingenious hypotheses that then sometimes develop vigorous lives of their own. Patience, caution, restraint, and modesty are virtues historians might better prize more highly than the boldness and inventiveness they now are pleased to honor. In the present case it is not impossible that Jabin was used by the author as a dynastic name, that "king of Canaan" was an ancient designation of this dynasty, and that reference to Hazor is to the historical royal city of the Jabin dynasty rather than to a present reality. Josh. 11:10 tells us that "Hazor beforetime was the head of all those kingdoms," and documents from Egypt and Mari attest to Hazor's preeminence in this region throughout the second millennium B.C. until it was destroyed. See A. Malamat, "Hazor, 'The Head of All Those Kingdoms,'" *JBL* 79 (1960):12-19.

18. Cf. Gen. 41:55; Ex. 5:15; 14:10; 15:25; Num. 12:13; Deut. 26:7; Josh. 24:7; Judg. 10:12; 2 Kings 6:5; 8:3, 5; Ps. 107:6, 28; Isa. 19:20. These all use the verb *ṣā'aq*. Actually the author of Judges seems to have preferred the related verb *zā'aq* (see 3:9, 15; 6:6,7; 10:10, 14; and for its use elsewhere, see, e.g., Ex. 2:23; 1 Sam. 7:8, 19; 12:8, 10; 1 Chron. 5:20; Ps. 107:13, 19; Jer. 11:11-12; Hos. 8:2; Joel 1:14; Jonah 1:5; Mic. 3:4).

Perhaps the choice here was dictated by a desire for differentiation between this cry for help and the calling out *(zā'aq)* of troops in vv. 10, 13.

19. The name is non-Semitic. If Albright is right, it is Luvian, which links Sisera with the Philistines or related Sea Peoples (originally from the Aegean region). See William F. Albright, *Yahweh and the Gods of Canaan* (Garden City, N.Y.: Doubleday, 1968), p. 51; "Prolegomenon" to C. F. Burney, *The Book of Judges* (New York: Ktav, 1970), p. 15.

20. Sisera was the real key to his power, as David was temporarily for Saul (1 Sam. 17-18) and as Naaman was for the king of Aram (2 Kings 5:1).

21. See the Bible encyclopedias and atlases for the several suggestions. The name appears to be descriptive, but whether it refers to a wooded area or to plowlands is unclear, and though Haggoyim seems clearly to be "of the nations" it is uncertain whether it is descriptive of a mixture (or coalition) of ethnic communities or is related to an ethnic group relatively recently migrating to the area (see Hos. 12:23).

22. The Hebrew pronoun ("he") refers to the one named in the previous main clause.

23. The number surely indicates a coalition; cf. "the kings" of 5:19.

24. The "chariots of iron" were chariots with certain iron fittings, perhaps axles and hubs. The expression is similar to "throne of ivory" (1 Kings 10:18), "house of ivory" (22:39; Amos 3:15), "palaces of ivory" (Ps. 45:8), 'deck of ivory' (Ezek. 27:6), "beds of ivory" (Amos 6:4), "shields of gold" (2 Sam. 8:7; 10:16-17; 14:26), "couches of gold and silver" (Esther 1:6), "idols of silver and idols of gold" (Isa. 2:20; cf. 30:22; 40:19). See James D. Muhly, "How Iron Technology Changed the Ancient World and Gave the Philistines a Military Edge," *BAR* 8 (November-December 1982):40-54.

25. Most interpreters have taken note of the meanings of the names (in context their subtle relevance to the story can hardly be missed), but they have not pursued the matter sufficiently. That Hebrew authors often made narrative use of such meanings can hardly be disputed. A greater sensitivity to this practice sheds light on many a passage.

26. See Deut. 1:44; Ps. 118:12; Isa. 7:18.

27. Sugar, lacking honey, was the main sweetener of the ancients.

28. Significantly, the same meteorological phenomenon that is called *bĕrāqîm* here is called *lappidîm* in Ex. 20:18. The two terms occur as synonyms also in Nah. 2:4 (5).

29. Cf. also the names Ahinoam (My [divine] Brother is Delightfulness) and Elnaam (God is Delightfulness).

30. See Gen. 14:3; 2 Chron. 20:35-37; Dan. 11:6, 23.

31. Some interpreters related Heber's name to a much less common cognate noun referring to a group, clan, or band (Hos. 6:9), but this seems much less likely.

32. *IDB*, s.v. "Kenites," by George M. Landes.

33. For a similar construction, see 2 Kings 22:14.

34. As prophetess, she is the one who is acted on by the Spirit of Yahweh (cf. Num. 11:29; 24:2; 2 Sam. 23:2; 1 Kings 18:12; 2 Kings 2:16), and as the one who stirs Barak to action, who supports him in carrying out his mission, and who sends him into battle, she effects in this event what elsewhere in Judges is effected by the Spirit (3:10; 6:40; 11:29; 13:25; 14:6, 19; 15:14).

35. Date palms grew profusely in the Jordan Valley (Jericho was known as the City of Palms, Deut. 34:3; Judg. 1:16; 3:13) and at oases (Ex. 15:27; Num. 3:9) but could also be found in the hill country by springs or in gardens where cultivated (*ZPEB*, s.v. "Palm Tree," by W. E. Shewell-Cooper).

36. *IDB*, s.v. "Palm Tree," by J. C. Trevor.

37. That dates were used for food in Palestine cannot be doubted, but explicit reference to this fruit is absent in the Old Testament, unless, as is likely, it is included in references to honey and raisins (see Shewell-Cooper, "Palm Tree").

38. Sweetness and honey(comb) were conventional metaphors for that which provided benefits, delight and, refreshment (Job 21:33; Pss. 19:10; 55:14; 19:103; Prov. 3:24; 9:17; 13:19; 16:24; 20:17; 24:13-14; 27:7; Eccles. 5:12; 11:7; Song of Sol. 2:3, 14; 4:11; 5:1, 16; cf. 1 Sam. 14:27, 29; Ps. 81:16; Ezek. 16:13).

39. James S. Ackerman has plausibly argued that this account of Deborah's commissioning of Barak fits the call schema detected by W. Richter (*Die sogenannte vorprophetischen Berufungsberichte* [Göttingen: Vandendhoeck and Ruprecht, 1970]) elsewhere in the Old Testament. The schema is composed of five elements: (1) allusion to distress, (2) commission (to go and act), (3) objection (by the one commissioned), (4) assurance (that God will be with the one commissioned), and (5) a sign (confirming the promise). See "Prophecy and Warfare in Early Israel: A Study of the Deborah-Barak Story," *BASOR* 220 (1975):5-13. But even if such a schema did exist as a stereotype form (whatever its genesis), it here provides only a part of the skeleton of the narrative; it does not affect the artistry.

40. This is surely the "city of refuge" mentioned in Josh. 20:7.

41. Like Judah later (15:11) but in contrast to Othniel and Ehud. Ackerman's conclusion ("Prophecy," p. 11) that, because of the holy war ideology of premonarchic Israel, no military leader would have (or could be expected to have) initiated a war in behalf of the tribes without an express commission from Yahweh (probably in a cultic situation) is based on such a long chain of questionable hypotheses that it cannot be taken seriously. His explanations for the absence of this factor in the cases of Othniel, Ehud, and Jephthah are lame. Moreover, the author of Judges certainly did not so understand the situation. The introduction to his work (1:1—3:6) clearly indicates that he interpreted this period in the light of the ministries of Moses and Joshua as these are presented in Deuteronomy and Joshua. On his view Israel was under standing orders to conquer and hold the land in Yahweh's name and had Yahweh's standing promise to be with them in this undertaking, if they remained faithful to Him. Moreover, it appears significant that whereas Othniel and Ehud needed no special commission from Yahweh, Barak did, and he responded hesitantly. So did Gideon, who required a series of special signs to confirm Yahweh's commission and promise (6:36-40; 7:9-15). In the days of Jephthah no one in Israel would take the lead (10:18), so the Israelites sent for an outlaw chief they had earlier expelled from the land. And Samson could be drawn into conflict with the Philistines only through his passion for Philistine women. Meanwhile, the Judahites would remain cravenly subservient to the Philistines (15:9-13). It seems clear enough that this progressive degeneration in Israel is one of the author's themes.

42. See, e.g., 1 Sam. 23:19.

43. This is because the action here refers to assembling a force to do battle, not to immediate preparation for attack.

44. R. C. Boling so renders the verb there, and also here and in v. 7 (*Judges*, AB [Garden City, N.Y.: Doubleday, 1975], pp. 95-96, 287); see also J. A. Soggin, *Judges* (Philadelphia: Westminster, 1981), pp. 65, 296). Its usual sense is to draw (as with a cord or rope: Isa. 5:18; Hos. 11:4; or with love: Song of Sol. 1:4; Jer. 31:3; or to draw a bow: often), to drag off (Jer. 31:3; Ezek. 32:20), to prolong (Pss. 36:10; 85:5; Isa. 13:22), or to extend (Ps. 109:12). In Job 21:33 the verb seems to refer to forming a processional line, as F. I. Andersen and D. N. Freedman recognize in *Hosea*, AB (Garden City, N.Y.: Doubleday, 1983), p. 458. If that sense is applicable here, Barak would be commanded to draw a procession of fighting men with him (that is, lead them) to Mount Tabor.

45. Cf. Abraham (Gen. 14:14) and Jephthah (Judg. 11:3).
46. Chapter 5 speaks of a broader tribal assemblage. It may be that Deborah summoned others also, as she had Barak, but that Barak was commissioned to muster the two tribes most directly affected and that this formed the major Israelite contingent.
47. Alonzo-Schökel's suggestion that the author here employs an ironical wordplay on Barak (lightning) and "go" is undoubtedly right ("Erzählkunst," p. 160).
48. The LXX has an expanded text at this point, reflecting precisely this concern that reads, "For I do not know the day on which the Lord will prosper the angel with me," which probably represents a *Vorlage* that could better have been rendered: "For I do not know the day on which the angel of the Lord will cause me to prosper [succeed]." However, attempts to validate this expanded form of the text (see, e.g., Ackerman, "Prophecy," p. 10) are not very convincing. Nowhere is the angel of Yahweh the subject of the presumed verb *(ṣālaḥ)*, which may account for the improbable LXX rendering. And the more likely idiom for the author here would have been "prosper my way *(darkî)*," cf. v. 9; 18:5; see also Gen. 24:56; Deut. 28:29; Josh. 1:8; Ps. 37:7; Isa. 48:15.
49. For this participle expressing present action see Gen. 24:42; 28:20; Deut. 1:33; Judg. 14:3; 18:5; Ps. 101:6; Isa. 65:2.
50. Hebrew *mākar* (sell) and *nātan* (give, cf. v. 7) are often synonymous, but the former, being more vivid, sharpens the contrast between the original promise and its present revision.
51. As Murray acutely observes in "Narrative Structure," p. 175.
52. It is fruitless to speculate concerning whether Deborah thinks or knows more than she says.
53. Noted already by Murray ("Narrative Structure," p. 170). The idiom occurs a number of times elsewhere (Judg. 5:15; 1 Sam. 25:27; 2 Sam. 15:16-18; 1 Kings 20:10; 2 Kings 3:9—not always in the sense "under . . . command") but is much less common than 'aḥărāyw, which the author uses in v. 14. It is also the normal idiom for going "on foot" (Ex. 12:11; Num. 20:19; Deut. 2:28; Ps. 66:6).
54. Alonzo-Schökel's perplexity over the placement of v. 11 (shared by most commentators) and Murray's elaborate explanations are unnecessary. (Lindars, who shows no awareness of the studies by Alonzo-Schökel and Murray, follows the more traditional course of dismissing v. 11 as a bit of Deuteronomistic editing ["Deborah's Song," p. 163 n. 11].) The author had good narrative reasons to place it just here and to formulate it as he did, naming Heber the Kenite first and Kadesh as his place of encampment last.
55. The "Oak in Zaanannim" is mentioned also in Josh. 19:33, where it is assigned to the tribe of Naphtali, but its precise location is unknown.
56. See Gen. 12:6; 13:18; 18:1; Judg. 6:11, 19; 9:6, 37; 1 Kings 14:23; 16:4; Isa. 1:29; 57:5; Ezek. 6:13; 20:28; Hos. 4:13.
57. Examples could be multiplied. See, e.g., Gen. 15:18; 20:12, 24; 21:34; 27:12; Deut. 9:23; Josh. 6:2; Judg. 1:2; 7:9, 14-15; 18:10.
58. See also Num. 10:35; Josh. 10:11-14; 2 Sam. 5:24; 22:8-20; Ps. 68:17-18; Hab. 3:8-15.
59. Ex. 14:24; 23:27; Deut. 2:15; Josh. 10:10; Judg. 4:15; 1 Sam. 22:15; Pss. 18:14; 144:6.
60. Or its symbolic representation, as in Ex. 14:24.
61. See also Ps. 97:2-3.
62. A duplicate of 2 Sam. 22.

63. Therefore many have posited a textual corruption (either dittography of the following *lipnê bārāq* or an accidental anticipation of the same phrase in v. 16). But *hāmam lipnê* is also rare, found only in Josh. 10:10, unless *hāmam* controls the preposition in 1 Sam. 7:10. Even *nāpal lĕpî ḥereb* (v. 16) is unusual, found elsewhere only in Josh. 8:24 (in a clause not found in LXX). It seems best, therefore, to accept the unanimous text tradition as transmitted.

64. See the structural analysis above.

65. See the structural analysis above.

66. See Judg. 15:18; 2 Sam. 24:14; Lam. 1:7.

67. The author names the destinations at which they arrived, not the goals they were pursuing. Barak had no special interest in Harosheth Haggoyim; he was pursuing Sisera (or so he thought). When Sisera fled the Kishon, it was no doubt Heber's protection he sought; he ended up in Jael's tent.

68. Alonzo-Schökel rightly suggests that Jael's "going out to meet" Sisera was purposeful; he points to Gen. 30:16; Prov. 7:10, 15 as parallels ("Erzählkunst," p. 163).

69. Cf. Gen. 19:2, where Lot rises to meet the angels that have come to investigate Sodom and says to them, "Sirs, turn aside to your servant's house."

70. The parallels and contrasts are striking: Deborah summons Barak, addresses him with an imperative, and motivates him with a promise; Sisera comes to Jael, she addresses him with an imperative, and she motivates him with a (implied) promise.

71. The meaning of Hebrew *sĕmîkâ* is uncertain, but the context suggests concealment rather than comfort as the purpose. Does the author intend by paronomasia to link and contrast the acts of Deborah and Jael here? Having summoned Barak, Deborah commands him to *māšak* the tribes, an act that will make him a very public figure. Jael invites Sisera into her tent and covers him with a *sĕmîkâ*, which conceals him.

72. As did Abraham, when three strangers appeared at his tent (Gen. 18:8). It was no doubt goat milk that she brought him (Prov. 27:27). Burney's suggestion (*Judges*, p. 93) that the drink referred to was strongly soporific is intriguing but seems hardly supported by Gen. 18:8. References in the Old Testament emphasize rather its refreshing and nourishing effects (see, e.g., Song of Sol. 5:1; Isa. 7:22; 55:1; 60:1; Ezek. 25:4; Joel 3:18).

73. Just as Ruth approached Boaz (Ruth 3:7).

74. The Hebrew noun occurs only in this context (see also v. 22; 5:26) and in Song of Sol. 4:3; 6:7. It is uncertain as to precisely what part of the head it refers to (see the commentaries).

75. Another rare word (elsewhere only 1:14 and its parallel, Josh. 15:1), but context indicates the generally accepted sense.

76. *Wattiqqaḥ . . . wattāsem . . . wattābô' . . . wattitqaʿ . . . wattisnaḥ* .

77. *Wĕhûʾ nirdām wayyāʿap wayyāmôt*.

78. The usual custom after a victory, cf. 1 Sam. 17:53; 31:8; 2 Chron. 20:25.

79. The Hebrew verb can signify either, but the imperative usage for "come" is relatively rare (see Num. 22:6, 11, 17; 23:7; Judg. 9:14; Isa. 55:1, 3) and thus the more remarkable here.

80. See n. 44 above.

81. Failure to give context its due has led to strange conclusions. Both Murray and Lindars, for example, propose that the present narrative has a feminist theme. That is to ignore even the stereotype frame within which the story is set. It is also to diminish the

significance of the plot and its relationship to the plots of the other narratives in the central cycle. In all these accounts, however, theme and plot are tightly bound together. All have to do with the politics of the kingdom of God. To suggest otherwise is to trivialize them.

82. See also n. 41 above.

83. Cf. 3:20-21; 7:20; see also by contrast Yahweh's word to Gideon (7:2) and the testimonies of Jonathan (1 Sam. 14:6) and David (1 Sam. 17:36-37).

ELMER B. SMICK (Ph. D., The Dropsie
College for Hebrew and Cognate
Learning) is professor of Old Testa-
ment at Gordon-Conwell Theological
Seminary.

4

Architectonics, Structured Poems, and Rhetorical Devices in the Book of Job

Elmer B. Smick

The Egyptian Middle Kingdom document entitled "A Dispute over Sui-
cide,"[1] in which a man dialogues with his soul, displays the same A-B-A
pattern (prose-poetry-prose) as the book of Job. The victim, like Job, looks
toward death (the west) as his only release and, like Job, pleads for divine
vindication but lacks the theological insight of the biblical book. The author of Job also displays a literary genius that matches his theological pro-
fundity. F. I. Andersen[2] broke new ground by showing how Eliphaz's
speech in chapters 4 and 5 has a symmetrical introverted structure as follows:

    A. Opening remark (4:2)
      B. Exhortation (4:3-6)
        C. God's dealing with men (4:7-11)
          D. The revelation of truth (4:12-21)
        C' God's dealing with men (5:1-16)
      B' Exhortation (5:17-26)
    A' Closing remark (5:27)

There are other balanced structures throughout the book, witnessing to
a creative composition, not merely an arbitrary compilation. The overall
structure of the book appears to be far more detailed than merely A-B-A.
The two most helpful recent contributions in this matter are those of

Claus Westermann and J. F. A. Sawyer.[3] Taking a cue from each of these sources, the following detailed structure seems plausible.

The Structure of Job
(by chapters)

Prologue	Job's Opening Lament	Dialogue— Dispute (three cycles)	Interlude on Wisdom	Monologues (three series)	Job's Closing Contri- bution	Epilogue
1-2	3	4-14 15-21 22-27	28	29-31 (Job) 32-37 (Elihu) 38-41 (God)	40:3-5; 42:1-6	42:7-17

The book is a literary masterpiece that draws from many genres with a heavy emphasis on legal disputation. The argument breaks down in the third cycle, and Job is left to deliver a peroration on a theme he has repeatedly brought up: his own vindication (chaps. 29-31). The wisdom poem of chapter 28 should be viewed, then, not as the words of Job but as the words of the unknown author who interjects this speech as a lesson on how the failure of all parties in the dispute is evidence of a lack of wisdom.[4] The author, whose words appear otherwise only in the prose portions, has not chosen to introduce himself in those portions and so does not introduce himself here. In praise of true wisdom he centers this structural apex (chap. 28) between the three cycles of dialogue-dispute and the three monologues: Job's (chaps. 29-31), Elihu's (chaps. 32-37), and God's (chap. 38-41). (Job's words of contrition—40:3-5 and 42:1-6—are divided to provide a response to each divine speech. The first is preparatory to the second.) In chapters 29-31 Job turns directly to God for a legal decision that he is innocent of the charges the counselors have leveled against him. Elihu's monologue is another human perspective on why Job has suffered. More needed to be said on the value of divine chastisement and the redemptive purpose of suffering.

God's monologue presents the divine perspective. Job is not condemned as one who is being punished for sin, but neither is he given a logical or legal reason for his suffering. It remains a mystery to Job, although the reader is ready for Job's restoration in the epilogue because he has had the heavenly vantage point of the prologue. So the architectonics and the theological significance of the book are beautifully tied together.

Job 13:28 —14:6

A brief but highly structured poem in 13:28 —14:6 introduces the theme: the plight of the human race. Impure and worthy of punishment, man needs pity from the sovereign God. G. B. Gray and Marvin J. Pope think 14:4 is a misplaced verse, whereas F. I. Andersen sees it as pivotal and therefore very important. Andersen's problem, however, seems to be his introverted structure (vv. 3 and 5 going together, as do 2 and 6). I think it is more likely that verses 2 and 5 are related, as are verses 3 and 6, with verse 4 as the apex. The introductory tricolon in 13:28 —14:1a establishes the tone of the poem. Even if "man born of woman" is placed with what follows, the structure remains intact. By taking it with what precedes, the tricolon beginning "Few of days" parallels the tricolon in verse 5 as the bicolon in verse 3 parallels the bicolon in verse 6.

13:28	He wastes away like something rotten,	
	like a garment eaten by moths—	*Introduction*
14:1	man born of woman.	
	Few of days and full of trouble,	
14:2	he springs up like a flower and withers away;	*cf. v. 5*
	like a fleeting shadow he does not endure.	
14:3	Do you fix your eye on such a one?	*cf. v. 6*
	Will you bring him before you for judgment?	
14:4	Who can bring what is pure from the impure?	*Apex*
	No one!	
14:5	Man's days are determined;	
	you have decreed the number of his months	*cf. v. 2*
	and have set limits he cannot exceed.	
14:6	So look away from him and let him alone,	*cf. v 3*
	till he has put in his time like a hired hand.	

Job 27

The place of chapter 27 in the discourse has been a knotty problem. Various reasons are given for the change from "Then Job answered and said" (6:1; 9:1; 12:1; 16:1; 19:1; 21:1; 23:1; 26:1) to "And then Job continued his discourse and said" (27:1; 29:1). E. Dhorme feels the new formula was not original in 27:1 but got there by accident because of a jumbled text.[5] It clearly begins a separate discourse in 29:1, so here (27:1) the author may have intended a similar use, that is, a separate and concluding statement by Job to balance his introductory speech in chapter 3. Dhorme also takes the final stanza, on the fate of the wicked (27:13-23), to be a fragment of Zophar's missing final speech.[6] Others consider it a later scribe's attempt to make Job sound orthodox. But Job never categorically denied God's justice. He differed with his friends on how it is carried out, especially with regard to himself. He feels God has denied him justice but still believes God is somehow just and will vindicate him. Refusal to accept the possibility of incongruous rhetoric baffles modern interpreters and makes them want to attribute Job's remarks to the counselors. It also baffled Elihu in 34:5-9. We all believe with Elihu that God never does wrong (34:10). But when tragedy strikes, we may doubt God's goodness. Job throws the mystery into God's lap, as it were, and leaves it there. His paradoxical words in 27:1 are an appeal to God against God. God has denied him justice, and yet his oath is based on the truth that God is just. The final stanza (27:13-23), then, is a discursive rhetorical device designed to reinforce Job's imprecation in verses 7-10. The grammatical problems of verse 23 with which Pope wrestles are solved if this verse is understood as an inclusion with verse 13.[7] The reading of the two verses would be as follows:

> 27:13   Here is the fate God allots to the wicked,
>   the heritage a ruthless man receives from the Almighty:
>   (The description follows in vv. 14-22.)

> 27:23   He [God] claps His hands in derision
>   and hisses at him from His dwelling.[8]

Job 28

The purpose and function of chapter 28 has brought about considerable debate. Many view it as extraneous and make no effort to integrate it with the rest of the book. Dhorme's suggestion that its purpose is to express a general judgment on the previous chapters is most perceptive.[9] Because the dialogue has reached an impasse, the author now makes his own comment on the powerlessness of man's efforts to penetrate secrets that belong only to God. No speaker is identified at the beginning of the poem, although one might assume the author meant it to be Job. But the change goes beyond the usual discursiveness to a complete change in literary genre. The tone is so irenic that one can hardly assume Job is speaking. When Job is heard again in chapter 29, he is still in the midst of his struggle. As both Dhorme and Andersen observe, this is a calm meditation compared with Job's hot words. As shown in the structural diagram of the book, the author uses another threefold symmetrical pattern within the A-B-A pattern. He inserts between the threefold dialogue-dispute (chaps. 3-27) and the three monologues (chaps. 29-41) his own wisdom poem as an apex. The drive toward symmetry as an important esthetic principle of Old Testament poetry has triumphed again. The internal structure of chapter 28 is as follows:

> Introduction (vv. 1-2): All treasure has a source
> I. First stanza (vv. 3-11): The discovery of treasure
> Refrain and response (vv. 12-14): Wisdom is elusive
> II. Second stanza (vv. 15-19): Wisdom as treasure
> Refrain and response (vv. 20-22): Wisdom is elusive
> III. Third stanza (vv. 23-27): God and wisdom
> Conclusion (v. 28): The source of wisdom

The theme of the chapter is stated twice in the refrain, which appears in verses 12 and 20. Job has been frustrated and unable to find a wisdom solution to the mystery behind his suffering. The counselors with their pseudo-wisdom (cf. 11:5-6; 12:2) have only been a hindrance. So this theme—"Where can you find wisdom?"—is certainly not extraneous. The poem develops the theme with skill by first concentrating on man's inquisitive nature and technological ability, which enables him to find the riches of the earth no matter how difficult they are to obtain (vv. 1-11). The second stanza dwells on the value of wisdom and its scarcity compared with even the rarest treasures on earth (vv. 13-19). The third stanza (vv. 21-28) finally addresses the question asked in the refrain. Wisdom has a source, but it is so elusive that only God knows the way to it. That is because He is omniscient (v. 24) and is wisdom's master (v. 27). Man finds it only when he fears God and honors Him as God (v. 28). The chapter as the literary apex of the book anticipates the theophany but does so without creating a climax. In God alone lies the answer to the mystery Job and his friends have sought to fathom.

Many reasons are given for taking 28:28 as an editorial appendage, making the poem an agnostic statement about man and wisdom. The arguments, however, are not so strong as they appear to be.

(1) The introductory formula "And he said to man" is said to be too short for a poetic line and hence was a splice.[10] But Psalm 50:16 is the same kind of formula followed by a series of synonymous bicola.[11] Including the formula in the balance of lines creates a tricolon (cf. vv. 3 and 4) with an acceptable syllable count of 6/9/6 (cf. Prov. 4:4).

(2) The form of the divine name *'ădōnāy*, used only here in Job, is thought to prove that this verse was added. But it merely supports the present contention that the entire chapter must be the words of the author, whose terms for God in the narrative reflected Israelite usage in contrast to the language of the non-Israelite characters. Many manuscripts have *yhwh* (cf. *BHS* n. 28c).

(3) According to Pope, there is too sharp a cleavage between "metaphysical wisdom" and "practical wisdom." The latter (v. 28) was supposedly added by the conservative school as an antidote to the agnostic tenor of the poem. But note how "wisdom" (*ḥokmâ*) is balanced by "understanding" (*bînâ*) in verses 12, 20, and 28. By asking the question about the source of wisdom, the refrains set the stage for the conclusion. Moreover, the poem opened with a statement about the source of man's treasures and now closes with a statement about the source of this greater treasure, wisdom. The entire poem is the creation of a single hand.

Job 29

Chapter 29 is another classic example of Semitic rhetoric with all the elements of good symmetrical style. It is unfortunate that scholars have again imposed their own notions of what the rhetoric should be and so have changed the order of the verses and obscured the beauty.[12] Verses 21-25 are moved up to follow v. 10. In my opinion the order of the verses in the Hebrew text presents the author's original symmetrical intention. The pattern is as follows:

> Blessing, vv. 2-6
> Honor, vv. 7-11
> Job's benevolence, vv. 12-17
> Blessing, vv. 18-20
> Honor, vv. 21-25

The chapter deals with both active and passive aspects of Job's former life. He was blessed by God and honored by men. But he was also socially active, a benefactor and leader. His benevolence was an important part of the high position he held in his society, where social righteousness was expected of every ruling elder. The Ugaritic literature and Hammurapi's law-code both stress the responsibility of rulers to protect the poor and champion the cause of widows and orphans.[13] Job in asserting his benevolence places a description of it in the climatic position in this oration, with the key line (v. 14) in the exact middle of the poem. This verse sums up his benevolence in a striking metaphor about his being clothed with righteousness. Such benevolence established his right to the honor and blessing the surrounding verses describe. This chapter is preparing the reader for chapter 30.

JOB 30

The contrast between chapters 29 and 30 is purposeful and forceful. The threefold use of "But now" in 30:1, 9, and 16 ties the chapter together and reveals the author's contrastive intention. Moreover, the very first verb seems to be used to heighten the effect. In 29:24 Job said, "I laughed (*sḥq*) at them [at his people who were discouraged], and now a brood of ruffians laughs at me." Throughout verses 1-15 he expands on this theme: the loss of his dignity. If one feels Job exaggerated his honor in chapter 29, the hyperbole on his loss of honor in chapter 30 is even more extreme. Verses 3-8 are typical. Having your peers mock you is bad, but to prove how honorless he was, Job tells how he was mocked by boys whose fathers he could not trust to handle his sheep dogs. This lengthy description of these good-for-nothing fathers is a special brand of rhetoric. The modern Western mind prefers understatement, so when Semitic literature indulges in overstatement, such hyperbole becomes a mystery to the average Western reader. To define every facet of their debauchery, to state it in six different ways, is not meant to glory in it but to heighten the pathetic nature of his dishonor.

To achieve a full measure of contrast Job dwells on the negative side of the three themes of chapter 29 in the following order: honor, blessing, and benevolence. The removal of God's blessing is far worse than affliction by men, so it is put in the climactic central position. The arrangement is as follows:

I. No honor from men (vv. 1-15)
   A. The mockers (vv. 1-10; cf. 29:7-11)
   B. The attacker (vv. 11-15; cf. 29:21-25)

    II. No blessing from God (vv. 16-23; cf. 29:2-6, 18-20)
        A. Job suffers (vv. 16-17)
        B. God afflicts (vv. 18-19)
        C. Job pleads (v. 20)
        D. God afflicts (vv. 21-23)
    III. No benevolence toward Job (vv. 24-31; cf. 29:12-17)
        A. Job, the merciful, gets no mercy (vv. 24-26)
        B. Result: his present condition (vv. 27-31)

JOB 31

Chapter 31 as to its literary format is a negative testament by which Job will close the matter of whether he is being punished for his sins. After such a statement, in the jurisprudence of the ancient Near East, the burden of proof fell on the court. That is why verse 40 says, "The words of Job are ended." Each disavowal had to be accompanied by an oath that called for the same punishment the offense deserved on the basis of the principle of *lex talionis* (vv. 5-10). Because the charges against Job were wide and varied, he must give a similarly wide disavowal. He had already done this in a general way (cf. 23:10-12), but now he specifies and calls for condemnation and punishment from both God and man (vv. 8, 11, 12, 14, 22, 23) if he is guilty of any of these sins.

Even though this is a poetic statement and should not be interpreted as if it were a legal brief, Job adds his signature as a gesture to show his intentions to make it an official disclaimer of any indictment brought against him (v. 35).

Scholars again have rearranged the contents of the chapter by putting together any verses that touch on the same subject. I agree with Andersen that by moving whatever annoys "their tidy minds" they do harm to the "living art of the whole poem." He points out, however, that this is poetry from a sufferer sitting on an ash-heap. But there is still a goodly measure of orderly rhetoric in these passionate and explosive utterances. This poem has a structure of themes built around the repeated oath formula. The formula does not slavishly employ an apodosis to follow every "if" clause. It can be implied (vv. 29-34). Also, several totally different "if" clauses may be given before a single apodosis completes the formula (vv. 16-22, 24-28). In verses 5-8 the formula is used with two "if" clauses on basically the same theme followed by one apodosis. Verses 9-12 have a complete formula with protasis and apodosis followed by a moral observation also coupled to a word of divine sanction, which serves as an apodosis. The following is an attempt to show the thematic structure:

Job's Oaths of Allegiance to God

Introduction: No lusting for the fertility goddess (vv. 1-4; see below)

Covenant ban (v. 1)	Lusting with the eye/ God's eye
Divine sanction (vv. 2-4)	

A. First list of seven oaths (vv. 5-22)

    1. Oath (v. 5)
      Self-imprecation
      and divine sanction (v. 6)
    2. Oath (v. 7)   1-2 Falsehood and
                                     deceit/God's scales

      Self-imprecation (v. 8)
    3. Oath (v. 9)

                                   3 Adultery/God's fire

      Self-imprecation (v. 10)
      and divine sanction (vv. 11-12)
    4. Oath (v. 13)

                                 4 Mistreatment of
                                   slaves/God's court

      Self-imprecation
      and divine sanction (vv. 14-15)
    5. Oath (vv. 16-18)
    6. Oath (vv. 19-20)   5-7 Neglect of needy
                                     and abuse of
                                     helpless/God's terror

    7. Oath (v. 21)
      Self-imprecation (v. 22)
      and divine sanction (v. 23)

B. Second list of seven oaths (vv. 24-34)

    1. Oath (v. 24)
    2. Oath (v. 25)   1-3 Idolatry (gold or gods)
    3. Oath (v. 26-27)
      Self-imprecation
      and divine sanction (v. 28)
    4. Oath (v. 29)   4 Hate of enemy
    5. Oath (v. 30)   5 Cursing

6. Oath (vv. 31-32)	6 Selfishness
7. Oath (vv. 33-34)	7 Hypocrisy

C. The climax (vv. 35-37): Job presents his signed defense and challenge that God indict him on specific charges

D. The anticlimax (vv. 38-40): A rhetorical device

Oath (vv. 38, 39)

Avarice

Self-imprecation (v. 40)

Verses 1-4 need to be examined from the standpoint of subject and form. Why does the chapter begin like this? Why would a statement concerning sexual lust be at the head of the list, and why is not the oath formula used here? Some have emended the text, and others have considered verse 1 misplaced, belonging to verses 9-12.[14] Pope's observation that this would leave verses 2-4 unconnected is worthy, for these verses form a poetic unit.[15] The covenant ban on Job's eyes (v. 1) parallels God's all-seeing eye (v. 4), and these verses enclose verses 2-3, which speak of God's judgment on the wicked, whose sins He sees.

The lines are, then, an introduction to Job's catalog of oaths protesting his loyalty to God. By declaring a covenant ban on his own eyes in conjunction with his sovereign's ability to see all, Job appropriately brings to the fore the covenant theme that underlies and gives meaning to the oaths he is about to make. But there is still more to it. The making of a covenant with his eyes is not merely a promise not to lust after a girl. The sin he has in mind is far more fundamental, or it would not have commanded this position in the poem. Job is emphatically denying an insidious and widespread form of idolatry: devotion to the *bĕtûlâ*, "the maiden," the goddess of fertility. This Venus of the Semitic world was variously known as the Maiden Anat in Ugaritic,[16] Ashtoreth in preexilic Israel,[17] and Ishtar in Babylonian sources, wherein she is described as "laden with vitality, charm and voluptuousness."[18] She is probably the "Queen of Heaven" mentioned in Jeremiah 7:18 and 44:16-19.[19] Pope still chose to emend Job 31:1, even though he admits that with this interpretation the difficulties that led to the emendation vanish.[20] Even token worship of those lesser deities in the West Semitic realm, of the sun and moon, is disavowed in the middle of the poem (vv. 26-27). This disavowal of the temptation to lust (look intently) at the sex-goddess is considered of prime importance to Job. As the consort of Baal, she plays a key role and is called *btlt 'nt,* "the Maiden Anat," in Ugaritic.[21]

JOB 38-41

The broad structure of the divine speeches does not reveal the same drive toward symmetry, although the Leviathan part of the second speech appears to present a central climax between its two major divisions. The following structure appears likely:

First Speech (38:1—39:30)

Introductory challenge to Job (38:2-3)
Subject: The Lord of nature
  I. The Creator (38:4-15)
    A. of the earth (vv. 4-7)
    B. of the sea (vv. 8-11)
    C. of day and night (vv. 12-15)
 II. The Ruler of inanimate nature (38:16-38)
    A. the depths and expanses (vv. 16-18)
    B. light and darkness (vv. 19-21)
    C. weather (vv. 22-30)
    D. the stars (vv. 31-33)
    E. floods (vv. 34-38)
III. The Ruler of animate nature (38:39—39:30)
    A. nourishment (38:39-41)
    B. procreation (39:1-4)
    C. wild freedom (vv. 5-8)
    D. intractable strength (vv. 9-12)
    E. incongruous speed (vv. 13-18)
    F. fearsome strength (vv. 19-25)
    G. flight of the predator (vv. 26-30)

Second Speech
(40:7—41:34 [MT 40:7—41:26])

Introductory challenge to Job (40:7)
Subject: The Lord of history
  I. Prologue (40:8-14): Lord over the moral order
    A. Rebuke of Job (v. 8)
    B. God's majestic wrath: the ultimate control of wickedness (vv. 9-
       14)

   II. The Beast par excellence (40:15-23)
     A. His might (vv. 15-18); four bicola
     B. A primordial creator under God's control (v. 19): climax
     C. His security (vv. 20-23); four bicola
  III. The sea monster (40:24 — 41:30 [MT 40:24 — 41:26])
     A. Man (Job) and Leviathan (40:24 — 41:10 [MT 40:24 — 41:2])
     B. God and Leviathan under God's control (41:11-12 [MT vv. 3-4]): climax
     C. Description of Leviathan (vv. 13-24 [MT vv. 5-16])
     D. The mighty (gods) and Leviathan (vv. 25-34 [MT vv. 17-26])

The architectonics of the second divine speech take this interesting form:

Prologue (40:8-14)
A. God's justice and power (vv. 8-9); rhetorical questions
B. Man's impotence against evil (vv. 10-14); irony

Example 1: Behemoth (40:15-24)
A. Description (vv. 15-18)
B. Relationship to God (v. 19): apex
C. Description (vv. 20-23)
D. Relationship to man (v. 24): impotence

Example 2: Leviathan (41:1-34)
A. Relationship to man (vv. 1-10)
B. Relationship to God (v. 11): apex
C. Description (vv. 12-34)
  1. human impotence (vv. 13-14)
  2. Leviathan's fierceness (vv. 15-32)
  3. the greatest earthly power (vv. 33-34)

The message of the prologue (40:8-14) provides the clue to the correct interpretation of the descriptions of Behemoth and Leviathan. Yahweh acting as His own defense attorney moves now to the very heart of His case. The real problem has been Job's misunderstanding of God's attitude toward wickedness. These verses call into question the contention of those who say that the God of the book of Job is amoral and that one purpose of the book is to set aside the old biblical doctrine of justice and retribution.[22] Here God addresses Himself to the moral question and rebukes Job for daring to question His justice (v. 8). Job has been discrediting *(pārar,* "to frustrate") God's justice by suggesting God was guilty of failing to run the world in the way Job imagined it should be run (e.g. 9:21-24; 24:1-12). Job's preoccupation with his own vindication has obscured the real issue: that God alone has the power and majesty it takes to combat evil. The imperatives in verses 10-11 that call on Job to display the attributes of deity are obviously intended to prove to Job how helpless he is against the reality of the forces of evil in this world. Verse 14 places the emphasis on deliverance from evil. The message is that Job's right hand cannot save, but God's can. Indeed, if Job could do what he has claimed God has failed to do, then he does not need God at all—a horrible implication, for Job has never denied that God is sovereign. His problems stem from that very belief. Robert Gordis's notion that God is tacitly conceding that He has not been able to achieve completely His goal of obliterating evil is just the opposite of what this speech is all about.[23] God states the fact that wickedness exists and that He alone has the power to uphold His own honor by crushing it. Deliverance from all evil rests with God not with man (vv. 9-14). Westermann has noted that the imperatives in many of these verses really have questions behind them.[24] "Then adorn yourself with glory and splendor" means "Are you so adorned?" God has increased Job's awareness of his own creatureliness in the first speech. Job must now acknowledge God not only as Creator but as Savior (v. 14b). It is precisely these two attributes of God that stand behind the Yahweh speeches. This prologue in verses 8-14 shows how the lengthy descriptions of the two creatures Behemoth and Leviathan serve the purpose of the book in a subtle and yet forceful way.

The second speech is not a mere afterthought about two creatures left out of the first speech. Here God accomplishes more than in the first speech, where He merely humbled Job by showing him how He is Creator and Sustainer of the natural world. Now He will convince Job He is also Lord of the moral order, one whose justice Job cannot discredit. And appropriately Job's response this time is repentance (42:1-6). The concentration on these two awesome creatures, placed as they are after the assertion of Yahweh's justice and maintenance of moral order, lends weight to the contention that they are symbolic, though their features are drawn from animals like the hippopotamus and crocodile. Although both words are used without symbolic significance (Pss. 8:8; 50:10; 78:22; 104:26; Joel 1:20; 2:22; Hab. 2:17), the biblical authors freely drew on figures from a rich linguistic reservoir. So Psalm 74:12-14 uses language about the Canaanite notion of a many-headed Leviathan. The figure is historicized and used metaphorically of Egypt at the Red Sea.

The same is true of Isaiah 27:1, where again the mythic chaos figure Leviathan is historicized to represent the evil power in the endtime. It is important to stress that this terminology in Mesopotamian and Canaanite myth is usually tied to natural phenomena, not to historical events. Here in Job it is not a particular historical event, but as the poem's prologue (vv. 8-14) suggests, the theme is God's action against all creatures who dare assert themselves against Him.[25]

Genesis 3:1 and Isaiah 27:1 present the Old Testament view of the beginning and the end of the history of evil in the world. They mark a major ideological difference between the Old Testament view of the origin and disposition of evil and that of Canaanite myth. On the other hand the serpent imagery is a continuity that cannot be ignored.[26] Similar imagery is found in Revelation 12-13, where a beast (Behemoth) as well as a dragon (Leviathan) represent the epitome of evil in the world. Revelation 12:9 says: "The great dragon was hurled down—that ancient serpent called the devil or Satan, who leads the whole world astray. He was hurled to the earth, and his angels with him" (NIV).

There is no apocalyptic tone to this part of Job, merely a free use of the same Canaanite imagery Isaiah and the psalmist knew so well. Those who regard these creatures as literal animals must admit that the description in Job is an exaggeration of the appearance of the power of hippopotami and crocodiles. Hermann Gunkel, Thomas K. Cheyne, and Marvin Pope see them as purely mythological creatures. I suggest that the mythological terminology is used to present graphic descriptions of cosmic powers such as the Satan in the prologue. But the accuser cannot be openly mentioned here without revealing to Job information he must not know if he is to continue as a model to those who also must suffer in ignorance of God's explicit purpose for their suffering.

Both creatures share two qualities. First is the obvious (on the surface) quality of a beast with oversize bovine or crocodilian features. This meets the needs of the uninformed (as to events of the prologue) Job, who is learning a lesson about Yahweh's omnipotence. Second is the hidden quality of a cosmic creature (the accuser of the prologue) whose creation preceded (40:19) and whose power outranks (41:33) all other creatures.

Most are agreed that in 41:11-12 God states that He alone has the power to control Leviathan and therefore He is the only Supreme Being. In these verses the climax of the poem is reached. Westermann claims this is the original conclusion of the whole poem.[27] A perfectly acceptable position, for such a climax is in the middle of the poem.

Before this climax the stress was on human impotence in the presence of Leviathan. After the climax (vv. 12-34) the poem becomes a masterful description that goes beyond anything ascribable to a mere crocodile or whale. It translates as follows, beginning in 41:18:

> His sneezings flash forth lightning,
>   his eyes are like the glow of dawn.
> Flames stream from his mouth;
>   sparks of fire leap forth.
> From his nostrils pours smoke,
>   as from a pot heated by burning brushwood.
> His breath sets coals ablaze;
>   a flame pours from his mouth.

Verse 25 reads,

> "When he arises, the heavenly beings are afraid;
>   they are besides themselves because of the crashing."

Swords, javelins, arrows, clubs, slingstones are useless against him, according to verses 26-29. And verse 33 states:

> Upon earth there is not his equal;
>   he was made without fear.
> He looks down on all that is lofty;
>   he is king over all proud beings.

Is this merely a crocodile, or should it be understood in light of Isaiah 27:1?

By telling of His dominion over Behemoth and Leviathan, the Lord is illustrating what He said in 40:8-14. He is celebrating His moral triumph over the forces of evil. The Satan—the accuser—has been proved wrong, though Job does not know it. The author and the reader see the entire picture, which Job and his friends never knew. No rational theory of suffering is substituted for the faulty one the friends proffered. The lesson is like that of Genesis 3, where the evil one is permitted to test and tempt only to be ultimately exposed and condemned. God has permitted the accuser to touch Job as part of His plan to prove that his accusations are false and so humiliate Satan. Far from using Job as a pawn, God has a higher purpose in allowing the cosmic struggle between Himself and the accuser. As an innocent sufferer, a prototype of the Suffering Servant, Job is brought to a higher level of spiritual understanding: "My ears had heard of you, but now my eyes have seen you" (42:5). But when the contest is over, God still does not reveal His reason to Job. Job never finds out what the reader knows. That is why Job could be restored without destroying the integrity of the account. To understand this is to understand why the forces of moral disorder are veiled underneath mythopoeic language about ferocious, uncontrollable creatures. Once again it should be emphasized that if the specific reason for his suffering had been revealed to Job, even at this point, the value of the account as a comfort to others who must suffer in ignorance would have been diminished if not canceled.

NOTES

1. *ANET*, p. 405-7.

2. F. I. Andersen, *Job: An Introduction and Commentary* (Downers Grove, Ill.: InterVarsity, 1976), p. 111.

3. Claus Westermann, *The Structure of the Book of Job: A Form-Critical Analysis* (Philadephia: Fortress, 1981); J. F. A. Sawyer, "The Authorship and Structure of the Book of Job," *Studia Biblica* 1 (1978):253-57.

4. See N. C. Habel, "Of Things Beyond Me: Wisdom in the Book of Job," *Currents in Theology and Mission* 10 (1983):142-54.

5. E. Dhorme, *A Commentary on the Book of Job* (Camden: Nelson, 1967), p. 379. Dhorme begins Zophar in verse 13, Marvin J. Pope (*Job*, 3d ed., AB 15 [Garden City, N.Y.: Doubleday, 1979]) in v. 8.

6. Dhorme, *Commentary*, p. 386.

7. Pope, *Job*, p. 194.

8. For *māqôm* as God's "place, abode" see Hos. 5:15; Mic. 1:3; Isa. 26:21; 1 Kings 8:30; 2 Chron. 6:21.

9. Dhorme, *Commentary*, p. li. Y. Tsamodi adopts the same view in his article "The Wisdom Hymn (Job 28)—Its Place in the Book of Job," *Beth Mikra* 28 (1982/83):268-77 (Hebrew).

10. Pope, *Job*, p. 206.

11. The monocolon "To the wicked God says" is a kind of anacrusis just as here in 28:28. Such a device was always counted as part of the form parallelism (the balance) while outside the thought parallelism.

12. Dhorme is followed by Skehan, Pope, and the NEB.

13. Hammurapi asserts his obedience to a divine call "to cause justice to prevail in the land, to destroy the wicked and the evil, that the strong might not oppress the weak" (*ANET*, p. 164). As a shepherd he was commissioned "to guide the people aright" and "establish law and justice in the language of the land, thereby promoting the welfare of the people" (*ANET*, p. 165). Similarly at Ugarit, Yassib son of King Keret accused his father of failing to practice social justice:

> "Thou judgest not the cause of the widow,
>   Nor adjudicat'st the case of the wretched;
> Driv'st not out them that prey on the poor,
> Feed'st not the fatherless before thee,
> The widow behind thy back." (*ANET*, p. 149)

14. Cf. NEB.
15. Pope, *Job*, p. 228.
16. *ANET*, pp. 132-33.
17. Judg. 2:13; 10:16; 1 Sam. 7:3-4; 1 Kings 11:5, 33.
18. *ANET*, p. 383.
19. Cf. Pope, *Job*, p. 228.
20. Ibid., p. 229.
21. See Hans W. Wolff's material on the sex cult in *Hosea* (Philadelphia: Fortress, 1974), p. 14. It would strengthen the case if a reference to the goddess using only *btlt* were available. However, in Prov. 6:25 lusting (*ḥmd*) in the heart after a prostitute is not unlike Job's statement. But *ḥmd* is not used here. Job uses here the Hithpoel of *bîn*, "to give full attention to." Earlier (9:11) he had used the Qal/Hiphil of *bîn* parallel with *rā'â* ("to see") to complain about his inability to see God. On the other hand, the fertility goddess was everywhere to be seen.
22. Cf. M. Tsevat, "The Meaning of the Book of Job," *HUCA* 37, pp. 102-5.
23. Robert Gordis, *The Book of Job: Commentary* (New York: Jewish Theological Seminary, 1978), p. 475.
24. Westermann, *Structure*, p. 105.
25. Jewish apocalyptic literature like 4 Ezra 6:51-54 treats Leviathan.
26. See *ANET*, pp. 137-38.
27. Westermann, *Structure*, p. 119.

THOMAS E. MCCOMISKEY (Ph. D.,
Brandeis University) is professor of
Old Testament and Semitic lan-
guages at Trinity Evangelical Divinity
School.

5

The Hymnic Elements of the Prophecy of Amos:
A Study of Form-Critical Methodology

Thomas E. McComiskey

The methodology of form criticism has provided the biblical scholar with one more tool to use in the study of the literary history of the Old Testament books. Its most important contribution has been in its isolation of certain literary types and in its insistence on a careful delineation of the life settings of those types. Like most schools of biblical criticism, it has had its staunch supporters and its vehement detractors, but it continues to dominate the field of Old Testament studies as it has for decades.

A few conservative scholars may be found who allow form-critical approaches to bring them to the point where they see complex accretive levels in many Old Testament books. However, conservative scholars have generally tended to use form criticism, if at all, in a very limited way, choosing those aspects of the methodology that do not conflict with the constructs of their critical presuppositions and rejecting those that do. In spite of the serious reservations that most conservatives have about some aspects of form-critical methodology, serious critiques of it from a conservative viewpoint have not kept pace with the vast amount of material being produced from a form-critical perspective.[1] But the methodology of form criticism has not escaped the searching questions of those who are not conservative. The observation of James Muilenburg in his presidential address to the annual meeting of the Society of Biblical Literature in 1968 is still applicable, if largely unheeded. In that address Muilenburg critiqued form-critical methodology in this way:

> Form criticism by its very nature is bound to generalize because it is concerned with what is common to all the representatives of a genre, and therefore applies an external measure to the individual pericopes. It does not focus sufficient attention upon what is unique and unrepeatable, upon the particularity of the formulation. . . . Exclusive attention to the *Gattung* may actually obscure the thought and intention of the writer or speaker. . . . It is the creative synthesis of the particular formulation of the pericope with its content that makes it the distinctive composition that it is.[2]

Muilenburg went on in this article to plead for a balancing of form-critical methodologies with "rhetorical criticism." And though a few scholars have responded,[3] most have not. The result is that many commentaries written from a form-critical perspective use the methodology uncritically.[4] Such an uncritical approach has several profound implications. One of them is that it greatly complicates the task of the biblical theologian. By *biblical theology* I do not mean simply biblically-based theology, although that may be appropriate as well. Rather, what is meant is that system of theology that determines by exegetical means the contribution of each biblical writer to a given theological theme. The preliminary application of form-critical methodology to a prophetic book, for example, requires the expenditure of much energy on the part of the biblical theologian in determining the authentic sayings of the prophet. James L. Mays in his work on Micah concludes: "The sayings which can be attributed to Micah with confidence are collected in chs. 1-3."[5]

That is not a sufficient reason for rejecting form criticism out of hand, but it does warrant giving it critical attention, particularly when the great disagreement that exists among form-critical scholars with regard to the conclusions to which the methodology has led them is observed.

The hymnic elements of the prophecy of Amos provide an unusually productive context in which to conduct this examination of form criticism. The reason for this is that there is almost universal agreement among critical scholars as to the criteria by which the historical provenance of the doxologies may be determined. Another reason for the appropriateness of the hymnic elements for this study is that conservatives are forced to do their form-critical homework in interpreting them. When these pericopes

(4:13; 5:8-9; 9:5-6) have been identified as "hymns" or "hymn-like," the genre has been identified. If their origin is located in some form of the Israelite cultus, the *Sitz im Leben*[6] has been identified. Even if one concludes that they are from the pen of Amos, one has determined that the "setting" is a literary one.

This study will examine the ways in which form criticism approaches the doxologies in the prophecy of Amos and will use these exalted hymns of praise as the catalyst for a critique of the form-critical method.

THE INTRUSIVE NATURE OF THE DOXOLOGIES

The apparently intrusive nature of the hymnic elements in Amos is an important argument for critics of the literary and form-critical schools.[7] If the hymns fit awkwardly into the structure of the book and have a tenuous relationship with the surrounding context, the question of the possibility of intrusion arises and must be considered.

Of the three doxologies, only the second can be said to be clearly structurally intrusive. The first (4:13) occurs at the end of a logical section and forms an apt conclusion to the threat of judgment in the preceding verse. That verse sets forth the ominous warning: "Prepare to meet your God, O Israel!" The doxology that follows is theophanic in nature. It depicts Yahweh as stepping into time and treading on the heights of the earth. This is similar to a theophanic depiction in Micah 1:3-7. Both theophanies picture Yahweh as striding across the heights of the earth, and both use the same terminology for that depiction.[8] It may be affirmed, then, that the content and language of the theophanic depiction in the first hymn was current during the eighth century, when both Micah and Amos prophesied. Conceptually and theologically it is not anomalous to the period in which Amos lived. Indeed, similar types of theophanic depictions may be found much earlier (Judg. 5:4-5; 2 Sam. 22:8-16).[9]

The theophany in Micah presages divine judgment as Yahweh steps into time and history to effect His will. The theophanic depiction in the doxology of Amos 4:13 must be said to have the same function, for it immediately follows the announcement that an encounter between Yahweh and the people is imminent. The theme of the hymn is exactly consonant with the theme of the immediately preceding context and is thus in conceptual agreement with it.

An important argument for the insertional nature of the first doxology is the apparent corruption of the text just preceding it. The language seems clumsy, and its clausal structure appears to be broken. This is understood to be an indication of later interference with the text.[10] The desultory nature of verse 12 may be observed in its failure to state what the threatened punishment is and in its apparently clumsy repetition of the word *'e'ĕseh* ("I will do"). It says, in announcing the judgment, "Therefore thus I will do to you, O Israel; because I will do this to you. . . ." The failure to cite the nature of the punishment seems out of keeping with Amos's careful attention to that aspect of prophetic *kerygma* elsewhere in the prophecy.[11] Either this statement is a literary device calculated by the author to create an aura of uncertainty by purposefully omitting a reference to the judgment, or it is textually corrupt. The former possibility has much to commend it. Indeed, the same device can be found in the prophecy of Amos in the oracles against Judah, Israel, and the surrounding nations. In that section there is a recurring suffix for which there is no apparent referent. The phrase, which occurs in 1:3, 6, 9, 11, 13; 2:1, 4, 6, is *lô' 'ăšîbennû*[12] ("I will not revoke it"). Because this verb occurs eight times in these oracles in precisely the same fashion, the lack of a clear referent cannot easily be attributed to a corrupt text. It must be understood as an integral element of the oracles against the nations.

Various suggestions have been made as to what the referent may be,[13] but it is difficult to construe it as anything other than the threat of divine punishment that God had determined and that He would not withdraw.[14] In view of the fact that it is for "transgressions" *(piš'ê)*, it must refer to punishment. But the punishment is not cited. The lack of a clear identification of the punishment would have created a dread uncertainty in the minds of Amos's hearers and would have made the statement the more powerful and awesome in its implications. Edward B. Pusey asks: "What was this which God would not turn back? Amos does not express it. Silence is often more emphatic than words."[15]

Whatever the referents suggested for the suffix,[16] the fact remains that one is not cited. If the incredulous suggestion is made that a later hand systematically erased the pronouncements of doom throughout this section, several problems arise. Where would the statement of doom have been placed in the numerical formulas? These statements allow no room for an additional element. If it is suggested that a section of the text before verse 3 has been lost in transmission, then all objectivity has fled, for the assertion is completely hypothetical. In short, there is little evidence that brings the authenticity of this formula, as it is used in the undisputed oracles, into serious question.[17] This is strong evidence for the possibility that the purposeful omission of the nature of an impending judgment was a characteristic of the style of Amos's prophetic oracles.

A similar motif is found in the oracle against Israel in 2:6-16. The authenticity of this section is universally acknowledged. In this oracle Amos described the sins of the rebellious society in the northern kingdom (2:6-8). He reminded them of God's gracious acts on their behalf (vv. 9-11). After he described their rebellion in one short verse (v. 12), Amos depicted the Lord as pronouncing His judgment on them. But instead of a specific reference to the exile, the prophet used a series of metaphorical statements that describe an impending calamity but that tantalizingly avoid a specific statement telling what the calamity will be. He said they would be pressed down like a cart (v. 13), the strong would become weak (v. 14), and the men of war would die (v. 15). Then he concluded by stating that "the mighty shall flee away naked in that day" (v. 16). Amos held out the prospect of an awful calamity, but he did not say what the calamity was to be. Yet Amos could refer to that time of uncertainty as "in that day." It was a specific time, but one can hardly speak of a specific punishment. The vagueness of the description intensifies the threat because of the wonder, uncertainty, and dreadful insecurity it engenders. It is certain and yet undefined, and therein lies its awful force.

Inasmuch as the apparently purposeful omission of a stated judgment may be found in undisputed portions of Amos, it may be wondered if form-critical methodology is as balanced as it might be in its conclusions relative to the context preceding the first hymn. If Amos purposefully omitted a reference to a specific judgment in two passages generally attributed to him, the possibility that the same motif was used in 4:12 deserves more serious consideration than it has been given. The omission of such a statement would explain the fact that the two verbs *'e'ĕseh* ("I will do") occur in such close proximity and appear to sustain an awkward relationship to each other.

The second hymnic element (5:8-9) seems to interrupt the flow of thought in the context. It is preceded and followed by negative characterizations of the people of Amos's day. If the hymn is removed from its present position, the remaining contexts blend together into one extended condemnation of the ungodly society in which Amos lived.

It may be argued that the hymn is not structurally or syntactically intrusive because of the change in the grammatical modes in which the people were addressed or characterized in the sections preceding and following the hymn. In the preceding verses (6-7)[18] the structure is that of second-person plural imperatives followed by a plural participle and a third-person plural perfect. In the context that follows the hymn, the structure is comprised of third-person plural verbs in verse 10 with the subsequent pronouncement of judgment in verse 11 in the second-person plural. Because the statement preceding the second doxology begins with a direct address to the people and the statement following it consists mainly of a depiction of them it may appear that a new pericope begins at verse 10. Understood in this way the hymn would thus form an apt conclusion to the preceding context and would not be structurally intrusive.

There are several problems associated with this suggestion, however, chief of which is that this complex use of grammatical persons may be observed elsewhere in the book within logical units. For example, in the oracle against Israel in 2:6-11 there is a similar pattern observable in the verbs that characterize or address the people. This pattern involves four distinct grammatical forms. The introductory formula is followed by an infinitive construed with a third-person suffix. This is followed by a plural participle. The rest of the oracle, except for one infinitive, is comprised of two series of verbs, one in the third-person plural (vv. 7-9) followed by a series in the second-person plural (vv. 10-11). Because the oracle is clearly defined by its content as well as the saying, "says the Lord," that begins and ends the oracle, it may be confidently concluded that the section is a unit. Thus the change following the hymn at 5:8-9 is not necessarily an indication of the beginning of a new pericope. It may also be noted that the preceding context ends with a verb in the third-person perfect, and the context that follows the doxology begins with similarly inflected verbs. There is thus a sense in which the hymn interrupts the context conceptually and structurally.

The apparent intrusiveness of a given pericope must be taken into account when the literary structure of a book is being considered. The interpreter must make a judgment as to whether an apparently intrusive element is the result of the author's style, an early editor's hand, or an accretion by a later redactor. Much depends on the presuppositions of the interpreter. But all too often the possibility that structural peculiarities are integral to the author's style is not given the consideration it deserves. The motif of "intrusion" is often used uncritically. Any assessment of the shaping of the book of Amos must involve a consideration of the writer's style if it is to be a balanced assessment.

An examination of the prophecy of Amos reveals another pericope that is clearly structurally intrusive. This is the description of the ten men who die in a house while attempting to hide from the divine wrath (6:9-10). A reading of verses 8 and 11 will demonstrate how closely these two verses that surround the pericope are related. Verse 8*b* says, "I abhor the pride of Jacob and hate his strongholds, and I will deliver up the city and all that is in it." Verse 11 states: "For, behold, the Lord commands, and the great house shall be smitten into fragments and the little house into bits."

It is apparent that the destruction of the city is the theme of both verses. Verse 11 begins with *kî* ("for") and must find its referent in verse 8, for there is nothing about the destruction of houses or cities in verses 9-10, which verses I suggest are intrusive. These verses state: "And if ten men remain in one house, they shall die. And when a man's kinsman, he who burns him, shall take him up to bring the bones out of the house, and shall say to him who is in the innermost part of the house, 'Is there still anyone with you?' he shall say 'No'; and he shall say, 'Hush! we must not mention the name of the Lord!'" The fact that these verses are written in prose, not in the poetic language of the surrounding context, also supports their intrusive nature. Thus it may be concluded that this section is a literary intrusion because it interrupts the flow of the section. It occurs before *kî*, which logically refers to the preceding context, and it is in prose, whereas its surrounding context is poetic. If verses 9-10 were written by Amos, and if the section has not been altered in the history of the transmission of the book, it may be affirmed that Amos did not find the "intrusion" an objectionable literary type.

The question of Amos's authorship of verses 9-10 is crucial. One may argue that just as the intrusive nature of the second doxology supports a late date for it, so one should ascribe the pericope of 6:9-10 to a later writer on the same grounds. Yet there is surprising agreement among modern commentators of all stripes that the section is to be attributed to Amos. To be sure, some have denied its authenticity,[19] but the style, atmosphere, and linguistic devices in these verses give strong support to the possibility of their having been written by Amos. Several things may be noted in this regard. First, there is the air of awful finality in this verse so typical of Amos's style. Second, the peculiar use of the unreferred suffix that was discussed earlier and concluded to be a characteristic of Amos's style is found in this passage. Just as the suffix on *'ăśîbennû* has no stated referent, so the suffixes of the second major clause of verse 10 have no stated referent. The first two clauses read literally: "And it will be that if ten men are left in a house and they die, and when his kinsman lifts him up, that is, the one who burns him, to carry the bones out of the house. . . ." It is readily apparent that the grammatical inflections move from ten men who died to one of them whose relative comes to dispose of the body. But this man who died is not cited in the text; his existence must be assumed. In short, the second clause contains suffixes that have no stated referent.

It is difficult to attribute this phenomenon to a later redactor or a school of disciples.[20] If this "intrusion" should be attributed to a group of Amos's disciples, it is necessary to posit a group of people who were not only loyal to Amos's ideals but who also slavishly copied his style to the extent that they, like him, omitted suffixal referents. Such a conclusion is forced and completely without historical evidence. If they copied Amos's style so closely, one wonders how their contributions to the literary development of the book may be identified, for it is divergences of style that betray the presence of the contributions of this school to the literary growth and development of the book. Third, the verse is characterized by the quick succession of various types of dependent clauses so typical of Amos's style. This phenomenon may be observed in the oracles of chapters 1 and 2 and in 3:9-11; 5:14-15; 6:1-7; and 8:4-6.[21] Fourth, the broken nature of the section reminds us of 3:12, where the style is clipped and nonessential words are omitted. If the last line of 3:12 is read literally, this may be observed. It describes those who will be rescued as "those who dwell in Samaria with the corner of a couch and in Damascus with a bed." It has been observed that a reference to the corpse that was to be burned was omitted in 6:9-10. This is strikingly similar to the style of 3:12.[22] Fifth, the superstitious Yahwism apparent in the prohibition against speaking the name of Yahweh lest He bring further calamity is hardly consonant with the religion of exilic and postexilic times. It fits best with the religious syncretism of the eighth century. Thus caution should be exercised in giving it an historical provenance beyond the time span from Amos to the Exile. Amos made several references to the popular Yahwism of his day. It apparently involved such Yahwistic elements as belief in the "day of the Lord" (5:18), affirmation of Yahweh's presence with His people (v. 14), and the observation of Levitical requirements (vv. 21-23). At least a formal sort of Yahwism was observed in the time of Amos. But at the same time the people could "swear by Ashimah of Samaria, and say, 'As thy god lives, O Dan,' and, 'As the way of Beersheba lives'" (8:14). In the statement of the man in Amos's picture who cringes among the corpses in the house, a Yahweh who acts not on the basis of one's relationship to Him but on the basis of the superstitious pronouncement of His name is found. This is not the Yahweh of Moses but the Yahweh of the pagan mind, a Yahweh who is little more than the pagan gods, whose activities were determined by what was done to anger or placate them. Such was the religion of Amos's day. Sixth, there is the extreme difficulty involved in explaining why a redactor in exilic or postexilic times would write these words.

The fact that this section appears to depict a plague rather than a siege of war does not provide sufficient reason for concluding that it is out of place in this context, for plague is often an accompaniment of war.

If the conclusion is correct that the stylistic evidence lends strong support to the possibility that the prophet Amos penned the words of 6:9-10, certain observations may be drawn about the literary type that has here been designated the "intrusion." Whether it is a device used purposefully for its dramatic effect or simply the result of the writer's spontaneity of thought is impossible to determine. It may be observed, however, that the device as it is used in 6:9-10 functions as an explicative element, that is, it is a vivid illustration of the previous statement. Its interruptive nature creates an aura of urgency. It is as though the writer was so caught up in the importance of what he was saying that he could not wait to underscore his urgent message with an illustration, even at the cost of interrupting the unity of the section.

This seems to be the function of the hymnic elements as well. As previously observed, the first hymn begins with the words *kî hinnēh* ("for, behold"); it is clearly explicative in function. And each doxology can be shown to illustrate poetically and theologically some aspect of the prophetic word in the preceding context.

The third doxology, like the first, is not conceptually or structurally intrusive and forms an appropriate conclusion to the preceding oracle.

THE SOPHISTICATED THEOLOGY OF THE DOXOLOGIES

In the process of form-critical evaluation of a pericope it is not enough that it appear intrusive; it must give some evidence of lateness as well before it is assigned to a period beyond that of the author.[23] In the case of the doxologies this is to be found in the concept of Yahweh as Creator. This concept is found only in the first doxology, where it depicts Yahweh as "He who forms the mountains, and creates the wind" (4:13). This is the only occurrence of *bārā'* ("create") in the hymns in the prophecy of Amos. J. L. Crenshaw states the matter in these words: "It is said that Yahweh was not thought of as Creator of the cosmos until the time of Second Isaiah, who emphasizes the fact in a context of new creation."[24] He also says, "The designation of Yahweh as Creator (*bōrē'*) of the universe is the bone of contention, especially significant since the Yahwistic creation account lacks a cosmogony."[25]

This contention is based on a supposition the implications of which have been given little attention by critical scholars of all schools. That supposition is that a Yahweh cosmogony did not exist early in Israelite history. Because the early J documents lack a cosmogony, there is a reluctance to posit the crystallization of such a cosmogony until the period of the Exile and Second Isaiah's masterful expression of Israelite monotheism. The implications of this conclusion are enormous. Such a conception of ancient Hebrew religious thought places the Hebrews millennia behind their pagan neighbors and, at least in the matter of cosmogony, places in serious question the widely held belief that the Hebrews borrowed many of their ideas about God from the cultures with which they had commerce. Are we to believe that Yahweh's role as Creator came into Hebrew religion only with an alleged Second Isaiah? This does not seem to be his understanding, for he asks his fellow countrymen, "Have you not known? . . . The Lord is the Creator of the ends of the earth" (40:28). He assumes that knowledge on their part.

The idea that Yahweh is the Creator of the universe is consonant with Amos's theology, although one does not find a concrete expression of that concept in the prophecy. This consonance may be seen in such passages as 4:6, where Yahweh sends famine, and 4:7, where He withholds the rain. These statements of the divine activity, though they do not prove that Amos attributed to Yahweh creative sovereignty over the universe, certainly complement that idea.

It is clear that Yahweh was more than simply a national God to Amos, for the prophet affirmed that Yahweh's presence pervades the universe. He said that if the people went to Sheol, they would find Yahweh there, and if they climbed to the heavens, Yahweh would bring them down (9:2). Such language, if not proof that Amos believed Yahweh created all things, is consonant with such a belief.

Most important, however, is the contention that Yahweh is not called "Creator" until the time of Second Isaiah. This is the crux of the matter. The argument of form criticism in this regard is linguistic as well as theological. If Yahweh is not found to be designated "Creator" until the late or early postexilic periods, it is likely that the concept developed late in Israelite history. Thus the hymns of Amos must be placed late because they reflect that theological concept.

Two verses that must be examined in this regard are Isaiah 37:16 and Jeremiah 27:5. Both verses attribute to Yahweh the role of fashioner of the universe. True, the word *'āsâ* is used in these verses, not *bārā'*, but they do affirm that Yahweh "made" *('āsâ)* the earth (Jer. 27:5) and the heavens (Isa. 37:16). Neither of these verses has escaped critical scrutiny.[26] Indeed, in a recent commentary on Isaiah 1-39, Ronald E. Clements has concluded that Isaiah 37:16 represents a Deuteronomic pericope in an extensive "Josianic redaction."[27] But in recent years the prose narratives of Jeremiah have come under increasingly more stylistic and linguistic examination, due largely to the work of John Bright,[28] and one is hard pressed to find a recent commentator on Jeremiah who will deny the integrity of Jeremiah 27:5. In the light of this, the contention that Second Isaiah is chiefly responsible for the formulation of the role of architect of the universe for Yahweh is questionable. Indeed the concept may probably be moved earlier to less than a century and a half beyond Amos.

There are several implications of the critical view that may be considered here. Chief of these is that several psalms that apply the term *bārā'* to Yahweh (Pss. 89:13 [MT 12]; 104:30; 148:5) must be placed during or after the time assigned to Second Isaiah. This is somewhat problematical for Psalm 104 because several scholars[29] have observed affinities between it and the Hymn to the Aten of Amunhotep IV.[30] This would require a preexilic provenance for the psalm[31] and thus a preexilic use of *bārā'* to depict the role of Yahweh in creation. Psalm 89 is placed by Mitchell Dahood in the "post-Davidic monarchic period."[32] Perhaps this is too early, for the language of the psalm seems to depict the early Exile—the walls have been breached and the strongholds laid in ruins (v. 40). The covenant with David seems now an empty promise (vv. 38-39).

Although this evidence is not conclusive, it does illustrate that the form-critical argumentation based on the use of *bārā'* involves more than the occurrences of the word in Second Isaiah. There is the strong likelihood that the word was used earlier than the late exilic period, and the argument that the occurrence of *bārā'* in a pericope is an indication of lateness should be understood to be somewhat tenuous because serious questions continue to surround the use of *bārā'* in the development of Israelite Yahwistic theology.

In comparison to the use of *'āsâ* to describe the role of God in creation, *bārā'* is used far fewer times in the Old Testament. The question may actually be one of stylistic usage rather than a reflection of the growth and development of theological thought in Israel. It is difficult to regard the one occurrence of *bārā'* in the hymns as a necessary indication of their late exilic origin.

A third argument for the lateness of the hymns is the title "Yahweh, God of Hosts is His name." Several forms of this title appear in Amos, but it is the occurrence of the word *šēm* ("name") in the title that gives it its late provenance, because that precise expression is not found in undisputed passages earlier than Second Isaiah. Crenshaw says, "It is not sufficient to show that *YHWH 'ēlōhê ṣēbā'ôt* was used prior to Amos; one must consider the entire refrain *YHWH 'ēlōhê ṣēbā'ôt šēmô*. Once this is done, a different picture emerges, and the probability of lateness increases tremendously."[33] The word *ṣēbā'ôt* occurs in divine titles in Amos on nine occasions[34] in different formulations,[35] but the formula *YHWH 'ēlōhê ṣēbā'ôt* with *šēmô* ("His name") in the first doxology is the critical issue.

Once again it may be observed that form criticism is very rigid in its categorizations. Because Second Isaiah uses this precise formulation of the divine name on four occasions[36] and it is not used in quite that form in undisputed passages earlier, the formula is regarded as a peculiarity of the late exilic or postexilic periods.

Within the constructs and presuppositions of form criticism this approach is valid. If one should appeal to the occurrence of the divine title *YHWH 'ēlōhê ṣēbā'ôt šēmô* in Amos 5:27, a usage outside the doxologies, one finds that its integrity is questioned because of the desultory nature of verses 25-27. The title in 5:27 is questioned also because it occurs with *'āmar* ("says"), a usage unusual in Amos. One may not appeal to the somewhat similar usage of the title in 6:8, for the line in which it occurs is also questioned, chiefly because the phrase "says the Lord, the God of Hosts" is not in the LXX. If one should refer to the somewhat similar *YHWH 'ēlōhê haṣṣēbā'ôt YHWH zikrô* in Hosea 12:6, one finds that this section is almost universally denied to Hosea.[37] The undisputed passages that remain are thus found no earlier than texts assigned to Second Isaiah. Form critics for the most part deal fairly and precisely with the data within the parameters of their presuppositions.

It may be observed, however, that the reasons given for the rejection of the title in Amos 5:27 are not necessarily conclusive. It has not been universally rejected by critical scholars. Samuel R. Driver[38] has cautioned against denying the authenticity of this phrase, and more recently K. Cramer argued for the authenticity of the word *šēmô* ("His name") in the title of 5:27.[39] The argument of Richard S. Cripps against the authenticity of portions of the divine title is based primarily on the fact that verses 25-26 do not fit together well, and this witnesses to the interference of a later hand in this section.[40] But the difficulty that scholars have with the integrity of these verses is due largely to their interpretation of this difficult passage that deals with the Israelites' images and their star-god. If the perspective of the passage is put into the future, then it does appear that something "is needed between the two verses."[41] However, if the verses are read in keeping with the Masoretic tradition, they set forth the disobedience of Israel in the past, and verse 27 may thus be understood as the pronouncement of judgment based on their past disobedience: "Therefore I will take you into exile beyond Damascus."[42]

This consideration is vital, for if the divine name in 5:27 is authentic, the form-critical argument for a late date for the doxologies based on the occurrence of $šĕmô$ in the title is invalid. Amos 5:27 would thus attest to a preexilic usage of the name found in the refrains of the doxologies. It must be observed that in the final analysis the validity of this form-critical argument depends on how a context is interpreted. It is a distinct possibility that the whole title of 5:27 is from the hand of Amos. Without the evidence of intrusiveness there is little warrant for doubting the authenticity of the title.

It must also be observed that the refrains in the doxologies are not uniform. The divine titles appear in the following order: In the first doxology (4:13) the title $YHWH$ $'ĕlōhê$ $ṣĕbā'ôt$ $šĕmô$ occurs. In the second (5:8-9) the refrain occurs not at the end of the hymn as in 4:13[43] but at the end of verse 8. The phrase is $YHWH$ $šĕmô$ ("Yahweh is His name"). And in the third hymn (9:5-6) there are two titles: $'ădōnāy$ $YHWH$ $haṣṣĕbā'ôt$ ("the Lord Yahweh of Hosts") and $YHWH$ $šĕmô$ ("Yahweh is His name"). In Second Isaiah only two forms of the title occur: "I am the Lord, that is my name" (42:8) and "The Lord of Hosts is His name" (47:4; 48:2; 51:15). It is readily apparent that none of the titles that occur in the doxologies in the prophecy of Amos occurs in Second Isaiah. The form-critical contention stands or falls with one word, namely, $šĕm$ ("name").

Several occurrences of similar phrases may be found in Jeremiah as well, but most of them are considered late redactions. However, the phrase "My name is Yahweh" occurs in a verse in Jeremiah that may be authentic: 16:21. Bright says of the pericope in 16:19-21: "The passage swarms with Jeremianic expressions, and the idea of the turning of the nations to Yahweh rests on very old tradition (cf. various pre-Exilic Psalms), was certainly

current in 'Deuteronomic' circles of Jeremiah's day (e.g., I Kings VIII 41-
43), and is not without echoes in the words of Jeremiah himself (e.g., IV 1-
2)."[44]

An examination of the word *šēm* in connection with the divine name reveals an occurrence of the phrase "Yahweh is His name" in Exodus 15:3.
The occurrence of this phrase necessitates consideration. Many older
scholars placed this song, often called the Song of Miriam (Ex. 15:1-18),
very late. But more recent scholarship has tended to support the antiquity
of the song.[45] Frank M. Cross and David N. Freedman, for example, argue
on the basis of Canaanite affinities that the poem "is scarcely later than the
twelfth century in its original form."[46] The dating of pericopes on the basis
of linguistic data is far more precise than dating them on critical assumptions. In the Song of Miriam there are clear linguistic and mythological
parallels that cast considerable doubt on the placement of this piece of material late in Israelite history. It thus may witness to a very early occurrence of the phrase "Yahweh is His name," which, it has been observed,
occurs only in Amos and not in Second Isaiah. Crenshaw dismisses this argument too lightly when he says, "Too much importance should not be attributed to this use of *YHWH šĕmô*, especially in view of divergent views in
regard to the date of the song."[47] It is true that the views of the provenance
of this song oscillate between a late date and an early date,[48] but as Brevard
S. Childs notes, "Of the various arguments brought forth the philological
arguments carry the most weight. The cumulative evidence forms an
impressive case for an early dating of the poem, particularly the tense system and the orthography."[49] When the evidence is evaluated, the philological material proves to be of greatest value because it is far more objective
and concrete than other criteria and should caution against too rigid an
application of the argument from the divine titles. The form critic may argue as Crenshaw does that "the cumulative evidence favors, nay, almost
demands, the assumption that the doxologies do not come from Amos,
and, in fact, are from a much later time,"[50] but the cumulative value of evidence depends entirely on the strength of the data that support it. True,
the preponderant usage of titles of that nature is found in Second Isaiah
and sections of Jeremiah attributed to the postexilic period, but these may
be stylistic choices of the writers.

The phrase *bĕyāh šĕmô* ("Yahweh is His name") in Psalm 68:5, a psalm
now regarded by many as early because of its affinities with Canaanite and
Phoenician,[51] may also be noted.

If the divine titles were static in their formulation, one might argue that they are crystallizations of Israelite thought and expression in its development throughout Israel's changing history. But they are not static. It is difficult to argue that the presence of the word *šēm* in a title is a mark of lateness if even one example of that phenomenon may be found earlier.

THE SETTING OF THE HYMNS

Other arguments for a late date for the doxologies could be considered,[52] but they are not within the scope of this article. Attention must now be given to the question of the setting of the hymns. John D. W. Watts characterized the hymns as "a Psalm from the Jahwistic cult." He placed them in the cultic setting of the annual fall festival. He concluded that "the prophet's speech of judgment led up to the singing of the hymn at its appropriate place in the celebration."[53] The conclusions of Watts have been met effectively by Crenshaw, who shows in part that some of the theories used by Watts to develop his thesis depend on his distinctive evaluation of the parameters of the hymns.[54] T. H. Gaster posits the setting as an ancient hymn "to the god Yahweh Sebaoth."[55] He finds illustrations of this in "Babylonian texts" and "Phoenician legends."[56]

Hans Walter Wolff understands the setting of the first hymn to be a redactor's response to the destruction of the altar at Bethel.[57] H. L. Bern sees the first two hymns as the cultic expression of the fear of God. The words of 5:8 are the answer of the community to the conditional threat of 5:6. The hymn of 9:5-6 differs from the others in that there is no exhortation to the community in the preceding context. He concludes that it is an imitative confession of a redactor who wished to confess his faith personally.[58]

Crenshaw believes the hymns to be a prophetic response to the Israelite "temptation to swear by foreign deities" after the "confrontation between Israelite and Assyro-Babylonian religion."[59]

Mays regards them as coming from a cultic source in Judah.[60] He holds that the three hymnic elements of Amos comprise one hymn and concludes that "nothing in the form or content of the hymn indicates that it could not have been current in Amos's day."[61] He continues: "The earliest tradents of Amos-material may have inserted the hymnic descriptions of Yahweh's supernatural might on which earth depends at the climax of Amos's oracles which seemed to them to involve a coming theophany."[62]

At the outset of the study of the setting of the hymns it must be noted that they evince a striking conceptual affinity to their immediate contexts. The first hymn is connected to the preceding context by strong ties, for it depicts in highly exalted language the words "prepare to meet your God."

The words *kî hinnēh* ("for, behold") underscore the conceptual connection of the hymn to its preceding context. A similar conceptual connection may be observed in the second hymn, for the destruction predicted in verse 6 is vividly illustrated by the destructive power of God in verse 9 of the hymn. The third hymn depicts Yahweh's presence as pervading the universe: He "builds His upper chambers in the heavens, and founds His vault upon the earth" (v. 6). This is consonant with the affirmation of verses 2-4 that there is no place in the universe where the people may go to escape Yahweh.

Although this phenomenon could be the result of a redactor's placing hymns of appropriate content at compatible points in the prophecy, it also supports other possibilities. One of them is that the doxologies are poetic representations of theological truth written by Amos himself to give awesome validation to the content of the oracle that precedes each doxology. According to this view, the setting would thus be a literary one.

This is the conclusion adopted here. It has not enjoyed enthusiastic support in the history of the interpretation of the prophecy of Amos. But it deserves consideration because of the consonance of the literary style of these doxologies with the style of generally undisputed portions of the book. This conclusion will provide the catalyst for a critique of form criticism and serve to place its methodology in sharper focus.

One of the most prevalent views of the setting of these doxologies is that they were hymns that were current in the Hebrew cultus of the exilic or postexilic periods. However, there is something that must be observed in this connection. Two of the doxologies are linked conceptually to a more distant oracle in the book. It is the oracle of 8:7-10 in which Yahweh swears by the pride of Jacob. The second doxology (5:8-9) speaks of day darkened into night (v. 8), and 8:9 says that God will darken the earth in daylight. The third doxology (9:5-6) says that all who dwell in the *'ereṣ* will mourn (v 5), whereas 8:8 says of the *'ereṣ* that "everyone mourns who dwells in it." The verbal and conceptual similarity of these clauses is striking. The clause in 8:8 reads *wĕ'ābal kol yôšēb bāh*, and the clause in 9:5 reads *wĕ'ābĕlû kol yôšĕbê bāh*. The difference is simply one of number.

Of greater significance is the linguistic affinity of the third hymn with a phrase in 8:8. With the exception of two words these references to the rising and receding of the Nile are verbally the same. Also, the second doxology uses the word *hāpak* ("turn") in 5:8. The word also occurs in the immediately preceding verse.

This evidence poses several problems for the view that holds that the doxologies were cultic hymns or, if they are grouped together, a cultic hymn of three stanzas, added in exilic or postexilic times. If the doxologies were composed for cultic use, independently of the text of Amos and incorporated into the text by a redactor, how can their striking verbal similarity to phraseology in Amos's oracles be explained? One may explain it by positing an extensive reworking of the text of Amos, but that is completely subjective. Conclusions must be reached on the evidence at hand.

Another possibility is that the doxologies were a cultic hymn (or cultic hymns) current in Amos's day[63] added by Amos, a redactor, or a "school of Amos." Several conservative scholars have allowed for this possibility.[64] The view is attractive, but it poses the same problem as the previous view. How is it that two phrases in the hymns are almost exactly verbatim with the Amos-material? Mays suggests with regard to the consonance between 8:8 and 9:5: "If Amos did use a line from the original hymn in his oracle ending at 8:8 . . . that would explain the attraction of this specific hymn to the Amos-material."[65] But why was the hymn added at such a distance from the point of attraction and in a completely different literary unit? The doxology occurs in the vision of the destruction of the Temple (9:1 ff.), whereas the consonant clause occurs in the vision of the summer fruit (8:1 ff.).

It is not enough to say that this similarity was the cause of their attraction. There must be an attempt to explain the similarity. It is difficult to explain this phenomenon as sheer coincidence. Perhaps Amos used language current in the prevailing cultus, but again this possibility is difficult to prove.

If, however, the data is viewed against the possibility of Amos's authorship of the doxologies, these problems are not as severe. It will be discovered that there is objective data with which to deal.

The objective material may be found in an aspect of Amos's literary style that will emerge from this study. Authentic Amos-material is characterized by the repetition of similar verbal and conceptual phraseology. This phenomenon ties the Amos-material together. It is woven into the fabric of the prophecy. Not only does this phenomenon mark the oracular material, but it extends into the doxologies as well. There are three clauses in the doxologies that find counterparts in nondoxological material in Amos. Inasmuch as this phenomenon is a peculiarity of Amos's style and pervades the hymns as well as the oracles, an objective factor exists that lends strong support to the view that the hymns are authentic Amos-material as well.

This phenomenon of repetitive phraseology occurs so frequently in the narrow compass of the book and with such precision that its significance cannot be denied. The following parallels serve to illustrate this phenomenon: *wĕšillahtî 'ēš* ("I will send fire") occurs in 1:4, 7; 2:2; *wĕhikrattî yôšēb* ("I will cut off the inhabitant") occurs in 1:5, 8; cf. 2:3; *wĕtômēk šēbeṭ* ("the one who holds the scepter") occurs in 1:5, 8; *wĕ'ākĕlâ 'armĕnōtêhā* ("It will devour her strongholds") occurs in 1:7, 14. The concept of turning justice to wormwood occurs in separate sections of Amos-material: 5:7, *hahôpkîm lĕla'ănâ mišpāṭ*; 6:12, *hăpaktem . . . ṣĕdāqâ lĕla'ănâ (/mišpāṭ)*. Trampling on the poor occurs three times: 2:7, *haššō'ăpîm 'al . . . dallîm*; 5:11, *bôšaskem 'al dāl;* 8:4, *haššo'ăpîm 'ebyôn*. A reference to "smiting the house" occurs twice: 3:15, *wĕhikkētî bêt;* 6:11, *wĕhikkâ habbayit.*

Thus generally undisputed Amos-material is marked by a repetition of similar clauses. Because this same stylistic peculiarity also embraces two of the doxologies, it may be concluded that this stamp of Amos's literary style is on them as well as on the oracle material.

Several other factors may be observed. The doxologies are refrains that have an appropriate relationship with each section to which they are connected. The use of the refrain may be shown to be integral to Amos's literary style, for it occurs elsewhere in the prophecy in different forms. For example, the refrain "says the Lord" occurs consistently in the undisputed oracles against the nations. The words "this also shall not be" function as a refrain in the vision of 7:1-9. And the frequent use of the formula *lō' 'ăšîbennû* in the oracles against the nations has previously been observed.

Also, the hymns function in the same way the intrusion of 6:9-10 functions: to illustrate the foregoing material. This also is consonant with Amos's literary style.

Objective literary data thus strongly support the authenticity of these hymnic elements. Data such as these are stronger evidence than those often appealed to in support of redactive accretions. There is no reason Amos could not have written these hymns to give awesome theological support to his pronouncements. They are woven into the fabric of the prophecy linguistically and conceptually. Amos demonstrates elsewhere his ability to fashion original verbal motifs in the history of prophetic material. It is not difficult to see these hymns as poetic expressions of truths that the prophet had set forth earlier in more prosaic language.

Form criticism has rendered service to biblical scholarship in many ways. It has drawn attention to literary types that enable us to go more deeply into the texts.[66] It has developed criteria by which accretive levels may be determined in the development of certain books such as Jeremiah, a book that witnesses to its own redactive history.

In the case of the doxologies, however, there is a tendency to base conclusions on evidence that may be seriously questioned. One wonders if the positive statements read in form-critical works should not be qualified or other options presented.

Form critics often assume complex redactive histories behind the materials with which they are working. Indeed there are pericopes in the Old Testament that may contain evidence of a later provenance than the books in which they occur, but sometimes pericopes are pronounced later accretions by form critics when the evidence is not strong. This basic assumption of form criticism needs further evaluation.

In recent years the tendency has been to divide certain prophetic books into increasingly more numerous literary units. Often the data appealed to for this are vague and speculative. And, as observed earlier, the processes of biblical theology become even more complex until uncertainty about the original words and theologies of the various authors of the prophetic corpus is all that is left.

There is also a tendency to give precedence to form-critical assumptions over matters of style when drawing conclusions. Stylistic criteria provide us with objective data and should provide balance in the application of critical methodologies.

Much of the evidence appealed to in support of the doxologies as redactive intrusions is questionable. A divine title, similar to those in the doxologies, was found that is regarded by many scholars as antedating the eighth century. It was also found that the alleged intrusiveness finds a counterpart in authentic Amos-material. Again, an appeal to the preponderance of evidence rather than to the quality and strength of that evidence was observed. Form-critical conclusions should be stated with greater fairness, objectivity, and balance. There is much at stake. In the prophetic books, not only is it the nature and identity of the prophetic word that is at stake but the authority of that word as well.

NOTES

1. For a recent critique of aspects of form criticism by a conservative see Carl E. Armerding, *The Old Testament and Criticism* (Grand Rapids: Eerdmans, 1983), pp. 43-66.
2. James Muilenburg, "Form Criticism and Beyond," *JBL* 88 (1969):1-18.
3. See for example J. R. Lundbom, *Jeremiah: A Study in Ancient Hebrew Rhetoric* (Missoula, Mont.: Scholars, 1975); William L. Holladay, *The Architecture of Jeremiah 1-20* (Lewisburg, Pa.: Bucknell U., 1976).
4. Some form-critical scholars balance the methodology with other approaches. Notable among these is Hans Walter Wolff, whose commentaries on Old Testament books combine form criticism with careful attention to the stylistic peculiarities of the individual writers.
5. James L. Mays, *Micah: A Commentary* (Philadelphia: Westminster, 1976), p. 21.
6. Note the conclusion of J. A. Motyer, *The Day of the Lion* (London: Inter-Varsity, 1974), p. 20, with regard to the questions of the literary type and setting of the doxologies: "The similarity of style shown by these three passages and their possible dissimilarity from the style of Amos are best explained by assuming that he was quoting here from some hymnic source."
7. Note the following comments: "Moreover verses 8 and 9 actually *interrupt* the flow of the exhortation contained in verses 6 and 7, and continued in verses 10 and 11" (Richard S. Cripps, *A Critical and Exegetical Commentary on the Book of Amos* [London: SPCK, 1929], p. 184); "Amos 4:13; 5:8f; 9:5f all stand distinct from their immediate context in style and subject. . . . The earliest tradents of Amos-material may have inserted the hymnic descriptions of Yahweh's supernatural might on which earth depends at the climax of Amos' oracles which seemed to them to involve a coming theophany" (James L. Mays, *Amos: A Commentary* [London: SCM, 1969], pp. 83-84); "The second doxology does not seem to fit its context at all, interrupting either 5:7, 10 or more probably 5:4-7; 14-15; and together with 5:13, setting off a passage containing authentic words of Amos (5:1-12)" (J. L. Crenshaw, *Hymnic Affirmations of Divine Justice* [Missoula, Mont.: Scholars, 1975], p. 8); "The real difficulty is the second doxology, chap. vv. 8-9 which does break the connection, in a sudden and violent way. Remove it, and the argument is consistent. We cannot read chap. v. without feeling that, whether Amos wrote these verses or not, they did not originally stand where they stand at present" (George Adam Smith, *The Book of the Twelve Prophets*, 2 vols. [New York: George H. Doran, n.d.], 1:204).

8. The similar terminology is in the words *wĕdôrēk 'al bāmôtê 'āreṣ* in Amos 4:13 and *wĕdārak 'al bāmôtê 'āreṣ* in Mic. 1:3.

9. Mays, *Micah*, p. 42, says concerning the theophanic depiction of Mic. 1:3: "This two-element description is a literary type which appears in hymnic (Judg. 5.4f.; Ps. 18.8-16 = II Sam. 22.8-16; Pss. 68.8-9; 77.17-20; 144.5f.) and prophetic materials (Nahum 1.2-6; Hab. 3.3-15; Amos 1.2)."

10. William Rainey Harper notes "that this later editor here as everywhere, ignored, consciously or unconsciously, the poetic form of the production which he thus modifies. We may well understand that in a multitude of cases the closing words of earlier sermons, having lost in later times the direct and specific reference which they were intended to convey, have given place to utterances presenting more modern thought and form" (*Amos and Hosea*, ICC [Edinburgh: T. and T. Clark, 1936], p. 102). "Diese Mahnung sich zu rüsten seinem Gotte entgegenzutreten, ist auffallend, weil sie 1) den Zusammenhang unterbricht, 2) durch *z't* auf ein inhaltlich noch gar nicht bestimmtes *kh* hinweist, 3) keinen klar erkennbaren Sinn gibt, da weder an Verteidigung noch Rechtfertigung zu denken ist, weil *kh* und *z't* sich nur auf die aus dauernder Unbussfertigkeit result, erende Vernichtung beziehen kann" (W. Nowack, *Die Kleinen Propheten* [Göttingen: Vandenhoeck and Ruprecht, 1903], p. 146). "The cumbersome transition nevertheless reveals that the whole was not a single composition" (John D. W. Watts, *Vision and Prophecy in Amos* [Leiden: Brill, 1958], p. 52). "The two introductory words *ky hnh* ("For [it is] so!") must be set aside as a secondary insertion into the old hymnic text" (Hans Walter Wolff, *Joel and Amos* [Philadelphia: Fortress, 1977], p. 216).

11. See for example 1:5, 8, 10, 14; 2:2, 5; 3:11, 15; 4:3 et al.

12. For a discussion of the various interpretations of the suffix see Wolff, *Joel and Amos*, p. 128. The same arguments are cited in J. Barton, *Amos's Oracles against the Nations: A Study of Amos 1.3-2.5* (Cambridge: Cambridge U., 1980), pp. 18-19.

13. The suggestion that the suffix refers to the turning back of the Assyrians (allowed by Cripps, *Amos*, p. 119, and E. Hammershaimb, *The Book of Amos: A Commentary* [Oxford: Blackwell, 1970], p. 25) is difficult because Assyria is not mentioned in the context and is never cited by Amos as an instrument of God's anger. But more difficult is the fact that Assyria did not effect the punishment ascribed to Judah by Amos 2:5. The ultimacy of the language of that verse and its consonance with 2 Kings 25:9 fit better with the Babylonian conquest of Jerusalem under Nebuchadnezzar. Wolff, *Joel and Amos*, p. 128, observes: "Apart from 1:15, exile is otherwise nowhere else threatened in these oracles." Wolff, however, attributes the statement to the Deuteronomist (ibid., p. 164).

14. The fact that the suffix is masculine rather than feminine does not militate against the conclusion that it refers to the threatened punishment. Though it is true that we would expect the feminine in cases where the referent is not presented in concrete terminology, the masculine may also be used in this way (*GKC* §135o). And, Amos's use is not always precise; see his application of a masculine plural suffix to the women against whom he spoke in 4:1 (*'ădōnêhem*).

15. Edward B. Pusey, *The Minor Prophets*, 2 vols. (London: Nisbet, 1906), 2:58.

16. It is unlikely that *qôl* ("voice") in v. 2 is the referent of the suffix on *'ăšîbennû* for a number of reasons. First, it is removed from *'ăšîbennû* by a considerable distance in the structure of vv. 2-3. Second, *kōh 'āmar YHWH* ("thus says Yahweh") is a formula that introduces a new logical unit. A linguistic or conceptual connection with the preceding context is thus questionable. Third, the physical impossibility of recalling one's voice renders the connection doubtful. It is not an idiom that may be found in the Old

Testament. Fourth, when the voice of God heralds divine judgment—as it does for example in Jer. 25:30-31—the voice of God is always distinct from the punishment itself. Fifth, inasmuch as that which is not revoked (*lô' 'ăšîbennû*) is for transgressions (*'al piš'ê*), the suffix (*-nû*) refers most appropriately to punishment for those transgressions rather than to the voice that heralds them.

17. The disputed oracles are 1:9-10; 1:11-12; 2:4-5. There is unanimous agreement that the remaining oracles reflect the message of Amos.

18. Watts disagrees with this division. He includes vv. 6-7 in the doxology. This rests in part on the rendering of the translation of v. 7 in the LXX, which has a singular subject, and on the presence of imperatives in v. 6, which he affirms are elements found in ancient Israelite hymnology (*Vision,* p. 73).

19. Harper, *Amos and Hosea,* p. 151, observes: "These verses are a later insertion . . . made in order to illustrate the last phrase of verse 8. This is evident because of (1) the marked interruption of the continuity of thought between verse 8 and verse 11; (2) the utterly strange and incongruous conception thus introduced; (3) the impossibility of arranging the material of these verses (viz. 9.10) in any poetical form, much less the form which characterizes the remainder of the piece."

20. Wolff, *Joel and Amos,* pp. 108-11, posits a "school of Amos" that promulgated the original sayings of the prophet. He says of this school that "its own divergent language can be recognized. In any given instance it is often difficult to distinguish between the *ipsissima verba* of the prophet and the new formulations and supplementations of the disciples" (ibid., p. 109). Wolff does not attribute the phenomenon of the unreferred suffixes in 6:9-10 to this school.

21. Wolff observes this phenomenon in the latter two passages but attributes the style to the "school of Amos" (ibid., p. 281).

22. The verse is attributed to Amos by Wolff, ibid., p. 197; Mays, *Amos,* p. 66; Harper, *Amos and Hosea,* p. 81.

23. Smith says on this: "It is only where a verse, besides interrupting the argument, seems to reflect a historical situation later than the prophet's day, that we can be sure it is not his own" (*Twelve Prophets,* p. 142).

24. Crenshaw, *Hymnic Affirmations,* p. 11.

25. Ibid.

26. B. Duhm, *Das Buch Jesaia* (Göttingen: Vandenhoeck and Ruprecht, 1922), p. 268, attributed the invocation of Hezekiah's prayer (Isa. 37:16) to a narrator. Ronald E. Clements, *Isaiah 1-39* (Grand Rapids: Eerdmans, 1980), p. 284, sees in it "a stamp and character which are very markedly Deuteronomic."

27. Clements, *Isaiah 1-39,* p. 284; cf. p. 6.

28. John Bright, *Jeremiah,* AB (Garden City, N.Y.: Doubleday, 1965) and "The Date of the Prose Sermons of Jeremiah," *JBL* 70 (1951):15-35. Bright says in the latter work: "It must therefore be borne in mind in the present discussion that the question is not: could or did Jeremiah say it? but: what date for it seems to be required by the evidence?" (p. 17).

29. J. Breasted, *The Dawn of Conscience* (New York, 1933), pp. 366-70; Mitchell Dahood, *Psalms,* AB, 3 vols. (Garden City, N.Y.: Doubleday, 1966-1970), 3:33-48.

30. *ANET,* pp. 370-71.

31. So Dahood, *Psalms,* 3:33.

32. Dahood, *Psalms,* 2:311.

33. Crenshaw, *Hymnic Affirmations*, p. 22.

34. 3:13; 4:13; 5:14, 15, 16, 27; 6:8, 14; 9:5.

35. *'ădōnây YHWH 'ĕlōhê haṣṣĕbā'ôt* (3:13); *YHWH 'ĕlōhê ṣĕbā'ôt* (4:13; 5:14, 15, 27; 6:8); *YHWH 'ĕlōhê ṣĕbā'ôt 'ădōnây* (5:16); *YHWH 'ĕlōhê haṣṣĕbā'ôt* (6:14); *'ădōnây YHWH haṣṣĕbā'ôt* (9:5).

36. Isa. 47:4; 48:2; 51:15; 54:5.

37. For a survey of those who consider Hos. 12:5 a gloss see Crenshaw, *Hymnic Affirmations*, p. 79.

38. Samuel R. Driver, *The Books of Joel and Amos* (Cambridge: Cambridge U., 1897), pp. 121-22.

39. K. Cramer, "Amos, Versuch einer theologischen Interpretation," *Beitrage zur Wissenschaft vom Alten und Neuen Testament*, 3 (1930):1-215.

40. "Loose as the present connection between verse 26 and verse 25, the speech could not have *ended* at verse 25: and if verse 27 is the conclusion of the discourse, some further denunciation or threat is needed between verses 25 and 27" (Cripps, *Amos*, p. 301).

41. Crenshaw, *Hymnic Affirmations*, p. 77.

42. For a discussion of this verse on the basis of the MT see C. F. Keil, *The Twelve Minor Prophets*, 2 vols. (Grand Rapids: Eerdmans, 1949), 1:289-96.

43. But see Wolff, who understands v. 9 as "a later addition." He holds that the text is "badly damaged and difficult to interpret" (*Joel and Amos*, p. 241).

44. Bright, *Jeremiah*, p. 113.

45. For a survey of some of the literature on this question see Crenshaw, *Hymnic Affirmations*, p. 87 n. 51.

46. Frank M. Cross, Jr., and David N. Freedman, "The Song of Miriam," *JNES* (1955):240.

47. Crenshaw, *Hymnic Affirmations*, p. 87.

48. See for example Martin Noth, *Exodus* (Philadelphia: Westminster, 1962), p. 123, who regards the poem as relatively late, and Cross and Freedman, "The Song of Miriam," who argue for an early date. Brevard Childs, *Exodus* (London: SCM, 1974), p. 247, argues that "Noth's position has relied too uncritically on the assumption that shortness in length reflects antiquity."

49. Childs, *Exodus*, pp. 245-46.

50. Crenshaw, *Hymnic Affirmations*, p. 24.

51. William F. Albright, "A Catalogue of Early Hebrew Lyric Poems [Psalm LXVII]," *HUCA* 23 (1950-51):1-39, understands the psalm as a collection of incipits that were recorded in the Solomonic period. He is followed by Dahood, who extends the principles set forth by Albright (*Psalms*, 3:130-52). See also S. Iwry, "Notes on Psalm 68," *JBL* 71 (1952):161-65.

52. The participial structure of the hymns is also used in support of their lateness because of the presence of similar structures in Job, late sections of Jeremiah, and Second Isaiah. It is difficult to determine why the creative work of God was celebrated in participial forms. Perhaps the distinctive nature of the participle contributed a mood or atmosphere to that which the writer wished to convey. Amos uses participles in his cosmic depiction of Yahweh forming locusts (7:1) and calling to contend by fire (7:4). But the participle is used frequently by Amos, and this may have no significance. There are brief catenae within a number of psalms that utilize participles to depict aspects of God's character and celebrate His creative power. Note the following from Book I of the Psalter: Pss. 9:12-13 (Eng. 11-12); 11:7; 18:51 (Eng. 50); 19:2 (Eng. 1); 22:29 (Eng.

28): 29:5, 7; 31:24; 33:4, 5, 7; 34:23 (Eng. 22). If it is objected that these sections also contain other verbal forms such as imperfects, it may be pointed out that this is true of the doxologies in Amos as well. Many of these psalms are now considered to be early. Dahood observes: "These considerations thus point to a pre-Exilic date for most of the psalms, and not a few of them . . . may well have been composed in the Davidic period" (*Psalms*, 2:xxx).

53. Watts, *Vision*, p. 65.

54. Crenshaw, *Hymnic Affirmations*, p. 38 and n. 140.

55. T. H. Gaster, "An Ancient Hymn in the Prophecies of Amos," *Journal of the Manchester Egyptian and Oriental Society* 19 (1935):23.

56. Ibid., p. 24.

57. Wolff, *Joel and Amos*, pp. 217-18.

58. H. L. Bern, *Die sogenannten hymnenfragmente im Amosbuch* (Frankfurt: Peter Lang, 1974), pp. 324-25.

59. Crenshaw, *Hymnic Affirmations*, p. 92.

60. Mays, *Amos*, p. 13.

61. Ibid., p. 83.

62. Ibid., p. 84.

63. Ibid., pp. 83-84.

64. See for example Motyer, *Day of the Lion*, p. 169 n. 1.

65. Mays, *Amos*, p. 84.

66. See in this regard Claus Westermann, *The Praise of God in the Psalms* (Richmond: John Knox, 1965).

Part II

Old Testament
Historical Research
Appraised

KENNETH L. BARKER (Ph. D., The
Dropsie College for Hebrew and Cognate Learning) is dean at Capital Bible Seminary.

6

The Antiquity and Historicity
of the Patriarchal Narratives

Kenneth L. Barker

In agreement with the consistent claim of Scripture itself, this chapter argues for the early date (roughly from the last century of the third millennium through about the first third of the second millennium B.C.) and historicity of the patriarchal episodes recorded in Genesis. Light on these episodes has come from the Mari letters, the Nuzi tablets, the Code of Hammurapi and other lawcodes, legal and social contracts of all types, and other texts.

The old critical view was that the details of the monarchic period were projected back into antiquity in order to achieve a glorified image of Israel's history. Thus those details do not present an accurate picture of the patriarchal age. This view is essentially echoed by Thomas L. Thompson:

> The results of my own investigations, if they are for the most part acceptable, seem sufficient to require a complete reappraisal of the current position on the historical character of the patriarchal narratives. These results support the minority position that the text of Genesis is not a historical document.[1]

Gaalyah Cornfeld similarly writes: "A penetrating analysis of the accounts recorded in Genesis does not permit us to consider them as a faithful representation of the actual history of the Patriarchs and their exploits."[2]

As will become clear, however, many patriarchal references, names, customs, and practices have been confirmed or elucidated, strongly suggesting that the biblical record does accurately reflect patriarchal life and customs. William F. Albright, after alluding to Julius Wellhausen's denial of the historicity and authenticity of the patriarchal narratives, asserts that "the theory of Wellhausen will not bear the test of archaeological examination."[3]

AUTHENTIC BACKGROUND EXAMPLES

For illustrative purposes I have selected nine authentic reflections of ancient Near Eastern background.

Genesis 12:16: Abraham and camels. The biblical indication that Abraham had camels at this time in Egypt has long been challenged by some scholars. Archaeology, however, attests isolated instances of their presence and limited use at this period and even earlier.[4]

Genesis 13:10-11: Lot's choice of the Jordan plain. The text indicates that the plain of the Jordan valley, where Lot chose to live, was once well watered "like the garden of the Lord." Yet today, because of the lack of water and the oppressive heat, it is not thought to be a desirable place to live. For this reason certain scholars had maintained that this area was absolutely barren in patriarchal times, thus contradicting the statement in Genesis 13. However, as a result of his surface explorations at Bab edh-Dhra (east of the Dead Sea), Albright wrote:

> The results of this and numerous other expeditions made by the writer into the Jordan Valley have definitely established the correctness of the very early Biblical tradition that the valley was very prosperous and densely peopled when Abraham came into the country. The population of the Jordan Valley decreased steadily thereafter, partly because of the catastrophe described in Genesis, and reached the lowest point in its history in the Israelite period, about 900 B.C.[5]

The biblical text itself reminds us that all this was "before the Lord destroyed Sodom and Gomorrah," obviously implying that the situation was different prior to that great conflagration. Archaeological surface explorations bear this out.

Genesis 14: its historical character. Certain scholars used to have a heyday with this chapter, charging it with being unhistorical, fictitious, full of errors, and impossible. But, as Albright puts it, "Genesis 14 can no longer be considered as unhistorical, in view of the many confirmations of details which we owe to recent finds."[6] These "many confirmations" include the validity of the names, proof of Mesopotamian incursions into Palestine and Syria, extensive travel in those days (there are wagon contracts forbidding that they be driven as far west as Palestine and Syria), and the line of march used by the invading coalition of kings.

Genesis 15:2-4: Eliezer as Abraham's heir. Kenneth A. Kitchen writes:

> Before he had children at all, Abraham had adopted Eliezer, a "son of his house" (cf. Gen. 15:3), as his heir. Possibly a slave, probably simply a member of the household, the inheritance-rights of such an adoptee were commonly guarded in Mesopotamian law, even against the subsequent birth of offspring (natural heirs) to the adoptor. Such a position was explicitly accepted by Abraham (Gen. 15:2-3) until he was told and commanded otherwise (Gen. 15:4).[7]

Genesis 15:20: the Hittites. The very existence of the Hittites was once doubted by a few scholars. And if they did exist, they were thought to be unimportant. But now, thanks to excavations at Boghazkoy in Turkey, so much is known about the Hittites and their ancient empire that entire books have been written about them.[8]

Genesis 16:2-3; 30:1-13: adopted sons through surrogates. These references deal with the custom of barren wives giving to their husbands surrogates to bear sons on their behalf whom they can then adopt as their own in order to provide male heirs. Such a custom is attested in Old Assyrian marriage contracts dating from the nineteenth century B.C., in the Code of Hammurapi, and in the Nuzi tablets.[9]

Genesis 21:32, 34; 26:1: Philistines before 1200 B.C. Inasmuch as it is usually maintained that the Philistines did not migrate to Canaan until after 1200 B.C., the mention of their presence there in the time of Abraham constitutes a problem to some scholars, who point to these references as an example of error or anachronism in the Bible. Kitchen has suggested a reasonable resolution of the difficulty:

> The "Philistines" of Genesis 26 are relatively peaceful and well Semitized, quite different in character from the alien Aegean warriors of the twelfth century B.C.; and we are entitled to ask whether the term "Philistines" in Genesis 26 is not in fact a term of the thirteenth/twelfth centuries B.C.

here applied to some earlier Aegean immigrants into Palestine who, like the later Philistines (Am. 9:7; Jer. 47:4), had come from Caphtor (Crete and the Aegean Isles).[10]

One view is that the "Philistines" of 2000 B.C. were Minoan and peaceful, whereas those of 1200 and following were Mycenean and warlike.

Genesis 23: Abraham, Ephron, and Hittite laws. When Abraham had to acquire a family burial plot in order to bury Sarah, he tried to purchase just the cave of Machpelah from Ephron the Hittite but had to buy instead the entire plot of ground on which it was located. Light has been shed on the possible reason for this by the Hittite laws. Law 47 stipulates that when a landowner sells only part of his property to someone else, the original and principal landowner must continue to pay all dues on the land. But if the landowner disposes of an entire tract, the new owner must pay the dues.[11] Apparently Abraham wanted only the cave, with no complications or further financial or social obligations, but Ephron knew that Abraham had to deal quickly in order to have a place to bury Sarah; so he insisted that Abraham buy the entire lot and assume responsibility for the dues as well. Abraham evidently agreed to this arrangement for the sake of family needs.

This is a better and more probable background to the story than the dialogue-document kind of contract known from the late eighth century B.C. and chiefly in the Neo-Babylonian period. Gene M. Tucker attempts to build a case for the latter,[12] but the result is the assertion that Genesis 23 is a late tradition and cannot be used as an example of an authentic patriarchal practice. Kitchen rightly rejects Tucker's contention.[13]

Genesis 37:28: the price of a slave. The price of twenty shekels of silver paid for Joseph in this verse is the correct average price for a slave in about the eighteenth century B.C. Earlier, slaves were cheaper; later, their price steadily increased.[14]

Additional illustrations could be given. For example, after discarding several comparative social customs that have recently been challenged, M. J. Selman still retains thirteen valid comparisons.[15] It should also be mentioned that there are numerous authentic reflections of specifically Egyptian background in Genesis 39-50.[16]

REACTION AND REPLY

Since Albright's death in 1971, a reaction has set in against the patriarchal picture presented above. A small group of scholars, among them

Thompson and John van Seters,[17] have been writing at length to debunk the views of Albright and his followers. Rather bluntly, Kitchen says that these "reactionaries" are seeking, in effect, to "put the clock back by 100 years."[18]

It must be acknowledged that these scholars have performed a useful service in demonstrating that the Nuzi materials must be used with greater caution.[19] Lamentably, however, they fail to measure up to the standard they would impose on others. Kitchen justifiably scores them because "they neglect the 3rd millennium BC entirely, along with whole sections of relevant evidence from the early 2nd millennium, and give exaggerated attention to 1st-millennium materials."[20] Besides, of the Nuzi parallels I have been able to examine, I have found only one to be completely wrong. Original reports from Nuzi led many to conclude that Rachel stole her father's household gods to gain inheritance rights for Jacob. A re-evaluation of both the Nuzi and the biblical texts has demonstrated this view to be false.[21] Kitchen correctly concludes that "Rachel simply took them for her own protection and blessing."[22] The most recent treatment of our subject is found in a book authored by William Sanford LaSor, David Allan Hubbard, and Frederic W. Bush.[23] After noting some of the modern challenges to the more moderate view of patriarchal traditions and texts, they write at length:

> Although these challenges have shown that some of the lines of evidence used to establish the historicity of the patriarchal traditions are invalid, there is still more than sufficient evidence from the Bible and extrabiblical texts to show that . . . this historicity is a warrantable conclusion.
>
> First, both a surface reading and a literary study of the patriarchal narratives reveal both their historiographical nature and intent. . . .
>
> Second . . . there is significant evidence that the patriarchal narratives reflect authentically the conditions pertaining in the ancient Near East in the early second millennium. The main lines of evidence are as follows:
>
> (1) The font of patriarchal names is abundantly exemplified among the Amorite population of the period and can be identified as Early West Semitic, i.e., as belonging to the languages of the West Semitic family extant in the second millennium in contradistinction to the first. . . .
>
> (2) Abraham's journey from northwest Mesopotamia (Haran) to Canaan accords well with a number of the conditions known to pertain during M[iddle] B[ronze] II A (2000/1950-1800). . . .
>
> (3) The pastoral nomadic life-style of the patriarchs fits the cultural milieu of the early second millennium. . . .

(4) Various social and legal customs occurring in the patriarchal narratives can be compared with a wide range of socio-juridical customs from both the second and first millennia, showing that these narratives authentically reflect the longstanding usage of the ancient Near East. . . .
(5) The general picture of patriarchal religion is early and authentic.[24]

Perhaps this is the best place to interact with van Seters' contention that, because the recent excavations at Beersheba indicate that the city was not founded until the Iron Age (twelfth century B.C.) and no earlier Canaanite city existed on the site, this proves that the strong patriarchal associations with Beersheba must be unhistorical.[25] Nahum M. Sarna points out:

However, he has overlooked the fact that not a single Biblical passage makes reference to any permanent settlement at Beersheba. The Biblical passages refer only to a well and to a cultic site (Genesis 21:19, 30-33; 26:32f.; 46:1). No king or ruler is mentioned and no patriarch ever has dealings with the inhabitants of Beersheba. The only description of Beersheba as a "city" in the patriarchal narratives is a late editorial note (Genesis 26:33) which clearly has nothing to do with the narrative context, and which views the material through the eyes of a later age.[26]

CONCLUSION

In the light of all this, what should be our approach? Although some deny the antiquity and historicity of the patriarchal narratives, a more reasonable approach—particularly in view of the evidence presented above—is that of Albright and his school: "to grant the basic authenticity of the texts and traditions until they are shown to be otherwise by historical and archaeological study."[27] Certainly the basic reliability of the historical narratives of the Old Testament has been confirmed time and time again. Segal writes: "Archaeology has taught us that the background of the patriarchal stories suits well the culture and conditions prevailing in the first half of the second millennium B.C.E."[28]

Thus Thompson and van Seters have not made their case by attacking a few problems in a limited body of materials, such as the Nuzi texts. Sarna predicts: "But in the end I believe Van Seters' major thesis that the patriarchal narratives were composed in, and reflect, late first millennium milieu will be proven wrong."[29] I am inclined to agree.

Finally, Selman rightly concludes:

> Since the large majority of these examples show that the patriarchal customs can be compared without difficulty with a wide range of material from the ancient Near East, it may be concluded that the patriarchal narratives accurately reflect a social and historical setting which belongs to the second and first millennia B.C. More precise dates must of course be derived from other considerations, but neither van Seters's preference for first millennium material nor Thompson's assessment of the essentially nonhistorical character of the narratives can be supported by the evidence of the social customs. From the independent viewpoint of the historian, therefore, the social parallels make the historical existence of the patriarchs more likely.[30]

Based on this survey of the current data, we may continue to believe in the antiquity and historicity of the patriarchal narratives—a belief shared by my dear friend and esteemed former colleague, Gleason Archer.[31]

NOTES

1. Thomas L. Thompson, *The Historicity of the Patriarchal Narratives: The Quest for the Historical Abraham* (Berlin: de Gruyter, 1974), p. 2. John van Seters also considers the patriarchal narratives to be totally unhistorical; see *Abraham in History and Tradition* (New Haven, Conn.: Yale U., 1975).

2. Gaalyah Cornfeld, *Archaeology of the Bible: Book by Book* (New York: Harper, 1976), p. 17, citing Mazar with approval.

3. William F. Albright, *The Archaeology of Palestine and the Bible* (Cambridge: American Schools of Oriental Research, 1974 reprint), p. 129. See also John Bright, *A History of Israel* (Philadelphia: Westminster, 1972), pp. 67-102; Nahum M. Sarna, "Abraham in History," *BAR* 3 (December 1977):5-9; G. Ernest Wright, *Biblical Archaeology* (Philadelphia: Westminster, 1962), pp. 40-52.

4. See Kenneth A. Kitchen, *Ancient Orient and Old Testament* (Chicago: InterVarsity, 1966), pp. 79-80; A. R. Millard, "Methods of Studying the Patriarchal Narratives as Ancient Texts," in *Essays on the Patriarchal Narratives*, ed. A. R. Millard and Donald J. Wiseman (Leicester: Inter-Varsity, 1980), pp. 49-50; E. M. Yamauchi, *The Stones and the Scriptures* (Philadelphia: Lippincott, 1972), pp. 42-43. See also the essay in this volume that follows by John J. Davis.

5. Albright, *Archaeology*, p. 48.

6. William F. Albright, "Recent Discoveries in Bible Lands," in Robert Young, *Analytical Concordance to the Bible* (Grand Rapids: Eerdmans, n.d.), Supplement 32; see also "Abraham the Hebrew: A New Archaeological Interpretation," *BASOR* 163 (October 1961):49-50 nn. 66-68.

7. Kenneth A. Kitchen, *The Bible in Its World* (Exeter: Paternoster, 1977), p. 70; see also *ANET*, p. 545 or *ANESTP*, p. 109.

8. See C. W. Ceram, *The Secret of the Hittites* (New York: Shocken, 1973); O. R. Gurney, *The Hittites* (Harmondsworth: Penguin, 1954); J. G. Macqueen, *The Hittites and Their Contemporaries in Asia Minor* (Boulder: Westview, 1975); see also *ZPEB*, s.v. "Hittites," by H. A. Hoffner, Jr., 3:165-72, which deals with the problem of the identity of the Hittites mentioned in the Old Testament.

9. See M. J. Selman, "Comparative Customs and the Patriarchal Age," in *Essays*, p. 127; *ANET*, p. 543 or *ANESTP*, p. 107.

10. Kitchen, *Ancient Orient*, p. 80; cf. E. E. Hindson, *The Philistines and the Old Testament* (Grand Rapids: Baker, 1971), pp. 94-95.

11. See *ANET,* p. 191.

12. Gene M. Tucker, "The Legal Background of Genesis 23," *JBL* 85 (1966):77-84.

13. Kitchen, *Ancient Orient,* pp. 154-56; *Bible in Its World,* p. 71; see also Donald J. Wiseman, "Abraham in History and Tradition," *BibSac* 134 (April-June 1977):130 n. 29.

14. Kitchen, *Ancient Orient,* pp. 52-53.

15. Selman, "Comparative Customs," pp. 125-29.

16. See Kitchen, *Bible in Its World,* p. 74; "The Old Testament in Its Context," *TSFB* 59 (Spring 1971):7-8; in *ISBE* (rev.), s.v. "Joseph," 2:1126-30.

17. See n. 1.

18. Kitchen, *Bible in Its World,* p. 58.

19. See especially M. J. Selman, "The Social Environment of the Patriarchs," *TB* 27 (1976):114-36; "Comparative Methods and the Patriarchal Narratives," *Themelios* 3 (September 1977):9-16; "Comparative Customs," pp. 93-138.

20. Kitchen, *Bible in Its World,* p. 58.

21. See Moshe Greenberg, "Another Look at Rachel's Theft of the Teraphim," *JBL* 81 (1962):239-48.

22. Kitchen, *Bible in Its World,* p. 70.

23. William Sanford LaSor, David Allan Hubbard and Frederic W. Bush, *Old Testament Survey: The Message, Form, and Background of the Old Testament* (Grand Rapids: Eerdmans, 1982).

24. Ibid., pp. 101-6.

25. Van Seters, *Abraham,* pp. 111-12.

26. Sarna, "Abraham," p. 9.

27. Walter E. Rast, *Tradition History and the Old Testament* (Philadelphia: Fortress, 1972), p. 31.

28. M. H. Segal, "The Composition of the Pentateuch: A Fresh Examination," *Scripta Hierosolymitana* 8 (1961):99.

29. Sarna, "Abraham," p. 9.

30. Selman, "Comparative Customs," p. 128.

31. See Gleason L. Archer, Jr., *SOTI* (Chicago: Moody, 1974), pp. 165-72.

JOHN J. DAVIS (Th. D., Grace Theolog-
ical Seminary) is professor of Old
Testament and archaeology at Grace
Theological Seminary.

7

The Camel in Biblical Narratives

John J. Davis

The camel, which was one of the largest animals in the ancient Near
East, continues to hold special fascination for archaeologists and ethnog-
raphers. Its ability to go without water for up to five days is legendary.
Standing six to seven feet high at the shoulders, adult camels weigh
between a thousand and fifteen hundred pounds and are able to cover approximately twenty-five miles a day with an average speed of five to seven
miles an hour.[1]

The camel, a member of the genus *Camelus,* exists today in two species:[2]
Camelus dromedarius, the one-humped Arabian camel common to North
Africa and the Middle East, and *Camelus bactrianus* with two humps, normally associated with the steppes of central Asia and north Australia,
where it was introduced during the last century. Camels have thirty-six
teeth in all, including three cuspidate on each side above, six incisors, and
two cuspidate on each side below. The camel is a ruminant and chews the
cud like the sheep or ox, but the stomach possesses only three compart-
ments instead of four as in other ruminants. It has long been thought that
one of the stomachs or the humps provided the unusual supply of water
that enabled this beast of burden to travel in the desert without water for
days at a time. More detailed studies on the physiology of the camel, however, have indicated that neither of these provides the fluids necessary to
sustain the camel in desert travel.[3]

Experiments conducted by Knut Schmidt-Nielsen, together with T. R.

Houpy and S. A. Jarnum, with camels in the Sahara Desert have indicated that the camel tolerates dehydration much better than other domestic animals due to its ability to maintain the volume of its blood. Under normal conditions plasma water in both man and camel accounts for about a twelfth of total body water.[4] When a camel loses approximately a fourth of its body water, the blood volume under the same conditions will drop by a third.[5] Also important to the camel's survival in the desert on minimal amounts of water is its ability to allow body temperatures to rise before sweating. According to recent studies, the camel's body temperature can rise to 105 degrees before it begins to sweat freely.[6]

The camel, regarded as low in intelligence and often possessing a nasty disposition, is a slow breeder, becoming mature only when five years old. Females give birth to a single young one approximately every three years or at even longer intervals.[7] Both the dromedary and the bactrian reach full maturity at about seventeen years but have been known to live up to fifty years.

In addition to the camel's ability to survive without water for three or four days, it is also anatomically and physiologically well-adapted to survive as a domestic servant in desert environments. The nostrils can close to narrow slits and help to filter out blowing sand, whereas the eyes are well protected by overhanging brows and abundant lashes. The hooves of the camel are ideally suited for traversing desert regions. The toes are not completely separated, and the main part of the foot rests on a large pad that underlies the proximal joints of the digits. Apparently it is the lack of separation between the two toes that underlies the expression "Do not part the hoof" in Leviticus 11:4/Deuteronomy 14:7.

In biblical times the camel was used for a wide range of purposes. In addition to its employment as a pack animal, the camel provided transportation, milk, meat for eating, and skin for leather. The longer hair from the neck of the camel was employed for both fuel and as a source of sal ammoniac. According to William F. Albright, Arabs of Byzantine times even utilized the camel for sacrifice.[8]

Among archaeologists the study of ancient methods of animal husbandry has been complicated by their inability to distinguish between wild and domestic animals. Even when animal bones appeared in early archaeological contexts, no sure statement could be made concerning the origin or function of that animal within the urban context. On the basis of recent analytic techniques, however, it would appear that the distinction of domestic species from their wild counterparts will be part of archaeological processes.

> Examination of the bones in standard petrographic thin-section and X-ray diffractometer studies indicate that there are well defined characteristics that distinguish specimens of wild animal bone from those of domestic animals. Clearly this is of vital importance in determining the cultural status of food animal remains, particularly in the Near East, where wild ancestral forms and domestic animals of the same species could have co-existed.[9]

A promising third method for differentiating wild from domestic bone types is revealed by the internal structure. By magnifying between five and ten times the pattern of structure between domestic and wild bones, distinctions are apparent. "The lacunae in bones of wild animals are rounded, whereas those in the bones of domestic animals are more rectangular."[10] In addition to bone analysis and identification, the broader study of camel husbandry in social and economic contexts is shedding important light on the nature and extent of early desert cultures.[11]

Clearly the improved identification of animal bones and the ability to differentiate between domestic and wild species will be of significant benefit to the student of Scripture.

THE ANTIQUITY OF THE CAMEL

Though not bearing on biblical history directly, it is significant that in recent years the presence of camel remains in prehistoric Pleistocene deposits is now well documented. Camel bones have been discovered in North Africa,[12] India,[13] Russia and Romania,[14] and Arabia.[15]

Of special interest have been the finds of Pleistocene skeletal materials at Sabha and in the Rishpon (Arsuf) dunes in Israel.[16] Camel materials were also discovered at a Pleistocene site in the Jordan valley.[17]

From the Neolithic period (c. 8000-4500 B.C.) the presence of the camel is evidenced in remains found in the Jordan valley.[18] In a Yarmukian stratum (c. 7000 B.C.) near the southern shore of the Sea of Galilee, many stone and bone implements, as well as fragmentary pottery, were found in association with bone remains of camel, cattle, horse, and gazelle.[19] More important for the student of Scripture, however, is the appearance of the camel in domestic contexts dating back to the Bronze Age both in Egypt and Canaan. It was during this period of time that the domestication of the camel most likely took place.

The domestication of the camel has long been the subject of speculation and lively debate. Because of the paucity of evidence, archaeologists in past decades have had to speculate as to both the date and place of domestication. The lack of specific evidence caused William F. Albright to conclude: "In short, the effective domestication of the camel cannot antedate the outgoing Bronze Age, though partial and sporadic domestication may go back several centuries earlier."[20] John van Seters argues that "only with the first millennium B.C. was the camel fully domesticated as a riding and burden-carrying animal."[21] Two observations need to be made with regard to these views on this matter. First, it should be noted that, in many of the Palestinian digs prior to 1950, animal bones were regarded as having little or no importance. As Michael Ripinsky put it; "Nobody will ever know what quantities of camel bones, before they could be even identified, were discarded by uninformed field archaeologists who were only looking for artifacts."[22] It has only been in the most recent decades that careful attention has been given to faunal materials from the various archaeological loci at a given site.[23] It should also be observed that the camel is, for the most part, a species not commonly used around urban centers. Much of the past archaeological activity in Palestine has centered on interior hill-country sites, in which the camel played a very small role. Sites located and adjacent to trade routes are more likely to provide substantive artifactual material for analysis.

From an archaeological point of view the observation of Paula Wapnish regarding the disposition of faunal remains is significant.

> Faunal remains recovered from archaeological deposits represent the end product of the effects of human activity and the conditions of deposition. Potentially, they measure the proportions of the kinds of animals killed at different times in the past and the way the carcasses were utilized. Unfortunately, of the processes involved with animal use—breeding, nurturing, working, killing, consuming, and discarding—only the last is directly reflected in the archaeological record. Information about the other activities must be generated through analogy.[24]

In spite of these difficulties, however, the evidence for the early domestication of the camel is growing at a significant rate. A number of writers today place the domestication of the camel as early as the fourth millennium B.C.[25] Others assign the date of domestication either to the Early Bronze[26] or to various points in the Middle or Late Bronze Age periods.[27]

The evidence from Egypt for knowledge of the camel in the Predynastic and Dynastic periods is now substantial. Although the appearance of the figurine or painted figure on a vessel does not prove domestication of the animal, in every case the cumulative impact of such evidence is impressive testimony to at least limited domestication in these early periods.[28] One of the more interesting discoveries was made in 1927-28 during a third season of work in gypsum quarries and workshops in the northern Faiyum scarp. Among the objects found was a two-strand twist of hair-cord more than three feet in length. After microscopic study of the hair it was clear that this was a piece of cord made from camel hair, dating to the Third or possibly early Fourth Dynasty in Egypt.[29] Of even earlier provenance in Egypt was a stylized camel head found at Maadi in 1930 and dated to the Predynastic period.[30] Also from the Predynastic age is a drawing of what appears to be a dromedary.[31]

In Palestine, camel bones have been discovered in Middle Bronze layers at Gezer,[32] Megiddo,[33] Taanach[34] and the Late Bronze Age at Tell Jemmeh.[35] Equally important is the information relative to a knowledge of camels in early Mesopotamia and Syria. This information has been comprehensively discussed by Harold Stigers[36] and Frederick Zeuner.[37] The data from Mesopotamia and northern Syria are of particular interest to the Bible student, for the mention of the camel in connection with patriarchal narratives has frequently been designated as anachronistic.[38] The archaeological data, along with inscriptional information, would seem to invalidate such a criticism of the biblical text.

That the camel was known and listed among domestic animals during the Old Babylonian period is supported by a Sumerian lexical text from Ugarit.[39] Another Sumerian text from Nippur, also dating from the Old Babylonian period, contains a reference to camel's milk, which appears to be clear evidence of the domestic use of the camel.[40] Donald J. Wiseman[41] and A. Goetze[42] argued that the translation of line 59 of Alalakh text 269 should read *ša.gal* ^{anše} *gam.mal* ("one [measure of] camel fodder"). W. G. Lambert, however, has contested this rendition, suggesting that the reading should be *dàra.maš*, meaning "stag" rather than "camel," as suggested by Wiseman.[43] It would appear, therefore, that final judgment on this text and its value to the camel debate will need to be suspended until further transcriptional work can be done on the text by an independent party.

The use of the camel during the Iron Age for both domestic and military activities is now well known from inscriptions and other forms of archaeological data. The expansion of the Assyrian empire brought them in more consistent contact with northern Arabs using dromedaries. A number of Assyrian inscriptions and reliefs portray the now widespread use of the camel, especially by Arab tribesmen.[44] The comparative samplings of animal bones found at Tell Jemmeh is of particular interest here.[45] "Compared with cattle, equids, gazelles, pigs and birds, camels constitute about 25% of the Assyrian faunal sample, between 35 and 47% of the Neo-Babylonian/Persian sample, and 14% of the Hellenistic sample."[46] Camel-bone materials from Iron Age layers have also been documented at Tell Hesban.[47]

In the light of the above data, two general conclusions are possible. First, it is abundantly clear that the camel was known in most lands of the ancient Near East prior to the third millennium B.C. Second, it appears that the camel was not only known in the earlier periods but was probably domesticated sometime prior to the second millennium B.C. The extent of that domestication will need to be clarified geographically by future disciplined field techniques that give greater attention to animal bones and their identification.

THE CAMEL IN BIBLICAL HISTORY

In all likelihood it is *Camelus dromedarius,* the one-humped camel, that appears in most biblical texts. The common Hebrew word for camel is *gāmāl* and appears fifty-four times in the Old Testament. This word is also the linguistic root of the Greek transliteration *kamēlos* and our English word camel. Although this term may apply to either of the principal species, most are agreed that it is the Arabian dromedary that is alluded to most frequently. Two other words are used in the Hebrew text to designate the camel. The masculine noun *beker* appears in Isaiah 60:6 and probably refers to a young camel. The feminine form of the same noun appears in Jeremiah 2:23 and describes the animal as a young, wild female in the bearing years, which rushes about in heat. The second word is *karkārâ,* found in Isaiah 66:20 as a beast of burden.

The noun *rekes* was translated as "camel" in some older versions, but as Esther 8:14 shows, it was a swift steed, likely a horse. Therefore it would appear that in 1 Kings 4:28 Solomon did not keep camels in his military stables but swift steeds. The word *'ăhaštārān* has occasionally been translated "camel" in Esther 8:10, 14. The word occurs only in these texts and represents a Persian loan word meaning "royal" and stands here in apposition to the word mules. Therefore it would appear that the RSV translation of the latter part of verse 10 more accurately reflects the intention of the original: "mounted couriers riding on swift horses that were used in the king's service, bred from the royal stud."

A statistical analysis of occurrences of the three words for camel in the Old Testament indicates that 49 percent of the references (28 of 57) relate to the patriarchal age, 14 percent (8 of 57) to the Exodus, conquest, and settlement periods, and 30 percent (17 of 57) refer to the monarchal period. Four of the total number of references, that is, 7 percent, have to do with eschatological or prophetic passages. In all but one case (Jer. 2:23) it would appear that the domestic dromedary was in view.

Although the Hebrews obviously utilized the camel for transportation, they were not permitted to eat the meat, because even though camels chew the cud, their hooves are not divided (cf. Lev. 11:4; Deut. 14:7). If the meat of the animal were regarded as ceremonially unclean, it can also be surmised that milk from the camel was also not to be drunk. The reference to Jacob's thirty "milk camels with their colts" (Gen. 32:14) only has reference to "nursing" female camels.[48] It further appears from 2 Kings 1:8 and Zechariah 13:4 that some Israelites may have worn rough camel skins.

The New Testament word for camel *(kamēlos)* appears six times, all of which are in the gospels (Matt. 3:4; 19:24; 23:24; Mark 1:6; 10:25; Luke 18:25). Two of the references are to the camel's-hair clothing of John the Baptizer, and the other four deal in proverbial comparisons. Camel's hair (Greek *tiches kamēlou*) was a rough material woven from the hair found on the back and hump of the camel. A softer cloth was produced from the finer hair taken from beneath the animal. John's rough clothing was in keeping with his ascetic manner of life, and it appears that the rough, hairy garment may have been a distinguishing mark of a prophet (cf. Zech. 13:14). It is significant that references to the camel in both the Old and New Testaments are in accord with ethnographic and archaeological data regarding their use on the landscapes of the ancient Near East. The employment of the camel for transportation falls into two distinct contexts. Peaceful uses included travel from Canaan to Paddan Aram by Eliezer and the return accompanied by Rebekah (Gen. 24) and Jacob's journey from Paddan Aram to Canaan along with his family (31:17). When the Midianites attacked regions in central Canaan from the east, they utilized the camel for part of their transportation (Judg. 6:5; 7:12; 8:21, 26). The desert fighting Amalekites also utilized the camel according to 1 Samuel 30:17 and Isaiah 21:7.

Camels were also used widely for carrying merchandise of various kinds. Genesis 37:25 makes special reference to spices, whereas the caravans of Job 6:18-19 and Isaiah 21:13 probably have reference to general goods for trade. Note also that jewelry and clothes were transported on camels from Abraham to the family of Laban (Gen. 24:53) as well as food from the Israelites to David (1 Chron. 12:40). Most famous was the shipment of spices, gold, and precious stones from the queen of Sheba to Solomon mentioned in 1 Kings 10:2. The Israelite domination of the frontier districts of Syria, including Zobah, Damascus, Haran, Ammon, Moab, and Edom to the south, gave Solomon a virtual monopoly on caravan commerce between Arabia and the north and from the Red Sea to Palmyra.[49] Products of Damascus from Ben-hadad to Elisha were transported by camel (2 Kings 8:9) as were other materials from Judah to Egypt (Isa. 30:6).

The Bible also makes specific reference to the equipment used with the camel and the special care required by this beast. The saddle is referred to in Genesis 31:34 and was likely held on with a girth (24:32). Such a saddlebag or box is pictured in a relief on a stone slab discovered at Tell Halaf and dated to the ninth century B.C.[50] The animal is said to have "kneeled" (Gen. 24:1) for rest and loading. Only animals of the size of a camel would need to do this. A relief from Byblos from the eighteenth century B.C. depicts such a camel kneeling, indicating its use as a beast of burden.[51]

When Esarhaddon marched down the Philistine coast to Egypt in 671 B.C., he records the fact that he received camels from the Arabs to be used as water carriers for the army.[52] Dromedaries played a role in Ashurbanipal's wars against the Arabs of the Syrian Desert.[53]

The proverbial use of the camel in New Testament passages has drawn special attention from commentators. In three gospels (Matt. 19:24; Mark 10:25; Luke 18:25) Jesus stated that it was "easier for a camel to go through the eye of a needle than for a rich man to enter the kingdom of God." Because the camel was the largest common animal in Palestine and the eye of the needle the smallest commonly observed aperture, the imagery was self-explanatory. John Calvin[54] and others, however, understood the word *kamēlon* to mean a "cable" or "rope" rather than the camel. With this imagery it was the large rope used by sailors, rather than the camel, that could not be pulled through the eye of the needle.

Others[55] have suggested that the "eye of the needle" does not refer to a literal bone, ivory, or metal needle but to a small gate in the wall of a city or domestic structure. George Williams describes this interpretation as follows: "At sundown the great gate of an eastern city is closed, but a much smaller gate, called the needle's eye, is kept open for a little while. Through it, with difficulty, a camel may be pushed; but he must first be unloaded. It may be to this that the Lord referred."[56] However inventive this suggestion is, it has no foundation in common entry systems of ancient Near Eastern walls. It would appear that the best understanding of Jesus' expression is to take the camel and needle at face value. The impossibility of an Arabian camel passing through the eye of a needle drove home the theological truth of the kingdom in a most unique way. It is of interest that Talmudic literature uses a similar parabolic idea when referring to an elephant passing through the eye of the needle.[57]

The other idiomatic use of the term camel by Jesus appears in Matthew 23:24, where He calls the Pharisees "blind guides, who strain at a gnat and swallow a camel." Again, because gnats and camels were both common, the imagery carried significant theological impact.

The frequency with which the camel is mentioned in Scripture and the broad historical periods its use represents, along with important domestic ranges of activity, make this an interesting and provocative study. With recent archaeological discoveries, nagging problems relating to the early use of the camel have been largely resolved, and even greater light is being shed on the domestic economies of various peoples as they related to the camel and camel caravans. It is hoped that new discoveries will further aid the student of Scripture in the precise interpretation of specific passages and to better understand their theological and practical importance.

NOTES

1. R. J. Forbes, *Studies in Ancient Technology,* 2d rev. ed. (Leiden: Brill, 1965), p. 194.
2. I. L. Mason has recently challenged this division in "Origin, History and Distribution of Domestic Camels," *International Foundation for Science Provisional Report* 6 (1979):21-32. His contention is that because the two types produce fertile offspring of both sexes they should be regarded as two forms of one species.
3. Knut Schmidt-Nelson, "The Physiology of the Camel," *Scientific American* 201/6 (1959):141.
4. Ibid., p. 142.
5. Ibid.
6. Ibid., p. 146.
7. Frederick E. Zeuner, *A History of Domesticated Animals* (New York: Harper, 1963), p. 363.
8. William F. Albright, *From the Stone Age to Christianity* (Baltimore: Johns Hopkins, 1957), p. 165.
9. Isabella M. Drew, Dexter Perkins, Jr., and Patricia Daly, "Prehistoric Domestication of Animals: Effects on Bone Structure," *Science* 171 (1971):280.
10. Ibid., p. 282.
11. For examples of such recent studies see Louis E. Sweet, "Camel Pastoralism in North Arabia and the Minimal Camping Unity," in *Man, Culture and Animals,* ed. Anthony Leeds and Andrew Vayda (Washington, D.C.: American Association for the Advancement of Science, 1965), pp. 129- 52; Charles A. Reed, "The Pattern of Animal Domestication in the Prehistoric Near East," in *The Domestication and Exploitation of Plants and Animals,* ed. Peter J. Ucko and G. W. Dimbleby (Chicago, 1968), pp. 361-80; Rainer Berger and Reiner Portsch, "The Domestication of Plants and Animals in Europe and the Near East," *Or* 42 (1973):214-27; Dexter Perkins, Jr., "The Beginnings of Animal Domestication in the Near East," *American Journal of Archeology* 77 (1973):279-82; Daniel da Cruz, "The Camel in Retrospect," *Aramco World* (1981):43- 48.
12. A. Gauther, "Camelus Thomasi from the Northern Sudan and Its Bearing on the Relationship C. Thomasi-C. Bactrianus," *Journal of Paleontology* 40/6 (1966):1368-72. See also Forbes, *Studies,* p. 194; Zeuner, *History,* p. 356.
13. Michael M. Ripinsky, "Pleistocene Camel Distribution in the Old World," *Antiquity* 56 (1982):48.

14. Ibid., p. 49.
15. Michael M. Ripinsky, "The Camel in Ancient Arabia," *Antiquity* 49 (1975):295.
16. Ripinsky, "Pleistocene," p. 48.
17. Ibid., p. 49; see also "The Camel in Ancient Arabia," p. 295.
18. M. Stekelis, "A New Neolithic Industry," *IEJ* (1950-51):16; Ripinsky, "Pleistocene," p. 49.
19. Ripinsky, "Pleistocene," p. 49.
20. Albright, *Stone Age*, p. 165. See also S. Z. Leiman, "The Camel in the Patriarchal Narrative," *The Yavneh Review* (1967):16-26, for a review of this position with bibliographic sources. Albright's position is also presented in the posthumously published article, "The Historical Framework of Palestinian Archaeology Between 2100 and 1600 B.C.," *BASOR* 209 (1973):12-18.
21. John van Seters, *Abraham in History and Tradition* (New Haven, Conn.: Yale U., 1975), p. 17.
22. Michael M. Ripinsky, "Camel Ancestry and Domestication in Egypt and the Sahara," *Archaeology* 36/3 (1983):27.
23. Cf., e.g., the careful work done at the sites of Tell Jemmeh (Paula Wapnish, "Camel Caravans and Camel Pastoralists at Tell Jemmeh," *JANESCU* 13 [1981]:101-21), Tell Hesban (O. S. LaBianca, "The Zooarchaeological Remains from Tell Hesbân," *AUSS* 11 [1973]:133-44; O. S. LaBianca and Asta S. LaBianca, "Domestic Animals of the Early Roman Period at Tell Hesbân," *AUSS* 14 [1976]:205-16; Joachim Boessneck and Angela von den Driesch, "Preliminary Analysis of the Animal Bones from Tell Hesbân," *AUSS* 16 [1978]:259-87), and Pella (Robert H. Smith, "Preliminary Report on a Second Season of Excavation at Pella, Jordan, Spring, 1980," *Annual of the Department of Antiquities* 25 [1981]:320).
24. Wapnish, "Camel Caravans," p. 107.
25. H. G. Epstein, *The Origin of the Domestic Animals of Africa* (New York: Africana, 1971), p. 574; Ripinsky, "Camel Ancestry," p. 23; Mason, "Origin," p. 23.
26. R. Bulliet, *The Camel and the Wheel* (Cambridge, Mass.: Harvard U., 1975), p. 47.
27. Zeuner, *History,* pp. 342-44; Roland de Vaux, *The Early History of Israel* (Philadelphia: Westminster, 1978), p. 223; Kenneth A. Kitchen, *Ancient Orient and Old Testament* (Chicago: InterVarsity, 1966), p. 79; Joseph P. Free, "Abraham's Camels," *JNES* 3 (1944):187-93; John J. Davis, *Paradise to Prison* (Grand Rapids: Baker, 1975), p. 228.
28. See the evidence presented by Forbes, *Studies*, pp. 196-200; Free, "Abraham's Camels," pp. 189-92; Zeuner, *History,* pp. 350-52; Ripinsky, "Camel Ancestry," p. 25.
29. C. Caton-Thompson, "The Camel in Dynastic Egypt," *Man* 34/24 (1934):21.
30. Michael M. Ripinsky, "The Camel in Archaeology of North Africa and the Nile Valley," *Popular Archaeology* 3/6-7 (1974):11-12.
31. V. Gordon Childe, *New Light on the Most Ancient East* (New York: Norton, 1957), p. 51, fig. 19.
32. R. A. S. Macalister, *The Excavation of Gezer: 1902-1905 and 1907-1909*, p. 2 n. 9.
33. B. S. J. Isserlin, "On Some Possible Early Occurrences of the Camel in Palestine," *PEQ* (1950-51):51.
34. Ibid.
35. Wapnish, "Camel Caravans," p. 102.

36. Harold G. Stigers, *A Commentary on Genesis* (Grand Rapids: Zondervan, 1976), p. 196.
37. Zeuner, *History*, pp. 345-47.
38. John Bright, *History of Israel* (Philadelphia: Westminster, 1959), pp. 72-73.
39. W. G. Lambert, "The Domesticated Camel in the Second Millennium—Evidence from Alalakah and Ugarit," *BASOR* 160 (1960):42.
40. Kitchen, *Ancient Orient*, p. 79.
41. Donald J. Wiseman, "Ration Lists from Alalakh VII," *Journal of Cuneiform Studies* 13 (1959):29.
42. A. Goetze, "Remarks on the Ration Lists from Alalakh VII," *Journal of Cuneiform Studies* 13 (1959):29.
43. Lambert, "Domesticated Camel," p. 42.
44. See Zeuner, *History*, pp. 345-47; Wapnish, "Camel Caravans," pp. 115-17.
45. Wapnish, "Camel Caravans," pp. 117-18.
46. Ibid., p. 102.
47. LaBianca, "Zooarchaeological Remains," p. 141.
48. See BDB, s.v. *yānaq*, p. 413.
49. Merrill F. Unger, *Israel and the Aramaeans of Damascus* (Grand Rapids: Zondervan, 1957), p. 52.
50. See Davis, *Paradise*, p. 252.
51. See R. K. Harrison, *Old Testament Times* (Grand Rapids: Eerdmans, 1970), pp. 80-81.
52. Wapnish, "Camel Caravans," p. 115.
53. Ibid.
54. John Calvin, *Commentary on a Harmony of the Evangelists* (Grand Rapids: Eerdmans, 1949), 2:401.
55. See G. Campbell Morgan, *The Gospel According to Matthew* (New York: Revell, 1929), p. 241; Melancthon W. Jacobs, *Notes on the Gospels* (New York, 1853), p. 196; J. N. Darby, *Annotations on the New Testament* (Cambridge, 1829), p. 34.
56. George Williams, *The Student's Commentary on the Holy Scriptures* (London: Oliphants, 1949), p. 719.
57. See discussion and bibliography in Edward B. Nickolson, *A New Commentary on the Gospel According to Matthew* (London, 1881), p. 167.

CARL G. RASMUSSEN (Ph. D., The
Dropsie College for Hebrew and Cog-
nate Learning) is professor of Old
Testament at Bethel College, St.
Paul, Minnesota.

8

The Economic Importance of Caravan Trade for the Solomonic Empire

Carl G. Rasmussen

The reigns of David and Solomon are consistently depicted by the biblical writers as the high points of the Israelite monarchy. The greatness of
this era is highlighted in many ways, one of the most prominent being the
description of the fabulous wealth amassed by David and his son Solomon.
This accumulation of riches reached its climax during the reign of Solomon and was exhibited through a variety of means. For example, in the
building of the Temple in Jerusalem, gold was used extensively in plating
certain rooms and in fabricating the Temple accouterments (1 Kings 6-7; 2
Chron. 3-4). Twenty-three tons overlaid the Most Holy Place alone (2
Chron. 3:8). In addition to precious metals such as gold, silver, bronze,
and iron; and to costly fabrics of purple, crimson, and violet; expensive cedar, cypress, and algum woods were used in the building process (1 Kings
5:8-10; 2 Chron. 2:7, 10). At the dedication of the Temple the king sacri-
ficed an extravagant number of cattle (22,000) and sheep and goats
(120,000; see 1 Kings 8:63; 2 Chron. 7:5).

Certainly Solomon's personal building projects in Jerusalem were no
less lavish than his religious one. His palace was built along the lines of a
bīt ḫilāni palace.[1] His throne was made of ivory and overlaid with gold (1
Kings 10:18-20; 2 Chron. 9:17-19), his drinking vessels were made of gold
not silver (1 Kings 10:21; 2 Chron. 9:20), and it was noted that he made

"silver and gold as common in Jerusalem as stones, and cedar as plentiful as sycamore-fig trees in the foothills" (1 Kings 10:27; 2 Chron. 1:15; 9:27 NIV*). In addition, 2,625 pounds of gold were used in fabricating ceremonial shields (1 Kings 10:16-17; 2 Chron. 9:15-16). Even his daily provisions as described in 1 Kings 4:22-23 reveal the luxury of life in his court, as do the recorded comments of the queen of Sheba during her stay in Jerusalem (1 Kings 10:1-13; 2 Chron. 9:1-12).

Further, Y. Ikeda has recently argued that Solomon's accumulation and trade of horses and chariots can be thought of in military terms as well as in terms of a display of wealth.[2] Whether for ceremonial or for military purposes, the accumulation and maintenance of horses and chariots was a very costly affair.[3] His building/rebuilding of strategic centers such as Jerusalem, Hazor, Megiddo, Gezer, lower Beth-horon, Baalath, Tadmor, and Tamar, as well as his store cities and "towns" for his chariots and horses (1 Kings 9:15-19; 2 Chron. 8:4-6), must also have been expensive endeavors. In addition, the internal maintenance of his kingdom (1 Kings 4:1-6) and that of controlling vassal states, such as Edom, Moab, Ammon, and Aram, also needed to be financed. All of this data indicates that a large amount of wealth was needed to create and maintain the Solomonic kingdom. Thus the chronicler could write of the promise, which had been fulfilled, that God would give to Solomon "wealth, riches and honor, such as no king who was before you ever had and none after you will have" (2 Chron. 1:12).

The question that flows naturally from the above data is: From what sources did revenue stream into the coffers of Solomon in such magnitude that he was able to build his empire and maintain his lavish kingdom? One source could have been the production and exportation of goods or services that were in demand in neighboring countries. Nelson Glueck's older suggestion that Solomon amassed great wealth through the mining of copper at Timnah and then exported it to the surrounding nations never had textual support, and B. Rothenberg's recent excavations at Timnah have demonstrated that the mines were not in operation during the days of Solomon.[4]

In addition, other raw materials, such as gold, silver, tin, iron, precious stones, and ivory, were not native to the land of Israel, whereas the best quality trees were found in Lebanon. At certain points in history, particularly during the Greco-Roman periods (332 B.C.-A.D. 324) when northern portions of Cis- and Transjordan were under intense cultivation, grain was exported from Palestine (for biblical data see, e.g., Acts 12:20). But S. Ahituv, from his study of the economic base of Canaan during the Late Bronze

Age (c. 1550-1200 B.C.), has shown that Canaan had little to offer her neighbors in terms of agricultural products such as grains, oil, wine, and livestock.[5] To be sure, Solomon gave Hiram, king of Tyre, wheat, barley, wine, and olive oil for the men who were cutting timber in Lebanon (1 Kings 5:11; 2 Chron. 2:10), but there is no indication in the text that great wealth was accumulated by Solomon through the export of these or any other raw materials.[6] A reasonable assumption is that conditions had not changed appreciably from those of the fourteenth and thirteenth centuries described by Ahituv and that agricultural products were primarily consumed by the residents of Canaan itself.

On the other hand, there were internal sources of revenue or revenue equivalents that were available to the king. His subjects could be conscripted on a regular or irregular basis in order to serve on state-mandated projects or in the army (1 Kings 5:13-18; 9:15, 21-23; 1 Chron. 27:1-15; 2 Chron. 8:7-10). They were also required to help support the royal court on a regular basis (1 Kings 4:1-19, 27-28). Indeed it is implied that at the time of the accession of Rehoboam, the "yoke" that Solomon had placed on the people of the north had been significant (1 Kings 12:14; 2 Chron. 10:14). It is difficult, however, to see how these internal transfers of goods and services could have brought to Jerusalem raw materials such as cedar, cypress, almugwood, spices, precious stones, silver, ivory, apes, and especially gold, all of which were derived from foreign sources (1 Kings 10:2, 11-12; 2 Chron. 9:1, 9-10).

Another internal source of wealth would have been the revenues and products gathered from the royal estates. It has been plausibly suggested that during the period of David's consolidation of the state, former Canaanite territories came to be the possession of the crown.[7] David appointed overseers to be in charge of the royal storehouses; the storehouses in the outlying districts, towns, villages, and watchtowers; the field workers; the vineyards; the produce of the vineyards; the olive and sycamore-fig trees; the supplies of olive oil; the herds; the camels; the donkeys; and the flocks, all of which were part of the king's property (1 Chron. 27:25-31; 28:1). It can be assumed that such arrangements were carried over into the reign of Solomon, during whose rule revenue from the royal estates would have been supplemented through taxation.

Other sources of revenue for the Davidic-Solomonic court would have been from booty collected after the defeat of various nations and from tribute that subsequently flowed into Jerusalem on a regular basis. For example, after the defeat of the Arameans at Helam, seven hundred chariots fell into Israelite hands (2 Sam. 10:15-19; cf. 1 Chron. 19:16-19). At the final defeat of Hadadezer, David took chariots, horses, gold shields, and "a great quantity of bronze" as booty (2 Sam. 8:3-4, 7-8; 1 Chron. 18:3-4, 7-8), and the Arameans "became subject to him and brought tribute" (2 Sam. 8:6; 1 Chron. 18:6). Indeed Tou (Toi), king of Hamath, sent his son Joram (Hadoram) to Jerusalem with "articles of silver and gold and bronze" (2 Sam. 8:9-11; 1 Chron. 18:9-11). To the south the Moabites were subjugated by David and "brought [him] tribute" (2 Sam. 8:2; 1 Chron. 18:2, 11), and garrisons were placed in Edom (2 Sam. 8:14; 1 Kings 11:15-16; 1 Chron. 8:11, 13). Thus at the outset of the united monarchy great amounts of capital were transferred to Jerusalem, and in subsequent years tribute continued to flow in from vassal states.

At its greatest extent Solomon's kingdom is reported to have stretched from Tiphsah on the Euphrates River in the north to the Brook of Egypt (=Wadi el-Arish in northern Sinai)[8] in the south (1 Kings 4:20-25; 2 Chron. 9:26). In the north this meant that kingdoms such as Hamath, Aram-Zobah, Beth Rehob, and Aram-Damascus were under his control. On his eastern boundary the Ammonites, Moabites, and Edomites were subject to him, whereas to the south his effective area of control must have reached to Ezion Geber on the Red Sea, from which his maritime expeditions departed (1 Kings 9:26-28; 2 Chron. 8:17-18).[9] The only nearby territories that remained outside his direct control were cities such as Tyre, Sidon, and Byblos, all situated along the Phoenician coast.[10]

Given the extent of the Solomonic empire, it is obvious that he controlled the great trunk route that ran from Egypt in the southwest, across northern Sinai to Gaza, and from there, via Aphek, Megiddo, and Hazor, on to Damascus. From Damascus the route continued on to the neo-Hittite states to the north or turned northeast toward the normally powerful civilization centers along the Euphrates and Tigris rivers. Along this trunk route Solomon fortified strategic centers such as Hazor, Megiddo, and Gezer (1 Kings 9:15), and by this means he was able not only to effectively rule the countryside surrounding these old Canaanite centers but also to control and to service the caravans passing through his territory. It must be remembered, however, that during most of the period of the united monarchy, both Egypt and the civilizations along the Euphrates and Tigris rivers were relatively weak and that commerce between these two centers may have been rather limited.

To the east, Solomon's rule over Edom, Moab, Ammon, Gilead, and Damascus meant that he controlled all the branches of the Transjordanian highway, sometimes known as the "King's Highway" (Num. 21:22; but cf. 20:17). The value of controlling this route may not be as apparent as that of controlling the more westerly trunk route, but its importance may have been as great or greater during certain historical periods.

The major reason why the control of this route had value was because it connected Israel, Damascus, Hamath, Assyria, Asia Minor, and even Europe with southern Arabia (modern Yemen, South Yemen, and Oman). In today's world economy the produce of the latter countries is not too significant, but in ancient times their products, namely, frankincense and myrrh, were in great demand. According to the testimony of classical authors as well as modern researchers, frankincense was only grown in the Dhofar district of Oman (ancient Hadramawt), South Yemen (ancient Hadramawt and Qataban), and northern Somalia (ancient Punt[?] in the horn of Africa), whereas myrrh was grown in the above places as well as in Yemen (ancient Saba) and portions of Ethiopia.[11]

In the ancient world incense was in great demand, for it was included as part of the offerings to various deities from earliest historical times.[12] It can be debated as to whether Arabian frankincense or local varieties of incense were used during the very early periods, but the negativism of N. Groom and Paula Wapnish about the nonusage of south Arabian frankincense in the Levant and Egypt during the second millennium B.C. seems to be rather extreme.[13] Indeed, if the Mosaic authorship of the Pentateuch is maintained (i.e., it was written prior to c. 1400 B.C.),[14] then the reference to "pure frankincense" as a component of the special incense compound that was to be burned in the Tabernacle (Ex. 30:34-36) implies that the production and transport of frankincense from south Arabia is much older than the sixth century.

It is generally believed that the appearance of camels in the western fringes of the north Arabian and Syrian deserts was coincidental with the opening of the frankincense route from south Arabia. In this regard R. Bulliet has argued that the Arabian-Transjordanian north-south frankincense route was opened as early as the beginning of the second millennium B.C., albeit on a small scale,[15] for this would account for the evidence indicating the presence of camels at the northern terminus of this route in the early and mid-second millennium.[16] The appearance of small numbers of camels in north Syria during the early second millennium would also fit in well with the limited usage of camels in the patriarchal narratives.[17] Bulliet has developed the reasonable thesis that after northern Semites became aware of the sources of raw frankincense they moved into south Arabia during the second millennium B.C., and it was they who provided the impetus for the widespread cultivation of frankincense and myrrh.[18] This would put the beginning of the caravan trade between Arabia and the north a bit earlier than William F. Albright's suggestion that it began during the Late Bronze Age (1550-1200 B.C.)[19] and that the use of the camel in the Syrian desert became quite common at the beginning of the Iron Age (1200-1000 B.C.).[20]

Besides being offered as a sacrifice to the gods, frankincense had many other uses, namely, to purify houses, cities, and people, to mask unpleasant odors, and so forth.[21] During the Roman period (63 B.C.-A.D. 324) when huge amounts were consumed, an ounce of frankincense is said to have been as expensive as an ounce of gold.[22] G. Van Beek has estimated that during the second century A.D. a person would normally have had to work two weeks in order to purchase a pound of high-quality frankincense.[23]

Myrrh, on the other hand, was a fragrance included in the production of perfumes and other cosmetics. It was one of the elements used by the Israelites in the production of the anointing oil, which in turn was used to anoint the Tent of Meeting and its contents as well as the priests (Ex. 30:22-33). These references should not be taken as late anachronisms[24] but rather as a fifteenth-century testimony to the usage of myrrh.[25] Indeed the term for myrrh is also mentioned in extrabiblical documents of the fourteenth century, including a ritual text from Ugarit and two Amarna letters.[26] In Egypt myrrh was used for embalming, whereas in many countries it was used for medicinal purposes.[27]

Because frankincense and myrrh were low-bulk luxury items that were grown only in southern Arabia and in the horn of Africa, they needed to be transported from these remote growing areas to the consuming centers such as Egypt, Greece, Italy, Israel, and Syria, as well as the states situated along the Euphrates and Tigris rivers. Incense and other luxury goods were assembled in centers such as Shabwah, Tumna, and Marib for shipment northward.[28] Caravans would depart from these centers and follow the overland route that ran just east of the western coastal mountains of Arabia, north-northwestward to Yathrib (Media). From there a branch of the route headed northeast toward Babylon, whereas the more traveled routes continued northwest via Dedan (al-Ula) or Tema to Maan in southern Transjordan.[29] The journey from Marib to Maan covered about 1,355 miles and took about 63 days in classical times.[30] From there the route continued to Rabbath Ammon, through Ramoth Gilead, and on to Damascus and to points north, northwest, and northeast. Solomon's building of

Tadmor as well as store cities in Hamath (2 Chron. 4:3-4) may reflect his control of the northern terminus of this route. Solomon's kingdom sat astride this north-south route, and it is reasonable to assume that he was able to collect tolls from the caravans passing through this territory as well as provide for their needs.

In addition, routes branched off the northern portion of the Transjordanian route to the west, heading for ports on the Mediterranean Sea. One east-west connecting route ran from Ramoth Gilead to Tyre via the southern shore of the Sea of Galilee. From there it turned northward to Hazor and Abel Beth Maacah and then headed westward to Tyre, passing through upper Galilee. This section that led through upper Galilee may well have been the much discussed "Way of the Sea."[31]

A southerly branch of this northern east-west route could have connected Ramoth Gilead with Acco via the Jezreel valley or lower Galilee, the so-called "Darb al-Hawarnah."[32] In any case once the luxury goods reached the Mediterranean Sea they could be shipped by Hiram's fleet to all points of the Mediterranean world.[33]

The desire to control the Transjordanian highway can be seen in the interplay of Assyrian, Aramean, Israelite, and Arab activities along its northern section.[34] Whoever controlled this section could exact tolls and tariffs from caravans heading west, north, or east.[35] In the ninth century, during the early years of Assyrian expansion westward, Shalmaneser III (858-824 B.C.) fought against a coalition of western kings at the battle of Qarqar (853). Among the kings present was Gindibu the Arab, who supplied a thousand camels, probably for transport,[36] to the coalition.[37] Why would Gindibu ally himself against the Assyrian ruler? A logical explanation is that he had a stake in maintaining friendly relations with a strong Israel and a strong Damascus, so that his shipments of luxury goods from southern Arabia could pass unhampered through Israelite and Aramean territories to the Mediterranean Sea as well as to points northward.[38] Later, in the eighth century, Zabibe, queen of the Arabs, along with Rezin of Damascus, Menahem of Samaria, and Hiram of Tyre, paid tribute to Tiglath-Pileser III (745-727 B.C.).[39] Why should Zabibe have paid? She and her tribe(s) could have retreated into the desert and thus avoided the imposition of tribute. Possibly she and the rulers of terminal and transit points such as Tyre, Byblos, Israel, and Damascus were interested in keeping the trade routes open for their mutual economic benefit.[40] Later Samsi, queen of the Arabs, was defeated by Tiglath-Pileser III, and among the booty mentioned were 30,000 camels and 5,000 measures of spices.[41] Thus it is evident that the Arabs were deeply involved in the attempt to prevent Tiglath-Pileser from taking control of the northern end of the Transjordanian highway. Their success against the Assyrians was short-lived, for within a brief period of time the Assyrians had gained control of the area. Yet the Arabs kept the routes open by merely shifting their allegiance to the Assyrians. This can be seen in the fact that distant Arab tribes were paying Sargon II (721-705 B.C.) tribute as they attempted to keep the route open.[42] In fact, by the end of the eighth century Sargon controlled not only the Transjordanian highway but also the trunk road as far as Gaza.[43] Thus it can be seen, even as early as the ninth and eighth centuries B.C., that Arab tribes were making every effort to come to terms in one way or another with those powers that controlled the northern transit and terminal points of the Transjordanian highway.[44]

The other important route that connected the Transjordanian highway with ports on the Mediterranean Sea ran from "Maan" in Transjordan to "Gaza" on the coast.[45] This route, or an approximate equivalent to it, is well known from its usage during the Roman and Byzantine periods (63 B.C.-A.D. 640), at which time it was first controlled by the Nabateans and then the Romans.

From the Transjordanian highway several roads branched off leading northwest toward Gaza. One descended into the Wadi Arabah close to the oasis of Gharandal, another descended from Petra via the Wadi Musa, and to the north another ran from Bosrah to Punon via the Wadi Feidan. From the Wadi Arabah various roads led through the Negev highlands to the Negev basin on to "Gaza." One of these, for example, led from Moa in the Arabah through Moahile near the Ramon crater and past Oboda and Elusa on its way to Gaza. Z. Meshel and Y. Tsafrir have surveyed portions of this route,[46] and R. Cohen has excavated several forts located in its southeastern portion. As a result of these excavations Cohen has argued that the route was in use continuously from the third-second centuries B.C. until the fourth century A.D.[47] This would be the period during which huge quantities of frankincense were shipped to Greece and Rome from southern Arabia via the emporium at Gaza.

There is also evidence for the usage of this route during the Hellenistic (332-63 B.C.) and Persian (586-333 B.C.) periods and even as far back as the eighth century B.C. The Assyrians, for example, exhibited considerable interest in controlling the Gaza area from the days of Tiglath-Pileser III onward. It was during the days of Tiglath-Pileser III and Sargon II that southern Philistia came under Assyrian control. An Assyrian "*kāru* [emporium] of Egypt" was established near the "Brook of Egypt."[48] The Assyrians took control of the Meunites who lived in the region and received tribute from a certain Adbeel who evidently was headquartered in the Negev and northern Sinai.[49] Local chiefs were put in control of traffic through the area. Now besides Assyria's control of the obvious northeast to southwest connection to Egypt, the terminus of the incense route was firmly in her hands.

It should also be noted that just prior to the Assyrian consolidation of control in the Gaza area, the Judahite king, Hezekiah (728-696 B.C.), was militarily active in the region. He had warred against the Philistines, capturing Gath, Jabneh, and Ashdod, against the "Arabs who lived in Gur Baal, and against the Meunites" (2 Chron. 26:6-8). It is possible to interpret his activities in this area as an attempt to control the terminus of the incense/spice route, so that its profits would accrue to him.[50] Spices were included among the treasures that he showed to the delegation from Babylon (2 Kings 20:13; 2 Chron. 22:27; Isa. 39:2).

Because the Negev region and the Gaza coastal area were so important as transit and terminal points for the incense/spice routes from the eighth century B.C. through the Byzantine period, it is reasonable to infer that they would have been almost as important during the Solomonic era (970-931 B.C.), when frankincense and other spices were also considered to be of such great value. To be sure, the written records of Egypt and Mesopotamia are silent on the subject, but during this period of their weakness, they are silent on almost all matters relating to Israel until the campaign of the Egyptian king Shishak (c. 925 B.C.).[51]

Thus the basic source of information regarding the Solomonic era is the biblical text. This source strongly implies that Solomon controlled the Transjordanian highway from Edom to Damascus to Tadmor to Tiphsah and that he also controlled all connecting routes that led to the ports of Tyre and Acco on the Mediterranean Sea. In addition it relates how the queen of Sheba arrived in "Jerusalem with a very great caravan—with camels carrying spices, large quantities of gold, and precious stones" (1 Kings 10:2; see further 10:1-13; 2 Chron. 9:1-12).[52] Immediately after that story it is noted that Solomon received "revenues from merchants and traders and from all the Arabian kings and governors of the land" (1 Kings 10:14; 2 Chron. 9:14). Although the Bible continually places emphasis on the glory and wisdom of Solomon, certainly an underlying motivation for the above actions would be the desire of the "queen of Sheba" and the "Arabian kings" to keep the trade routes open and the associated tolls and tariffs as low as possible.[53]

The Arabs may have attempted to circumvent Solomon's monopoly on the northern routes to the Mediterranean by using the southern Maan-Gaza connection. But it is proposed that Solomon countered this attempt by establishing a series of forts in the Negev in order to monitor the caravans passing from Maan to Gaza. Indeed recent surface explorations and excavations have shown that Solomon established some forty forts in the Negev highlands and Negev basin. These fortresses, many of which have been excavated by R. Cohen, are usually enclosed by casement walls and are rectangular, oval, or square in shape. They are generally small in size, fifty yards square, and in addition, small farmsteads including four-roomed houses, terraced fields, dammed wadis, and cisterns are often located close by. The dating of these fortresses is somewhat problematic, but Cohen's arguments, based on the ceramic finds and historical evidence (Shishak's destruction of seventy settlements in the Negev in 925 B.C.), seem decisive in dating them to the tenth century.[54] Cohen believes that these fortresses/farmsteads were built primarily to protect the southern flank of Solomon's kingdom from raids from the desert tribes. This may have been partially the case, but certainly they would have also served to protect, monitor, and service the caravans passing through this region.[55]

It is evident that Solomon controlled all of the routes passing through his territory: the north-south trunk and Transjordanian highways as well as the east-west connecting routes to the Mediterranean. Surely considerable revenues would have accrued to him, for he was able to coerce all caravans passing through his territory to pay tolls and to pay for services such as food, lodging, and "protection." This source of revenue would have brought a considerable amount of wealth to the kingdom without having to assume the export of almost nonexistent mineral resources or the export of limited high-bulk, agricultural products. It would have been with these revenues, along with that gained through the collection of booty and tribute, that Solomon built and maintained his lavish state.

In view of this it seems very probable that the record found in the Persian archives several hundred years after the days of Solomon by the Persian king Artaxerxes (464-423 B.C.) could very well be a reference to the policies of Solomon. This record states that Jerusalem had "had powerful kings ruling over the whole of Trans-Euphrates, and [that] taxes, tribute and duty were paid to them" (Ezra 4:19). Thus it preserved the memory of the coerciveness of the Solomonic state as it accumulated tremendous amounts of wealth from its control of the trade routes.

NOTES

* All Scripture citations in this chapter, unless otherwise noted, are taken from the NIV.

1. D. Ussishkin, "King Solomon's Palaces," *BA* 36/3 (September 1973):78-105.

2. Y. Ikeda, "Solomon's Trade in Horses and Chariots in Its International Setting," in *Studies in the Period of David and Solomon and Other Essays,* ed. T. Ishida (Winona Lake, Ind.: Eisenbrauns, 1982), pp. 215-38.

3. C. Hauer, Jr. "The Economics of National Security in Solomonic Israel," *Journal for the Study of the Old Testament* 18 (1980):63-73.

4. See Nelson Glueck, "Ezion-geber," *BA* 28 (1965):70-87, esp. p. 73; H. Shanks, "Nelson Glueck and King Solomon—A Romance That Ended," *BAR* (March 1975):10-16; B. Rothenberg, *Timna* (London: Thames and Hudson, 1972), pp. 63, 180.

5. S. Ahituv, "Economic Factors in the Egyptian Conquest of Canaan," *IEJ* 28 (1978):93-105.

6. See also H. J. Katzenstein, *The History of Tyre* (Jerusalem: Shocken Institute, 1973), p. 99.

7. Y. Aharoni, *Land of the Bible,* rev. ed. (Philadelphia: Westminster, 1979), pp. 294-96.

8. A. F. Rainey, "Toponymic Problems: The Brook of Egypt," *Tel Aviv* 9 (1982):131-32.

9. The location of Ezion-geber is problematic, for the old identification of it with Tell el-Kheleifeh can no longer be maintained due to the lack of tenth-century (Solomonic) remains; see G. Pratico, "Tell el-Kheleifeh 1938-1940: A Forthcoming Reappraisal," *BA* (1982):120-21.

10. Katzenstein, *History,* pp. 96-101.

11. On these locations see N. Groom, *Frankincense and Myrrh: A Study of the Arabian Incense Trade* (London: Longmans, 1981), pp. 96-120.

12. Ibid., pp. 1-5.

13. Ibid., pp. 22-37 passim, 231; Paula Wapnish, "Camel Caravans and Camel Pastoralists at Tell Jemmeh," *JANESCU* 13 (1981):111-12.

14. Gleason L. Archer, Jr., *SOTI* (Chicago: Moody, 1975), pp. 105-76.

15. R. Bulliet, *The Camel and the Wheel* (Cambridge, Mass.: Harvard U., 1975), pp. 60-67.

16. Ibid., p. 92, but cf. the rather extreme position of Wapnish, "Camel," p. 121, who states that "camels were not a major means of transport before 600 B.C.E."

17. Only ten are mentioned in the narrative of Abraham's servant's journey to Aram Naharaim to secure a wife for Isaac (Gen. 24:10). On the question of camels in the patriarchal narratives see Kenneth A. Kitchen, *Ancient Orient and Old Testament* (Chicago: Inter-Varsity, 1966), pp. 79-80; Bulliet, *Camel,* p. 35.

18. Bulliet, *Camel,* p. 36.

19. William F. Albright, "Midianite Donkey Caravans," in *Translating and Understanding the Old Testament,* ed. H. T. Frank and W. L. Reed (Nashville: Abingdon, 1970), p. 202. Albright's position (pp. 204-5) was that donkey caravans initiated this trade no later than the fifteenth century B.C. and that camel caravans took over the route soon after 1200. As it stands, this position allows for camel caravans during the Solomonic era, but in light of Bulliet's evidence it seems more likely that camel caravans were in use earlier than Albright maintained.

20. Ibid., pp. 204-5; see especially Judg. 6:5; 7:12: "Their camels could no more be counted than sand on the seashore"; see also Bulliet, *Camel,* p. 77.

21. Groom, *Frankincense,* p. 8; see also M. D. Fowler, "Excavated Incense Burners: A Case for Identifying a Site as Sacred?" *PEQ* 117 (January-June, 1985):25-26.

22. Groom, *Frankincense,* p. 8.

23. G. van Beek, "Frankincense and Myrrh," in *BAR,* ed. E. F. Campbell, Jr., and D. N. Freedman (New York: Doubleday, 1964), 2:119.

24. As in Groom, *Frankincense,* p. 31.

25. Even the Egyptian queen Hatshepsut (1503-1482 B.C.) made use of myrrh as "an ointment for the divine limbs"; see ibid., p. 25.

26. See Albright, "Midianite," pp. 203-4, for discussion and references.

27. Groom, *Frankincense,* pp. 19-20.

28. Ibid., p. 170. Possibly spices from India and elsewhere were brought to these centers and were transported northward as well. For example, cinnamon, native to Ceylon, was in use in Egypt during the reign of Ramses III (1198-1166 B.C.). Van Beek, "Frankincense," p. 110, has plausibly suggested that it was brought there via southern Arabia.

29. See I. Eph'al, *The Ancient Arabs* (Jerusalem: Magnes, 1984), p. 241; van Beek, "Frankincense," p. 107.

30. Groom, *Frankincense,* p. 213.

31. A. F. Rainey, "Toponymic Problems: The Way of the Sea," *Tel Aviv* 8 (1981):146-49.

32. D. Baly, *The Geography of the Bible,* rev. ed. (New York: Harper, 1974), p. 100.

33. For a description and discussion of the near monopoly enjoyed by the Phoenicians with reference to Mediterranean transport at this time see Katzenstein, *History,* pp. 77-115 *passim.*

34. Later the Babylonians, Persians, Greeks, Nabateans, Romans, and Arabs would vie for control of the area.

35. Groom, *Frankincense,* p. 10, notes that the high cost of frankincense and myrrh in the Greek and Roman markets "was in a great measure due to the considerable expense of transporting the commodity over a very great distance through many different states and tribal areas, to each of which customs and service charges had to be paid." Using figures from Pliny (first century A.D.), Groom (*Frankincense,* pp. 159-61) adds that the price of frankincense had doubled from the time it left Shabwah to the time it arrived in Gaza, the increase being due to transport costs and tolls incurred along the way.

36. At this date camels were probably used primarily for transport of equipment, for it was not until later (c. 500 B.C.) that a special "north Arabian" saddle was developed that allowed the riders of camels a more secure platform from which to fight; Bulliet, *Camel,* pp. 90-99.

37. *ANET,* pp. 278-79.

38. Eph'al, *Ancient Arabs,* p. 76.

39. *ANET,* p. 283.

40. Eph'al, *Ancient Arabs,* pp. 82-83.

41. *ANET,* pp. 283-84; see Eph'al, *Ancient Arabs,* pp. 85-87, for a discussion of the text.

42. For the text see *ANET,* p. 286; for a discussion of their distant location see Eph'al, *Ancient Arabs,* pp. 87-92.

43. Eph'al, *Ancient Arabs,* pp. 101-11.

44. Ibid., p. 91.

45. "Maan" refers to any of the major centers in the Petra/Maan region that served as a major transit point/junction. The site changed from period to period. On the Mediterranean, "Gaza" was the chief port during most periods, but it must be recognized that any ports along the coast (e.g., Ashkelon, Ashdod, Joppa) could be used as shipping points.

46. Z. Meshel and Y. Tsafrir, "The Nabataean Road from Avedat to Shaar Ramon," *PEQ* 106 (1974) 103-8; *PEQ* 107 (1975) 3-21.

47. R. Cohen, "New Light on the Date of the Petra Gaza Road," *BA* 45/4 (Fall 1982):246.

48. See N. Naaman, "The Brook of Egypt and Assyrian Policy on the Border of Egypt," *Tel Aviv* 6/1-2 (1979):68-90; "The Shihor of Egypt and Shur That Is Before Egypt," *Tel Aviv* 7/1-2 (1980):95-109; R. Reich, "The Identification of the 'Sealed *Kāru* of Egypt,'" *IEJ* 34/1 (1984):32-38.

49. Eph'al, *Ancient Arabs,* p. 91.

50. On this whole argument see ibid., p. 107 n. 363. For an extensive presentation of the biblical data of how various Judahite monarchs attempted to control the Gaza area and the Negev routes see S. Yeivin, 'Did the Kingdoms of Israel Have a Maritime Policy?" *JQR* 50 (1960):193- 228.

51. See for example Kenneth A. Kitchen, *The Third Intermediate Period in Egypt (1100-650 B.C.)* (Warminster: Aris and Phillips, 1973), pp. 3-81; D. B. Redford, "Studies in Relations Between Palestine and Egypt During the First Millennium B.C. II. The Twenty-Second Dynasty," *JAOS* 93 (1973):3-17.

52. For a discussion of this visit see John Bright, *A History of Israel,* 3d ed. (Philadelphia: Westminster, 1981), p. 215; A. Malamat, "A Political Look at the Kingdom of David and Solomon and Its Relations with Egypt," in *Studies in the Period of David and Solomon and Other Essays,* p. 191; J. B. Pritchard, ed., *Solomon and Sheba* (London: Phaidon, 1974).

53. In commenting on the visit of the queen of Sheba it is usually suggested that Solomon offered in exchange "finished products . . . high-value, low-bulk goods of some sort" (Malamat, "A Political Look," p. 191). Usually no specific items are listed as export possibilities because there probably are none. It is more reasonable to assume that Solomon exchanged tariff and toll concessions as suggested here. It does not make much difference whether the land of Sheba is located in south Arabia, as many commentators

believe, or whether it is some kind of merchant colony in north Arabia (Groom, *Frankincense*, pp. 41-45), for in either case the incense had to pass through Solomonic territory on its way to the Mediterranean ports.

54. R. Cohen, "The Fortresses King Solomon Built to Protect His Southern Border," *BAR* 11/3 (May/June, 1985):56-70 and the literature cited regarding earlier explorers such as Glueck and Aharoni. See, however, a minor revision, R. Cohen, "Solomon's Negev Defense Line Contained Three Fewer [From more than Forty] Fortresses," *BAR* 12/4 (July/August, 1986):40-45.

55. During much of antiquity the Egyptians not only exported grain grown in the Nile valley but also materials that had been imported from the south. For example, at various times frankincense and myrrh were shipped from south Arabia by boat to ports along the western shore of the Red Sea. From there the goods were transported overland to the Nile River, where they were loaded on boats and shipped to the Mediterranean port of Alexandria. This option seems to have been closed during the days of Solomon, for Egypt was a divided country at that time. The rulers of Dynasty XXI resided in and ruled from the delta city of Tanis and had very poor relations with the preists of Thebes, who effectively controlled the southern portion of Egypt. See Kitchen, *Third Intermediate Period in Egypt*, p. 3; Malamat, "A Political Look," p. 198. During the days of Shishak (935-914 B.C.), Upper and Lower Egypt were again united (cf. e.g. Redford, "Studies," pp. 11-13), and it is probable that one of the objectives of Shishak's campaign into Israel was to close off the usage of the Maan-Gaza connection so that goods from southern Arabia and the horn of Africa would again flow through Egypt, rather than through Israel. See Yeivin, "Did the Kingdoms," pp. 193-95, 207, 209-15; Z.Herzog, "Enclosed Settlements in the Negeb and the Wilderness of Beer-sheba," *BASOR* 250 (1983), p. 48; Malamat, "A Political Look," p. 204.

EDWIN M. YAMAUCHI (Ph. D., Brandeis University) is professor of history at Miami University, Oxford, Ohio.

9

Postbiblical Traditions About Ezra and Nehemiah

Edwin M. Yamauchi

EZRA AND NEHEMIAH

Gleason Archer has contributed much to Old Testament studies both by his teaching and by his writing. It is an honor for me to join other colleagues in recognizing the distinguished career of such a *sôphēr*, who like Ezra has so faithfully expounded God's Word.

Archer has helpfully discussed some of the key problems in the books of Ezra and Nehemiah in his widely used survey of the Old Testament[1] and in his useful *Encyclopedia of Bible Difficulties*.[2] Elsewhere I have also addressed such issues as the archaeological background of Ezra,[3] the archaeological background of Nehemiah,[4] the role of Nehemiah as a royal cupbearer,[5] and the question of the contemporaneity of Ezra and Nehemiah.[6]

In the following essay I would like to trace some of the apocryphal stories and pseudepigraphical works associated with Ezra and with Nehemiah. Though Ezra preceded Nehemiah, I will discuss the latter first, inasmuch as Ezra attracted the greater and longer attention down through the centuries. The task of tracing such postbiblical traditions has been greatly facilitated by the publication in 1983 of the first volume of *The Old Testament Pseudepigraphia*.[7]

TRADITIONS ABOUT NEHEMIAH

It is striking that neither Philo[8] nor the New Testament refers to Ezra or to Nehemiah. H. Shires compares the prayer for rulers in Ezra 6:10 with 1 Timothy 2:1-2, the attitude of humility in Ezra 9:6 with Luke 18:13, and the phrase "holy city" of Nehemiah 11:1, 18 with Matthew 4:5.[9] Jacob Myers detects a possible allusion to Nehemiah 9:6 in Acts 4:24.[10] Josephus's account that parallels Ezra and Nehemiah introduces many errors.[11]

Nehemiah was extolled in Sirach 49:13 (dated c. 180 B.C.): "The memory of Nehemiah also is lasting; he raised for us the walls that had fallen, and set up the gates and bars and rebuilt our ruined houses." Some curious traditions about Nehemiah are found in 2 Maccabees (first century B.C.). There is a reference to "the feast of the fire given when Nehemiah, who built the temple and the altar, offered sacrifices" in 1:18, and 2:13 reports: "The same things are reported in the records and in the memoirs of Nehemiah, and also that he founded a library and collected the books about the kings and prophets, and the writings of David, and letters of kings about votive offerings."

In *Antiquities* 11.183, Josephus speaks of Nehemiah's life and death as follows: "Then, after performing many other splendid and praiseworthy public services, Nehemiah died at an advanced age. He was a man of kind and just nature and most anxious to serve his countrymen; and he left the walls of Jerusalem as his eternal monument."

TRADITIONS ABOUT EZRA

Though Ben Sirach (Sir. 49:11-13) in his catalog of famous men lists Nehemiah, he fails to mention Ezra. The omission, however, can be explained. For one thing Ben Sirach was primarily concerned with men who were builders. According to some scholars Ben Sirach betrays a Sadducean bias and according to others an anti-Levitical bias, either of which would explain Ezra's omission.[12]

The Talmud (*Megilla* 16b) tells us that Ezra was a disciple of the aged Baruch, who had been Jeremiah's scribe. The rabbis held that "if Moses had not anticipated him, Ezra would have received the Torah" (*Sanh.* 21b). *Baba Bathra* 14b-16a credits Ezra with the authorship of the books of Ezra and Chronicles.[13]

Baba Qamma 82a ascribes to Ezra ten *takkanot*, or regulations, which cover such miscellaneous practices as (1) holding the court on Mondays and Thursdays, (2) washing clothes on Thursdays and not Fridays, (3) eating garlic on Friday as an aphrodisiac,[14] (4) the combing of a woman's hair before taking a ritual bath, and so for th.[15]

The Old Testament tells us nothing of Ezra's end. Josephus (*Ant.* 11.158) relates that Ezra died at the age of 120 in Jerusalem: "And it was his fate, after being honored by the people, to die an old man and be buried with great magnificence in Jerusalem." Later traditions spoke of his burial at Abu Ghosh or south of Nablus.[16]

From the eleventh century A.D., Jews in Mesopotamia held that Ezra was buried near the Persian Gulf at al-'Uzair (*'Uzayr* is Arabic for "Ezra") on the right bank of the Tigris in southern Iraq.[17]

Both Josephus and the rabbinic traditions ascribe the establishment of the "great synagogue" to Ezra. E. Bickerman suggests that the "men of the great synagogue" should not be understood as an institution but rather as the generation between Cyrus and Alexander because one cannot find any traces of a "great synagogue" outside of the Talmud.[18]

Samaritan tradition preserved in the medieval *Liber Josuae* blames "the cursed Ezra" for the excommunication of the Samaritans from the Jewish community.[19] Though it is possible that such a tradition may stem from the Old Testament period of Ezra and Nehemiah, it more probably reflects later hostility between the two communities.

The high regard with which the Jews of Arabia held Ezra may be reflected in the strange accusation found in Quran 9:30: "And the Jews say: 'Ezra is the son of Allah,' and the Christians say: 'The Messiah is the son of Allah.'" Late tradition holds that Ezra tried to persuade the Jews of Yemen in southwest Arabia to return to Palestine, but they refused to come because they knew that the second Temple would be destroyed.[20]

FIRST ESDRAS

Esdras is the Greek transliteration of the name Ezra. The arrangement and naming of the apocryphal and pseudepigraphal Ezra/Esdras books are complicated because the canonical books of Ezra-Nehemiah were also called Esdras in the LXX and Vulgate. A chart can best clarify the relationship of the various titles:

Version	OT Ezra	OT Nehemiah	A Paraphrase of Ezra, etc.	A Latin Apocalypse
LXX		2 Esdras	1 Esdras	
Vg	1 Esdras	2 Esdras	3 Esdras	4 Esdras
KJV, RSV	Ezra	Nehemiah	1 Esdras	2 Esdras

In the following discussion 1 Esdras will be used as the title of the apocryphal work of the third column and 2 Esdras or 4 Ezra for the pseudepigraphal work of the fourth column inasmuch as this latter name is now preferred by scholars.

First Esdras, which is the first book of the Apocrypha, differs from the other apocryphal books in that it is a divergent account for the most part of the canonical books of Ezra-Nehemiah. First Esdras parallels the last two chapters of 2 Chronicles, all of Ezra, and thirteen verses of Nehemiah from the section on Ezra (Neh. 7:73 through chap. 12). The following chart indicates the parallels:

1 Esdras	Parallels
1:1-20	2 Chron. 35:1-19
1:21-22	[without parallel]
1:23-55	2 Chron. 35:20—36:21
2:1-3a	2 Chron. 36:22-23; Ezra 1:1-3a
2:3b-11	Ezra 1:3b-11
2:12-26	Ezra 4:7-24
3:1—5:6	[without parallel]
5:7-71	Ezra 2:1—4:5
6:1—9:36	Ezra 5:1—10:44
9:37-55	Neh. 7:73 [MT 7:72]—8:13

In striking contrast to Ezra-Nehemiah, the writer of 1 Esdras concentrates exclusively on the ministry of Ezra. In the parallel to Nehemiah 8:9 the name of Nehemiah is omitted. As the Ezra narrative that is now found in Nehemiah 7:72— 8:12 is placed in 1 Esdras 8:88 —9:36 immediately after the events of Ezra 10, it is sometimes claimed that the 1 Esdras account is superior in that it avoids the gap of thirteen years found in the Hebrew text between Ezra's arrival and the reading of the law.

The Greek text of 1 Esdras in the LXX is written in elegant Greek in contrast with the painfully literal LXX text of Ezra-Nehemiah.[21] The latter had been considered by Charles C. Torrey[22] as the work of Theodotion (second century A.D.), but it is more probably a Palestinian translation by a forerunner of Theodotion.

There is a variety of theories about the origins of 1 Esdras, whose composition is dated c. 150 B.C.[23] As the beginning and end of 1 Esdras are quite abrupt and as it ignores Nehemiah, K. F. Pohlmann has suggested that it is a fragment of an old Greek translation of the chronicler's work on Ezra before the Nehemiah memoirs were attached to it.[24]

Frank M. Cross and his students have argued that 1 Esdras is based on a shorter Hebrew *Vorlage*, which is earlier than and superior to the MT.[25] Though 1 Esdras may have preserved a superior text in some cases, as in the lists of names,[26] the added narrative materials have no independent value. About 20 percent of the Aramaic documents are mistranslated in 1 Esdras.[27]

The one independent passage is the entertaining story of the guardsmen, one of whom was Zerubbabel, in 1 Esdras 3:1—5:6. The guardsmen attempt to answer the riddle of what is the strongest power in the world. The answers given were: (1) the king; (2) wine; (3) women; (4) "but truth is victor over all things."

It is noteworthy that Josephus (*Ant.* 11) chose to follow 1 Esdras rather than the MT/LXX, perhaps because of its superior Greek. Josephus compounds the errors of 1 Esdras in his narrative. Both Ezra and Nehemiah are placed by him in the reign of Xerxes instead of in the reign of Artaxerxes I.[28]

Though 1 Esdras was not highly regarded among other Jewish writers —it is not, for example, quoted in the Talmud—it became popular among Christians. It is found in Origen's *Hexapla*. Augustine believed that he could find in it a prophecy of Christ, but Jerome was scornful of it. In later editions of the Vulgate it was sometimes included as an appendix to the New Testament. Neither 1 Esdras nor 2 Esdras (see below) have been included in Roman Catholic translations of the Scriptures, such as the *Douay-Confraternity*, *New American Bible*, or the *Jerusalem Bible*, but they are included in the RSV Apocrypha. Luther was so contemptuous of what he called that *figmentum Iudaicum* that he reported: "The third book of Esdras I threw into the Elbe."[29]

SECOND ESDRAS

The pseudepigraphal work called 2 Esdras in the English versions, 4 Esdras in the Vulgate, and most commonly 4 Ezra by scholars is preserved in its entirety only in Latin recensions of the seventh to thirteenth centuries A.D. Most scholars believe that the original, central section, which is an apocalypse (chaps. 3-14), was composed in Hebrew or Aramaic by a Jewish author about A.D. 100.[30] We have but three verses of chapter 15 in Greek (*P. Oxy.* 1010). The work was translated into several languages including an important Armenian version, which goes back to a Greek original according to M. E. Stone.[31]

The RSV restores seventy verses left out of many of the manuscripts between 7:35 and 7:36 for doctrinal reasons. These verses emphatically deny the efficacy of prayers for the dead: "So no one shall ever pray for another on that day . . . for then everyone shall bear his own righteousness or unrighteousness" (RSV 7:105).

Chapters 1-2, sometimes called 5 Ezra (see below), were added by a Christian in the middle of the second century, and chapters 15-16 were appended perhaps as late as A.D. 270.

Chapters 3-14 relate seven visions by which the angel Uriel instructs Ezra about the problem of evil and the destiny of souls after death. Ezra protests the punishment of mankind, whereas Uriel defends God's justice. Scholars have been divided as to whether Ezra or Uriel represents the author's viewpoint.[32] A. L. Thompson concludes his analysis of 2 Esdras = 4 Ezra as follows:

> The author of IV Ezra has been depicted both as a pessimistic hater of Gentiles (Rosenthal) as well as a sensitive lover of all mankind (Gunkel, Montefiore); both as a faithful Pharisee (Mundle) and as a detached apocalyptist (Oesterley, Neusner). One thing is clear, however, and that is that IV Ezra witnesses to the fact that when God's people fall on hard times, the spirit of his people is not thereby to be crushed.[33]

There is a clear reference to the destruction of Jerusalem in A.D. 70 in 2 Esdras 3:1, which refers to "the thirteenth year after the destruction of our city." Though there are references to the role of an eschatological Messiah, he was not conceived of as "the answer to the questions that Ezra was asking."[34]

Second Esdras 14:1-48 describes how God commanded Ezra to dictate the Scriptures in forty days to five rapidly-writing scribes, who produced twenty-four canonical books and seventy secret books. They wrote in an unknown script (Aramaic?) for forty days.

Bruce M. Metzger notes that Christopher Columbus used a passage in 2 Esdras 6:42, which led him to believe that there were six parts of land to one part of water, to gain the support of Ferdinand and Isabella for his epochal voyage in 1492.[35]

FIFTH EZRA

The first two chapters now included in 4 Ezra are sometimes designated 5 Ezra. This was quite clearly a separate Christian composition. G. N. Stanton has argued that it was composed soon after the Bar Kochba revolt in the early second century A.D. and that it reflects "Matthean Christianity."[36] If it was indeed composed this early, it would even antedate the earliest Latin church Father, Tertullian.[37] Fifth Ezra was the source of a number of phrases in the Catholic liturgy: *Requiem aeternam dona eis, Domine-* —"Give them eternal rest, Lord" (2:34); *Lux perpetua luceat eis*—"May the eternal light shine upon them" (2:35); *Accipite iucunditatem gloriae vestrae*—"Receive the joy of your glory" (2:36); *Gratias agite ei qui vos ad caelestia regna vocavit*—"Give thanks to Him who called you to heavenly kingdoms" (2:37).

OTHER EZRA PSEUDEPIGRAPHA

A number of other pseudepigraphal works, including the *Greek Apocalypse of Ezra*, were inspired by 2 Esdras = 4 Ezra. This work, which may be dated at some time after the second century and before the ninth century, contains a striking description of Ezra's descent into Tartarus. There he sees Herod punished on a fiery throne, eavesdroppers with fiery axles upon their ears, and an incestuous man hanging from his eyelids. He also views the terrible visage of the Antichrist.[38]

A related Latin work, the *Vision of Ezra*, dated between the fourth and seventh centuries, expands on Ezra's descent into Tartarus. The list of those suffering torments is expanded to include those who sinned with women on the Lord's day, those who failed to confess, those who were inhospitable, and women who killed babies conceived in adultery. It is quite possible that works like the *Visio Beati Esdrae* may have helped to inspire Dante's *Inferno*.[39]

Late in the Middle Ages astrological almanacs called *kalandologia* were attributed to Ezra. *The Revelation of Ezra* (ninth century A.D.) predicts the nature of the year from the day on which the year began.[40]

CONCLUSION

The impact of Nehemiah and Ezra was felt after their times. Though Nehemiah may have had the more prestigious position as the Persian king's cupbearer, it was Ezra's role as a *sôphēr* ("scribe") that attracted various attempts to ascribe all kinds of writings to him. Though little read today by the average reader and even the scholar, these apocryphal and pseudepigraphal works once exercised considerable influence and deserve our renewed attention today.[41]

NOTES

1. Gleason L. Archer, Jr., *SOTI* (Chicago: Moody, 1974), pp. 410-16.
2. Gleason L. Archer, Jr., *Encyclopedia of Bible Difficulties* (Grand Rapids: Zondervan, 1982), pp. 229-33.
3. Edwin M. Yamauchi, "The Archaeological Background of Ezra," *BibSac* 137 (1980):195-211.
4. Edwin M. Yamauchi, "The Archaeological Background of Nehemiah," *BibSac* 137 (1980):291-309.
5. Edwin M. Yamauchi, "Was Nehemiah the Cupbearer a Eunuch?" *ZAW* 92 (1980):132-42.
6. Edwin M. Yamauchi, "The Reverse Order of Ezra/Nehemiah Reconsidered," *Themelios* 5/3 (1980):7-13.
7. J. H. Charlesworth, *The Old Testament Pseudepigrapha*, vol. 1 (Garden City, N.Y.: Doubleday, 1983) (hereafter abbreviated *OTP*).
8. It has been suggested that Philo was referring to Ezra 8:2 in *The Confession of Tongues* 149, but this is most dubious. See F. H. Colson and G. H. Whitaker, *Philo*, Loeb Classical Library (London: Heinemann, 1932), 4:91, 557.
9. H. M. Shires, *Finding the Old Testament in the New* (Philadelphia: Westminster, 1974), p. 219.
10. Jacob M. Myers, *Ezra-Nehemiah* (Garden City, N.Y.: Doubleday, 1965), p. LXXV.
11. See my "Josephus and the Scriptures," *Fides et Historia* 13 (1980), pp. 50-51.
12. P. Höffken, "Warum schwieg Jesus Sirach über Esra," *ZAW* 87 (1975):184-201.
13. On the questions of authorship and the "chronicler" see the Introduction to my commentary on Ezra-Nehemiah in *The Expositor's Bible Commentary*, ed. Frank E. Gaebelein (Grand Rapids: Zondervan, forthcoming).
14. See my "Magic in the Biblical World," *TB* 34 (1983):180-81.
15. S. Zeitlin, "Takkanot Ezra," *JQR* (1917-18):62-74.
16. M. Munk, "Esra Hasofer nach Talmud und Midrasch," *Jahrbuch der Jüdisch-literarischen Gesellschaft* 22 (1931):228-29.
17. D. S. Sassoon, "The History of the Jews in Basra," *JQR* 17 (1926-27) 407-69.
18. E. Bickerman, "Viri magnae congregationis," *Revue biblique* 55 (1948):397-402.
19. J. D. Purvis, *The Samaritan Pentateuch and the Origin of the Samaritan Sect* (Cambridge, Mass.: Harvard U., 1968), p. 98.

20. L. Ginzberg, ed., *The Legends of the Jews* (Philadelphia: Jewish Publication Society, 1928), 6:432.
21. R. Hanhart, ed., *Esdrae Liber I* (Göttingen: Vandenhoeck and Ruprecht, 1974).
22. Charles C. Torrey, *Ezra Studies*, ed. W. F. Stinespring (1910; reprint, New York: Ktav, 1970), pp. 11-36, 66-82.
23. L. Rost, *Judaism Outside the Hebrew Canon* (Nashville: Abingdon, 1976), pp. 98-99.
24. K.-F. Pohlmann, *Studien zum dritten Esra* (Göttingen: Vandenhoeck and Ruprecht, 1970). For a critique see H. G. M. Williamson, *Israel in the Book of Chronicles* (Cambridge: Cambridge U., 1977), pp. 23-29.
25. Frank M. Cross, "A Reconstruction of the Judean Restoration," *JBL* 94 (1975):7-8; R. Klein, "Old Readings in I Esdras," *Harvard Theological Review* 62 (1969):99-107.
26. H. L. Allrik, "The Lists of Zerubbabel (Nehemiah 7 and Ezra 2) and the Hebrew Numerical Notation," *BASOR* 136 (1954):21-27; R. Klein, "Old Readings in I Esdras: The List of Returnees from Babylon (Ezra 2/Nehemiah 7)," *Harvard Theological Review* 62 (1969):99-107.
27. C. Hensley, "The Official Persian Documents in the Book of Ezra" (Dissertation; Liverpool U., 1977), p. 139.
28. C. G. Tuland, "Josephus, *Antiquities*, Book XI, Correction or Confirmation of Biblical Post-Exilic Records?" *AUSS* 4 (1966):176-92.
29. Myers, *Ezra-Nehemiah*, p. 18.
30. F. Zimmerman, "The Underlying Documents of IV Ezra," *JQR* 51 (1960):107-30.
31. M. E. Stone, *The Armenian Version of IV Ezra* (Missoula: Scholars, 1979).
32. A. P. Hayman, "The Problem of Pseudonymity in the Ezra Apocalypse," *Journal for the Study of Judaism in the Persian, Hellenistic and Roman Periods* 6 (1975):47-56.
33. A. L. Thompson, *Responsibility for Evil in the Theodicy of IV Ezra* (Missoula, Mont.: Scholars, 1977), p. 342.
34. M. E. Stone, "The Concept of the Messiah in IV Ezra," *Religions in Antiquity*, ed. J. Neusner (Leiden: Brill, 1968), p. 312.
35. B. M. Metzger, "The Fourth Book of Ezra," *OTP*, p. 523; cf. S. E. Morison, *Christopher Columbus, Mariner* (New York: New American Library, 1955), pp. 19, 115.
36. G. N. Stanton, "5 Ezra and Matthean Christianity in the Second Century," *JTS* n.s. 28 (1977):67-83.
37. J. Daniélou, "Le Ve Esdras et le Judéo-Christianisme Latin au second siècle," *Ex Orbe Religionum I: Studia Geo Widengren Oblata* (Leiden: Brill, 1972):163.
38. M. E. Stone, "Greek Apocalypse of Ezra," *OTP*, p. 575.
39. J. R. Mueller and G. A. Robbins, "Vision of Ezra," *OTP*, p. 585.
40. D. A. Fiensy, "Revelation of Ezra," *OTP*, pp. 601-4; M. E. Stone, "The Metamorphosis of Ezra: Jewish Apocalypse and Medieval Vision," *JTS* n.s. 33 (1982):14-16.
41. See R. A. Kraft, "'Ezra' Materials in Judaism and Christianity," *Aufstieg und Niedergang der römischen Welt*, ed. H. Temporini and W. Haase (Berlin: de Gruyter, 1979), 2.19.1, 119-36.

Part III

Old Testament
Exegetical Conclusions
Applied

BARRY J. BEITZEL (Ph. D., The Dropsie
University) is professor of Old Testament and Semitic languages at Trinity Evangelical Divinity School.

10

The Right of the Firstborn (Pî Šnayim) in the Old Testament (Deut. 21:15-17)

Barry J. Beitzel

Primogeniture is defined in the dictionary and understood in patriarchal societies as the custom or law by which the property of an estate passed to the authority and discretion of the eldest son. The institution should be viewed as the cultural mechanism through which the patripotestal author-itarianism that so thoroughly characterized patriarchal/clanal politics would have been transmitted to the next generation, as it effectively guar-anteed to the firstborn son the right of estate succession. As a widespread and persistent socio-legal establishment from high antiquity, primogeni-ture was practiced in ancient cultures from China to western Africa. With some modifications it was subsequently employed at certain places within the classical world and still later as a component of feudalism in European history.

However, more recent inheritance practices in Western civilization, likewise operating as a function of political thought, have adopted a more democratic orientation, and most recently in some quarters they have tended to assume an egalitarian posture. It is therefore possible for us in the West to fail to discern the far-reaching and dramatic implications that radiated from this axial reality embedded deeply within patriarchal culture.

But indeed profound were the consequences of such a custom. So encompassing in patriarchal society was the demand for the birth of a male offspring that some modern authorities have argued that the institution of marriage itself would have been perceived as never fully consummated until the birth of the first son.[1] In point of fact, marriage contracts from the time of the biblical patriarchs would seem to support this contention. From the site of Alalakh (western Syria), for example, a marriage contract was exhumed that stipulates that a wife had only seven years in which to provide her husband with a male child.[2] From a similar document excavated at Kanish (central Turkey), one discovers a situation in which a certain woman—Ḥuatala by name—was obliged to provide such an offspring within only two years.[3] Presumably, then, at the conclusion of a designated period of time, should the woman have failed in this provision, her husband could have been legally freed from marital obligations, and whatever formal relationship had previously existed simply could have been dissolved. In this context one is reminded of the traumatic and tenuous circumstances, both psychologically and socio-economically, that would have vexed Sarah (Gen. 16:1), Rebekah (25:21), Rachel (29:31), and Hannah (1 Sam. 1:2, 6-7; cf. Gen. 20:18).

The purpose of primogeniture then was the systematic and orderly transference of social, legal, and religious authority within the family structure. The firstborn male was made the principal heir and was given a sizeable portion of the estate because it was he who was to perpetuate the family name and lineage[4] and who was to bear the chief burden for the continuance and welfare of the family,[5] being especially responsible for the economic and social necessities of his mother until the time of her death[6] and of his unwed sisters to the point of their marriages.[7] In this latter regard it is pertinent to recall the role of Laban in giving his sister Rebekah in marriage to Isaac (Gen. 24:29-33, 50-61; cf. 25:20; 28:5).[8] The presumption of the Genesis narrative is that Rebekah's father was deceased, and so her brother was discharging his legal obligations on her behalf. The preeminence of the firstborn, moreover, sometimes extended into the religious sphere, as he would function in the role of clanal priest.[9] In short, one could say that patriarchal society invested the position of firstborn with high honor and uncontested authority (cf. Ex. 4:22; Jer. 31:9; Ps. 89:27). It becomes clearer, then, why the New Testament writers should choose this term (*prōtotokos*, the LXX term for MT *běkôr)* and rightly apply it to the person and work of Christ (Heb. 1:6; cf. Rom. 8:29; Col. 1:15).

What has been less clear, however, is the size of the portion given to the firstborn, the actual amount of the estate that became his personal property. The reason for this, quite simply, is that cuneiform documents that address the subject—in the form of law codes or inheritance texts— either do not stipulate its size or do not offer a uniform testimony regarding its size. Sometimes, for example, the firstborn was bequeathed an "additional portion," a "preferential portion" *(elâtum)*[10] or a "double portion" *(šinnišu ina zitti)*;[11] at other times he shared equally in the estate,[12] he received a special gift *(qīštum)*,[13] or he inherited as much as two-thirds of the entire estate (see below).

In the Bible the only passage that specifically treats this question is Deuteronomy 21:15-17. This law imagines a situation in which a man has two wives, one of whom he loves and the other of whom he dislikes, and a son by each wife. To complicate the matter, however, the firstborn of these two sons is a child of the unloved wife. The purpose of the law was to prevent the father from arbitrarily exercising parental prerogative, as it enjoined him to bestow impartially the birthright on his eldest son, because he was the first issue of the father's procreative powers. This legislation, then, was designed to safeguard the rights of the firstborn against what otherwise might have been the natural human inclination of the father. We should note here parenthetically, as will become important later, that this situation is remarkably reminiscent of the relationship that had existed between the patriarch Jacob and his two wives (Gen. 29-31). In any event, the law in Deuteronomy stipulates that the firstborn son was personally entitled to *pî šnayim* of his father's estate. This somewhat strange Hebrew expression derives from the words "mouth" and "two" and could be literally translated "a mouth of two." It seems that the phrase is almost universally translated "double portion" or "double share" and is understood to denote twice as much of the estate as each of the other portions.[14]

Now the idiom *pî šnayim* occurs in only two other Old Testament texts. In the first of these (2 Kings 2:9) Elisha responds to his mentor's urging by beseeching Elijah for *pî šnayim* of the latter's spirit. The other occurrence of the expression is found in Zechariah's oracle of impending judgment on the inhabitants of Jerusalem because they have repudiated their king. He declares (Zech. 13:8) that *pî šnayim* of Jerusalem's population will perish, whereas *haššělîšît* of them will be kept alive, though they will be refined by fire. What is luminous about this latter passage is that *pî šnayim* is used precisely in opposition to *haššělîšît*, which is the normal Hebrew fraction "one-third." Accordingly, most Bible versions take the Zechariah text to be saying that "two-thirds" (i.e., *pî šnayim*) of the population will perish and that "one-third" will be spared.[15]

What is so arresting about this final observation is that the standard Akkadian lexeme for the fraction "two-thirds" (*šinipû/āt*)[16] is also composed of the words for "two" (*šinā*) and "mouth" (*pûm*).[17] Although the Akkadian word is not found in Phoenician[18] or Ugaritic,[19] it is a loanword into Old Aramaic where it appears as *snb(y)*[20] and probably means "two-thirds of a mina." Furthermore, from as early as the Fifth Dynasty the standard Egyptian hieroglyph for the same fraction (*r'wy*) was composed of the sign for "mouth" plus two short vertical strokes.[21] This combination of an unambiguous context in Zechariah and a uniform linguistic composition in the ancient world surrounding Israel renders probable the hypothesis that the expression *pî šnayim* should be consistently rendered "two-thirds" in the Bible.

It has long been recognized in comparative Semitics and Egyptian that a complementary fraction, that is, a fraction in which the numerator is one number less than the denominator, is often expressed by using parts of the body.[22] Hebrew, for example, expresses the fraction "four-fifths" by the phrase "four hands" as is unmistakably the case in Genesis 47:24, where as part of the Pharaoh's land reform Joseph tells his subjects that "one-fifth" (*ḥămîšît*) of the land's produce had to be given over to the state, but that "four-fifths" (literally, "four hands") of it could be retained by the citizens.[23] On the other hand, Nehemiah 11:1 expresses the fraction "nine-tenths" by the phrase "nine hands." In discussing the repopulating of post-exilic Jerusalem, the passage states that lots were cast in order to bring one out of ten individuals to live in the holy city, whereas the remaining "nine-tenths" (literally, "nine hands") of the population would continue to live in the surrounding towns.[24] Hence it is possible to see how the present hypothesis is predicated on linguistic precedent. Now of course any interpretation of Deuteronomy 21:15-17, in which only two sons and necessarily therefore only three portions are being meted out, would lead to the practical conclusion that the firstborn should inherit "two-thirds" of the estate as described. But as is true elsewhere in Deuteronomy, laws are often cast into their simplest possible mold, using the lowest common denominator. And so we submit, as a consequence, that balance of probability favors interpreting *pî šnayim* in Deuteronomy hypothetically (i.e., philologically and semantically the word itself means "two-thirds") and not practically (i.e., only three portions are being distributed under the circumstances).

Historical precedent for such an interpretation comes from a number of sources. In an adoption document from Mari (eastern Syria)[25] a certain Yahatti-El is denominated as the heir apparent and is promised "two-thirds" ḫatti-El is denominated as the heir apparent and is promised "two-thirds" (*šittān*) of the entirety of his father's estate.[26] Another Old Babylonian text, presumably from Larsa (south-central Iraq), deals with the emancipation and subsequent adoption of a slave named Ḫablum.[27] According to this tablet, though Ḫablum was adopted, should he later have children a certain Maṣam-Ili , whom we can only conclude was the eldest son, would nevertheless inherit "two-thirds" (*šittān*) of the father's estate, whereas Ḫablum and his sons would share the remainder equally. Third, in an Old Babylonian text from Tell Harmal (vicinity of Baghdad) a certain Nanna-mansum is said to have inherited "two-thirds" (*šittān*) of an estate, whereas his two brothers—Igmil-Sin and Warḫum-magir —were to divide the remainder equally.[28] This text is especially illuminating in the present discussion because it describes the apportionment of an estate among three individuals, and it naturally refers therefore to more than three portions. As a consequence, one is enabled to recognize that *šittān*, as we have also argued above for *pî šnayim*, must be construed hypothetically and not merely under the circumstances of a particular law. Fourth, several neo-Babylonian documents divide estates proportionately into "two-thirds" and "one-third."[29] One of these, a marriage contract, spells out the circumstances in which a certain man was marrying his second wife: His first wife was barren. But the text goes on to specify that should the first wife later bear a son, this son would receive "two-thirds" (*šittān qātēn*)[30] of the estate, whereas a child of the second wife, the woman whose marriage is here being contracted, was eligible to receive only "one-third" (*šalšu*).[31] In another of these, an estate was divided between two daughters, the elder receiving "two-thirds" (*šittān qātēn*) and the younger receiving "one-third'" (*šalšu*).[32] Fifth, in a similar pattern, the neo-Babylonian laws stipulate that the children of a man's first wife are to receive "two-thirds" (*šittān qātēn*) of his estate, whereas sons of a second wife should receive only "one-third" (*šalšu*).[33] Clearly, then, to suggest that the right of the firstborn according to Deuteronomy was "two-thirds" of the entire estate can be anchored in what appears to have been an ancient and persistent, if not exclusive, tradition of inheritance. Moreover, in a culture where the purpose of primogeniture was to guarantee estate succession, the present hypothesis insures that the firstborn should become the bona fide successor, the majority stockholder, if you will, the one who inherited a majority and not just a plurality of his father's estate. And in point of fact, a glance at standard Hebrew lexica and grammars will disclose that this is precisely how many of these sources understand *pî šnayim*.[34]

expression *pî šnayim* is always taken to mean "twice as much," and other words for the fraction "two-thirds" are employed in both Mishnaic Hebrew[35] and Palestinian Aramaic.[36] These references, beginning with those contained in Ecclesiasticus (second century B.C.), have been conveniently collected and discussed in the seminal article by Solomon Gandz.[37] Likewise the same tradition is reflected in the Targums, Peshitta, and LXX, as well as in Philo and Josephus. But one must bear in mind that these are all late sources. It is a truism that many words and phrases in biblical Hebrew underwent changes of one sort or another and came to mean something quite different in later periods.[38]

This all leads to the conclusion that *pî šnayim* originally meant "two-thirds," the original sense being clearly reflected in Zechariah as well as in comparative Semitic and Egyptian lexicography, but that it later evolved in its meaning to "two parts, double portion," as already pointed out by a number of authoritative sources, including Gandz and the *Encyclopaedia Judaica*.[39]

Why then would influential sources no less than Gandz and the *Encyclopaedia Judaica* recognize on the one hand the original meaning of *pî šnayim* and yet render the expression in Deuteronomy 21:17 "double portion?" Is this not curiously inconsistent? The answer, in a word, is no. For anyone will translate phrases and idiom in Deuteronomy or any other book in accordance with when he dates the book, and both Gandz and *Encyclopaedia Judaica* assign a late date to the composition of Deuteronomy.[40] In fact, it seems to me that a realization of this point may help crystallize the issue before us, namely, how one is to translate *pî šnayim* in Deuteronomy: If one dates the book in an earlier preexilic context, he ought logically to assign the earlier meaning to *pî šnayim,* as clearly seen in ancient Near Eastern lexicography and attested as late as the time of Zechariah; if on the other hand one chooses to affix an extremely late date to Deuteronomy, he ought logically to construe *pî šnayim* in its evolutional meaning, as witnessed in the apocrypha, Mishna, Talmud, and derivative sources. That is to say, there appears to me to be a gaping discrepancy in the logic of one who argues in favor of a preexilic date for Deuteronomy while simultaneously assigning a translation to *pî šnayim* that is simply undocumented before the Talmudic period and is in point of fact a rendition that flies in the face of the original common meaning of the idiom in Akkadian, Aramaic, Egyptian, and the book of Zechariah.

It remains, then, for one to understand the thrust of the legislation of Deuteronomy 21:15-17 in light of patriarchal practices according to which

Deuteronomy 21:15-17 in light of patriarchal practices according to which in one instance Isaac inherited all of Abraham's estate (Gen. 25:5-6), and in another instance Jacob passed over Reuben, his firstborn and son of Leah whom he disliked, in favor of Joseph, the eldest son of his beloved Rachel (Gen. 29-31; 48-49). Deuteronomy both here and elsewhere seems to be imposing explicit regulation over a realm that was left more or less open to the Hebrew patriarchs. To take another example, the patriarch Abraham is said to have married his stepsister (Gen. 20:12), yet such a marital arrangement is expressly forbidden in Deuteronomic legislation (Deut. 27:22; cf. Lev. 18:9). Again, the regimentation imposed on the practice of Levirate marriages (Deut. 25:5-10) seems designed precisely to prevent a recurrence of the travesty committed by the patriarch Judah against Tamar (Gen. 38). It is to be noted in passing that many of these legal modifications involve the subjects of marriage and inheritance, but perhaps this is only a consequence of the preoccupation of the book of Genesis with such topics. Be that as it may, though these innovations in Deuteronomy do not necessarily imply that the biblical patriarchs acted with capricious whim about such matters, they do assert categorically that whatever had been the patriarchal practice would be no longer valid or acceptable.[41]

NOTES

1. Among the recent discussions see M. Selman, "Comparative Methods and the Patriarchal Narratives," *Themelios* 3 (1977):9-16; T. Frymer-Kensky, "Patriarchal Family Relationships and Near Eastern Law," *BA* 44 (1981):209-14, and literature cited there; M. Morrison, "The Jacob and Laban Narrative in Light of Near Eastern Sources," *BA* 46 (1983):155-64; J. Scullion, "Some Reflections on the Present State of the Patriarchal Studies," *AbrN* 21 (1982-83):50-65.

2. Text *ATT* 8/51, published by Donald J. Wiseman, *The Alalakh Tablets*, Occasional Publications of the British Institute of Archaeology at Ankara 2 (London, 1953):55 and pl. XXIII.

3. Text *ICK* I.3, published by B. Hrozný, *Inscriptions Cunéiformes du Kultépé* (Praha: Státní pedagogické nakladatelství, 1952), 1.14-15. This text was discussed extensively by J. Lewy, "On Some Institutions of the Old Assyrian Empire," *HUCA* 27 (1956):8-10, where all relevant literature is quoted. The reader may refer to the more recent translation in *ANET* 543a (4); cf. R. Frankena, "Some Remarks on the Semitic Background of Chapters XXIX-XXXI of the Book of Genesis," *Oudtestamentische Studiën* 17 (1972):63. Interestingly enough, a transportation contract from Kanish (*ICK* I.67) also mentions this same Huatala, and it indicates that she was still the wife of La-qep, the same individual listed in the marriage contract. For a translation of the latter text the reader is advised to consult M. T. Larsen, *Old Assyrian Caravan Procedures* (Istanbul: Nederlands historisch-archaeologisch Instituut in het Nabije Oosten, 1967), p. 47.

4. *TDOT*, s.v. *"bĕkôr,"* by M. Tsevat, 2:125-26; *IDBSup*, s.v. "First- Born," by J. Milgrom, p. 337; *Encyclopaedia Judaica* (hereafter *EncJud*), s.v. "Firstborn," by B. Levine, 6:1306; P. W. Pestman, "The Law of Succession in Ancient Egypt," *Essays on Oriental Laws of Succession* (Leiden: Brill, 1969), pp. 64-66; *Encyclopedia of Religious Knowledge*, s.v. "Birth-right," p. 243.

5. *IDB*, s.v. "First-born," by V. H. Kooy, 2:271.

6. *People's Bible Encyclopedia*, s.v. "Firstborn in Israel," 1:372; cf. G. R. Driver and J. C. Miles, *The Babylonian Laws* (Oxford: Clarendon, 1955), 1:334-35.

7. *The New Schaff-Herzog Encyclopedia*, s.v. "Family and Marriage Relations, Hebrew," by I. Benzinger, 4:277; *Universal Jewish Encyclopedia*, s.v. "Birthright," by M. Lehrer, 2:383; *Universal Jewish Encyclopedia*, s.v. "Primogeniture," by M. Cohen, 8:644.

8. Compare the *ṭuppi aḫḫūti* texts at Nuzi, cf. *CAD*, A1. 187b.

The Right of the Firstborn in the Old Testament (Deut. 21:15-17)   187

Terms, s.v. "Firstborn," by D. Kaufman, p. 187; *Encyclopedia of Religion and Ethics*, s.v. "Firstborn (Hebrew)," by J. Strahan, 5:35-36; *The Jewish Encyclopedia*, s.v. "Primogeniture," by I. Casanowicz, 10:199.

10. *CAD*, E. 78a; cf. I. Mendelsohn, "On the Preferential Status of the Eldest Son," *BASOR* 156 (1959):39, for texts from Nippur and Larsa.

11. *CAD*, Z. 140-1a; for Nuzi examples see *ANET*, p. 220 (3); for the Middle Assyrian laws refer to *ANET*, p. 185 (#1); cf. M. David, "Ein Beitrag zum mittelassyrischen Erbrecht," *Essays on Oriental Laws*, pp. 79-81. Concerning the distinction between the *elâtum* and *šinnišu ina zitti* portions and what each denotes, I cannot offer a satisfactory explanation; cf. discussion of F. Kraus, "Erbrechtliche Terminologie im alten Mesopotamien," *Essays on Oriental Laws*, pp. 54-56.

12. E.g., Code of Hammurapi, par. 167, 170 (consult Driver and Miles, *Babylonian Laws*, 1:331; cf. *ANET*, p. 173); the Lipit Ishtar Law Code, par. 24 (Mendelsohn, "Preferential Status," p. 40); and texts from Harmal (M. deJ. Ellis, "The Division of Property at Tell Harmal," *Journal of Cuneiform Studies* 26 [1974]:133-48) and Nuzi (J. van Seters, *Abraham in History and Tradition* [New Haven, Conn., and London: Yale U., 1975], p. 89 and n. 79).

13. *CAD*, Q. 277 (2a); e.g. Code of Hammurapi, par. 165.

14. This is the translation of JPSV, RSV, NEB, JB, *Confraternity Version, Douay, Geneva, KJV, NKJV, NIV, NASB, ASV, Berkeley. The Old Testament: An American Translation* was the only version I could locate that translated the phrase "two-thirds." My random sample of Deuteronomy commentaries included Richard Clifford, *Deuteronomy* (Wilmington: Michael Glazier, 1982), p. 113; John Calvin, *Calvin's Commentaries*, 22 vols. (Edinburgh: Calvin Translation Society, 1849), 3:173-74; Meredith G. Kline, *Treaty of the Great King*, (Grand Rapids: Eerdmans, 1963), p. 108; Gerhard von Rad, *Deuteronomy*, OTL (Philadelphia: Westminster, 1966), pp. 137-38; Abraham Cohen, *The Soncino Chumash* (Hindhead, Surrey: Soncino, 1947), p. 1099n.; Samuel R. Driver, *A Critical and Exegetical Commentary on Deuteronomy*, ICC (Edinburgh: T. & T. Clark, 1895), p. 246; *La Sainte Bible*, p. 647; Peter C. Craigie, *The Book of Deuteronomy*, NICOT (Grand Rapids: Eerdmans, 1976), p. 283 n. 19; John A. Thompson, *Deuteronomy: An Introduction and Commentary*, TOTC (London: InterVarsity, 1974), p. 229; J. K. F. Keil and F. J. Delitzsch, *Biblical Commentary on the Old Testament*, 25 vols. (Grand Rapids: Eerdmans, n.d.), 1:407—all of which rendered the phrase "double portion" or its equivalent.

15. So JPSV, RSV, JB, NEB, *Confraternity*, NIV, etc.

16. The morphology and semantics of *šinipûlāt* are clear enough. A problem arises concerning its derivation, which ultimately revolves around its exact relationship to Sumerian *ša.na.bi*. It is claimed that *šinipûlāt* is Semitic (e.g., A. Goetze, "Number Idioms in Old Babylonian," *JNES* 5 [1946]:202 n. 81; F. Rundgren, "Parallelen zu Akk. *šinēpūm* '2/3'," *Journal of Cuneiform Studies* 9 [1955]:29-30) or that it is a Sumerian loanword (e.g., E. A. Speiser, "Of Shoes and Shekels," *BASOR* 77 [1940]:18-20; S. Lieberman, *Sumerian Loanwords in Old Babylonian Akkadian* [Missoula, Mont.: Scholars, 1977], pp. 476-77 #621). However, because *ša.na.bi* reflects no transparent Sumerian etymology, it is not related to the Sumerian word for "two" (*min/mene*; so M. Civil, "Studies on Early Dynastic Lexicography I," *Oriens Antiquus* 21 [1982]:7), and the word is written syllabically at the site of Fara as *ša₄.na.bi*, it seems most plausible to assume that *ša₄.na.bi* is an Akkadian loanword in Sumerian. I wish to acknowledge my indebtedness to Joan Westenholz, of the Oriental Institute, with whom I had the opportunity of discussing this problem.

17. This is the etymological explanation advocated in *GAG*, p. 93 par. 70i; *AHW,* 1242b; cf. further W. von Soden, "Zu den semitischen und akkadischen Kardinalzahlen und ihrer Konstruktion," *Zeitschrift für Assyriologie* 73 (1983):84. His proposal is followed, *inter alia,* by R. Borger, *Babylonisch-Assyrische Lesestücke* (Rome: Pontifical Biblical Institute, 1963), 1:lxxxiii; A. Goetze, *JNES* 5 (1946):202 n. 81.

18. According to J. Friedrich and W. Röllig, *Phönizisch-Punische Grammatick,* AnOr 46 (Rome: Pontifical Biblical Institute, 1970):124 par. 246.

19. *Pace* Ludwig Köhler and Walter Baumgartner, *Lexicon in Veteris Testamenti Libros* (Leiden: Brill, 1958), 2:753b (hereafter KB); P. Watson, "A Note on the 'Double Portion' of Deuteronomy 21:17 and II Kings 2:9," *Restoration Quarterly* 8 (1965) 71; *UT,* p. 50 par. 7.57; p. 493a (#2455), but see p. 555; cf. D. Hillers, "Ugaritic *ŠNPT* 'Wave-Offering'," *BASOR* 198 (1970):42.

20. H. Lidzbarsky, *Handbuch der nordsemitischen Epigraphik* (Weimar: Felber, 1898), 1:202, 329; C.-F. Jean and J. Hoftijzer, *Dictionnaire des inscriptions sémitiques de l'ouest* (Leiden: Brill, 1965) 195; S. Kaufman, *The Akkadian Influences on Aramaic,* Assyriological Studies 19 (Chicago: Chicago U., 1974), p. 103 and n. 361.

21. A. H. Gardiner, *Egyptian Grammar: Being an Introduction to the Study of Hieroglyphics,* 3d ed. (London: Oxford U., 1957), pp. 196-97 par. 265; p. 452 (#D22); E. Edel, *Altägyptische Grammatik,* AnOr 34 (Rome: Pontifical Biblical Institute, 1955):1. 179 par. 411.

22. For Egyptian the reader is advised to consult Gardiner, *Grammar,* pp. 196-98 par. 265-66; p. 452 (#D23); cf. p. 451 (##D11, 13-16); Edel, *Grammatik* 1. 178-179 par. 411; for Ethiopic see S. Moscati et al., *An Introduction to the Comparative Grammar of the Semitic Languages* (Wiesbaden: Harrassowitz, 1969), p. 119 par. 14.10; for Akkadian refer to A. Sachs, "Notes on Fractional Expressions in Old Babylonian Mathematical Texts," *JNES* 5 (1946):213-14; for Hebrew see A. B. Davidson, *Hebrew Syntax,* 3d ed. (Edinburgh: T. & T. Clark, 1964), p. 56 par. 38 R5; *EncJud,* s.v. "Numbers, Typical and Important," by I. Abrahams, 10 col. 154-55.

23. So translated by JPSV, RSV, JB, NEB, NKJV, NIV, NASB; cf. H. Bauer and P. Leander, *Historische Grammatick der hebräischen Sprache* (Hildesheim: Olms, 1962), 1:629 par. 79a'.

24. So translated by RSV, NKJV, NASB. Parts of the body are also used to express multiples: "two hands" translates "two divisions" (2 Kings 11:7; cf. *haššēlišit*), "three feet" translates "three times" (Ex. 23:14; Num. 22:28, 32, 33), "five hands" translates "five times" (Gen. 43:34); "ten hands" translates "ten times" (2 Sam. 19:43 [MT 44]; Dan. 1:20).

25. *ARM,* 8.1.

26. For *šittān* = "two-thirds" the reader is advised to consult *GAG* 93 par. 70i; *AHW* 1252a; cf. Borger, *Lesestücke,* p. lxxxiii. The exact relationship between the synonyms *šinipūlāt* and *šittān* is difficult to assess; the former is regularly found in mathematical texts (e.g., A. Sachs, "Notes" 203-14) and a handful of other places, whereas the latter is found more frequently, if not exclusively, (*ARM,* 10. 134.8-9, where *šittān* is used opposite to *šaluštum*) in contexts dealing with inheritance.

27. See M. Anbar, "Textes de l'époque babylonienne ancienne," *Revue d'Assyriologie* 69 (1975):131-33.

28. Text IM52624, published by Ellis, "Division," pp. 142-48, but note that she translated *šittān* "double share." As noted above, my translation of *šittān* is informed by von Soden's lexicographical research (*AHW,* 1252a).

29. Consult M. San Nicolò and A. Ungnad, *Neubabylonische Rechts—und Verwaltungsur-kunden* (Leipzig: J. C. Hinrichs, 1929), ##1, 12, 15, 19.

30. On which see above, n. 24.

31. For *šalšu* = "one-third" consult *AHW* 1150; *GAG* 93 par. 70h.

32. In this regard it is pertinent to recall the case of the daughters of Zelophehad (Num. 27:1-11).

33. See *ANET*, pp. 197-98, for a translation of this law.

34. The reader should examine BDB, p. 1041a; W. Gesenius and F. Buhl, *Hebräisches und aramäisches Handwörterbuch über das Alte Testament* (Berlin: Springer-Verlag, 1915), p. 635a; C. J. Labaschagne, *"Mund," Theologisches Handwörterbuch zum Alten Testament*, 2. col. 408; P. Joüon, *Grammaire de l'Hébreu Biblique*, 2d ed. (Rome: Pontifical Biblical Institute, 1947), p. 267 par. 101b (cf. how he specifically contrasts *pî šnayim* and *šnayim* ("double," Ex. 22:4, 7, 9 [MT 3, 6, 8]); cf. *mišneh* = "double/two-fold," Job 42:10; Isa. 61:7); M. Noth, *Die Ursprünge des alten Israel im Lichte neuer Quellen* (Cologne: Westdeutscher, 1961), pp. 19-20; van Seters, *Abraham* 92; *EncJud*, 12. col. 1255; *TWOT*, 2:718 (contra 2:942b). All of these sources specifically assign the meaning "two-thirds" to the Deuterormoy passage. KB, 2:754a, and W. H. Holladay, *A Concise Hebrew and Aramaic Lexicon of the Old Testament* (Grand Rapids: Eerdmans, 1974), p. 289b, cite the meaning "two-thirds," but they do not apply this meaning to our text; *contra* J. Fürst, *A Hebrew and Chaldee Lexicon* (Leipzig: Bernhard Tauchnitz, 1885), p. 1116b. For different reasons 1 Sam. 1:5; 13:21 cannot be introduced into the present discussion. The passage in chap. 1 contains a textual problem (cf. LXX *plēn*; translation of RSV; JB vis-à-vis NIV; NASB), and in chap. 13 *pîm* is the name of a Hebrew weight (taken by some authorities as "two-thirds of a shekel," so Speiser, "Of Shoes," p. 19; *IDB*, s.v. "Pim," by O. R. Sellers, 3:817- 18; *ZPEB*, s.v. "Weights and Measures," by F. B. Huey, Jr., 5:921b; H. W. Hertzberg, *I and II Samuel* [Philadelphia: Westminster, 1974], p. 102).

35. So M. Segal, *A Grammar of Mishnaic Hebrew* (Oxford: Clarendon, 1927), p. 197 par. 402.

36. So G. Dalman, *Grammatik des Jüdisch-Palästinischen Aramäisch* (Darmstadt: Wissenschaftliche Buchgesellschaft, 1981), p. 133 par. 23.1.

37. S. Gandz, "Complementary Fractions in Bible and Talmud," *Louis Ginsberg Jubilee Volume* (New York: American Academy for Jewish Research, 1945), pp. 143-57 (reprinted in S. Gandz, *Studies in Hebrew Astronomy and Mathematics* [New York: Ktav, 1970], pp. 530-44).

38. This point has already been argued cogently by J. Barr, *Comparative Philology and the Text of the Old Testament* (Oxford: Clarendon, 1968). Refer more recently to E. Y. Kutscher, *History of the Hebrew Language* (Jerusalem: Magnes, 1982); cf. Segal, *Grammar*, p. 5.

39. E.g., Gandz, "Complementary" 149; I. Abrahams, *EncJud*, 12. col. 1255; *IDB*, s.v. "Number," by M. H. Pope, 3:562b. In my estimation the nature of Elisha's request should be understood in the context of the original meaning of *pî šnayim*. He was not asking to become twice the man of God as was Elijah nor that he would be able to perform twice the number of miracles. Rather, his request entailed becoming the great prophet's *bona fide* successor, the one who should inherit his prophetic role. Later, at the time of Elijah's translation, when Elisha realized that his request would be granted, he exclaimed: "My father, my father!" Immediately thereafter Elisha set out to reproduce, in effect, his predecessor's miracle at the Jordan River. Whether this was done for

the express purpose of authenticating his newly-acquired authority cannot be said. But the miracle seems to have had this effect on the prophets from the school who, we are told as they came out and bowed before him, confessed: "The spirit of Elijah rests upon Elisha." The reader is advised to consult J. Montgomery, *The Book of Kings,* ICC (Edinburgh: T. & T. Clark, 1951), pp. 353-54; Keil and Delitzsch, *Biblical Commentary,* pp. 292-97.

40. See especially Gandz, "Complementary," p. 149.

41. To take this line of reasoning a step further, one observes that Jacob is said to have married two sisters within a period of one week (Gen. 29:15- 30), whereas this practice was strictly forbidden according to subsequent law (Lev. 18:18). It appears that even within pentateuchal codification itself, certain modifications were introduced in Deuteronomy. For instance, Lev. 22:18-25, though disallowing unblemished animals to be used in burnt offerings, sometimes permitted slightly blemished animals as peace offerings. But according to Deut. 17:1, it was impermissible to bring a blemished beast for any offering (cf. 15:21). Ex. 22:16 offered to the father of a seduced girl the option of demanding any damages he liked of her seducer; Deut. 22:29, contrariwise, imposed a ceiling on the damages (fifty shekels of silver) and insisted, moreover, on marriage. And one can observe clues in the Deuteronomic rendition of the decalogue (Deut. 5) that suggest a slightly updated version from Ex. 20. Many other specimens of this sort of innovation have been collected by G. J. Wenham, "Development Within the Old Testament Law" (essay read to an Old Testament colloquium at Trinity Evangelical Divinity School, May 22, 1984); cf. H. McKeating, "Sanctions Against Adultery in Ancient Israelite Society, with Some Reflections on Methodology in the Study of Old Testament Ethics," *Journal for the Study of the Old Testament* 11 (1979):63-71. Finally, if there is validity to what is expressed in this note, it logically follows that Deuteronomy is predicated on Exodus and Leviticus, that is, Leviticus (P) antedates Deuteronomy.

It is a distinct pleasure for me to have been invited to contribute an essay in a volume dedicated to Gleason Archer, distinguished scholar, esteemed colleague, and cherished friend. He is also a linguist extraordinaire; his facility in languages, whether Semitic, classical, or modern, amazes even those of us who have had the opportunity of working beside him through the years. I recall an incident that occurred a few years ago in conjunction with one of my own research projects. A volume that was seminal to the project was written, to my chagrin, in Danish. Having no proficiency whatever in that language, I needed to find a translator. Now I hesitated to contact Gleason, naively supposing that perhaps that was one language he had never tackled, and I really did not want to put him into a situation where he might have to tell me that he did not know Danish. But after trying unsuccessfully for about three days to find a translator, in desperation I decided to throw caution to the wind and contact Gleason. Graciously, he promptly sat down in my office, opened the book, and proceeded to offer me a polished translation of a page or two without a single lexical aid. Astounded, I confessed my initial reluctance to come to him and told him the story of this paragraph. Gleason responded: "Oh well, it was no problem at all, since Danish is so similar to Swedish." How foolish of me; I should have known that all along.

JESSE L. BOYD III (Ph. D., Oriental Institute, University of Chicago) is librarian at Trinity Valley School, Fort Worth, Texas.

11

An Example of
the Influence of Egyptian
on the Development of the Hebrew Language
During the Second Millennium B.C.

Jesse L. Boyd III

The importance of the study of ancient Egyptian for the elucidation of the Pentateuch cannot be overstated even today, so many years after the decipherment of the Rosetta stone.[1] In fact, second-millennium documents of the Levant require at least a rudimentary knowledge of the language in order to isolate the loanwords in Ugaritic[2] or the Amarna letters.[3] With the reprinting of A. Erman and H. Grapow, *Wörterbuch der aegyptischen Sprache* (Berlin, 1982), the advanced state at which the Chicago Assyrian Dictionary now finds itself, the completion of W. von Soden's three-volume *Akkadisches Handwörterbuch* (Wiesbaden, 1965-81) and W. Leslau's three-volume *Etymological Dictionary of Gurage* (Wiesbaden, 1979), and the reappearance of R. Payne Smith's monumental *Thesaurus Syriacus* (2 vols. plus supplement; Hildesheim/New York, 1981), the scholar is in a strong position for comparative lexicographical research from various angles.[4] In the case of Egyptian, the student is offered a wide range of possibilities for comparative philology with the tools presently available to him.[5] In the case of the Pentateuch, it is possible to note the vocabulary borrowed from the Egyptian lexical stock by the Hebrew writer. In fact, an attempt was undertaken by M. Ellenbogen in his *Foreign Words in the Old Testament: Their Origin and Etymology* (London, 1962) in which he included all the words that he believed to have been loaned from Egyptian into biblical Hebrew.[6]

In addition to loanwords from Egyptian, the latter language may have had some influence on Hebrew grammar and syntax. A more difficult task, certainly, is undertaken where grammar and syntax are concerned. However, if the ancient Hebrews lived in Goshen for several centuries, it would not be impossible for their own language, in its formative stage then, to have been affected directly by that of the dominant culture. It is within this category of syntax and grammar that I wish to make a small contribution in honor of Gleason Archer. The following observations stem directly from his insight, instruction, and inspiration, particularly in his hieroglyphics course, when I had the privilege of being his student at Trinity Evangelical Divinity School from 1968 to 1970.

Throughout the Old Testament occurs this refrain: "And the Lord spoke to . . . saying. . . ." It is a clause repeatedly attested in the Pentateuch. For example, in Exodus 30:11 Moses is addressed by Yahweh: *waydabbēr YHWH 'el mōšeh lē'mōr* (LXX: *kai elalēsen kyrios pros Mōysēn legōn;* Vg: *locutusque est Dominus ad Mosen dicens).* In this case, as in the overwhelming majority of others, the main verb is *dibbēr,* "to speak" (= Greek *laleō*[7]) followed by the infinitive construct of *'āmar,* "to say" (= Greek *legō*[8]) plus the prefixed preposition *lĕ-.* This construction (*dabbēr . . . lē-'mōr*) is rendered in a literal sense by the LXX, where the participle *legōn* is employed for *lē'mōr.*[9] Similarly, the employment of *legōn* with verbs of speaking in the New Testament (e.g., see John 1:15: *kekragen legōn*) reflects the influence of the Hebrew construction directly or through the LXX usage or both.[10]

Because no such construction equivalent to the Hebrew *dabbēr . . . lē-'mōr* is attested in any other Semitic language, the question arises whether this one is unique to Hebrew. If it is not peculiar to Hebrew, then its origin must be found outside the Semitic family. I propose to find it in Egyptian, where the phoneme *l* is not attested but is replaced by *r.*[11] Indeed, the Northwest Semitic preposition *l-,* "to, for," and the Egyptian preposition *r-,* "to, for," are the same formally and logically.[12] Hence the construction *r-ḏd* (*r-* preposition plus the infinitive of the verb *ḏd* , "to say") and the Hebrew *lē'mōr* appear to be interchangeable, the Egyptian *r-* and the Hebrew *l-* being phonetically cognate and the verbs *ḏd* and *'āmar* being semantically cognate. Gardiner points out the following functions of *r-ḏd* in Middle Egyptian:

> 1. When the main verb either has nothing to do with speaking, or else only hints at it, the phrase *r-ḏd* , "saying," lit. "in order to say," is often used.
>   Ex.: "I went round my enclosure rejoicing—*ir-tw nn mi m*—and saying: how (comes it that) this is done?"[13]

> 2. In Dyn. XII *r-ḏd* is already found quite tautologically after verbs of saying.
>   Ex.: *ḥʿ-n ḏd-n-f n-sn r-ḏd*
>   "Then he said to them saying . . . ."[14]

Although both usages of *r-ḏd* are enlightening, it is the second that throws clear light on the question at hand, and it is interesting to note that Gardiner is emphatic that the use of *r-ḏd* after verbs of saying does not allow for the translation "that."[15] The case is the same for Hebrew. Under no condition is *lē'mōr* to be understood as similar in meaning to the Greek *hoti*.[16] For all practical purposes *lē'mōr* has preserved, via translation, an ancient Egyptian syntactical construction, one that has been carried over into the New Testament via the LXX by the participle *legōn*.

NOTES

1. For a recent account of the decipherment of Egyptian hieroglyphics, including the Rosetta Stone, see Cyrus H. Gordon, *Forgotten Scripts: Their Ongoing Discovery and Decipherment,* 2d ed. (New York: Basic, 1982), pp. 19-39.

2. A substantive attempt was made by W. A. Ward in "Comparative Studies in Egyptian and Ugaritic," *JNES* 20 (1961):31-40. Other references to Egyptian words attested in Ugaritic may be found scattered throughout the scholarly literature, but the fact of the matter is that Ugaritic studies still remain without any major comparative lexicon, although they continue to survive with J. Aistleitner's *Wörterbuch der ugaritischen Sprache,* 4th ed. (Berlin: Akademie-Verlag, 1974) and the glossary in *UT.* The reediting of G. R. Driver's *Canaanite Myths and Legends* by J. C. L. Gibson has provided, among other things, a much improved and more easily accessible glossary for Ugaritic; however, the comparative data are incomplete to say the least. The most consistent attempt at Ugaritic lexicographic research has been that of M. Dietrich and O. Loretz in *Ugarit-Forschungen* since its inception in 1969; yet, the employment of comparative Semitic data as supporting evidence for words of Semitic origin is not overwhelming in most cases. I have also attempted a small contribution in an unpublished dissertation entitled "A Collection and Examination of the Ugaritic Vocabulary Contained in the Akkadian Texts from Ras Shamra" (Chicago, 1975).

3. Note J. A. Knudtzon's collection in *Vorderasiatische Bibliothek*, 2:1549-51. A. F. Rainey gives a short list of Egyptian words that he thinks are attested in the Amarna tablets (AOAT 8, 2d ed., p. 114). To my knowledge, however, no definitive study in this regard has been attempted.

4. Numerous standard lexicographic reference works are available in the field of comparative Semitic linguistics. For the Arabist the Librairie du Liban (Beirut) has reprinted, within the last twenty years, three standard works, all of which are necessary reference tools for comparative philology: R. Dozy, *Supplément aux dictionnaires arabes,* 2 vols. (1968); Georg Wilhelm Freytag, *Lexicon Arabico-Latinum,* 4 vols. in 2 (1975); Edward W. Lane, *An Arabic-English Lexicon,* 8 vols. (1968). Other lexicographic publications of recent years include the following: A. Avanzini, *Glossaire des inscriptions de l'Arabie du Sud,* 2 vols. (Firenze, 1977-1980); A. F. L. Beeston et al., *Dictionnaire sabéen* (Louvain-la-Neuve/Beirut, 1982); J. C. Biella, *Dictionary of Old South Arabic: Sabaean Dialect* (Chico: Scholars, 1982); T. M. Johnstone, *Ḥarsūsi Lexicon* (London, 1977) and *Jibbāli Lexicon* (Oxford: Clarendon, 1981).

5. In addition to Erman and Grapow, the following lexicographic reference works are of importance for the study of the Egyptian and Coptic languages (the following list is intended to be just a sampling from what is available): J. Cerny, *Coptic Etymological Dictionary* (Cambridge, 1976); W. E. Crum, *A Coptic Dictionary* (Oxford: Clarendon, 1939); W. Erichsen, *Demotisches Glossar* (Milan, 1972; Copenhagen, 1954); R. Faulkner, *A Concise Dictionary of Middle Egyptian* (Oxford, 1962); R. Kasser, *Compléments au Dictionnarie copte de Crum* (Cairo, 1964); W. Westendorf, *Koptisches Handwörterbuch* (Heidelberg: C. Winter Universitätsverlag, 1965-1977).

6. Among the words that Ellenbogen considers to be of Egyptian origin the following are attested in the Pentateuch: *'ebyôn*, "poor"; *'abnēṭ*, "girdle"; *'aḥlāmâ*, "precious stone"; *'epâ*, "ephah"; *gōme*, "papyrus"; *hîn*, "liquid measure"; *ḥōtām*, "seal, signet ring"; *tabba'aṭ*, "seal, signet ring"; *ṭene'*, "basket"; *yĕ'ōr*, "river, canal, the Nile"; *lešem*, "white-blue feldspar (?), jacinth, opal"; *paḥ*, "plate"; *par'ōh*, "Pharaoh"; *ṣî*, "ship, boat"; *šeš*, "Egyptian linen." See also T. O. Lambdin, "Egyptian Loan Words in the Old Testament," *JAOS* 73 (1953):145-55. Excluded of course are all words common to Afro-Asiatic. Recent works including vocabulary common to Semitic and Hamitic include M. Cohen, *Essai comparatif sur le vocabulaire et la phonétique du chamito-sémitique* (Paris, 1969); I. M. Diakonoff, *Semito-Hamitic Languages: An Essay in Classification* (Moscow, 1965), pp. 41-53; A. B. Dolgopolsky, "Semitic and East Cushitic: Sound Correspondence and Cognate Sets," in *Ethiopian Studies Dedicated to Wolf Leslau*, ed. S. Segert and A. J. E. Bodrogligeti (Wiesbaden, 1983), pp. 123-42. A large number of roots shared by Egyptian and Semitic are considered so common as to be entered into works of general knowledge as, e.g., *A General Introductory Guide to the Egyptian Collection in the British Museum* (London: British Museum, 1969). For further information one should consult C. T. Hodge, "Afroasiatic: An Overview," in *Current Trends in Linguistics*, ed. T. A. Sebeok (The Hague/Paris, 1970), 6:237-54, and J. Vergote, "Egyptian," in ibid., 6:531-57, both of which include extensive bibliographies.

7. F. Buhl, *Wilhelm Gesenius' Hebräisches und Aramäisches Handwörterbuch über das Alte Testament*, 17th ed. (Berlin: Springer, 1962), p. 153b.

8. Ibid., p. 50.

9. F. Blass and A. Debrunner, *A Greek Grammar of the New Testament and Other Early Christian Literature*, trans. and rev. Robert W. Funk (Chicago: U. of Chicago, 1961), p. 76a, para. 135 (4).

10. Ibid., pp. 204b para. 397 (3); pp. 216b-17a para. 420.

11. The most famous example of the *l/r* interchange between Hebrew and Egyptian, at least from the point of view of biblical scholars, is attested in the spelling of "Israel" in the stela of Mer-ne-Ptah (c.1225 B.C.), line 38: *ysrïr* (for a translation of the stela see *ANET*, pp. 376-78).

12. Cf. J. M. Sola-Sole, *L'infinitif sémitique* (Paris, 1961), p. 81 para. 29; A. Gardiner, *Middle Egyptian*, 3d ed. (Oxford/London, 1966), p. 125 para. 163.

13. Gardiner, *Middle Egyptian*, p. 173 para. 223.

14. Ibid., p. 174 para. 224; see also the remarks of G. Lefebvre, *Grammaire de l'égyptien classique*, 2d ed. (Cairo, 1955), pp. 200-201 para. 396 (1), regarding the uses of *r-dd*. For the employment of *r-dd* and its reduction to *dd* in Late Egyptian see A. Erman, *Neuägyptische Grammatik*, 2d ed. (Hildesheim, 1968), pp. 207-8 paras. 428-30; see also W. Spiegelberg, *Demotische Grammatik*, 2d ed. (Heidelberg, 1975), pp. 190-91 paras. 428-29; W. C. Till, *Koptische Grammatik*, 3d ed. (Leipzig, 1966), pp. 181 ff., for the evolution of the form and functions of *r-dd* throughout the evolution of Egyptian.

15. Gardiner, *Middle Egyptian*, p. 174 para. 224.

16. See Blass-Debrunner, *Greek Grammar*, p. 204 para. 397 (3).

WALTER C. KAISER, JR. (Ph. D., Brandeis University) is professor of Old Testament and Semitic languages, academic dean, and vice president of education at Trinity Evangelical Divinity School.

12

Integrating Wisdom Theology into Old Testament Theology: Ecclesiastes 3:10-15

Walter C. Kaiser, Jr.

The successful integration or paralleling of wisdom theology to the rest of the Old Testament materials still constitutes one of the greatest challenges to Old Testament theology. Conventional wisdom on this topic repeatedly points to a wide divergence between the historical and prophetic traditions in the Old Testament on the one hand and to its wisdom teachings on the other. The former are closely tied to a particular people (Israel), a particular series of historical events (such as the Exodus), and a particular purpose (usually ensconced in some form of salvation-history). In contrast to this, the wisdom materials focus on the here and now of everyday life instead of past history, the individual rather than the nation, and the various social settings and needs of all men of all nations in contradistinction to a single setting (usually the cult) of a single nation (Israel).[1]

Admittedly this scheme cannot be faulted in its general outlines. It must not be taken so seriously, however, that it is absolutized into an ironclad perspective that will allow no contrary evidence from the biblical texts.[2] Suffice it to say at this point that wisdom does participate in the total canonical context of the Old Testament, and given its internal claims, it may fairly be linked with the establishment of Israel's monarchy. This gives it both a covenantal and historical background against which it may be understood.

But wisdom presents a second challenge: Can a unifying theology be identified even within the wisdom literature? Gerhard von Rad concluded that the wisdom materials possessed no guiding concept or integrating rule. That "no wisdom, no understanding, no counsel" was valid in Yahweh's eyes led von Rad to see "a reticence towards attempting great, sweeping explanations" in wisdom literature: "The perceptions achieved are not built into a comprehensive system. On the contrary, they are basically left in the form in which they were originally expressed, and, without the slightest need for harmonization, perceptions of a different kind could be placed alongside them."[3] Furthermore, every event and experience of life was viewed by the wisdom movement, according to von Rad, from the dual perspective of human sagacity and Yahweh's overriding order of events. One of his key texts was Proverbs 21:31: "The horse is made ready for the day of battle, but victory belongs to the Lord." Therefore no man could guarantee his own success through using human wisdom; there was also the incalculable activity of God. Therein lay von Rad's dialectical estimation of wisdom theology.

Walther Zimmerli was of the same opinion as von Rad: "Wisdom has no relation to the history between God and Israel."[4] But surely both von Rad and Zimmerli have overstated themselves, for the wisdom of Proverbs, Qoheleth, Job, and the wisdom Psalms is definitely centered and has its origin in God. The situation is as Samuel Terrien has argued:

> (1) Job yields only to the intervention of Yahweh from the whirlwind . . .
> (2) Qoheleth on his part risks the airing of his doubts [?] only because he
> knows that in the end God "acts in such a way that human beings may
> fear in his presence" (3:14), and (3) [in Proverbs] it is wisdom personified
> as a woman who invites humankind to come to her in order to receive
> the fruits of her bounty, . . . as in the Mosaic theophany or in the pro-
> phetic vision, . . . from beyond [i.e., from God].[5]

The theocentricity of the sapiential sections of the Old Testament is one of its most distinguishing features.

Rather than forcing a hiatus between wisdom as human sagacity and the *tôrâ*, or the prophetic word as a revelation from God, "wisdom" (*ḥokmâ*), personified as a feminine characteristic of God, exhibits in her unique relationship to God, in her activity, and in her revelatory functions the close connection between the gifts she proffers and the God who gave these gifts and sent her. Terrien's analysis of this unprecedented role of wisdom as found in Proverbs 8:22-31 is most convincing.[6] Such wisdom transcends time, is fully proximate to, and is the object of God's delight and is thereby also the object of the delight of men.

Accordingly, without portraying the God of Israel as manifesting Himself in history, wisdom does portray God as revealing Himself through His attribute of wisdom, with a special application of that wisdom to the mundane affairs of everyday life. But the point that Terrien has made about Proverbs 8:22-31 can be extended to another enigmatic yet extremely significant text: Ecclesiastes 3:10-15. Here as well the writer sets forth his whole case as the argument reaches its central point.

It is therefore most appropriate that we investigate wisdom's most oft-repeated advice, to "fear God/the Lord." My contention in this chapter will be that this directive from wisdom to fear the Lord not only serves as wisdom's most all-embracing statement but also functioned as one of the formal connectors between the wisdom writers and the theology of the *tôrâ* and prophets. Such connection, integrating wisdom with creation theology and the God of the word and the God of all history, including the future salvation of all who believe, is to be found in Ecclesiastes 3:10-15.

Since 1871, commentators have referred to Ecclesiastes 3:11 as a *Walpurgisnachts-Traum*, an exegetical nightmare.[7] Nevertheless, in spite of its several difficulties, an analysis of this verse may supply not only the key to the entire chapter, as James L. Crenshaw properly argues,[8] but to the whole book of Ecclesiastes and perhaps the wisdom movement as a whole. The reason for such a bold claim can be found in the issues the text embraces: (1) creation theology ("He has made everything beautiful"), (2) order and time ("in its time"), (3) divine causality and internal anthropology ("also He has put eternity into the heart of man"), (4) humanistic secularity and divine revelation ("yet so that a [man/woman] cannot find out what God has done from the beginning to the end"), and in verse 14*b* (5) divine purpose and wisdom's motto ("the fear of God").

Inasmuch as verse 14 states what would appear to be the purpose of all the divine activity, and because many scholars regard the phrase *yir'at 'ĕlōhîm*, "the fear of God," to be one of the central affirmations of wisdom literature, it will be examined first.

THE FEAR OF YAHWEH/GOD

No one needs to make a case for the centrality of either this phrase or the repeated maxim that "the fear of Yahweh is the beginning of wisdom"

(Prov. 9:10; Ps. 111:10; cf. Prov. 1:7; 15:33). It served as the motto for the collection of Proverbs (Prov. 1:7), the "conclusion" (*sôp*) of Qoheleth's argument (Eccles. 12:13), and the source of the wisdom offered to the reader of Job during the break provided by the eye of the storm (cf. Job 28:28). It is hardly a random choice; the fear of Yahweh is that first step to finding a meaningful life for Old Testament men and women.

The expression was not a late invention of an enterprising "priestly" hand, for it may be found in an early polytheistic context: Akkadian *palḫ ilī*, "fear of the gods"; Aramaic *dḥl 'lhy*, "fearing the gods."[9] The fear of the gods/God was so endemic to the thinking of the cultures of antiquity that all attempts to isolate this phrase as an example of an alleged "religious" branch of wisdom are exposed as a contrived and twentieth-century retrojection on the biblical materials.[10]

Two major monographs on the fear of Yahweh/God[11] in recent years, one by Joachin Becker,[12] the other by Louis Derousseaux,[13] "have shown conclusively that words deriving from the same root (here *yr'*) cannot always be given the same semantic breadth. So the participle [*nôrā'*] does mean 'terrible' but the noun [*yir'âh*] never means 'terror.' "[14] Only once, in Exodus 20:20, is there a reference to "sacred fear."[15] Rather, for the biblical writers "the fear of Yahweh" is "the beginning or principle of wisdom." The Hebrew *rē'šît* points to the "beginning" or first and controlling principle[16] of wisdom just as Proverbs 9:10 has the nonambiguous *tĕḥillâ*, "beginning," of the same claim. Thus the fear of the Lord is the "principle," "base," "*Grundlage*," or "kernel-motive"[17] of wisdom. For Qoheleth, then, wise living, acting, and thinking has no foundation and no controlling ground principle apart from the fear of Yahweh.

But exactly what is this *yir'at YHWH*? It must be acknowledged from the start that the fear of God/Yahweh cannot be separated from the realm of religious practice or the cult. For example, in 2 Kings 17:24-28 the newly-deported populations that the king of Assyria resettled in the Northern Kingdom were plagued with lions because "they did not fear Yahweh" or know "the law [*mišpāṭ* = "ordinance," or cultic rules] of the god(s) of the land."[18] Priests were sent, then, and they "taught them how they should fear Yahweh." Michael L. Barré makes two incisive points here: (1) The concept of the fear of (the) god(s) is a concept endemic to many areas of the ancient Near East without necessitating the positing of theories of prophetic influence, priestly tradition, or various schools of wisdom, and (2) wisdom themes included the cult and man's full response to God. "Arguments to the contrary are no more convincing than the outmoded view that the O.T. prophets were inherently 'anti-cultic' because they criticized this aspect of Israel's religious existence."[19]

The fear of God/Yahweh is an invitation to (1) modesty (see the parallelism between the fear of God and humility in Prov. 15:33; 22:4), (2) moral obedience (as in 1:7; 9:10), and (3) accepting a religious foundation for one's life (as 3:5-7 elucidates in the fullest commentary available).

Henri Blocher saw the connection between wisdom/fear of the Lord and the rest of Old Testament theology:

> The role of the fear of the Lord in wisdom is intimately connected with [the] main tenets of Old Testament faith. It agrees with its anthropology, with its unified view of the inner man and its concentration in the *heart* (cf. Pr. 4:23). . . . It flows as a necessary consequence from creational monotheism. . . . Reality is all one piece; nothing is independent of God, and nothing can be truly interpreted independently of God. . . . One can even go further and relate to radical monotheism the so-called "secular" aspect of wisdom: it could not surface with a pan-sacral mentality, for it requires a clear distinction between Creator and creature; the fear of the Lord is the principle of demythologisation.[20]

But this connection must be spelled out even more clearly. Starting with Abraham's response to God's promise in Genesis 22:12 when he willingly offered up his son Isaac ("Now I know that you fear God"), Hans Walter Wolff found the "fear of God/the Lord" to be one of the most dominant themes linking the Mosaic materials with the patriarchal promise. His judgment was that "God's normative word for Mount Sinai to all Israel is directed towards the same goal that he had set for the patriarchs: fear of God, which produced obedience through trust in God's promise."[21]

Thus whether it was Joseph (Gen. 42:18), Job (Job 1:1, 8-9; 2:3), the midwives (Ex. 1:17), or all Israel at the Exodus (14:31; 20:20; Lev. 19:14, 32; 25:17, 36, 43), the fear of the Lord became the unified response to the God who saves, delivers, and promises His word. In the book of Deuteronomy the number of references to the fear of the Lord increased and became another way of expressing one's love for God and trust in His word (Deut. 4:10; 5:26; 6:2, 13, 24; 8:6; 10:12, 20; 13:4; 14:23; 17:19; 28:58; 31:12-13).

To fear Yahweh was to commit oneself to faith (as did some of that "mixed multitude" of Egyptians, Ex. 9:20, 30; cf. 12:38). Did not Solomon also pray for "all the peoples of the earth" who would come to "know [His] name and fear [Him]" in 1 Kings 8:43?

Why then should we be surprised when the wisdom books made this phrase the dominant note of their own theology? And why also should modern exegetes and biblical theologians be so reluctant to acknowledge the appropriateness of designating this theme as the one that ties together wisdom with the rest of Old Testament theology? Even apart from any references to such things as the nation Israel, the Exodus, or the Passover, it is possible to discern that the writers of the wisdom books had not lost sight of (1) the source of wisdom as coming from God, (2) the promise,[22] to which the fear of God was merely a response, or (3) *tôrâ* with its commands for which the fear of God served as an expression of a prior work of grace. Thus promise, *tôrâ*, and the prophets not only fit but actually form one consistent, unified theme with the wisdom materials.

CREATION THEOLOGY

The purpose of all the divine actions according to Ecclesiastes 3:14 was that men should "fear him" (JB), "feel awe in his presence" (NEB), "revere him" (NIV), and this served as the central theme for much of wisdom theology. But what about the exegetical nightmare of Ecclesiastes 3:11? How could this single verse serve as the theme not only for the unit in which it is found or even the whole book of Ecclesiastes (as I have argued elsewhere[23]) but also for all of wisdom theology? Simply because it is so purposely comprehensive in the themes that it tackles.

Ecclesiastes 3:11 begins by asserting that "He made everything beautiful." No special significance should be placed on Qoheleth's use of *'āsâ*, "make," instead of *bārā'*, "create"[24] (these terms are routinely interchangeable in Genesis and Isaiah; the small differences in their meanings hardly affect overall creation theology), or on his use of *yāpeh*, "beautiful," instead of the *ṭôb*, "good,"[25] that Genesis uses (Eccles. 5:18 [MT 17] uses them interchangeably).

Qoheleth's point is simply that everything within the universe, including the universe itself (which the creation narratives refer to as "the heavens and the earth"), was made by the Creator. Here also is the point of Zimmerli's assessment that Old Testament "wisdom thinks resolutely within the framework of a theology of creation."[26] Because the "teacher's" (= Qoheleth's) goal was to encourage a true "humanism" (in its classical sense) and a genuine response to the "secular," he had to begin with God as Creator. The only viable alternative would have been to make all things sacred, reflecting an incipient pantheism or pan-sacralism that would have blurred the subject/object distinction from the start. But that would have robbed him of the theology of work, pleasure, relaxation, and the intellectual quest. In Qoheleth man is called to a legitimate type of "worldliness" in which he receives from the Creator's hand the "gifts" of life, such as eating, drinking, and earning a living, riches, marriage, friends, and much more.

For all this proper emphasis on creation, however, one must be wary of making too sharp a disjunction between God's creating work and His redeeming work. The biblical writers can speak of the two together, as the "victory over the chaos monster" theme demonstrates.[27] Furthermore, creation theology has little or no relevance except to the individual who has come to "fear Yahweh." Without the God of redemption, the God of creation makes little or no sense. It is the redeemed individual, one who has come to "fear God," who can be the true "worldly" person and who can come to terms with creation theology.

ORDER AND TIME

For all the affairs of life, argues the teacher in 3:1-8, God has set a time. Both the length of time (*žemān* = "season") and the particular events (*'ēt*, LXX *kairoi*) along that time band are divinely ordained. This lesson is pressed home in fourteen pairs of opposites with twenty-eight references to "time/times."

Qoheleth's argument is that the plan of God encompasses everything from birth to death: The term of life is set for men as it is for plants. All of life unfolds under divine appointment: birth, death; growth, harvest; joys, sorrows; acquiring, losing; speaking up, being silent; war, peace. There is beauty to this plan encompassing all events and relationships in life. What is more, there is one other divine appointment: the desire divinely implanted in the hearts of men to know how this plan all fits together.

There is no attempt to divide time or the orders of creation into secular and sacred. Instead, all time and appointments come from God. "Everything" was made by God and made "beautiful in its time" *(bě'ittô)*.

However, it is reading too much into the text to affirm the unstated. Neither wisdom literature nor Qoheleth denies the authority of the spoken word of revelation. Nor do they ground their counsel in the decrees of creation.[28] True, there is what J. C. Rylaarsdam calls a horizontal revelation[29] (what the older theologies referred to as "common grace" or general revelation), but as Crenshaw also observes, "this does not mean that the sage was bereft of normative [i.e., revelatory] 'words'; on the contrary, the original creative deed established an order that remained normative for all time."[30]

The whole section of Ecclesiastes 3:1—5:17[31] concludes in 5:18-20 with these assessments of the plan of God: (1) His proposed course of living is "good" in that it is without moral problems (v. 18a); (2) His plan can be described as "beautiful," possessing practical, aesthetic, and moral perfections (v. 18b); (3) neither the plan of God nor religion were meant to stifle man's pleasure and joy in possessions or life itself (v. 18c); (4) men/women who will receive God's gift of enjoyment will not brood over their impermanence but will take one day at a time as a gift from God (vv. 18d-19); and (5) God "answers," that is, makes His person correspond to men/women and keeps them delighted with gladness in the plan of God (v. 20b).

DIVINE CAUSALITY AND INTERNAL ANTHROPOLOGY

The most enigmatic clause in Ecclesiastes 3:11 is "also He has put eternity into the heart of man." Of the four major suggestions for the meaning of 'ōlām—world, eternity, course of the world, and knowledge or ignorance[32] —"eternity" is probably the best. Crenshaw, however, read remorse in 3:11b and felt that 3:21 dismissed any ideas of "eternity" as the meaning here with an "almost flippant rhetorical question."[33]

However, the RSV translation of 3:21 as "Who knows whether the spirit of man goes upward and the spirit of the beast goes down to earth?" is deficient on grammatical grounds. The verbs "to go upward" (hā'ōlâ) and "to go downward" (hayyōredet) are active participles with the article indicated, at least in the Masoretic tradition, by the presence of the a-vowel. If the prefix had been the sign of the interrogative, it would have been vocalized with e before the first participle and ă before the second. This interpretation of man's spirit going upward (to meet God) is consistent with the threat that wicked judges will face God in the judgment to come (3:17) and with "the dust returning to the earth as it was, and the spirit returning to God who gave it" (12:7). The introductory words "who knows" (mî yôdēa') do not always lead us to expect an interrogative to follow, for in nine instances of this expression it is followed three times by a question (Esther 4:14; Eccles. 2:19; 6:12); three times by the imperfect verb, with a meaning something like "perhaps" (Prov. 24:24; Joel 2:4; Jonah 3:9); and three times, including our present passage, by a direct object (Ps. 90:11; Eccles. 3:21; 8:1).[34] Thus the teacher's point is that there are not many who take to heart the fact that the spirit of man goes upward (presumably to God), whereas the spirit of the beasts goes down to the earth. Therefore "eternity" is a reality to be dealt with in this book.

Even so, why has eternity been placed "in their hearts"? Here internal anthropology and divine causality come together. A deep-seated, compulsive drive to know the character, composition, beauty, meaning, purpose, and destiny of all created things has been placed in the core of a person's being by his Creator (apparently as a copyright mark that all persons are made in the *imago Dei*). This has left its stamp on men and women who remain incurably inquisitive about the total meaning, the appropriateness, and the fit of all that is, both secular and sacred.

Thus each person struggles to know how all of life fits together, even at the level of his or her most inward being; he or she has been granted this task from God.

HUMANISTIC SECULARITY AND DIVINE REVELATION

Ecclesiastes 3:11 concludes, "Yet so that [man/woman] cannot find out what God has done from the beginning to the end." That is not to say that the teacher has reverted to the numinous fear of God.[35] Rudolf Otto's connection[36] of the fear of God with dread cannot be established. Instead, Qoheleth is only making the same point that Augustine made at the beginning of his confessions: "Thou madest us for thyself, and our heart is restless until it repose in thee." The point is not that men and women are incapable of such knowledge or that God was unwilling to disclose Himself to the wisdom teachers. Rather, true knowledge about any facet of creation is partial, selective, unrelated, and often meaningless until men come to "fear God." Deliberately, God has withheld from mankind the ability to know "A" from "Z," the "beginning" (*rô'š*) from the "end" (*sôp*; 3:11).

This is no Promethean challenge. It is only a revelatory perspective that humanism, secularism, aesthetic appreciation, and intellectual investigation are all disjointed on the mundane, horizontal level, without relationships to one another, "so that" men and women might come to "fear God." In this sense "the fear of the Lord/God is the principle of wisdom." That is why the "fear of God" is also the *sôp*, "conclusion," of Qoheleth's argument (12:13).

In the final analysis, wisdom is a religious question. Although it embraces true secularity and humaneness in all its mundane proportions, it has a proper inception without which biblical wisdom is almost inconceivable. A failure to place the fear of the Lord at the heart of wisdom theology is to substitute an alternative purpose other than the one explicitly adopted in texts like Proverbs 1:7, Ecclesiastes 12:13-14, and Job 28:28.

Furthermore, this "fear of the Lord/God" already has its roots in the history of salvation. It functions in antecedent texts as a response of trust and belief to the unfolding promise-plan of God.[37] Only within this context does a creation theology take on the significance it should in analyzing wisdom literature.

Ecclesiastes 3:11, then, summarizes the teacher's whole argument, and in context (3:10-15) it serves equally well as a summary for the entire wisdom corpus. God has made the totality of the created order beautiful, all in its proper time and sequence. Furthermore, He has given man a desire and capacity to know the eternity of it all, yet with this one wrinkle, that no one can truly discern anything from "A" to "Z"—"so that" all may come to fear God. The divine gift of enjoying all the stuff of life will come, but only as a response to the total revelation.

NOTES

1. What is now regarded as the classical expression of this contrast is found in Walther Zimmerli, "The Place and Limit of Wisdom in the Framework of Old Testament Theology," *Scottish Journal of Theology* 17 (1964):146-58. See also John Goldingay, "The 'Salvation History' Perspective and the 'Wisdom' Perspective Within the Context of Biblical Theology," *The Evangelical Quarterly* 51 (1979):194-207 (hereafter *EvQ*).

2. As argued by David A. Hubbard, "The Wisdom Movement and Israel's Covenant Faith," *TB* 17 (1966):7-8.

3. Gerhard von Rad, *Wisdom in Israel* (Nashville: Abingdon, 1972), pp. 310-11.

4. Zimmerli, "The Place and Limit," p. 147.

5. Samuel Terrien, "The Play of Wisdom: Turning Point in Biblical Theology," *Horizons in Biblical Theology* 3 (1981):133.

6. Ibid., pp. 134-37.

7. H. Graetz, *Kohelet oder der Salomonische Prediger* (1871), p. 3, as cited by James L. Crenshaw, "The Eternal Gospel (Eccl. 3:11)," in *Essays in Old Testament Ethics*, ed. J. Crenshaw and J. Willis (New York: Ktav, 1974), pp. 28, 51. "The interpretation of Qoheleth in 2,000 years '*ist ein förmlicher exegetischer Walpurgisnachts-Traum.*'"

8. Crenshaw, "Eternal Gospel," p. 28.

9. Michael L. Barré, "'Fear of God' and the World View of Wisdom," *Biblical Theology Bulletin* 11 (1981):41-42, cites W. G. Lambert, *Babylonian Wisdom Literature* (London: Oxford U.), pp. 71, 105, and R. Lebrun, *Hymnes et prières hittites* (Louvain-la-Neuve: Centre d'Histoire des Religions, 1980), pp. 133-49, for Hittite examples.

10. W. McKane, *The Prophets and Wise Men* (London: SCM), p. 48; *Proverbs: A New Approach* (Philadelphia: Westminster, 1970), p. 348. See my criticism of McKane et al. in "Wisdom Theology and the Centre of Old Testament Theology," *EvQ* 50 (1978):143 n. 41. Especially significant is the form-critical study of Kenneth A. Kitchen, "Proverbs and Wisdom Books of the Ancient Near East: The Factual History of a Literary Form," *TB* 28 (1977):69-114. Kitchen concludes that "the theory of separate origins and dates for Proverbs 1-9 and 10-24 is refuted by the direct comparative testimony of some 15 [instructional ancient Near Eastern wisdom compositions] of all periods, while the supposed late linguistic and conceptual evidence on dating turns out to be fallacious—again, set aside by well-dated external reference material" (p. 108). Kitchen faults much OT scholarship on procedural grounds. For many scholars, "*Formgeschichte* is predominantly a theoretical exercise and largely myopic. Hebrew books are rarely considered as wholes or in terms of the larger units, but instead attention is concentrated

on the differentiation of very small units of various types, whose evolution and agglomeration are alike set out upon theoretical grounds. Cultural contexts (*Sitz im Leben*) are invented at will. No attempt is made to establish a true literary history of genres anchored in a firm frame of factual evidence" (p. 109).

11. The change of the divine name does not significantly affect the usage of the phrase according to H. A. Brongers, "La Crainte du Seigneur (*Jir'at Jhwh, Jir'at 'Elohim)," Oud-testamentische Studiën* 5 (1948):163 n. 11.

12. J. Becker, *Gottesfurcht im Alten Testament* (Rome: Pontifical Biblical Institute, 1965).

13. L. Derousseaux, *La Crainte de Dieu dans L'Ancien Testament* (Paris: Cerf, 1970). See also Frank Michaëli, "La Sagesse et la crainte de Dieu," *Hokhma* 2 (1976):40ff.

14. Henri Blocher, "The Fear of the Lord as the 'Principle' of Wisdom," *TB* 28 (1977):7.

15. Derousseaux, *Crainte*, p. 168, as cited by Blocher, "Fear of the Lord," p. 7.

16. Derek Kidner uses this phrase (*The Proverbs* [London: Tyndale, 1964], p. 59).

17. These last three suggestions are cited by Blocher, "Fear of the Lord," pp. 12-15 n. 77, from Wanke ("*rō'š,*" *Theologisches Handwörterbuch zum Alten Testament* [1976], 2:712 [*Kernmotif*]); Arthur Weiser, *Die Psalmen* (1950), p. 465 (*Grundlage*); A. Barucq, *Le Livre des Proverbs* (Paris: Gabalda, 1964), p. 49 ("base").

18. As pointed out by Barré, "'Fear' and World View," p. 42.

19. Ibid., p. 43.

20. Blocher, "Fear of the Lord," pp. 23-24.

21. Hans W. Wolff, *The Vitality of Old Testament Traditions,* ed. W. Brueggemann and Hans W. Wolff (Atlanta: Knox, 1975), p. 75.

22. The "promise," or the promise-plan of God, is in its most rudimentary form that divine word in which God pledges to be and to do a number of things for Eve, Shem, Abraham, Isaac, Jacob, and David and thereby to be and to do a number of things for all the nations of the earth. See my thesis for the promise as the center to OT theology in *Towards an Old Testament Theology* (Grand Rapids: Zondervan, 1978).

23. Walter C. Kaiser, Jr., *Ecclesiastes: Total Life* (Chicago: Moody, 1979), pp. 15-17, 66-68.

24. As Crenshaw, "Eternal Gospel," p. 29, suggests.

25. Ibid., p. 30, finds Qoheleth's affirmation "grudging" in comparison to Sir. 39:16: *ma'ásê 'ēl kullām ṭôbîm*, "The works of God, all of them, are good." But this is based on a contrived distinction between an aesthetic value for *yāpeh* and an ethical significance for *ṭôb*. Qoheleth's term embraces both values.

26. Zimmerli, "The Place and Limit," p. 148.

27. Goldingay, "Perspective in Biblical Theology," pp. 201-2.

28. As Crenshaw argues ("Eternal Gospel," p. 33).

29. J. C. Rylaarsdam, *Revelation in Jewish Literature* (Chicago: U. of Chicago, 1946).

30. Crenshaw, "Eternal Gospel," p. 33.

31. See my argument for a fourfold division of the book in *Ecclesiastes,* pp. 17-24.

32. Crenshaw, "Eternal Gospel," p. 40 n. 53.

33. Ibid.

34. Kaiser, *Ecclesiastes*, pp. 70-71, citing Herbert C. Leupold, *Exposition of Ecclesiastes* (Columbus, O.: Wartburg, 1952), pp. 99-101.

35. Crenshaw, "Eternal Gospel," p. 44.

36. Blocher, "Fear of the Lord," p. 7, points to Plath's studies, which show that the same root (here *yr'*) cannot always have the same semantic breadth. While *nôrā'* does mean "terrible," the noun *yir'â* never means "terror." Thus the *mysterium tremendum et fascinosum* is misapplied.

37. See Kaiser, "Wisdom Theology," pp. 137-45.

RONALD F. YOUNGBLOOD (Ph. D., The
Dropsie University) is professor of
Old Testament and Hebrew at Bethel
Theological Seminary West, San Die-
go.

13

Qoheleth's "Dark House" (Eccles. 12:5)

Ronald F. Youngblood

> The Semitic root '-l-m has given rise to a range of semantic develop-
> ments in the various Semitic languages. It is evident that, in general, the
> derivatives of the root cluster around a number of central ideas which do
> not appear to be related. This leaves open the possibility that some words
> for long understood as belonging to one semantic group may in fact be-
> long to another. If the context suits an alternative meaning just as well
> as, or even better than, the traditional sense, we have grounds for pro-
> posing a new understanding of some well-known terms.[1]

The above paragraph serves to remind us that striking the proper balance between etymology on the one hand and context on the other[2] is an
important prerequisite for breakthroughs in biblical interpretation. The
purpose of the present essay is to suggest the possibility of just such a
breakthrough in Ecclesiastes 12:5 by providing a new understanding of the
phrase *bêt 'ôlām*[3] there.

THE TRANSLATION "ETERNAL HOME" IN ECCLESIASTES 12:5

It goes without saying that *byt 'wlm* is almost universally translated
"eternal home" or its equivalent by commentators and in English versions.[4] The use of **byt*, "house," in the sense of "tomb, netherworld" is

common enough in the Semitic languages generally[5] and is not in dispute here. An unexceptionable Old Testament example is Job 30:23: "I know you will bring me down to death, / to the 'house' appointed for all the living." Another possible example, one that at first blush would seem to clinch the traditional rendering of *byt 'wlm* in Ecclesiastes 12:5, is Psalm 49:11 (MT 49:12): "Their tombs will remain their houses forever (*btymw l'wlm*), / their dwellings for endless generations (*mškntm ldr wdr*), / though they had named lands after themselves." But the relevance of Psalm 49:11 is considerably weakened by the observation that "tombs" in the above translation is based on the LXX and Syriac and that the MT is better translated as follows: "In their thoughts their houses will remain forever, /. . . for they have named lands after themselves."[6]

That *'ôlām* means "long time, eternity" in the vast majority of its Old Testament occurrences is also not at issue here. I wish only to question whether it means that in the phrase *byt 'wlm* in Ecclesiastes 12:5. It will not do simply to refer to passages like Ezekiel 26:20[7] to shed light on this text, for if *'(w)lm* means something else in Ecclesiastes 12:5 it may well have the same nuance in Ezekiel 26:20 and elsewhere. In fact, the combination *byt 'wlm* may turn out to be the key that, mutatis mutandis, unlocks the significance of other parallel texts in the Old Testament.

In any case, the traditional translation "eternal home" or the like is understood variously by its host of adherents. Most commonly it is taken to signify "tomb, grave," whether defined as the "permanent home" of the dead (as during the rabbinic period)[8] or as reflecting "the perception of death as eternal, in other words, the association of the concrete notions of death and the netherworld with the abstract idea of endless time."[9] H. C. Leupold, however, understands the phrase quite differently:

> In determining what "the eternal home" (*beth 'olam*) means it is not accurate enough to say that it is the grave and then to cite many very apt parallels from antiquity. . . . This first assigns a man to a place that is to be his *permanent* habitation ("eternal") and then presently (v. 7) informs us that at least a part of his being does not stay there but goes back to God who gave it. A most peculiar kind of *eternal* home! . . . The term "eternal home" refers to a state of being.[10]

But if by "state of being" Leupold is referring to an early foregleam of the later full-blown doctrine of eternal life, Derek Kidner would politely demur: "The expression, *his eternal home,* speaks here only of finality; not of the Christian's prospect of 'a house not made with hands, eternal in the heavens' (2 Cor. 5:1)."[11]

The "parallels" that Leupold refers to above are indeed numerous,[12] but they must not be used uncritically. It is quite common, for example, to cite the Egyptian phrase "house of eternity," implying (if not directly stating) that Qoheleth's phrase is dependent on it.[13] Recent studies, however, have demonstrated that Egyptian influence on the book of Ecclesiastes and on Qoheleth's conceptual world was relatively minimal when compared to the impact of other ancient cultures on the book and its author.

QOHELETH'S MESOPOTAMIAN/UGARITIC/PHOENICIAN BACKGROUND

Tremper Longman finds in Akkadian "didactic autobiographies" the closest ancient parallels to the overall structure of Ecclesiastes.[14] Anson Rainey states that the mercantile interests expressed in the book lead him to conclude that "Qoheleth would appear to be rooted in the commercial tradition of Mesopotamian society."[15] It has long been recognized that one of the most impressive external literary parallels to a passage in Ecclesiastes is the barmaid Siduri's advice to Gilgamesh as compared to Qoheleth's advice to his readers. The relationship between the two texts is striking indeed:

Gilgamesh X iii 3-14[16]	*Ecclesiastes 9:7-9*
When the gods created mankind, Death for mankind they set aside, Life in their own hands retaining. Thou, Gilgamesh, let full be thy belly, Make thou merry by day and by night. Of each day make thou a feast of rejoicing. Day and night dance thou and play!	Go, eat your food with gladness, and drink your wine with a joyful heart for it is now that God favors what you do.
Let thy garments be sparkling fresh, Thy head be washed; bathe thou in water.	Always be clothed in white, and always anoint your head with oil.
Pay heed to the little one that holds on to thy hand, Let thy spouse delight in thy bosom!	Enjoy life with your wife, whom you love, all the day of this meaningless life that God

214 A Tribute to Gleason Archer

has given you under the sun—
all your meaningless days.

For this is the task of [mankind]!   For this is your lot in life and
in your toilsome labor under
the sun.[17]

A large number of additional parallels from the Akkadian horizon can easily be adduced, and several will be referred to below.

Rainey has proposed a north Israelite origin for the book of Ecclesiastes, citing linguistic and dialectal peculiarities that have affinities with Ugaritic and Phoenician.[18] Mitchell Dahood has collected numerous cogent Phoenician and Ugaritic parallels to various passages in Qoheleth,[19] and Ernst Jenni (among others[20])has noted precise Punic and Palmyrene cognates to *byt 'wlm* in Ecclesiastes 12:5, the contexts of which cognates point to the meaning "grave"[21] for this colorful phrase.

An especially intriguing parallel to *byt 'wlm* is the term *b'lm*, found at the end of the first line of the tenth-century-B.C. Phoenician inscription on the Ahiram sarcophagus. The *b-* is almost surely not the preposition "in" here, for *'lm* is never prefixed with *b-* in Northwest Semitic (including the Old Testament). As Hayim Tawil suggests, citing Aramaic *by 'lm'*, "cemetery," as a parallel, *b'lm* in Ahiram is most likely an abbreviation of *b(y)t '(w)lm*.[22] The Babylonian Talmud uses Aramaic terms like *bê midrāšâ* (cf. Hebrew *bêt hammidrāš*) and *bê rab* in the sense of "school." An Old Testament example is *bě'eštěrâ* (Josh. 21:27), contracted from *bêt 'eštěrâ*.[23] In Ahiram , then, *b'lm*, abbreviated from *bt 'lm*, stands for **bb'lm*, "in the grave" (the preposition *b-* does not have to be written when it precedes a word beginning with the same letter).[24] Less plausible is the proposal of Dahood, who sees in the *'lm* of *b'lm* an (elliptical) equivalent of *bt 'lm* and reads the *b-* as the preposition.[25]

LIFE AS "LIGHT" AND DEATH AS "DARKNESS"
Weep for the dead,
for he lacks the light (Sir. 22:11a).[26]

As the title of this essay suggests, I am proposing that "dark house" is a better contextual translation of *byt 'wlm* in Ecclesiastes 12:5 than is "eternal home" or the equivalent. I should therefore like to proceed step by step toward the likelihood of that rendering.

In the ancient world, "light" and "darkness" were ubiquitous symbols of life and death respectively. Referring to Egyptian descriptions of the afterlife, Hellmut Brunner writes: "As in the OT, conditions in the realm of the dead are presented in negative terms: if light is a feature of earthly life, then the dead are in gloom and darkness."[27] In Mesopotamia the situation was much the same, for to live was to experience daylight rather than darkness. A passage from the Gilgamesh cycle is typical:

> Is it so much—after wandering and roaming
>   around in the desert—
> to lie down to rest in the bowels of the
>   earth?
> I have lain down to sleep full many a time
>   all the[se] years!
> [No!] Let my eyes see the sun
>   and let me sate myself with daylight!
> *Is darkness far off?*
>   *How much daylight is there?*
> When may a dead man ever see the
>   sun's splendor?[28]

Consider also a passage from the Dumuzi cycle:

> "It [sic] it is demanded, 0 lad, I
>   will go with you the road of no return. . . ."
> She goes, she goes, to the breast of the nether world.
> The daylight fades away, the daylight fades
>   away, to the deepest nether world.[29]

The Akkadian language, like Hebrew, has an especially rich vocabulary to express the concept of darkness. Derivatives of the verbs *da'āmu, ekēlu,* and *eṭû,* all of which mean "to be dark," are attested in contexts of death and the grave. Here are a few examples:

bināti šu ussappiḫū zumuršu da'ummatu umtalli[30]
His limbs are torn apart; darkness fills his body.

ina ekleti qereb qabrim[31]
In darkness, in the midst of the grave . . . .

nişirtašu šanûmma ikkal ekliš ittanallak[32]
His treasure someone else will enjoy; in darkness he will walk about.

The parallels to Ecclesiastes of this last excerpt are striking. For the first clause see Ecclesiastes 6:2;[33] for the second, it is only needful to note that *ekliš ittanallak* is the semantic equivalent of *bahōšek yêlēk*, "in darkness he walks" (Eccles. 6:4).

Old Testament examples of light = life and death = darkness are common throughout, but especially in Job (e.g., Job 10:21-22; 15:22; 17:13; 18:18; 38:17). Typical is Job 33:30, where Elihu portrays God as one who desires "to turn back [a man's] soul from the pit, that the light of life may shine on him."

"Darkness" as a Poetic Name for Sheol
The subjects of the kingdom will be thrown outside, into the darkness, where there will be weeping and gnashing of teeth (Matt. 8:12).

Job 33:30, quoted above at the end of the previous section, implies that "the pit" (one of the names for Sheol, "the grave," "the netherworld")[34] is a place of darkness and in fact may be described in terms of darkness itself. "The darkness actually becomes the characteristic term for the realm of the dead."[35] The song of Hannah says (1 Sam. 2:9) that God "will guard the feet of His saints, but the wicked will be silenced[36] in darkness."

Although *hōšek* (used here) is by far the most common Hebrew word for the "darkness" of Sheol (see, e.g., Job 10:21; 15:22, 23, 30; 18:18; 20:26; Ps. 88:12 [MT 88:13]; Isa. 45:19), other terms are attested as well: *mahšāk* Ps. 88:18 [MT 88:19]), plural *mahăšakkîm* (88:6 [MT 88:7]); *hăšēkâ*, *māʿûp*, and *ʾăpēlâ* (Isa. 8:22; latter term only, Jer. 23:12); *ʾōpel* and *ʿêpâ* (Job 10:22), and last but not least, *şalmāwet* (Job 10:21, 22).[37]

As is well known, the Hebrew word *şlmwt* has been analyzed in two quite distinct ways. The traditional understanding is that of the MT: *şalmāwet*, "shadow of death," the rendering shared almost throughout by the LXX (see n. 37). This analysis seems to be supported also (if not clinched) by Job 38:17, where "gates of death (*māwet*)" is paralleled by "gates of the shadow of death (*şalmāwet*)." But inasmuch as the LXX paraphrases *şlmwt* as *Hadēs* here, and because a rabbinic tradition states that *şlmwt* is one of the seven names of Gehenna,[38] Job 38:17 is not definitive for the vocalization *şalmāwet*.

The other major analysis of *şlmwt* is to read it *şalmût* or the like, understanding it as an abstract noun from the root ṣlm (*ẓlm), "to be dark."[39] Akkadian ṣalāmu means "to become dark, black," and the adjective ṣalmu means "black, dark." Arabic ẓalama IV likewise means "to be dark," and ẓulmat (plural ẓulumāt) means "darkness." Ugaritic ẓlmt, though appearing only as a proper name, probably means "Darkness" (as will be shown below). The eminent Jewish scholar Rashi, in commenting on Psalm 23:4, says simply that "ṣlmwt always means ḥšk."

An interesting position on this matter is that taken by D. Winton Thomas,[40] who decides that ṣalmāwet (which he prefers to translate literally as "a shadow of death") is correct as over against ṣalmût but that it nevertheless means "(deep) darkness" in the light of the superlative force (so he claims) often borne by *mwt. He was anticipated to some degree by Franz Delitzsch, who, however, in a somewhat convoluted argument, cannot seem to make up his mind between ṣalmût from the root ṣlm/ẓlm and ṣalmāwet from ṣl(l)/ẓl(l) plus mwt.[41]

THE RELATIONSHIP BETWEEN "DARKNESS" AND "ETERNITY"

Conceptually, the idea of experiencing eternal darkness in the regions below suggested itself readily to the minds of the ancients. Mesopotamian man sought to understand why the beneficent fresh waters were "banned to live in eternal darkness below the earth."[42] Similarly, in an ancient Egyptian song a widow laments her husband's death: "One cannot recount one's experiences but one rests in one place of eternity in darkness."[43]

Linguistically, it has often been proposed that the Semitic root 'lm in the nominal sense of "long duration," "eternity" is the same as 'lm in the verbal sense of "to conceal," "to be dark."[44] That the Hebrew root 'lm may be used as a synonym for the root ḥšk, "to be dark," is confirmed by comparing Job 38:2, "Who is this that darkens my counsel" (maḥšîk 'ēṣâ), with 42:3, "Who is this that obscures my counsel" (ma'lîm 'ēṣâ). The recognition of the parallelism between ḥsk and 'lm leads to the possibility that 'wlm means "darkness" in texts like Lamentations 3:6 = Psalm 143:3 (mētê 'ôlām, "the dead who live in darkness"?).

THE ROOT 'LM IN ECCLESIASTES

Of the eight occurrences of 'lm in Ecclesiastes, five are preceded by the preposition lĕ- (l'wlm: 1:4; 2:16; 3:14; 9:6; l'lmym: 1:10) and have the usual meaning "for a long time," "forever." A sixth is ne'lām, "hidden thing" (12:14), demonstrating that Qoheleth knew the use of the root 'lm in the sense of "to be concealed/dark."

Each of the other two attestations is somewhat unique and presents its own problems of interpretation. The form *hā'ôlām* (3:11), with the definite article and written defectively *(h'lm)*, has been called "the most disputed word in the book."[45] The form *'ôlāmô* (12:5) is the only occurrence in the Old Testament of *'ôlām* with a pronominal suffix (see n. 3); it is written *plēnē* (*'wlmw*) in the Leningrad MS but defectively (*'lmw*) in the Ben Ḥayyim tradition.

'LM IN ECCLESIASTES 3:11

James Crenshaw nicely summarizes the history of the interpretation of *hā'ôlām* in Ecclesiastes 3:11 when he reminds us that "four basic solutions to the meaning of this word have inevitably suggested themselves: (1) eternity, (2) world, (3) course of the world, and (4) knowledge or ignorance."[46] Although Crenshaw himself chooses "eternity," he does so with more than one grain of salt.[47] Hans Walter Wolff, on the other hand, renders *hā'ôlām* in a closely related way ("the most distant time") and vigorously defends his translation.[48]

The renderings "world" (see KJV) and "course of the world" (or the like) have attracted numerous proponents as well, primarily on the basis of the well-attested "world" for *'ôlām* in postbiblical Hebrew. "Knowledge" has had somewhat fewer supporters,[49] resting as it does on a supposed Arabic cognate.

The translation "ignorance" in Ecclesiastes 3:11, however, has a long and distinguished history. The Bible of Miles Coverdale (1535), for example, renders as follows: "He hath planted ignoraunce also in the hertes of men, that they shulde not fynde out the grounde of his workes, which he doth from the beginninge to the ende."[50] Smith-Goodspeed's "ignorance" demonstrates their respect for their worthy predecessors, and James Moffatt's "mystery" is in the same tradition.

Among Old Testament commentators the translation "ignorance," "darkness" in various nuances is gaining favor as well. George A. Barton is typical:

> To say that "God has put eternity in their heart, so that they cannot find out the work of God from beginning to end," makes no sense. . . . From this same root *'elem*, frequently used in the Talmud . . . , means "that which is concealed," "secret," etc. The context in our verse compels us to render it "ignorance."[51]

John Gray makes the observation that "the word *'ôlām* is translated [here] in [early editions of] the RSV not as 'eternity', which ill accords with the general sense of the context, but as 'darkness', meaning thereby 'ignorance'."[52]

The discovery of the Ugaritic corpus of texts at Ras esh-Shamra in Syria beginning in 1929 has given welcome (if unexpected) support to the translation "darkness" or "ignorance" for *'ôlām* in passages where such a rendering is contextually suitable. Dahood's preference for "'darkness' in the sense of 'ignorance'" in Ecclesiastes 3:11 gains strength in the light of his observation that a Ugaritic cognate means "to grow dark," "to cover over."[53] Dahood has subsequently pointed out that *'ōraḥ 'ôlām* probably means "way of ignorance" in Job 22:15.[54]

In the consonantal text of the Old Testament, any occurrence of the root *'lm* can theoretically represent either **'lm* or **ǵlm*, because the phonemes *'* and *ǵ* both became *'* in Hebrew. As it so happens, **'* and **ǵ* remained distinct in Ugaritic, and *'lm* and *ǵlm* both appear in its lexicon. Ugaritic *'lm* is well attested with the meaning "long duration," "eternity." And although it is true that Ugaritic *ǵlm* and its feminine counterpart *ǵlmt* normally mean "young man" and "young woman" respectively,[55] it is also true that *ǵlm* can mean "dark," "to be dark" and that *ǵlmt* can mean "darkness."

In I Kings 19-20, *ǵlm ym* (admittedly a difficult phrase) probably means "a dark day" (literally "the darkness of the day"), paraphrased by H. L. Ginsberg as *"calamity."*[56] Hebrew semantic parallels include Job 3:4, "May that day turn to darkness" (*ḥōšek*); 15:23, "the day of darkness" (*yôm-ḥō-šek*); Ezekiel 30:18, "Dark will be the day" (*ḥāšak hayyôm*); and last but not least, Ecclesiastes 11:8, "the days of darkness" (*yĕmê haḥōšek*).

In II Kings i-ii 50, *[t]k mǵyh wǵlm* is translated by Ginsberg as "[Ev]en as he arrives, it grows dark."[57]

In fragment b of the Baal cycle, *ǵlmt and ẓlmt* are parallel, treated as proper names (Ghulumat and Zulumat) by Ginsberg but defined by him as both meaning "darkness."[58] G. R. Driver understands the words as common nouns and translates them "gloomy darkness" and "dark gloom" respectively.[59]

In summary, if and when Hebrew *'lm* means "darkness," it probably should be referred to **ǵlm* (rather than to **'lm*) on the basis of the Ugaritic evidence. The conceptual connection between "eternity" and "darkness" is not thereby necessarily broken, of course. In fact it may well be that **ǵlm* , a relatively rare word for "darkness," tends to be used when the author wishes to conjure up the idea of **'lm*, "eternity," at the same time.

"Darkness" in Ecclesiastes 1-11

Although Qoheleth was not overly preoccupied with the subject of darkness,[60] his frequent references to it lend a somber note to his writing. He tells us that "light is better than darkness" (2:13; see also 11:7) and that "the fool walks in darkness" (2:14). "All his days [a man] eats in darkness" (5:17). A stillborn child "departs in darkness, and in darkness its name is shrouded" (6:14). A man should enjoy however many years he lives, but "let him remember the days of darkness, for they will be many" (11:8).

In each of these verses Qoheleth uses *ḥōšek*, the most common Hebrew word for "darkness."

"Darkness" in Ecclesiastes 12:1-8

Students of Qoheleth have often commented on the lengthening shadows that cast their pall over Ecclesiastes 12:1-8. H. Wheeler Robinson notes that Ecclesiastes reaches its climax "in an eloquent but sombre picture of death."[61] Gerhard von Rad agrees: "In the great allegory of 12.2-6, [Qoheleth] mercilessly reveals how the manifestations of human life diminish with age, how it grows darker and darker around a man until 'the silver cord snaps and the golden bowl breaks'."[62] The pertinent lines of 12:1-8 read as follows:

> Remember your Creator[63] ...
> before the sun and the light
>   and the moon and the stars grow dark (*tḥšk*);
>   and the clouds return ... ;
> when ... those looking through the windows grow dim (*ḥškw*); ...
> Then man goes to his *byt 'wlm*. ...
> Remember Him—before the silver cord is severed,
>   or the golden bowl is broken; ...
> and the dust returns to the ground it came from. ...

That the severed cord and the broken bowl represent the final extinguishing of the light of life in the temple of the human body has often been demonstrated.[64]

It remains, then, only to show how *byt 'wlm* fits into such a context.

The Translation "Dark House" in Ecclesiastes 12:5

Commentators who have been willing to entertain the possibility of translating *byt 'wlm* as "dark house" or the like are few indeed. John Gray sees the possible relationship between the *'lm*, "ignorance/darkness," in 3:11 and the *'(w)lm* in 12:5 and is tempted to translate *byt 'wlmw* as "his dark house." But the supposed parallel Egyptian expression for grave, "house of eternity," makes him uncertain.[65] Although Wolff translates the Hebrew phrase as "his secluded house,"[66] indicating at the very least that he prefers the semantic range "hidden, concealed, dark" to "permanent, eternal," he too fails to see the potential of "dark house" as a rendering of *byt 'wlm*.

Occasional attempts have been made to find Akkadian parallels to Qoheleth's *byt 'wlm* and its Northwest Semitic cognates. Hayim Tawil, for example, suggests *šubat dārât(i)*, "dwelling place of eternity," but surely he exaggerates in referring to it as an "exact semantic equivalent."[67] A phrase like **bīt dārât(i)* would deserve such a description, but unfortunately no such phrase is attested (to my knowledge). Another suggestion is that of Delitzsch, who long ago proposed that "Assyr. *bit 'idii = byt 'd* of the under-world,"[68] connecting *"'idii"* with Hebrew *'d*, often a synonym of *'wlm* in the sense of eternity. As it so often happens in the commentaries of the venerable Delitzsch, he may have been writing better than he knew.

One of the best-known Akkadian descriptions of the netherworld is found in the Gilgamesh epic:

> *ireddanni ana bīt ekleti šubat Irkalla*[69]
> *ana bīti ša ēribūšu lā āṣû . . . .*
> *nūra lā immarāma ina eṭûti ašbā*[70]

> He brings me down to the "house of darkness," the
>   dwelling place of Irkalla,
> to the "house" whose entrants do not leave. . . .
> Light they do not see; in darkness they dwell.

In the parallel section of the story of the descent of Ishtar into the netherworld, *ana bīt ekleti* ("to the 'house of darkness'") is replaced by *ana bīti eṭê* ("to the 'dark house'"), the latter part of which was misread by Delitzsch. The parallels demonstrate that the concept "dark house" was not restricted to one form of expression but could be evoked by either *bīt ekleti* or *bītu eṭû*. Similarly, in Hebrew one can say, "If my home (*bêtî*)" for which I hope is the grave (*šě'ôl*), if I spread out my bed in darkness (*ḥōšek*). . ." (Job 17:13), or one can speak of going to "his 'dark house' (*bêt* 'ôlāmô)" (Eccles. 12:5). One can "go about in darkness (baḥōšek hôlēk)" (Eccles. 2:14; cf. also baḥōšek yêlēk in 6:4), "go (hôlēk)" to "the grave (šĕ'ôl)" (9:10), or "go to his 'dark house' (hôlēk . . . 'el-bêt 'ôlāmô)" (12:5). The varied lexicon of Hebrew wisdom literature is seen to match that of the Akkadian epics. If bêt 'ôlām means "dark house"—and I am here proposing that it does—then the Akkadian equivalents are bīt ekleti and bītu eṭû . The Akkadian milieu of Qoheleth lends additional plausibility to such a rendering.

R. B. Y. Scott, then, may well be missing the mark in his insistence that the use of 'ôlām meaning "darkness" in Ecclesiastes 3:11 "is unique in the OT."[71] Later interpretation of bêt 'ôlām as "eternal home," in which sense it is alleged to have migrated into various Greek and Latin expressions,[72] would thus be based on popular misunderstanding of the linguistic and cultural origins of the phrase.

SUMMARY AND CONCLUSION

It is here argued that conceptual and philological antecedents for Qoheleth and his world should be sought in a Mesopotamian/Ugaritic/Phoenician orbit rather than from Egypt or some other horizon; that "light" and "darkness" frequently serve as metaphors for life and death respectively in Ecclesiastes as well as in other Old Testament books; that "darkness" is often a poetic name for Sheol in Ecclesiastes, as elsewhere; that the obvious relationship between "eternity" and "darkness" can easily lead to confusion and/or differences of opinion when the reader encounters the Hebrew root 'lm, which can point to either; that in Ecclesiastes the five occurrences of 'lm preceded by lĕ- (1:4, 10; 2:16; 3:14; 9:6) bear the meaning "long duration, eternity," whereas the other three occurrences (3:11; 12:5, 14) are to be interpreted in the sense of "concealment, darkness"; that the former derive from an original 'lm and the latter from an original ĝlm, as differentiated also in Ugaritic; and that the near and remote contexts of Ecclesiastes 12:5 prefer "dark house" rather than "eternal home" for bêt 'ôlām, especially in the light of Akkadian parallels.

In any event, all would agree that Old Testament references to the afterlife are, for the most part, shrouded in darkness when compared to the fuller revelation of the New Testament. Clearer understanding could come only with the arrival of the Messiah, "our Savior, Christ Jesus, who has destroyed death and has brought life and immortality to light through the gospel" (2 Tim. 1:10).

NOTES

1. J. A. Thompson, "The Root '-*l-m* in Semitic Languages and Some Proposed New Translations in Ugaritic and Hebrew," in *A Tribute to Arthur Vööbus: Studies in Early Christian Literature and Its Environment, Primarily in the Syrian East*, ed. R. H. Fischer (Chicago: Lutheran School of Theology, 1977), p. 159.

2. Cf. esp. James Barr, *The Semantics of Biblical Language* (London: Oxford U., 1961); *Comparative Philology and the Text of the Old Testament* (London: Oxford U., 1968).

3. Although the full phrase is *bêt 'ôlāmô*, the suffix *-ô* simply personalizes what in any event is a metaphorical abstraction. Curiously enough, only in Eccles. 12:5 does *'ôlām* appear with a pronominal suffix in the OT, as observed e.g. by E. Jenni, "Das Wort *'ôlām* im Alten Testament," *ZAW* 64 (1952):203, 222, 245.

4. A notable exception is "the house of his reward" in G. M. Lamsa, *The Holy Bible from Ancient Eastern Manuscripts*, 4th ed. (Philadelphia: Holman, 1957), p. 694, a translation based, however, on Syriac Peshitta MSS that do not predate the fifth century A.D.

5. See e.g. N. J. Tromp, *Primitive Conceptions of Death and the Nether World in the Old Testament*, BibOr 21 (Rome: Pontifical Biblical Institute, 1969):77-79, for a comprehensive treatment.

6. See Ps. 49:11 NIV (text and footnotes).

7. "I will bring you down with those who go down to the pit (*bôr*), the people of long ago (*'am 'ôlām*). I will make you dwell in the earth below (*'eres taḥtîyôt*), as in ancient ruins (*ḥrbwt m'lm*), with those who go down to the pit (*bôr*), and you will not return or take your place in the land of the living (*'ereṣ ḥayyîm*)."

8. Cf. e.g. L. A. Olan, *Judaism and Immortality* (New York: Union of American Hebrew Congregations, 1971), p. 51.

9. A. Cooper, "Ps 24:7-10: Mythology and Exegesis," *JBL* 102 (1983):42. Cooper sets forth the provocative thesis that in Psalm 24 the *piṯhê 'ôlām*, which he translates as "gates of eternity," are "none other than the gates of the netherworld" (pp. 42-43).

10. H. C. Leupold, *Exposition of Ecclesiastes* (Columbus, O.: Wartburg, 1952), p. 282 (italics his).

11. Derek Kidner, *A Time to Mourn, and A Time to Dance* (Downers Grove, Ill.: InterVarsity, 1976), p. 103. The TEV ("final resting place") nicely captures Kidner's interpretation.

12. For a typical list see Robert Gordis, *Koheleth—The Man and His World*, 3d ed. (New York: Schocken, 1968), p. 347.

13. See, e.g., Cooper, "Ps 24:7-10," p. 42 n. 32; R. B. Y. Scott, *Proverbs, Ecclesiastes,* AB 18 (Garden City, N.Y.: Doubleday, 1965), p. 255; cf. also Jenni, "Das Wort '*ōlām,*" p. 208.

14. Tremper Longman, III, "Comparative Methods in Old Testament Studies: Ecclesiasties [*sic*] Reconsidered," *TSFB* 7/4 (March-April 1984):9.

15. Anson F. Rainey, "A Study of Ecclesiastes," *Concordia Theological Monthly* 35 (1964):152.

16. The line count is that of the cuneiform text of the Old Babylonian version as transliterated in R. C. Thompson, *The Epic of Gilgamesh* (Oxford: Oxford U., 1930), pp. 53-54; the translation is that of E. A. Speiser in *ANET* (2d ed., 1955):90.

17. Gleason L. Archer understands the phrase "under the sun" throughout Ecclesiastes to indicate "that the author's perspective is that of this present, earthly life only, as distinct from the life beyond and the heavenly realm above" ("The Linguistic Evidence for the Date of 'Ecclesiastes,'" *JETS* 12 [1969]:177). Cf. the explanation of Longman, who states that the phrase means basically "apart from the revelation and knowledge of God" ("Comparative Methods," p. 9).

18. Rainey, "Study," pp. 148-49.

19. Mitchell J. Dahood, "Canaanite-Phoenician Influence in Qoheleth," *Bib* 33 (1952):201-21. Archer, "Linguistic Evidence," pp. 167-81, refers frequently to Dahood's seminal paper, usually with appreciation (especially as concerns the Canaanite-Phoenician linguistic parallels to Ecclesiastes).

20. Cf. e.g. H. Tawil, "A Note on the Ahiram Inscription," *JANESCU* 3/1 (Autumn 1970-71):35.

21. Jenni, "Das Wort '*ōlām,*" pp. 211, 217.

22. Tawil, "Note," pp. 35-36.

23. BDB, p. 129b; KB, p. 123b. "This contraction of Beth-ashterah is like that of Beth-shan to Beisan," the modern Arabic name of the site *(Westminster Dictionary of the Bible,* p. 64; see also *A Dictionary of the Bible* [ed. J. Hastings; Edinburgh: T. & T. Clark, 1898], 1:166; Jenni, "Das Wort '*ōlām,*" p. 208 n. 3)

24. See e.g. Tawil, "Note," p. 35 n. 16.

25. Mitchell Dahood, *Psalms,* AB, 3 vols. (Garden City, N.Y.: Doubleday, 1966-1970), 3:323.

26. Ecclesiasticus's fondness for and interaction with Ecclesiastes has often been noted; see e.g. G. A. Barton, *A Critical and Exegetical Commentary on the Book of Ecclesiastes,* ICC (New York: Scribner's, 1908), pp. 53-56; G. T. Sheppard, "The Epilogue to Qoheleth as Theological Commentary," *CBQ* 39 (1977):186-89; W. O. McCready, "Ben Sirach's Response to Koheleth—The Challenge of Change in the Ancient World," in *Religion's Response to Change,* ed. K. J. Sharpe (Auckland: U. Chaplaincy Publishing Trust, 1985). In fact, it is not impossible that the title Ecclesiasticus was eventually given to Sirach in conscious imitation of the title Ecclesiastes (which had been conferred on Qoheleth as an attempt to bring out the "convening" or "convoking" implications of the root *qhl).*

27. H. Brunner in *Near Eastern Religious Texts Relating to the Old Testament,* ed. W. Beyerlin (Philadelphia: Westminster, 1978), p. 11 (see also p. 16).

28. The translation is that of T. Jacobsen, *The Treasures of Darkness* (New Haven, Conn.: Yale U., 1976), p. 204 (italics mine). The crucial line in the Akkadian text (Gilg. M. i 14) reads: *rēqet ekletum kī maṣi nawirtum,* "Far away is the darkness (of death); how much daylight (remains)?" Cf. *CAD,* 7. 60.

29. The translation is that of T. Jacobsen in *Toward the Image of Tammuz*, ed. W. L. Moran (Cambridge, Mass.: Harvard U., 1970), p. 99.

30. Cuneiform Texts from Babylonian Tablets in the British Museum (hereafter *CT*) 17. 31:27-28. Cf. *CAD*, 3. 123.

31. *CT*, 17. 36:84-85. Cf. *CAD*, 7. 60.

32. *CT*, 39. 4:34. Cf. *CAD*, 4. 70. An example using *eţû* will be cited below.

33. That *'kl* often means "to enjoy" in Qoheleth is clear from 2:25, where *mî yō'kal* is parallel to *mî yāḥûš*.

34. This is not the place to enter the debate concerning whether Hebrew *šě'ôl* means "the grave" or "the netherworld." Neither translation fits comfortably every occurrence of the word, and in any event the allusive language of the OT can easily embrace pictorial descriptions of the netherworld without buying into the mythology that was part and parcel of the ancient pagan understanding of it.

35. J. Pedersen, *Israel: Its Life and Culture, I-II* (London: Oxford U., 1926), p. 464; see also Dahood, *Psalms*, 1:211. For a concise yet comprehensive treatment of Sheol, Sheol as the grave, light as life vs. darkness as death, etc., see Pedersen, *Israel*, pp. 460-70.

36. The deathly (no pun intended) silence of the tomb or netherworld is also a common motif among the ancients. Cf. e.g. Vergil *Aeneid* 2.755: *Horror ubique animo simul ipsa silentia terrent*, "Dread everywhere dismays my heart; so also does the very silence (of the night of death)."

37. In Job 10:22 LXX, *şlmwt* is rendered *aiōniou*—possibly misreading *şlmwt* as *'wlm*, but more likely making the common connection between "darkness" and "eternity" (see below). In Ps. 88:6 (MT 88:7) the LXX translates *bmşlwt* as though it were *bslmwt*—namely, *en skia , thanatou*.

38. *'Erub.* 19a.

39. Cf., e.g., E. Dhorme, *A Commentary on the Book of Job* (1967; reprint, Nashville: Nelson, 1984), pp. 26-27.

40. D. W. Thomas, "*Şalmāwet* in the Old Testament," *Journal of Semitic Studies* 7 (1962):191-200.

41. F. Delitzsch, *Biblical Commentary on the Psalms*, 2d ed. (Grand Rapids: Eerdmans, 1959), 1:330-31.

42. The expression is that of T. Jacobsen in H. and H. A. Frankfort et al., *The Intellectual Adventure of Ancient Man* (Chicago: U. of Chicago, 1946), p. 164 = H. and H. A. Frankfort et al., *Before Philosophy* (Harmondsworth: Penguin, 1949), p. 178.

43. H. Frankfort, *Ancient Egyptian Religion* (1948; reprint, New York: Harper, 1961), p. 108.

44. Thompson, "The Root '-1-m,'" pp. 161, 162; Jenni, "Das Wort *'ōlām*," p. 199. R. L. Alden has kindly supplied me with a copy of his unpublished paper, "The Root *'lm* and Its Derivatives," in which he also connects *'lm*, "long time," with *'lm*, "hide." Cf. also Barton, *Ecclesiastes*, p. 105. The Hebrew root *'lm*, however, represents two different original roots (see below).

45. D. C. Fleming in *The New Layman's Bible Commentary*, ed. G. C. D. Howley et al. (Grand Rapids: Zondervan, 1979), p. 743.

46. J. L Crenshaw, "The Eternal Gospel (Eccl. 3:11)," in *Essays in Old Testament Ethics*, ed. J. L. Crenshaw and J. T. Willis (New York: Ktav, 1974), p. 40. Cf. similarly Fleming in *The New Layman's*, pp. 743-44.

47. Crenshaw, "The Eternal Gospel," pp. 39, 42-43. G. von Rad suggests "distant future" but, like Crenshaw, makes his proposal with reservations *(Wisdom in Israel* [London:

SCM, 1972], p. 230). A. Heidel, who also appears to prefer "eternity," nevertheless confesses that Eccles. 3:11 is "not clear" to him (*The Gilgamesh Epic and Old Testament Parallels,* 2d ed. [Chicago: U. of Chicago, 1949], p. 149 n. 37).

48. Hans W. Wolff, "The Concept of Time in the Old Testament," *Concordia Theological Monthly* 45 (January 1974):41-42. Walter C. Kaiser, Jr., gives an equally vigorous defense of "eternity" in the essay immediately preceding this one in the present volume. See, however, n. 51 below.

49. E.g., Thompson, "The Root '-l-m,'" p. 165.

50. The popular Great Bible, published a few years later, reproduces Coverdale's translation of Eccles. 3:11 (apart from minor spelling differences, a common phenomenon in the sixteenth century) almost verbatim (the only change is "comprehend" for "fynde out").

51. Barton, *Ecclesiastes,* p. 105. Barton has, perhaps unwittingly, put his finger on a fatal flaw in the translation "eternity" here: In order to justify it, *mibbĕlî 'ăšer lô',* "so that not," has to be rendered "yet so that not"—a subtle but inadmissible change. "Ignorance" is the choice also of A. J. Grieve in *A Commentary on the Bible,* ed. A. S. Peake (London: Nelson, 1937), p. 413. After a lengthy discussion of the alternatives, O. S. Rankin states his preference for "forgetfulness" or "ignorance" (*The Interpreter's Bible,* ed. G. A. Buttrick et al., 12 vols. [Nashville: Abingdon, 1953-1956], 5:48-49). R. B. Y. Scott chooses "enigma" or "darkness" or "obscurity" (*Proverbs, Ecclesiastes,* p. 221).

52. J. Gray, *The Legacy of Canaan: The Ras Shamra Texts and Their Relevance to the Old Testament,* VTSup 5 (Leiden: Brill, 1957):200.

53. Mitchell Dahood, "Canaanite-Phoenician Influence in Qoheleth," *Bib* 33 (1952):206. Rainey, "A Study," p. 155 n. 78, takes exception to Dahood's argument for two reasons: "(1) there is already a noun derived from '*lm,* viz., *ta'ălumâ,* meaning 'hidden thing.'" But other words for "darkness" in Hebrew are multiple derivatives from the same root —e.g., cf. *ḥšk, ḥškh, mḥšk; 'pl, 'plh; 'yph, m'wp.* Such a phenomenon is exceedingly common in Hebrew as well as in other Semitic languages. "(2) The Ugaritic form he cites is not a verb but the common Ug. noun *ǵlm,* 'lad.'" But, although *ǵlm* often means "lad" in Ugaritic, it almost certainly means "to be dark" in the passages cited by Dahood (Rainey's renderings to the contrary notwithstanding), as we shall attempt to demonstrate below.

54. Mitchell Dahood, "Qoheleth and Northwest Semitic Philology," *Bib* 43 (1962):353-54.

55. The most famous occurrence of the Hebrew cognate of the feminine form is the celebrated *'almâ* of Isa. 7:14.

56. H. L. Ginsberg in *ANET,* p. 143.

57. Ibid., p. 147. Cf. also M. D. Coogan, *Stories from Ancient Canaan* (Philadelphia: Westminster, 1978), p. 69.

58. Ginsberg in *ANET,* p. 131 n. 11.

59. G. R. Driver, *Canaanite Myths and Legends* (Edinburgh: T. & T. Clark, 1956), p. 121.

60. Ironically, however, the early rabbis almost consigned the entire book to a darkness of its own; cf. *b. Šabb.* 30:72.

61. H. W. Robinson, *Inspiration and Revelation in the Old Testament* (Oxford: Clarendon, 1946), p. 258.

62. G. von Rad, *Wisdom,* p. 228. See also J. L. Crenshaw, "The Shadow of Death in Qoheleth," in *Israelite Wisdom: Essays in Honor of Samuel Terrien,* ed. J. G. Gammie et al. (Missoula, Mont.: Scholars, 1978):208-9.

63. E. Jenni, "Das Wort *'ōlām* im Alten Testament," *ZAW* 65 (1953):27 n. 4, wants to read *bwrk*, "your pit," here instead of *bwr'k*, "your Creator" (see also *BHS*). Attractive though such a reading might be, however, the consonantal text is against it.

64. Cf. e.g. E. H. Plumptre, *Ecclesiastes* (Cambridge, Mass.: Cambridge U., 1985), pp. 221-22.

65. Gray, *The Legacy of Canaan*, p. 200.

66. Hans W. Wolff, *Anthropology of the Old Testament* (Philadelphia: Fortress, 1974), p. 124.

67. Tawil, "A Note," p. 36.

68. F. Delitzsch, *Commentary on the Song of Songs and Ecclesiastes* (Grand Rapids: Eerdmans, 1970), p. 418.

69. Sumerian *IR.KAL.LA* = *IR.KAL.A(K)* = *IRI.GAL*, "big city," i.e., the netherworld. *IR-.KAL.LA* became a Sumerian loanword in Akkadian.

70. Gilg. VII iv 33-34, 39, paralleled in Ishtar's Descent i 4-5, 9 *(CT,* 15.45:4-5, 9).

71. Scott, *Proverbs, Ecclesiastes,* p. 221. It is tempting to see another example of *'ōlām,* "darkness," in 1 Kings 8:12-13 (= 2 Chron. 6:1-2), where "dwell *(škn)* in a dark cloud *('ărāpel)"* is parallel to "dwell *(yšb) 'ōlāmîm."*

72. So Jenni, "Das Wort *'ōlām,"* p. 28.

MEREDITH G. KLINE (The Dropsie College for Hebrew and Cognate Learning) is professor of Old Testament at
Gordon-Conwell Theological Seminary and at Westminster Theological
Seminary in California.

14

Death, Leviathan, and the Martyrs: Isaiah 24:1—27:1

Meredith G. Kline

A series of Isaianic oracles concerning the nations (chaps. 13-23) cul-
minates in a section popularly known as the Isaiah apocalypse[1] (chaps. 24-
27). From 27:2 on, the focus of this section is on Israel, its fall and fullness.[2] (More than is generally recognized, Paul tapped this vein for his
discussion of Israel in Romans 9-11.) In Isaiah 24:1—27:1 there is a
broader, universal perspective.[3] The present essay will concentrate on this
first part of the "apocalypse," treating it as a distinct composition and attempting to show how the subject of death, or better, the Lord's conquest
of death, permeates and structures its contents. Some contribution may
thereby be made to the higher critical debate, at least as to the unity of the
material. But my primary interest is in opening up exegetically Isaiah's
pastoral theology of death and resurrection and judgment. And in the process, I also want to explore the extraordinary influence exercised by
24:1—27:1 on subsequent biblical revelation, particularly on certain major
eschatological passages in the New Testament.

VICTORY OVER DEATH

Three passages celebrating Yahweh's victory over death occupy the key
positions in the structure of Isaiah 24:1—27:1.[4] They frame the composi-

tion with introduction (24:1-3) and conclusion (26:19—27:1) and form its central apex (25:6-8). Each, by means of its own distinctive image, graphically depicts a dramatic reversal that overtakes the realm of death.

THE DEVOURER DEVOURED

I shall start with Isaiah 25:6-8, the centerpiece of the composition,[5] and its picture of the eschatological banquet. To appreciate the point of this imagery it is necessary to recall the reputation of the grave as the great devourer. Sheol opens wide its spacious maw and swallows down victims insatiably.[6] But at the banquet for all peoples "in that day" (cf. v. 9) a remarkable reversal will take place. The Lord will become the devourer[7] and death, the famed and fearful swallower, will itself be swallowed up (v. 8).[8]

Perhaps the banquet scenario in 25:6-8 was prompted by the desire to exploit the identity of death as the swallower.[9] However, the divinely hosted banquet is a standard feature in visions of the life to come in biblical and extrabiblical literature. Moreover, the victory banquet is a regular element in the epic pattern of the conflict of the hero-deity and the monstrous power of disorder and death, which is in evidence elsewhere in the passage. In any case it was the communion meal of the elders of Israel on the mountain of God after the Exodus-triumph over the dragon (Ex. 24:9-11)[10] that provided the specific typological model for Isaiah 25:6-8. For "on this mountain," the location assigned to the banquet in 25:6-7, refers back to the 24:23 scene of the Glory epiphany before the elders on Mount Zion, and that in turn clearly recalls the banquet scene at Sinai (cf. Ex. 24:l0-ll).

The image of death as the swallower, alluded to in Isa. 25:6-8, leads naturally to the further image of death as a cover. Thus in the Numbers 16 narrative the earth opens its mouth and swallows the rebels (v. 32) and then closes over them and covers them (v. 33; cf. Ps. 106:17). The covering, concealing aspect of the grave is prominent in the concluding treatment of the victory over death in Isaiah 26:21, but it is probable that here in 25:7 there is also a reference to the grave, the swallower, as a cover over all peoples. In parallel with God's swallowing of death (v. 8) we read of His swallowing "the face of the wrapping that enfolds[11] all peoples, the woven thing woven over all the nations" (v. 7). This woven covering is most likely a shroud.[12] But this is apparently a figure for the grave, the universal shroud that covers all humanity in their common lot of death.[13] It could then be that the explanation of the "face"[14] of the shroud is to be found in the common expression "the face of the earth," inasmuch as it is this face, or surface, of the earth that constitutes the covering shroud over Sheol's occupants.[15] The two instances of Yahweh's swallowing *(bl')* would then together encompass as their twin objects death (v. 8) and Hades (v. 7).

Quoting Isaiah's forecast of the swallowing of death (25:8), Paul identifies this banquet of everlasting victory with the believers' ultimate putting on of the glory of incorruption and immortality (1 Cor. 15:54).[16] And the apostle John portrays this death of death in his account of the resurrection (the "second resurrection" in the first/second death/resurrection scheme of Rev. 20-21)[17] as a casting of death and Hades (or the "first death" in that same scheme) into "the second death," the lake of fire (Rev. 20:14; cf. 21:4).

THE VESSEL EMPTIED

Anticipating the master theme of Isaiah 24-26, the opening verses (24:1-3) foretell the Lord's mighty overthrow of death. The theme is expressed in terms that suggest that here at the beginning death is already being thought of as the greedy, gluttonous devourer, filled with generations on generations of mankind. In 25:8 the great reversal is a matter of the swallowing of the swallower. Here it takes the form of the upending and emptying out of what had been a filled container.[18]

"See, Yahweh pours out the netherworld and empties it out; He turns it upside down and scatters out its occupants" (v. 1). The verb *bqq*, "empty out," onomatopoetically imitates the gurgling sound of water plopping out of a bottle. It is here reinforced by the similar sounding *blq: bôqēq . . . ûbôlĕqâ.*[19] The use of *'ereṣ* for the netherworld is now well recognized.[20] In the present general context note, for example, "the realm *('ereṣ)* of the shades" (26:19).[21] The "face," *pānêhâ,* combined here with the verb *'wh,* "bend low,"[22] to express "turn upside down" apparently refers to the ground as surface of the grave,[23] which is compared to the top of a vessel bent over or upturned to pour out its contents.

According to the customary view of 24:1-3, it introduces the theme of the desolating of the earth, which is then traced further in the rest of chapter 24. But as interpreted above, this opening passage depicts the ultimate repair of the situation lamented in the immediately following verses and hence serves as an introduction not to chapter 24 alone but to the entirety of Isaiah 24-26. The interpretation of this passage as an opening statement of the main overall theme of the resurrection victory is corroborated by its closing formula: "For Yahweh has spoken this word" (v. 3).

Such an assurance of the certainty of fulfillment is better accounted for if what has just been foretold is not merely the desolation of the earth but the astounding prospect of the termination of the sway of death. Moreover, the one other place within Isaiah 24-26 where essentially this same formula of divine utterance appears is at the close of the climactic assertion of the resurrection in 25:6-8.

The resurrection-judgment, according to 24:1-3, is universal. This is suggested by the paired listing of the representatives of opposite ends of the socioeconomic spectrum of mankind (v. 2).[24] Subsequently the theme of the termination of death becomes more specifically occupied with the resurrection of the people of God. Thus in 25:6-8 and 26:19 and following, this theme finds expression within the genre of hymnic praise, the saints celebrating the resurrection as God's saving triumph that delivers them from the Satanic hosts. Not merely excluded from that salvation, the wicked are viewed along with death as the enemy from whom God rescues His own. But before the focus is narrowed down to the meaning of the resurrection for the redeemed, 24:1-3 presents the broader picture of a general resurrection, an emptying out of all the contents of the death-vessel without distinction.[25] All that death has swallowed down will be cast out at the resurrection. So death's historical role comes to an end: The first death undergoes the second death.

THE VEIL REMOVED

The covering aspect of Sheol, the natural concomitant of its identity as the devourer, is once again present in the final picture of the resurrection-victory over death in 26:19 and following. Previously the face of the earth (or netherworld) was viewed as the cover of a vessel (24:1) or as an enveloping shroud-cover (25:7), but here it is a veil-like covering that conceals the dead (26:21b). The blood of the slain sinks into the earth. The dead disappear into Sheol, concealed behind earth's covering of soil and stone. Death is the "hidden" place (Job 40:13). Resurrection is then an uncovering, an unveiling, a revealing of the concealed. "The earth shall disclose her blood and no more cover her slain" (Isa. 26:21b).

It is clear from the context that the slain in view are the martyrs, as typical of all the faithful. For the passage opens with the declaration that the dead who belong to the Lord shall arise in joy (v. 19), and it continues with a special encouragement to God's people in contemplation of their experience of death (v. 20).[26] Moreover, immediately connected with this revealing of the blood of the slain is the assurance of the divine advent to punish their wicked oppressors (v. 21a).

In this connection I want to point out the Isaianic roots of a misunderstood Pauline concept in Romans 8. To do so it will first be necessary to discuss the relationship of the context of Isaiah 26:19 to the context of 24:4. With its announcement of the uncovering of the earth and the resurrection-manifestation of the saints, the former passage answers redemptively to what the latter says about the earth in mourning over the curse of death and especially over the polluting stain of innocent blood. One indication that this mourning does have to do with death is the contrastive correspondence between the situation mourned in the context of 24:4 and the celebration of the conquest of death in chapter 25, especially verses 6-8. A comparison shows sorrow replaced by joy, sighs by songs of praise, the languishing of earth's fruit by a lavish feast of fat things full of marrow and flavorful wine, well refined. In Isaiah 24 the curse that is grieved over is one that "devours the earth," decimating its population (v. 6). This is the motif of death as the never-sated devourer, which 25:6-8 takes up in its answering prophecy of the devouring of the devourer.

In the context of 24:4, what makes the earth groan is that it is obliged to become the grave, to cover over the human dead. But the relationship of that passage to 25:6-8, which has a redemptive focus on God's people, argues for a special (even if not exclusive) concern with the death of the righteous in the former. Pointing in the same direction is the explanation given in 24:5 for the entrance of death and the resultant mourning of the earth: "The earth is profaned (*ḥānĕpâ*) under its inhabitants." In view of the use of *ḥnp* elsewhere for polluting the ground by spilling innocent blood on it,[27] it appears that the sin against God's covenant by reason of which the earth suffers defilement and mourns is hostility vented on the covenant faithful, resulting in their martyrdom.

When the profaned, mourning earth of the 24:4 section is understood in this way, it becomes apparent that 26:19 and the verses that follow, like 25:6-8, answers directly to the earlier passage, proclaiming the resurrection-conquest of death as the resolution of earth's grievance.[28] Earth's accursed role as concealing the grave of the not-yet-vindicated people of God comes to an end when the martyrs are revealed and arise and the cry of their blood is heard and honored in heaven.

Until that deliverance from death's curse, the earth bemoans its role as netherworld. Isaiah 24:4 pictures the realm of nature as joining together with man in sighs over death. This brings to mind at once the similar thought in Romans 8. Paul says that creation groans together with those who have the firstfruits of the Spirit (vv. 19-23). Even the more precise image of the groaning of birth-travail (Rom. 8:22) reflects the Isaiah 24-26 context. For in 26:16-18 God's people, struggling in the warfare against the enemy until God grants them the resurrection deliverance (v. 19), are likened to a woman crying out in birth pangs.[29] Moreover, just as the groaning of travail in 26:17-18 is followed by the resurrection-revealing of God's people (vv. 19-21), so in Romans 8 creation's groaning in birth pangs (v. 22) is in expectation of the resurrection of the children of God mentioned in the next verse (v. 23). Indeed, quite an extensive correspondence can be traced between these Pauline and Isaianic passages. Other features of 26:19—27:1 to be dealt with below are reflected in the latter part of Romans 8, such as the justification of believers in the face of Satanic accusation and the persuasion of God's presence and love in the experience of death. It is also remarkable that just as Isaiah moves from these themes into the question of Israel, its fall and fullness, in chapter 27, so does Paul in Romans 9-11 and (as we have observed) in such a way that his line of thought and imagery show dependence on Isaiah 27.

From this mutually illuminative relationship of Isaiah 24-26 and Romans 8 one perceives that the "bondage of corruption" over which, says Paul, the creation groans (Rom. 8:21) is the earth's being subjected to the fate of covering the blood of the innocent and concealing the corpses of the saints.[30] The term for corruption, *phthora,* is the one that describes physical death in the resurrection context of 1 Corinthians 15,[31] another passage with clear connections with Isaiah 24-26.[32] And in Romans 8, as we have seen, what the earth looks forward to in hope as its deliverance from this corruption is precisely the resurrection of the righteous. As the repeated references to their resurrection in verses 19, 21, and 23 indicate, that event is not merely the occasion of the earth's deliverance but is itself the liberation from the corruption over which the earth groans.[33] By reason of the swallowing up of death in resurrection-victory, "the reproach of God's people"—the vanity of corruption from which until now the earth groans to be released—"is removed from all the earth" (Isa. 25:8).

This discussion should not be closed without attention being drawn to another connection between Isaiah and Paul. Specifically, it again concerns Isaiah 24-26 and Romans. There is a general persuasion abroad that Genesis 3 is without influence on theological developments in the rest of the Old Testament.[34] And when Genesis 3 is thus regarded as an isolated, unfruitful phenomenon, Paul's federal-covenantal reconstruction in Romans 5 is left without a supportive canonical linkage. But Isaiah at least (not to assess other suggested connections) can be adduced as a bridge between Moses and Paul in this matter. What the prophet says in the context of 24:4 must be recognized as a significant source for the covenantal theology of death in Romans 5:12 and the verses that follow. Isaiah deals there with death as a curse. Like Paul, Isaiah teaches that death entered the world through the entrance of sin—indeed, through the sin of breaking "the ancient covenant" in Eden and that death so passed unto all men, devouring the earth's population, generation after generation (24:5-6; cf. v. 20).

VINDICATION OF THE MARTYRS

Associated with death in Isaiah 24-26 as allied enemies of the saints are Satan and, more conspicuously, his human accomplices. And the final proclamation of the resurrection in 26:21 depicts it not only as a redemption of believers from the prison of death (v. 21*d*) but as a vindication of the martyrs against these Satanic persecutors: "The earth shall disclose her blood" (v. 21*c*). The cry of the martyrs' blood will be heard. At the resurrection they will have their day in court.[35] For the Lord will come forth "to punish the inhabitants of the earth for their iniquity" (v. 21*ab*). Vindication of the Lord's people will not stop short of taking vengeance on their primeval adversary, the serpent-devil (27:1). What is said in 26:21—27:1 about the coming vindication of the saints is a concluding summation; the theme of the enemies and their subjugation is under development throughout chapters 24-26. This material shall be examined, dealing in turn with Satan and his demonic hosts and then with the evil world-power.

JUDGMENT ON LEVIATHAN

Included in the final portrayal of the resurrection triumph over death is the judgment of Leviathan (Isa. 27:1).[36] This serpentine symbol in the Bible often signalizes the demonic dimension of a situation. Sometimes the dragon is a figure for Satan himself, as in Revelation 12:9, 20:2, and here in Isaiah 27:1.[37] Inasmuch as the devil is the one who has the power of death (Heb. 2:14),[38] it is understandable that he and death should be found together here in common undertaking and common judgment. The same combination is found in Revelation 20:10-14.

There is indeed a curious overlap in the attributes and activities of death and the devil in biblical representations of them. They even share the same name, or epithet: Belial.[39] Like death, the devil is depicted as the swallower, if not through the Belial designation then at least in Revelation 12:4, where the dragon is seen ready to devour the messianic child, and in 1 Peter 5:8, where the Adversary is compared to a lion on the prowl,[40] seeking to devour believers. Similarly, Satan's human agents are portrayed as Sheol-like swallowers of the godly. The description of these enemies in Psalm 73:9 with gaping mouth reaching from heaven to earth reflects strikingly the description of Mot in the Ugaritic mythology.[41] And like the devil they are more specifically compared to lions eager to devour the righteous.[42] Death, on its side, shares with the Satan-Adversary in his identity as the enemy. Paul in his discussion of the resurrection in 1 Corinthians 15 characterizes death as "the last enemy" (v. 26), and possibly there is some (or even considerable) precedent in the Psalms for designating death as the foe.[43] Quite natural then is the conjunction of death and the devil in Isaiah 24:1—27:1. In particular, the aptness of Isaiah's concluding word on the judgment of Leviathan (27:1), appended to his final account of the resurrection-victory over death, can be appreciated.

The disclosure concerning Leviathan in 27:1 is adumbrated in 24:21-22. It is indicated there that the saints' warfare is on two levels. For behind the hostility displayed by earthly oppressors is a hidden, demonic enemy on high: "In that day Yahweh will punish the host of the height on high and the kings on the ground below" (v. 21). On high an army of evil beings is associated with the devil in his cause (cf. Rev. 12:7-9). God's judicial intervention[44] against them will come "after many days" (v. 22b), at the final cosmic catastrophe (v. 20) and the revelation of the Parousia-Glory (v. 23).[45] This judgment of the demonic host on high is the same as the judgment of Leviathan announced in 27:1.[46]

Something of the nature of the judgment on Leviathan referred to in 27:1 may be discerned from the equivalent disclosure in Revelation 20:10a. There the devil's doom takes the form of the lake of fire, the second death. That realm is one of forever-continuing torment (v. 10b), and accordingly, the fate of Satan and others relegated to it is not absolute erasure from existence. The second death is existence on the other side of an impassable gulf from the cosmos proper. To be cast into the lake of fire is to cease to figure or function in heaven and earth as the consummated kingdom of God. Satan slain, or banished to the second death, no longer participates in the creation proper. He no longer functions as the power of death or otherwise affects the glorified saints.[47] Such existence, cut off from rapport with God's realm of life, is a death-existence.

Implicit in the nature of the resurrection of God's people as a judgment-victory over the devil (27:1), the one who has the power of death, is the justification aspect of the vindication of the godly. For inseparable from Satan's identity as possessor of the power of death is his role as "the accuser of our brethren . . . who accuses them before God day and night."[48] It is through his tempting to sin and then prosecuting for sin (the ultimate duplicity) that he has come to wield the power of death. Therefore God's resurrection-conquest of Satan as possessor of the power of death is at the same time a triumph over him as the accuser of the brethren. And in the judicial ordeal before God's throne, to defeat the accuser in his quest for a verdict of condemnation is to seal the verdict of justification in behalf of the accused.[49]

The conclusion that the resurrection-victory of God's people involves their justification is also arrived at if the resurrection as a victory over death is considered. For death entered the world through sin, in condemnation for the breaking of the primeval covenant. Hence deliverance from death through resurrection in Christ is a reversal of condemnation. It publicly registers the verdict of justification secured by the merits of Christ. This verdict answers to the prayer of the blood of the martyrs that is disclosed at the resurrection (26:21), inasmuch as that blood has been pleading not only to be avenged through the judgment of the enemy but to be recognized as righteous blood, righteous through the advocacy of the blood of the Lamb (cf. Heb. 12:24; Rev. 12:11a). Agreeably, in the vision of the intermediate state in Revelation 6:9-11, the martyrs awaiting the final avenging of their blood on the earth-dwellers already receive a foretaste of that judgment by being acknowledged as justified through the bestowal of white robes, emblematic of their righteousness (cf. Rev. 19:8).

It follows that what 26:14, 19 say about not participating or participating in this resurrection may be construed as legal pronouncements of condemnation and justification respectively. These two verdicts are formulated as a clearly matching contrastive pair. The wicked dead, true to their name "sons of Belial/Perdition," will not rise again (v. 14).[50] But God's dead, something of a contradiction in terms according to the argument of Jesus for bodily resurrection,[51] shall come to life (v. 19).[52] The promise of resurrection,[53] "your dead shall live" (v. 19a), is a verdict of justification. It is comparable to "the just shall live," the justifying verdict pronounced on the righteous believer in Habakkuk 2:4. There too we find a contrasting verdict against the wicked.[54] The *lō'-yāšĕrâ* in v. 4a (however the grammar as a whole is construed) must refer to God's verdict of condemnation[55] on the proud sinner, a verdict to which "shall live" in v. 4b corresponds. And Paul, citing this passage in Galatians 3:11, confirms not only that "shall live" is a verdict but that it is indeed a verdict of justification. For he parallels this life obtained by the righteous through faith in Jesus Christ with the verdict of justification, which, he asserts, was not obtainable through the principle of works operative in the law.[56]

SUBJUGATION OF THE WORLD-CITY

The ancient dragon directs his assault on the faithful through the earthly agency of the dragonlike beast (cf. Rev. 12:17—13:7). Inevitably, at the judgment, the beast shares the dragon's doom in the lake of fire (cf. 20:10). The place prepared for the devil and his angels is the fitting fate of the seed of the serpent, for throughout history they have exhibited their father's spirit of self-assertion in blasphemous defiance of God and murderous hatred of His people.[57] An antichrist propensity infects the apostate city of man from the days of Cain onwards, erupting virulently in the reign of the sons of the gods at the climax of prediluvian history (Gen. 6:1-4) and in the final manifestation of the beast in the man of sin.

This two-tiered structure of the Satanic enterprise has already been encountered within Isaiah 24-26. In 24:21 the kings of the ground below and the demonic hosts above are listed together as the joint objects of divine vengeance.[58] Elsewhere Isaiah suggests the bond of identity between these companies by applying to the earthly forces of evil the term *mārôm*, which in 24:21 distinguishes "the host of the height on high" (*hammārôm bammārôm*). Thus 24:4 notes that even the "height (*mĕrôm*) of the people of the earth" are among the death mourners.[59] And 26:5 prophesies judgment against "the ones who dwell in the height (*mārôm*)," further identified as "the lofty city."

Under the present major heading of the vindication of the martyrs it is the enmity of Satan's earthly agents against God's people that calls for particular attention. Isaiah 25:10-12 contains a distinctive treatment of this enmity. Moab, inveterate foe of Israel, serves as representative of the hostile world. Disdainful of the presence of the Glory-hand of God on "this mountain" (v. 10), that is, Zion (cf. 24:23; 25:6), Moab extends[60] its grasping hands "in the midst of it" (v. 11a), to seize all it can from Israel.[61] The full extension of its clutching embrace is compared to a swimmer's stretching forth his hands in a sweeping stroke (v. 11*b*). In this greedy grabbing by Moab a replication of the insatiable appetite of Sheol-death[62] is again met with. Moab's rapacious lust is totally frustrated, however, as God brings down into the dust "his pride with the catch[63] of his hands" (v. 11*c*).

The enmity of the world-power is also mirrored in the prayers of the saints. Out of the midst of their struggle against the overwhelming might of the oppressor they raise their cry, seconding the call of the martyrs' blood for divine retribution. Isaiah 26:8-9*ab* describes the constancy of the saints in such expectant prayer for God's decisive acts of judgment,[64] indignant as they are at the obdurate obtuseness of the unrepentant, unrelenting wicked in the absence of such judgments (vv. 9*cd*, 10).[65] Verses 7 and 11 articulate their actual petitions.[66]

Again in 26:17-18 the antagonism of the world-power is reflected in the confession by the godly of their helplessness to prevail in the battle against the foe. In childbirth, as it were, they manage to bring forth only wind (vv. 17-18*ab*). They acknowledge: "Victory we cannot achieve (*na'āseh*) on the earth; the inhabitants of the earth do not fall" (v. 18*cd*).[67]

But what God's people cannot achieve for themselves He accomplishes for them: "Every achievement in our behalf (*ma'āsênû*) you have accomplished for us" (26:12). The section on their powerlessness to overcome the enemy (26:16-18) leads at once into the closing prophecy of the resurrection as the Lord's redemptive triumph, vindicating His people over against the world-power (26:19 ff.).

One subtle device tying the resurrection announced in 26:19 to the preceding description of the saints' battle with the world-power (v. 18) is the double use of the verb *npl*, "fall,"[68] to highlight the contrast being drawn. In verse 18*d* the godly lament their inability to make their enemies "fall" dead in battle. Then in verse 19 God is said to make His dew "fall" on the dead, bringing them to life.

Renderings of verse 19 as though it continued the figure of childbirth (v. 18*ab*) are unacceptable. The figure has meanwhile shifted in verse 18*c* to that of military salvation or victory. Moreover, *npl* is not attested elsewhere in biblical Hebrew for childbirth, whereas it is used for battle casualties (cf. Num. 14:29; Jer. 9:21). Also, consistently in this context "the inhabitants of the world" are the wicked foe (cf. esp. vv. 9, 21).

Again, to interpret *tpyl* in verse 19*b* as "give birth," with "earth" as subject, is to undo the parallelism between verses 19*c* and 19*d* and particularly to lose the obvious relationship, both sonant and semantic, between *tappîl* and *ṭal*, "dew." For the use of *npl* for the falling of dew on the ground see 2 Samuel 17:12. Therefore verse 19*cd* should read: "For the dew of dawn[69] is your [God's] dew, and on the land[70] of the shades you make it fall."[71] The "land of the shades" continues the focus of verse 19*ab* on "the dwellers in the dust," the martyred saints called "your [God's] dead." Restored by God's revivifying dew, they sing in the exultation of their vindication.

Most directly and emphatically the retribution-vindication aspect of the resurrection of the martyrs is expressed in 26:21. God's decisive intervention will take the form of a descent from His heavenly Temple (v. 21*a*; cf. Mic. 1:3) for the purpose of exacting recompense (v. 21*b*), and that with immediate reference to the appeal of martyrs' blood revealed (v. 21*c*) and the witness of God's slain released from the grave (v. 21*d*).

Once and again in Isaiah 24-26 the city is used as a figure for the hostile world-power. Judgment is in store for this city (24:10-12; 25:2, 12; 26:5-6) and its kings (24:22; 26:5, 14). In the case of both the city (25:12; 26:5-6) and its proud citizenry (26:5), these prophecies of final retribution are couched in the imagery of the primeval curse on the serpent (Gen. 3:14-15), the humbling in the dust and the trampling under foot. Isaiah thus anticipates the apostle John's theme of the dragonlike beast sharing the dragon's doom. He makes the same point more explicitly in his prophecy of the powers in the heavens and the kings on earth imprisoned together in the pit (24:21-22).

Perhaps the delineation of the judgment of the world-city is intended to conjure up the netherworld scene. The realm of the dead was conceptualized as a city with its entrance gates (cf. 24:12),[72] and various characteristic features of the netherworld appear in the picture of the devastated world-city in chapters 24-26. It is a joyless desolation (24:7-12),[73] an eternal[74] ruin (25:2),[75] laid low in the dust (25:12; 26:5-6).[76] On this interpretation the world-city is mocked with the irony of its downfall. It conspired with the prince of death to usurp the status of Zion, heavenly city of life, but it ends up as a necropolis, the netherworld city of the dead.[77]

From this land of no return the persecutors of the saints do not arise (26:14; cf. 24:20).[78] The contrast between their fate and the resurrection affirmed for the martyrs (26:19) underscores the vindicatory nature of the latter.

In sum, then, according to Isaiah 24-26 an army of enemies is associated with death in warfare against the saints, but divine vengeance will befall them all on the day of resurrection. A similar perspective informs Paul's teaching on the resurrection: Death is "the last enemy" to be abolished by Christ in a process that involves His putting "all His enemies under His feet" (1 Cor. 15:25-26).

INVITATION TO THE MARTYRS

Even before death is ultimately abolished, it undergoes for the martyr-people an intermediate transformation. In the light of their coming resurrection-vindication, death assumes for them a different face. It becomes something that can be welcomed. The language of invitation becomes appropriate for it: "Come, my people, enter into your inner rooms and close your doors about you. Hide yourselves for a brief moment, until the wrath has passed by" (Isa. 26:20). The term *ḥeder*, "inner room," used for private rooms like the bedchamber, is combined with death in Proverbs 7:27: "the chambers of death."[79] The house or room, particularly a sleeping chamber, is a natural image, elsewhere attested, for Sheol.[80] Certainly then the invitation of Isaiah 26:20, embedded as it is in a context of death and resurrection, is to be understood as welcoming God's people into the inner room of death, as into a sanctuary.

Quite clearly Isaiah is alluding to the enclosure of the Noahic family within the ark-house[81] for their passage through the waters of death. In the flood narrative Noah receives an invitation from God to enter[82] the virtual burial chamber (Gen. 7:1). There is a fastening of the door behind the occupants (Gen. 7:26).[83] The ark as burial room functions as a refuge until the time of wrath on the hostile world-power has passed.[84] Meanwhile the occupants of the ark anticipate their eventual resurrection-exit and the perfecting of their vindication.

According to Isaiah 26:20 death for the redeemed has been radically altered, from confining covering to covert.[85] This same view of the death of the righteous is expressed in 57:1-2. There it is seen as a gathering away from evil and an entering into peace and rest.[86] Sheol's repute as an "eternal house" is refuted by the interim character and indeed relative brevity attributed to its continuance in 26:20. Implicit in the temporal limit of "a brief moment" is the hope of the resurrection, when all the enemies have been abolished and there is no longer need for the refuge provided by death.[87] Meanwhile death has lost its terror. The great enemy is obliged to serve the saints as a friend. Yahweh's triumph over Mot has begun.

Subsequent biblical revelation concerning death reflects quite specifically the Isaianic disclosures, with the perception of death as a veritable blessing and the invitation to experience it as a temporary sanctuary until the resurrection-vindication.

In Daniel 12:13 the invitation, "Come my people," of Isaiah 26:20 is made individually personal. Daniel is invited: "As for you, come!"[88] Under discussion in the context are the persecution of the covenant people and the ultimate resurrection of glory for "the wise." The invitation is immediately preceded by a beatitude pronounced on those who wait in faith for the time of deliverance. That Daniel's invitation does indeed contemplate his death becomes evident once the verse is properly punctuated. "Until the end you shall rest.[89] And then at the end of the days you will stand [or arise] in your allotted inheritance."[90] In the first instance, as in the second, "the end" refers to a historical climax of collective eschatology, not to the individual end of Daniel.[91] It is rather the verb "rest" that refers to his death, in agreement with the earlier Isaianic assessment of the death of the godly.[92]

A series of passages in the book of Revelation presents again this distinctly Isaianic perspective on the death of the righteous: 2:10; 6:9-11; 14:13; 20:4-6.[93] In all these passages the godly are viewed as under persecution. The beast power, or even the devil himself, appears in the nearby contexts. But the saints are faithful unto death, and their martyr blood cries out for avenging.[94] Also, the intermediate state of death is perceived as a royal sabbatical resting until the historical strife is over.[95] This interval of waiting will be short.[96] And finally, the continuity of John, the New Testament seer, with Isaiah, the Old Testament prophet, is exhibited in their common portrayal of death as having been fundamentally changed for the redeemed of the Lord. In Revelation 20:4-6 this transformation is expressed by identifying the Christian's death as "the first resurrection."[97]

NOTES

1. The form-critical assessment expressed by this label is disputed, other genres (including cantata) being proposed.
2. At the close, however, the focus seems to widen (cf. 27:13).
3. Isa. 24:1—27:1 and 27:2-13 are alike in their eschatological extension to the final divine advent.
4. The customary chapter partitioning (except for the separation of 27:1 from chap. 26) appropriately marks the main divisions.
5. Within chap. 25 itself this passage stands in the center between two confessional sections (vv. 1-5; 9-12).
6. Isa. 5:14 speaks of Sheol making wide its throat (or enlarging its appetite) and opening its mouth without limit to engulf the multitudes descending therein. In the Ugaritic texts Mot, the god of death, is similarly described (*UT* 67, i 6-7). Cf. also Ex. 15:12; Num. 16:30, 32, 34; 26:10; Deut. 11:6; Ps. 106:17; Prov. 1:12; Hab. 2:5.
7. It is particularly as the consuming theophanic fire that God is the devourer (cf. e.g. Ex. 24:17; Deut. 4:24; 9:3; Ps. 21:9 [MT 10]; Isa. 29:6; 30:27, 30).
8. Announcements of God's judgments on His enemies frequently involve such radical reversals. The evil that they have purposed or perpetrated boomerangs against them.
9. Variations on this image recur as a kind of leitmotiv of the haunting presence of death throughout this composition.
10. Use of the dragon-conflict pattern for the Exodus history in poetic portions of the Bible is well known.
11. Cf. the use of *lwt* in 1 Sam. 21:9 (MT 10); 1 Kings 19:13.
12. Some take it as a mourning veil, others as the net by which death ensnares its victims, a widely attested image.
13. Cf. Hab. 2:5; Josh. 23:14.
14. The "face" of the shroud in Isa. 25:7 might also allude to the face-portraits on mummy cases and on coffins with anthropoid lids.
15. To be judged to eat dust forever was for the serpent to be cursed with death. But Yahweh's swallowing of the earth-cover of death and the grave is a banquet of resurrection life forever, a devouring-death of death. Anticipating this eschatological banquet is the sacramental supper of the Lord, in which a feasting on Christ's death celebrates His victory of life.

16. Cf. also 2 Tim. 1:10.

17. Cf. Meredith G. Kline, "The First Resurrection," *WTJ* 37 (1975):366-75.

18. Jer. 51:34 combines the imagery of Isa. 24:1-3; 25:6-8 in one picture of destruction in terms of devouring, monster-like swallowing, filling the maw, and emptying a vessel.

19. Nominal derivatives of these two verbs appear as synonyms in Nah. 2:10 (MT 11), a passage descriptive of the judgment of Nineveh, which has just been likened to a pool draining away (v. 8 [MT 9]). Also the emptying process in both passages is equated with a plundering (*bzz*) of the plunderer (Isa. 24:3; Nah. 2:9 [MT 10]). Cf. Jer. 48:11-12.

20. The word *'ereṣ* does not thereby denote two entirely distinct entities. It is rather that the earth as the receptacle and covering of the dead becomes functionally the grave or netherworld as one aspect of its total historical identity.

21. A parallel phrase in 26:19 is "the dwellers (*šōkĕnê*) of the dust," an equivalent of "its [the netherworld's] inhabitants (*yōšĕbêhā*)" in 24:1.

22. Cf. Ps. 38:6 (MT 7).

23. On the possible resumption of this concept of the face of the earth in 25:7 see above. The Sumerian myth *Inanna's Descent to the Netherworld* (117, 123) refers to an entrance gate Ganzir, called the "face" of the netherworld. The familiar imagery of the gates of death is found in Isa. 38:10. Cf. Ps. 9:13-14 (MT 14-15); Matt. 16:18; Rev. 1:18.

24. Similarly in Rev. 20:12 "the great and the small" indicates the totality of the dead who are delivered up by death and Hades and the sea to stand before the judgment throne (cf. also 19:18). The appearance of the sea with death and Hades in 20:13 is one of numerous instances of the conceptualization of death as the waters of the deep. This identification of the netherworld with the waters of the sea perhaps contributed to Isaiah's imaging of death as a bottle or skin whose liquid contents are to be poured out. Conceivably Rev. 20:12-13 reflects such an understanding of Isa. 24:1-3. Cf. B. F. Batto, "The Reed Sea: Requiescat in Pace," *JBL* 102 (1983):27-35; "Red Sea or Reed Sea?" *BAR* 10/4 (1984):57-63.

25. Nevertheless the resurrection experience means different things for the godly and the wicked, as appears in the perspective of 25:6-8; 26:19ff. In the language of Rev. 20, what is the second resurrection for those written in the book of life is the second death for those who are not.

26. On this see further below.

27. See Num. 35:33; Ps. 106:38.

28. The use of *nĕbēlâ*, "corpse," in 26:19 echoes *nābĕlâ*, "it [the earth] withers (or dies)," in 24:4. The verb *nābēl* contributes to the alliterative quality of 24:4, but its choice there was probably also prompted by the preceding imagery of the emptied pitcher (cf. *nēbel*, "skin bottle") and the following motif of the silenced music (cf. *nēbel*, a musical instrument).

29. A similar combination of ideas and imagery is found in Hos. 13:13-14.

30. Whatever wider reality might be suggested by "the whole creation" (Rom. 8:22), the critical element in the idea is the earth's character as grave of the saints. If one is not persuaded that the earth's groaning in Rom. 8:21 is specifically due to its entombment of the martyr-righteous, preferring still to see this verse as a reflection on Gen. 3:17 (i.e., as a general curse affecting all mankind), then it must at least be recognized that that curse consists particularly in the reversal of the earth's original subservient relationship to mankind whereby man now is overpowered by the earth and ultimately reduced to the condition of "dust unto dust" (Gen. 3:19).

31. See vv. 42, 50.

32. Note particularly the quotation of Isa. 25:8 in 1 Cor. 15:54. Verse 55 continues with a quotation from Hos. 13:14, which falls within a section of Hosea's prophecy where extensive interdependence with Isa. 26-27 has been noted. See n. 29 above and J. Day, "A Case of Inner Scriptural Interpretation: The Dependence of Isaiah 26:13 —27:11 on Hosea 13:4—14:10 (Eng. 9) and Its Relevance to Some Theories of the Redaction of the 'Isaiah Apocalypse,' " *JTS* 31 (1980):309-19.

33. In Rom. 8:19 the "revealing (*apokalypsis*) of the sons of God" for which creation waits is customarily identified as the manifestation of the saints with Christ in glory; cf., e.g., Col. 3:4. But discovery of the relation of Rom. 8 to Isa. 24-26 and of its concern with the earth's deliverance from profanation through the corruption of death suggests that the *apokalypsis* is the emergence of the righteous from their concealment in the earth (as in Isa. 26:21), the uncovering that is the prelude to the manifestation in glory. Cf. J. Plevnik, "The Taking Up of the Faithful and the Resurrection of the Dead in 1 Thessalonians 4:13-18," *CBQ* 46 (1984):274-83.

34. For a recent representative statement see L. R. Bailey, Sr., *Biblical Perspectives on Death* (Philadelphia: Fortress, 1979), p. 53. He insists that, apart from the possible exception of Gen. 2-3, mortality is not associated in the OT with guilt and punishment.

35. Cf. Gen. 4:10-11; Job 16:18; Rev. 6:9-11; 8:3 ff.; 11:18; 19:2.

36. Isa. 27:1 continues the judgment theme of 26:21 (note *pqd*, "punish," in both verses). Together the two verses deal with the final judgment of the evil occupants of both earth and heaven. Cf. 24:21-22. "In that day" in 27:1 forms an *inclusio* with 26:1. (It is a question whether the same phrase at the beginning of 27:2 introduces the following vineyard song, as is likely, or possibly belongs with 27:1.)

37. Isa. 27:1 closely resembles a passage in a mythological text from Ugarit (*UT* 67, i 1-3). Such mythological use of the dragon figure is a corruption of the tradition of the serpent-agent of Satan in the fall episode. In biblical texts like Isa. 27:1 the dragon imagery is a demythologized, poetic adaptation.

38. This characterization of the devil is explained by his critical role in the entrance of sin into the world, through which death also found entrance. Moreover a continuing agency of Satan in the infliction of death is suggested in Job 2:6 (and, on one interpretation, in 1 Cor. 5:5).

39. Note the parallelism of death and Belial in Ps. 18:4 (MT 5) and 2 Sam. 22:5. Belial (or Beliar) is used for Satan in 2 Cor. 6:15. This is of special interest for this Isaiah context. If *blyy'l* is derived from *bl'*, "swallow," cf. Isa. 25:7-8. If it is explained as *bly* plus *'lh*, "none comes up," cf. 26:14. In Job 7:9 *lō' ya'āleh* describes the one who descends into Sheol. Isa. 26:14 uses *qwm*, not *'lh*, but in Ps. 41:8 (MT 9) *qwm* with negative stands parallel to *blyy'l*.

40. Behind this usage is probably the judicial surveillance conducted by Satan with a view to his accusing function, as in Job 1:7 and 2:2.

41. Cf. *UT* 67, ii 1-3.

42. See e.g. Pss. 10:9; 17:12; 35:17, 25; cf. 5:9 (MT 19); 124:3-6.

43. Cf. e.g. Pss. 31:8 (MT 9); 61:3 (MT 4). For a survey of the evidence in the Psalms adduced by M. Dahood for death as the foe see N. J. Tromp, *Primitive Conceptions of Death and the Nether World in the Old Testament* (Rome: Pontifical Biblical Institute, 1969), pp. 110-19.

44. The verb *pqd*, "punish," used in the first colon of v. 21 is repeated at the close of v. 22 as an *inclusio*. Hence the same judgment is in view in each case. "After many days" (v. 22*b*) is equivalent to "in that day" (v. 21*a*).

45. "Before his elders will be the Glory" (v. 23). After the introduction (24:1-3) two sections on earth's desolation (vv. 4-13; 16*b*-22) alternate with two brief sections describing the final epiphany and the response thereto (vv. 14-16*a*; 23). Verses 14-16*a* form an intricate chiasm produced by lexical and morphological pairings. In the terminal parts of the chiasm the eschatological theophany is denoted as the Majesty (*g'wn*) and the Beauty (*ṣby*), in the middle parts as the Name (Yahweh). The Glory (*kbwd*) of v. 23 is the corresponding reference to the Parousia in the second epiphany section. Further on in 24:15 the *'l-kn* is perhaps to be taken as a divine title, "the Most High, the Upright." Following a suggestion of L. Viganò, W. H. Irwin argues for this in "The Punctuation of Isaiah 24:14-16*a* and 25:4*c*-5," *CBQ* 46 (1984):215-19. A chiastic structuring is, however, still preferable to Irwin's overall stichometric analysis.

46. A question arises as to the relation of the imprisonment in 24:22*a* and the binding of Satan in Rev. 20:2-3. If that imprisonment is equated with the judicial intervention announced in v. 21 and again in v. 22*b*, then it will not correspond to the thousand-year confinement of the devil in Rev. 20:2-3 but to his subsequent eternal doom (20:10). If, however, the imprisonment of v. 22*a* is understood as pluperfect with respect to the judgment of v. 21 (and thus too as preliminary to the same judgment as mentioned again in v. 22*b*), it would then be equivalent to Rev. 20:2-3, and the "many days" could correspond to the "thousand years." In this case the subject of the imprisonment might better be viewed as only the demonic host, not the earthly kings. The word *bôr*, "pit," often used as a synonym of Sheol, also denotes a place of confinement and torment for demons. See Luke 8:31 (cf. Matt. 8:29); Rev. 9:1, 2, 11; 11:7; 17:8; 20:1, 3.

47. The Son of God came so that through death He might "render inoperative" him that had the power of death (Heb. 2:14) and death itself (1 Cor. 15:26; 2 Tim. 1:10).

48. It is just after a reference to Satan in terms distinctly reminiscent of 27:1 that this identification of him as the Accuser is given in Rev. 12:10. The echo of 27:1 is all the clearer if the disputed adjective *bārîaḥ* means "primeval" and thus corresponds to the "ancient" serpent of Rev. 12:9.

49. Cf. Zech. 3.

50. Context must be ignored to take this as a denial of a universal resurrection. See the discussion of 24:1-3 above and n. 78 below.

51. See Matt. 22:32; Mark 12:27; Luke 20:38; cf. John 5:21.

52. For this meaning of *hyh* see 1 Kings 17:22; 2 Kings 13:21; Job 14:14; Ezek. 37:3, 5, 6, 9, 10, 14.

53. For a recent survey of the evidence for interpreting 26:19 and context in terms of physical resurrection see F. C. Hasel, "Resurrection in the Theology of Old Testament Apocalyptic," *ZAW* 92 (1980):271-76.

54. Heb. 10:37-38 connects Isa. 26 and Hab. 2 by (apparently) introducing its citation of Hab. 2:4 with the "yet a very little while" of Isa. 26:20 (LXX). Cf. the echo of Isa. 26:11 in Heb. 10:27. Also note in Hab. 2:5 the reference to the insatiable appetite of death, devourer of all peoples, the central concern and pervasive image of Isa. 24-26. Further, the patient waiting in faith for the eschatological divine intervention encouraged in Hab. 2:3 is a major emphasis in the Isaiah passage (e.g. 25:9; 26:3, 4, 8, 9, 20).

55. Preponderantly the verb *yšr* is used in the registering of assessments. Such is also the tradition of interpretation reflected in the LXX as quoted in Heb. 10:37.

56. The function of resurrection to life as the rendering of a verdict of justification should be borne in mind in dealing with Paul's expression "justification of life" (Rom. 5:18) and his statement that Jesus "was raised for our justification" (4:25). On the principle of works in the Mosaic economy see Meredith G. Kline, "Of Works and Grace," *Presbyterion* 9 (1983):85-92.

57. See n. 42 above for the attribution to these human enemies of the same lionlike rapacity that distinguishes the devil and death.

58. What is depicted as a single judgment episode here in 24:21-22 is related twice in the book of Revelation because of the thematic arrangement of its visions: once in Rev. 19 from the perspective of the beast and kings of the earth, and a second time in Rev. 20 from the perspective of the career of Satan.

59. Pretensions to deity by mortals are repeatedly mocked by reminders of mortality. See Gen. 6:3; Isa. 14:9 ff.; Ezek. 28:9; cf. Ps. 82:7.

60. This same idea is again expressed by the verb *prs* in a similar context in Lam. 1: "The adversary has spread out his hands over all her [Jerusalem's] desirable things" (v. 10a). Interestingly, the adversary who thus profanes the sanctuary is further defined in v. 10c in terms of the law of Deut. 23:3 (MT 4) forbidding the Moabites and Ammonites to enter the assembly of the Lord. Also note Moab's involvement in the destruction of Judah (2 Kings 24:2).

61. For this same imagery elsewhere in Isaiah see 10:10, 14: 11:14.

62. In the motif of Mot's prodigious appetite, his hands figure as scoops (cf. *UT* 67, i 19-20). By them he also grasps his victims (cf. *UT* 2059, 21-22). For similar biblical references to the hands of Sheol see Ps. 89:48 (MT 49); Hos. 13:14.

63. Like *pēras* earlier in v. 11, *'orbōt* is followed by "his hands" and should be understood in a way that brings out this connection. That is achieved if one regards the noun as related to *'rb*, "lie in ambush," and as denoting plunder or prey—here the treasure that had been seized by Moab's outstretched hands. This results in a further point of likeness of this agent of death to death, for the latter is pictured as ensnaring its prey (cf. e.g. Ps. 18:5 [MT 6]). So too is the devil (2 Tim. 2:26).

64. "Yes, for the way of your judgments we call upon you, Yahweh; our soul's longing is for (the revelation of) your memorial Name. In my soul I long for you in the night; yes, in my inmost spirit I yearn for you in the morning." In vv. 8, 9b God's "judgments" are His judicial acts of deliverance. The "Name" (v. 8) is the theophanic Presence or Parousia. Note the chiastic structure with the repetitive *ta'āwat-nāpeš* (v. 8b) and *napšî 'iwwîtîkā* (v. 9a) in the center and the corresponding *'ap* clauses with their semantically matched verbs in the first and fourth cola (vv. 8a, 9b).

65. "Only when your judgments are on the earth do the inhabitants of the world learn righteousness. If the wicked is shown compassion, he does not learn righteousness; in a land of fair dealings the one who is evil does not see the majesty of Yahweh." In vv. 9d, 10a *ṣedeq* refers to God's acts of judgment. In v. 10b the *waw* of *ûbal* is emphatic with postposition of the verb. Thus understood, an excellent parallelism obtains between the two cola of v. 10. In v. 9c, W. H. Irwin reads *kĕ'aššēr* "correct, set right," instead of *kî ka'ašer*; cf. his "Syntax and Style in Isaiah 26," *CBQ* 41 (1979):246.

66. "Let there be a way of justice for the righteous, O Upright One, may you make level the path of the righteous" (v. 7) "Yahweh, let your hand be lifted high; let those who do not see see. Let them be dismayed at the fury of your forces; by the fire of your enmity consume them" (v. 11). Verse 7 is an example of the form in which the b-element is a single word (here, as often, a vocative) serving both a-sections. The first colon contains an

interrupted construct chain. Possibly *mêšārîm* refers to the concrete *mēšarum*-act. Verse 11 is a further petition for the Parousia (cf. the "hand" of God and the angelic armies). Note again the theme of Yahweh as the true devourer who consumes the hostile would-be devourers.

67. On this see further below.

68. Enhancing the *npl* wordplay in 26:18 is the use of *nēbēlâ*, "corpse" (v. 19). As observed above (n. 28) this also recalls the verb *nbl* in 24:4, another context that is concerned with death and mourning and also contains a case of paronomasia using *npl* and *nbl*. Note the use of *npl* in 24:20 (itself a parallel to 26:14).

69. On *'ôrôt* as "lights, dawn" cf. *'ūrîm*, "East" (24:15). Dawn fits well with waking from sleep (*hāqîṣû*). For the association of dew and dawn cf. Ex. 16:13; Judg. 6:38; Ps. 110:3. On resurrection and dawn cf. Hos. 6:2-3. On light and life cf. Job 3:16; 33:28; Ps. 49:19 (MT 20); 56:13 (MT 14). Whether *'ôrôt* is understood as dawn, or herbs, or (Elysian) fields (so Mitchell Dahood, *Psalms*, AB, 3 vols. [Garden City, N.Y.: Doubleday, 1966-1970], 1:222-23), the idea is that of the enlivening effect of dew.

70. Cf. above (n. 21).

71. Dahood, *Psalms*, 1:223, takes *tpyl* from the verb *nbl*: "But the land of the shades will be parched." On this basis Irwin ("Syntax," p. 258) suggests a wordplay with *tappîl* calling to mind *tabbîl*, i.e., the earth gives birth to the shades it had parched. Earlier he took *tappîl* from *pll*, "moisten": "It will moisten the land of the shades" (*Isaiah 28-33: Translation with Philological Notes*, BibOr 30 [Rome: Pontifical Biblical Institute, 1977], p. 20).

72. Cf. e.g. Ps. 9:13 (MT 14), which contrasts the gates of death with the gates of Zion (v. 14 [MT 15]), and Isa. 38:10. On Mot's city cf. *UT* 51, viii 11.

73. Cf. Ps. 73:18-19; Ezek. 26:20.

74. On the use of "eternity" for the netherworld (including its gates) in the OT and literature of the biblical world see A. Cooper, "Ps. 24:7-10: Mythology and Exegesis," *JBL* 102 (1983):37-60.

75. If MT is followed, the third colon in 25:2 should be translated: "(You have turned) the city into a palace of strangers." The *mē'îr* of the first and third cola are thus treated identically. The full pattern, "from . . . to," established in the first colon continues with ellipsis of "from" in the second colon and "to" in the third. For the role of "strangers" as desolators see v. 5 (cf. Isa. 1:7). In the Sumerian composition *Lamentation over the Destruction of Ur* (p. 289ff.) the goddess Ningal bewails the fact that a "strange city" and "strange house" have replaced her demolished dwelling. The fall of Jerusalem is bemoaned in almost identical fashion in Lam. 5:2. J. A. Emerton emends the *mē'îr* in Isa. 25:2c to *mu'ar*, hophal participle of *'rr*, translating "the palace of foreigners is destroyed" ("A Textual Problem in Isaiah 25:2," *ZAW* 89 ([1977]:72). Cf. Isa. 23:13 for *'rr* with *'armôn*, "palace," paralleled moreover by *sym* and *lĕmappēlâ*, as in 25:2ab.

76. Cf. e.g. Gen. 3:19; Job 10:9; 17:16; 21:26; 34:15; Pss. 22:15 (MT 16); 90:3. In the Akkadian myth *Descent of Ishtar to the Netherworld*, dust and clay are said to be the fare of the netherworld (obv. 8). A fate decreed there is the curse of having the "food of plows" as food (rev. 23-24). Cf. Gen. 3:14.

77. This same ironic reversal becomes a major motif in Ezekiel's prophecy of Gog (Ezek. 39:11-16). God aspires to the mount of God but must settle for the immortality of the cemetery city of Hamonah.

78. Their resurrection experience is a passage from Sheol to the second death. They do not return to their historical freedom vis-à-vis the godly. They are not present in God's eternal cosmic kingdom of life to threaten again the peace of the righteous. Cf. above the discussion of the judgment on Leviathan; cf. also nn. 25, 50.

79. Cf. *ḥdry š'wl* in 1QH x 34. In Phoenician and Punic *ḥdr* means "grave, netherworld."

80. Cf. Tromp, *Primitive*, pp. 156-59.

81. Cf. Meredith G. Kline, *Kingdom Prologue* II (privately published, 1983), pp. 105-6.

82. As in Isa. 26:20, the verb is *bw'*.

83. As in Isa. 26:20, the verbal phrase is *sgr b'd*.

84. Isa. 26:20 also recalls the securing of the Israelites behind their bloodsmeared doors in Egypt while the Lord's judgment passed through (*'br*, Ex. 12:23, as in Isa. 26:20).

85. Cf. Job 14:13-15. Job longs for Sheol as a temporary hiding place from wrath until the resurrection.

86. Cf. Pss. 36:7-12 (MT 8-13); 57:1 (MT 2).

87. Heb. 10:37, apparently citing Isa. 26:20, identifies the brief time as that still remaining until the second coming of Christ. Cf. n. 54 above.

88. As in Isa. 26:20 the imperative is *lēk*.

89. The key to the verse division is this emphatic *waw* with postposition of the verb.

90. For *gôrāl* in this sense see Judg. 1:3; Ps. 125:3; cf. Col. 1:12.

91. On *qēṣ* see also Dan. 12:4, 6, 9, noting especially the correspondence of vv. 4 and 13.

92. As in Isa. 57:2 the verb is *nwḥ*. Cf. Job 3:17.

93. Rev. 14:13; 20:6 are in the form of beatitudes. Cf. Dan. 12:12.

94. See Rev. 6:10.

95. Esp. Rev. 6:11; 14:13.

96. Esp. Rev. 6:11; cf. 2:10.

97. See Kline, "The First Resurrection." Cf. Rev. 12:11. There the martyr victims are proclaimed victors. It is in and through their faithfulness unto death that they are overcomers, secured from the second death, assured of the second resurrection (cf. Rev. 2:11).

HERBERT M. WOLF (Ph. D., Brandeis
University) is associate professor of
theological studies at Wheaton Grad-
uate School.

15

The Relationship Between Isaiah's Final Servant Song (52:13—53:12) and Chapters 1-6

Herbert M. Wolf

As a young teacher beginning my second year in the classroom, I accepted an invitation to join a translation committee chaired by Gleason Archer. During those Saturday sessions that continued for about two years, I
came to appreciate first-hand Archer's linguistic and exegetical skills.
Whatever the passage under discussion and however complicated the issues might be, he never rested until arriving at a carefully reasoned solution. Over the years I have continued to be amazed at his ability to understand and explain the Scriptures, and I shall always be grateful for the
lessons in exegetical methodology that I learned from him.

One of the books to which Archer has given close attention is Isaiah. He
contributed the chapter on Isaiah for the *Wycliffe Bible Commentary*[1] and
devoted twenty-five pages to Isaiah in *A Survey of Old Testament Introduction*.[2] In the course of his writing he has ably defended the unity of Isaiah
as a product of the eighth-century prophet. Whether one looks at subject
matter, language and style, or theological ideas, there is no need to abandon the view that one person wrote the whole book. In this brief study of
Isaiah 53 and the early chapters of the book, I hope to bolster this view.

The four servant songs of Isaiah (chaps. 42, 49, 50, 52-53) are among the most famous chapters in the book, but unquestionably the final servant song (52:13 —53:12) has received the greatest acclaim. In this climactic chapter the servant suffers unspeakable sorrow and pain in order to bear the iniquity of the world. Despised and afflicted, he was "cut off from the land of the living" (v. 8), though he had done nothing to deserve such treatment. Yet in the midst of this description of terrible suffering it is also said that the servant will be highly exalted (52:13) and will win a great victory (53:12). How can this note of triumph be reconciled with the theme of suffering?

Christians, of course, believe that the servant is a prediction of Christ, the Lamb of God, who suffered in our place and then rose from the grave. Early Jewish interpretations, reflected by such sources as the LXX and the Targum of Jonathan, tended to identify the servant with the Messiah. Under pressure from Christian apologists, however, later interpreters argued that the servant represented the nation of Israel amid its great suffering or a godly segment of that nation who played a sort of "messianic" role until the Messiah Himself would arrive. Other commentators tried to link the servant with a particular prophet, such as Jeremiah or "Deutero-Isaiah," because the prophets are sometimes called God's "servants."[3]

In the process of interpreting this servant song in light of the entire book, a number of scholars have rightly pointed out the similarity between the words "raised and lifted up" in 52:13 and the description of "the Lord seated on a throne, high and exalted" in 6:1. It is my contention that there are several other important connections between this servant song and the early chapters of Isaiah, connections that can increase our understanding of 52:13—53:12 and at the same time underscore the unity of the book. Most of these additional parallels are found in chapters 1-2, especially 1:5-6, 2:11-17, and 2:22.

THE SUFFERING OF THE SERVANT (1:5-6; 53:4-5)

Perhaps the most striking parallel between Isaiah 53 and the early part of the book is the comparison between the suffering of the servant and the pitiful condition of Israel in 1:5-6. In the opening chapter Isaiah presents a scathing indictment of Israel's sinfulness as he confronts both the leaders and the people with their hypocrisy, unfaithfulness, dishonesty, and heartlessness. Unless they repent, judgment will be inevitable. In verses 5 and 6 the nation is portrayed as an individual who has suffered a terrible beating for his rebellion and yet refuses to change. His whole body is covered with "wounds and welts and open sores" (v. 6) that need to be cleansed and bandaged. Apparently this description is a metaphor for the destruction of the land, whose cities are burned and whose fields are ruined by foreign invaders (v. 7).

Although the connection is not easily seen in translation, there are several terms in 1:5-6 that also occur in 53:4-5. One is the word "beaten" *(tukkû,* v. 5), which corresponds with *mukkê 'ĕlōhîm* ("smitten by God") in 53:4. Both terms are hophal forms from the root *nkh,* "to hit, strike down, slay." Jeremiah was beaten at the order of the chief officer of the Temple, who took exception to his preaching (Jer. 20:1-2). Because of the sins of Jeroboam, the prophet Ahijah announced that "the Lord will strike Israel," sending the nation into captivity beyond the Euphrates River (1 Kings 14:15). When Uzzah touched the Ark of the Covenant to keep it from falling, "because of his irreverent act . . . God struck him down and he died" (2 Sam. 6:7).[4] The noun *makkâ,* "wound" or "sore" (1:6), also comes from the root *nkh.*

A second term is the word *ḥŏlî,* translated "injured" in 1:5 and "suffering" and "infirmities" in 53:3-4. "Illness" is probably the most basic meaning of *ḥŏlî* (cf. 38:9), but Israel's "whole head" has become ill because of the injuries she suffered as a result of being beaten (1:5). When Isaiah says that the servant "took up our infirmities and carried our sorrows" (53:4), he is primarily referring to the sins borne by Christ. Spiritual disease is the worst illness of all, and unless a remedy can be found, the result is eternal separation from God.

A third link between the two passages is the noun *habbûrâ,* another word for "wounds" or "welts" (1:6; 53:5) that is found only in these two verses in all of the prophetic writings.[5] According to Proverbs 20:30, "blows and wounds cleanse away evil," and the worst beatings were reserved for criminals or fools (19:29; 26:3). When Christ was condemned to die, He was struck repeatedly on the head and body by the soldiers who flogged Him (Matt. 27:26; Mark 15:19; John 19:1-3).

In the light of the similarities between 1:5-6 and 53:4-5 it seems clear that the servant suffered in almost the same way as the personified nation in chapter 1. Because of its moral and spiritual collapse, Israel deserved to be in such a pitiful condition, but the servant endured that same affliction and suffering so that he might deal with the source of the problem, the sin that plagued mankind. He was considered a moral and spiritual failure in order to bring peace and healing through his wounds.

If in fact there is a close connection between Israel in chapter 1 and the servant in chapter 53, does this not indicate that the servant is the nation, as argued by many Jewish interpreters? No one would deny that the servant does equal Israel in some passages, such as 41:8-9 and 42:19. But in passages such as the four servant songs (42:1-9; 49:1-7; 50:4-11; 52:13—53:12), it seems equally clear that the servant is an individual within Israel. Like the lamb led to the slaughter, he met death and "was assigned a grave with the wicked" (53:7-9). The servant died as a substitute for the nation of Israel and for "the many" outside of Israel. Israel suffered justly for her sin and rebellion, but the servant endured even worse punishment, though he had committed no sin whatever.

After the servant has suffered and died, Isaiah says that "he will see the light (of life) and be satisfied" (*yisba'*; 53:11). The verb *sb'* also occurs in 1:11 where the Lord complains to Israel that He has "more than enough (*sāba'tî*) of burnt offerings" and that the sheer number of sacrifices will not avail as long as sin controls their hearts. Hence in 1:11 the verb means "satiate" rather than "satisfy." But what a multitude of sacrifices could not do in the first chapter, the one perfect sacrifice of Christ accomplished in chapter 53. Through His death the demands of a holy God were fully satisfied.

THE EXALTATION OF THE SERVANT (2:11-17; 6:1; 52:13)

The most famous correlation between the final servant song and the earlier portions of Isaiah is the use of the verbs *rûm* and *nāsā'* in 52:13 and 6:1. Often overlooked, however, are the occurrences of these verbs in 2:12-14, along with the use of words derived from the verb *gābah*, a third word for "exalt" that is also found in 52:13. In each of these five instances as well as in 57:15, *rûm* precedes *nāsā'*. Outside of Isaiah *rûm* refers to God as exalted over the nations (Pss. 46:11; 99:2) or above the heavens (Pss. 57:5, 11; 113:4). Although there is some question whether "high and exalted" (Isa. 6:1) refers to the Lord or to the throne on which He is seated, the former interpretation is favored by the reference to "the high and lofty One" who speaks in 57:15. Likewise, it is the servant who "will be raised and lifted up and highly exalted" in 52:13.

In chapter 2 Isaiah contrasts the majesty of God with the pride and arrogance of men. The day of the Lord will bring terror and judgment against the nations and their proud leaders, and "the Lord alone will be exalted in that day" (2:11, 17). In three consecutive verses (12-14) the verbs *rûm* and *nāsā'* are applied to those who oppose God. They are called "the proud and lofty," those who are "exalted" and in need of humbling (v. 12). In 13 the cedars of Lebanon are "tall and lofty" *(hārāmîm wĕhannissā'îm)*, and these cedars are most likely a symbol of the kings and armies of Assyria (cf. 10:18, 33-34) that would be devastated by the Lord in 701 B.C. (cf. 37:36-38). The same pair of adjectives describes "the towering mountains" and "the high hills" (v. 14), probably another reference to the nations brought low before the Lord (cf. 41:15).

The "lofty tower" (v. 15) uses the adjective *gābôah*, derived from the same root *(gābah)* as the word for "pride" *(gābût)* found in verses 11 and 17; see also the word "proud" *(gē'eh)* used in verse 12. Chapter 5 also speaks of "the eyes of the arrogant" (v. 15) that will be brought low when "the Lord Almighty will be exalted by His justice" (v. 16). "Exalted" is an imperfect from the root *gābah*.

Like the other words for "high" and "lifted up," *gābah* and its derivatives have the connotation of "pride" and "arrogance" when used of men but of "exaltation" and "majesty" when used of God. Because God does not share His glory with others, the "day of the Lord" will bring judgment to mankind and put an end to man's proud ways. The creation must not usurp the place of the Creator.[6]

The majesty and holiness of God are graphically described in chapter 6, where Isaiah saw a vision of the sovereign Lord "seated on a throne, high and exalted." Overwhelmed by his own sin, Isaiah cried out in awe because he had seen "the King, the Lord Almighty" (v. 5). It is understandable why the words "high and exalted" are used in the glorious setting of chapter 6, but it is more difficult to explain their presence in 52:13 with reference to the servant who is about to endure humiliation and death. And 52:13 contains a third word for exaltation *(gābah)* that is not even found in chapter 6, although it does occur in 5:16 and its derivatives in 2:11, 15, 17. In a remarkable way the exaltation of the servant is closely compared with the glory of God Himself.

According to Claus Westermann, the success and exaltation of the servant can best be understood from the results of his suffering in 53:11-12. By his atoning death he will effect righteousness for many and will remove the curse of sin.[7] In 52:7-10 the prophet has spoken about the good news of Israel's release from captivity, and this note of joy leads into the final servant song in 52:13. In Romans 10:15 Paul quotes Isaiah 52:7 as he connects the good news of salvation with the work of Christ, and in Philippians 2:8-9 the apostle states that after Christ "became obedient to death . . . God exalted Him to the highest place." On the day of Pentecost Peter linked the resurrection of Christ to His exaltation to the Father's right hand (Acts 2:32-33). So whether attention is focused on the sovereign "Lord seated on a throne" (Isa. 6:1) or the victorious servant "raised and lifted up and highly exalted" (52:13), the similarity in expression is marvelous. Does this not indicate that one writer was at work in both places, using the same vocabulary to present his message? The suffering servant fully deserved this exaltation, but those human leaders who in pride and arrogance exalted themselves over nations and empires will be humbled and brought low (2:11-17). They too were considered to be "high" and "lofty," but their glory would fade quickly and God alone would be exalted.

THE REJECTION OF THE SERVANT (2:22; 53:3)

The final parallel to be noted between Isaiah 53 and the early chapters of the book is undoubtedly the least known, partially because translations obscure the connection. Yet it may be significant that both 2:22 and 53:3 contain forms of the same two verbs, *ḥādal* and *ḥāšab*, and this is the only place in the Old Testament (except for Job 19:14-15) where these verbs occur in such close proximity. In 53:3 the two words are translated "rejected" and "esteemed" respectively, and each occurs in conjunction with the strong opposition faced by the servant: "He was despised and rejected by men" and "he was despised, and we esteemed him not." The verb "despised" *(nibzeh)* is used in Daniel 11:21 to describe Antiochus IV Epiphanes, the Seleucid ruler who desecrated the Temple and tried to wipe out Judaism in a series of actions that precipitated the Maccabean revolt in 165 B.C. To this day Antiochus is ranked among the worst of the anti-Semitic persecutors. The plight of the servant can also be compared with the suffering of Job, who laments, "My kinsmen have gone away" *(ḥādĕlû,* 19:14), and "My guests and my maidservants count me a stranger" *(taḥšĕbûnî,* 19:15). Convinced that Job had been struck down by the hand of God because of his sin, both friends and relatives abandoned him (also cf. 19:19-21). In Isaiah 53:4 the suffering servant was likewise considered to be "stricken by God."

The close similarities between the experience of Job and the servant give credence to the traditional translation "rejected by men" in 53:3 for *ḥādal ʾîšîm.* In this phrase *ḥādal* is a construct form of the verbal adjective *ḥādēl,* and there is some question as to whether it should be understood in an active or passive sense. D. Winton Thomas, for instance, follows Driver in arguing that the servant is forsaking the company of men, staying aloof from men.[8] This interpretation lies behind the translation "He shrank from the sight of men" (NEB). Most interpreters support the passive sense of "rejected" or "forsaken" by men, even though BDB arrives at this translation as a development of the idea of "lacking men."[9] The verb *ḥādal* literally means "to cease," as in Isaiah 1:16 ("Stop doing wrong") or 24:8 ("The noise of the revelers has stopped").[10] Most likely the idea is that men have given up on the servant; they will have nothing to do with him, and hence he is "rejected by men." In their estimation he should be ignored and despised.

Turning now to Isaiah 2:22, it is to be noted that the thrust of the verse seems to be diametrically opposed to 53:3, even though the same vocabulary is employed. Once again the verb *ḥādal* cannot be translated easily, for a literal rendering would result in "Cease *(ḥidlû)* from man." To capture the idiom the translations use a variety of expressions: "Turn away from man" (RSV); "Trust no more in man" (JB); "Have no more to do with man" (NEB); "Let man alone" (NAB); "Stop regarding man" (NASB); "Stop trusting in man" (NIV). The reason why man cannot be trusted lies in his mortality. He "has but a breath in his nostrils. Of what account is he?" *(neḥšāb)*. Apparently Israel was putting her trust in princes rather than in God (Ps. 146:3). But proud and lofty men will be brought low by the judgment of God (Isa. 2:12). Too often Israel sought the assistance of the mighty leaders of Assyria or Egypt only to be sadly disappointed (cf. 30:1-3). If she puts her trust in her own officials or warriors, the prophet warns that God will soon take away all her leaders, probably by death or deportation (cf. 3:1-4).

One Jewish community that took this verse seriously was the separatist group at Qumran that produced the famous Dead Sea scrolls. Isaiah was one of the most popular books at Qumran, and perhaps this explains why 2:22 caught the separatists' attention. In 1QS v 17 this verse is cited in a section that encourages separation "from all the men of falsehood who walk in the way of wickedness."[11] Such men are not part of the covenant and are destined to face the wrath and vengeance of God. Just one line before the quotation of Isaiah 2:22, 1QS cites Exodus 23:7 with its exhortation to "keep far away from every false matter," and this is also interpreted to mean that any contact with the wicked must be avoided.[12] As is usually the case, the Qumran interpreters do not pay much attention to the context of either Exodus 23 or Isaiah 2, but the application they make is not totally out of line.

Ironically the warning of Isaiah 2:22 did not apply to the servant of chapter 53. If ever there was a man who should have been trusted and highly esteemed, it was the Son of Man who came as a light to the nations and to establish justice on earth. Here was no arrogant, self-centered tyrant but the very "Prince of Peace" Himself. And He was the one who had participated with the Father in breathing into man's nostrils "the breath of life" (Gen. 2:7). He was the Creator of life, and no man could take His life from Him unless He laid it down of His own accord (John 10:18). How powerful the Messiah was, and how thoroughly trustworthy! Yet He was openly and decisively rejected by His own people and sent to an ignominious death upon the cross.

CONCLUSION

The study of similarities between Isaiah 52:13 —53:12 and the early chapters of the book could be expanded to include a comparison between the messianic title "the Root of Jesse" in 11:10 and the description of the servant as "a root out of dry ground" in 53:2.[13] A number of verses from chapters 4, 9, and 11 speak of a king from the line of David who in several respects is like the servant of the Lord in Isaiah 42-53. These similarities between widely separated areas of the book strengthen the view that all of Isaiah came from the hand of the prophet himself. As Gleason Archer has written, "the Holy One of Israel" as a title "occurs frequently throughout Isaiah and only five times elsewhere in the Old Testament," and this one fact alone is "a sort of authoritative seal for all of his writing."[14] When one examines the other similarities between the various parts of the book, one is driven to the conclusion that Isaiah possesses remarkable unity and is not the product of two or more authors writing in different centuries.

NOTES

1. Gleason L. Archer, Jr., *Wycliffe Bible Commentary*, ed. C. F. Pfeiffer and E. F. Harrison (Chicago: Moody, 1962), pp. 605-54.

2. Gleason L. Archer, Jr., *SOTI* (Chicago: Moody, 1974), pp. 326-51.

3. Cf. Isa. 20:3; Jer. 25:4; Walther Zimmerli, *TDNT*, 5:676; Joseph A. Alexander, *Commentary on the Prophecies of Isaiah* (Grand Rapids: Zondervan, 1953), 2:285-86; F. Duane Lindsey, *The Servant Songs* (Chicago: Moody, 1985), pp. 11-16.

4. *TWOT*, s.v. *"makkâ,"* by Marvin R. Wilson, 2:578.

5. R. Margolioth, *The Indivisible Isaiah* (New York: Yeshiva U., 1964), p. 166.

6. Edward J. Young, *The Book of Isaiah*, 3 vols. (Grand Rapids: Eerdmans, 1965-72), 1:125-26.

7. Claus Westermann, *Isaiah 40-66* (London: SCM, 1969), p. 256.

8. D. Winton Thomas, "Some Observations on the Hebrew Root *Ḥādal*," *VTSup* 4 (1957):11.

9. BDB, p. 293.

10. BDB, pp. 292-93; *TWOT*, s.v. *"hādal,"* by E. Yamauchi, 1:264-65.

11. G. Vermes, *The Dead Sea Scrolls in English* (Baltimore: Penguin, 1968), p. 79.

12. P. Wernberg-Möller, *The Manual of Discipline* (Grand Rapids: Eerdmans, 1957), p. 28.

13. Cf. H. Wolf, *Interpreting Isaiah: The Suffering and Glory of the Messiah* (Grand Rapids: Zondervan, 1985).

14. Archer, *SOTI*, p. 345.

Rüdiger Pfeil (Ph. D. candidate, Wycliffe College, University of Toronto) is professor of Old Testament, Seminario Evangelico Asociado in Venezuela.

16

When Is a *Gôy* a "Goy"?
The Interpretation of Haggai 2:10-19

Rüdiger Pfeil

It has been Gleason Archer's privilege to challenge many theories accepted by a large proportion of modern scholars. His legal background makes him intolerant of insufficient evidence or inconsistencies in argumentation, and his extensive knowledge of ancient Semitic languages makes it possible for him to seek his own and sometimes new solutions to problems of Old Testament interpretation. It is my hope that this short case-history of the interpretation of Haggai 2:10-19 may serve to encourage similar challenges to the theological establishment.

In the fall of 520 B.C., eighteen years after the edict of Cyrus permitted the return of the Judahites to their native land, Haggai and Zechariah proclaimed their messages. The major focus of Haggai's prophecies was the reconstruction of the Temple. The people responded well to his messages so that the building began. When the foundation walls (Ezra 6:4) were finished a special ceremony was held. On this occasion Haggai pronounced the message of Haggai 2:10-14 concerning holiness. It received attention during our century because of Johann Wilhelm Rothstein's interpretation that considered it the basis of the split between Jews and Samaritans.[1]

This review of the history of interpretation of the text in recent scholarship intends not only to show how, in my view, the text ought to be interpreted but also to warn of the dangers of basing one's interpretation on theological theories instead of investigating the biblical sources themselves in a scholarly fashion.

Traditionally there have been four approaches to the text: (1) ceremonial, (2) ethical, (3) allegorical, and (4) a combination of all three.

The ceremonial interpretation takes the text literally as a discussion about the sanctity of sacrifices and service in the Temple. In the Talmud[2] this point of view is driven to a legalistic extreme with a debate on the correctness of the priest's answer. It is based on the idea that Haggai tested the priests to see whether they remembered the law correctly after the Exile. For Julius Wellhausen the issue is the degree of holiness (understood as ceremonial worship).[3] There is too much secular life, and there is too little service at the provisional altar. More holiness (or ceremonial worship) is needed, making the completion of the Temple construction urgent.

Many interpreters identify holiness and ethical behavior. They assume that the judgment in Haggai 2:14 addresses some transgression, such as a lack of cooperation in the Temple construction[4] or some other sinful action. Already the writers of the LXX added the following comments to the text: "Because of their unjust gains in the morning, they shall suffer pain from their labors. And you hate those who reprove in [the court of] the gate" (Hag. 2:14 [LXX]; cf. Amos 5:10).

A few scholars treat the text as an allegory. Then every element of the discussion in Haggai 2:10-14 is only a symbol for the real meaning. T. André's commentary may serve as an example for various possibilities. The man bearing holy meat is Israel, the garment represents Palestine, the skirt Jerusalem. The holy meat is identified with the altar, bread with products of the soil. In the second part Israel is symbolized by the defiled man, and the corpse stands for the ruined Temple. Accordingly the meaning is that the altar sanctified the land but not its products, whereas the ruined Temple defiled the sacrifices offered on the temporary altar.[5]

John Calvin combines the ceremonial interpretation with the doctrine of original sin. It is not enough to offer sacrifices and build the Temple unless it is done rightly. "Whatever we touch is polluted by us, except there be a real purity of heart to sanctify our works."[6] All our works are corrupt before God, "but when God purifies our hearts by faith, then our works begin to be approved."[7]

All these interpretations have in common that they consider Judah to be the people referred to in verse 4 and that they do not propose any major changes in the text of Haggai. This was drastically changed with the publication of Rothstein's booklet about Haggai.

ROTHSTEIN'S THESIS

Rothstein interpreted Haggai 2:10-14 on the basis of a comparison with Ezra 4:1-5. This he could do only after rearranging the historical setting of the first chapters of Ezra.[8]

According to the biblical text, the Jews were given permission in the first year of Cyrus, king of Persia, to return to their home country to reconstruct the Temple in Jerusalem (Ezra 1). Vessels from the first Temple were returned by the Persians to Sheshbazzar. Shortly after their arrival in Jerusalem the group of returnees began the construction of an altar (3:1-7) and laid the foundations of the Temple under the leadership of Jeshua (Joshua) and Zerubbabel (3:8-13). However, the work was stopped by people who are called the enemies of Judah (4:1) or "people of the land" (4:4). According to the biblical record, all these events took place shortly after the beginning of the reign of Cyrus (538 B.c.). Ezra 4:24 reports that the work on the Temple ceased until the second year of Darius (520). Then Haggai and Zechariah, by their prophecies, caused a new start of the building activities on Mount Zion (5:1-2). In spite of new adversities (5:3—6:12) the sanctuary was rebuilt and could be dedicated about four years later (6:13-22).

Rothstein accepts the historicity of Ezra 1 but changes the historical references in the following three chapters to make them agree with his theory.[9]

Already in an earlier work[10] he had developed the thesis that Sheshbazzar was the father of Zerubbabel and that the first attempt to build the Temple in 538/7 B.c. failed when Sheshbazzar fell victim to a denunciation before the Persian authorities. Rothstein rejects the idea that Sheshbazzar and Zerubbabel could be the same person and divides the first (537) and second (520) beginnings of the Temple construction between the two personalities. He arrives at the conclusion that Ezra 3-4 does not refer to the first event but to the second.[11] His reasoning here is circular: He bases his understanding of Ezra 4 on his particular interpretation of Haggai 1:10-14 and at the same time uses Ezra 4 as the basis for his understanding of the text in Haggai.[12]

Rothstein interprets the two passages as follows. The enemies of Judah and Benjamin, who are mostly Samaritans according to Ezra 4:17-23,[13] want to participate in the construction of the Temple (4:1-2). Because the priests do not take a firm position on the matter, Haggai proclaims the decision of the Lord, which declares those people unclean and unfit for participation in any type of service or worship on Mount Zion.[14] In other words, Haggai's judgment in Haggai 2:14 receives a new interpretation. Whereas before Rothstein "this people and this nation" was thought to refer to Judah as indicated by the context in Haggai, Rothstein makes it refer to the Samaritans, considering it in the context of Ezra 4.[15] As a result of Haggai's severe judgment, the Jewish leader Zerubbabel must have taken courage to reject the request of the Samaritans as reported in 4:3. The following intimidation by the Samaritans then necessitated words of encouragement to Zerubbabel (Hag. 2:20-23).

Among many very detailed arguments we see eight main reasons[16] for his conclusion that the people of Haggai 2:14 are not the Jews but the Samaritans.

1. There is no connection between 2:10-14 and verses 15-19.[17] Though it is clear that verses 15-19 refer to the Jews, this does not have to be the case in the former verses once they are separated.

2. The content of Haggai 2:10-14 does not indicate what could have caused Haggai to criticize the people harshly after they had been willing to participate in the construction.

3. It is not likely that the enthusiasm of the people who had begun the construction would have decreased so much that Haggai would have castigated them with the very harsh words of verse 14.

4. The expression "this people" in verse 14 implies depreciation. Rothstein recognizes that it is not used negatively in 2:4, but he doubts that it is original there.

5. Haggai 2:5 ("The Lord's Spirit abides among you") shows that the Jews were not regarded as unclean by Haggai.

6. A comparison with Zechariah 1:5-6 of the same historical period shows that the people needed to be set straight at times, but it does not speak about uncleanness.

7. The date of Ezra 4 is wrong. There Zerubbabel is closely connected with the construction, but according to Haggai, he began with the building only in 520 B.C. Consequently Ezra 3:8 and following and 4:1-5 were originally reports of the second year of Darius (520 B.C.) but were reassigned to the earlier period by a redactor.

8. There are many parallelisms between Ezra 3:8 — 4:5 and Haggai and the context of Zechariah 8:9 (Ezra 3:12a = Hag. 2:3; Ezra 4:4 = Zech. 8:9, 13; Ezra 4:1 = Hag. 2:1 = Zech. 8:9 ff.). Haggai 2:10-14 can be assigned to about one month after Zechariah 1:1 and accordingly to about the same time as Zechariah 8:9.[18]

Many of these points are repeated in scholarly commentaries about Haggai 2:10-14 after the publication of Rothstein's work. At the same time, however, special investigations negate the validity of the most important of these arguments.

Rothstein interprets Haggai 2:10-14 as an allegory. In the first question to the priests (Hag. 2:12) the hem of the garment represents the returnees from exile, the holy meat stands for the altar, the holy service, and its representatives, whereas the bread, pottage, and so forth, is identified with "this people."[19] In the second question (2:13) the correlation is between uncleanness and "this people," whereas the bread is connected with the returnees. Rothstein himself notices the inherent problem in an interpretation that has to assign different values to the same symbols in consecutive verses. But he blames this on the clumsiness of the author and nevertheless uses these equations as basis for his subsequent argumentation.

Similarly in many other points he uses as evidence theories with a low probability. This deficiency he tries to overcome by using a large number of arguments that lead to an internally consistent model of what could have happened according to Rothstein, namely, the "birthday of the separation between Jews and Samaritans."[20] However, the problem is that Rothstein bases one argument of low probability on another of the same kind, so that the probability of the result actually diminishes with the number of alleged proofs. Moreover, the fact that he can present a perfectly plausible and logical model of what could have happened does not mean that the model is true and that it indeed represents historical fact, especially if it could only be developed by changing the evidence of the biblical texts on which it is based.

Rothstein is aware of the deficiencies of his evidence but believes nonetheless that his conclusions do not leave much room for doubt:

> I know very well that my argumentation had to be based frequently on assumptions, guesses and opinion, which leaves impression of uncertainty concerning the results. However, in this it is not different from the

vast majority of OT investigations. On the contrary one has reason to doubt the conclusions of a thesis when its author claims absolute certainty for them. Therefore at the outset I do not claim more than probability for the results of my work. However, I believe I can hope that the argumentation will stand also the closest examination.[21]

In spite of these disclaimers he had expressed his firm convictions about the correctness of his results already: "I think when we carefully weigh everything that I considered according to its proper weight, there can hardly be any doubt now that those points which we saw ourselves forced to maintain have really been proven."[22]

The uncertainty of his reasoning was clearly seen by W. Bousset and C. Steuernagel, who reviewed Rothstein's book shortly after its publication. After praising Rothstein for making a valuable contribution to the study of Samaritan history Bousset continues: "I cannot treat the details of the intelligent and scholarly work here, but I do not consider its alleged results to be certain or convincing."[23]

Steuernagel, however, gives a more favorable impression of the work:[24]

> The author bases his thesis on a very careful but also very detailed analysis of all witnesses of the conditions of the time. He does not deny that these testimonies frequently are not sufficient to come to really certain ideas. Indeed some of his points are questionable. But this concerns only less important details; in the main point I suspect I would have to agree with him. This concerns especially the new interpretation of Hag 2:10-14 and the statement that the report in Ezra 4:1 ff. is historically reliable even though it is placed chronologically wrong by 3:8 and 4:5.[25]

That the details of his criticism are not really so trivial can be seen from the fact that he rejects Rothstein's identification of "the people of the land" in Ezra 4:4 with those rejected in Haggai 2:14,[26] the very center of Rothstein's thesis.

THE DEVELOPMENT FROM ROTHSTEIN TO KOCH

Considering the weaknesses of Rothstein's argumentation, which he himself admitted and which were recognized by these early reviewers of his work, it is surprising that his interpretation of Haggai 2:10-14 became generally accepted not only in German scholarship but also in English and Hebrew commentaries.

Although German Protestant scholarship soon treated Rothstein's theses as established facts, his position seems to have been unknown for a time in other countries. Four years after the publication of the book, H. G. Mitchell[27] gives a literal interpretation of Haggai 2:10-19, which he considers one unit. The people of Judah have become unclean.[28] Consequently they have defiled the sanctuary and the work of their hands, causing the continuation of calamities described in chapter 1. Haggai reproves them but also gives them encouragement in verses 15-19. Mitchell quotes several earlier commentators but ignores Rothstein.

P. F. Bloomhardt tried to work out a poetic metrical arrangement of Haggai.[29] Even though he quotes Rothstein's earlier thesis about the relationship between Sheshbazzar and Zerubbabel, he evidently did not know of Rothstein's new interpretation of Haggai 2:11-14.

Also in Catholic French theology the work of Rothstein is ignored for many years. Paul Joüon[30] quotes Ehrlich's *Randglossen* of 1912 and develops his own position that the Temple has become impure, but he does not mention Rothstein's thesis on the same topic.

Meanwhile Ernst Sellin's commentary on the minor prophets[31] became the main German source of reference for the study of the minor prophets at least until 1954. In it Sellin gave a full endorsement to Rothstein's work. One of the reasons[32] probably was that Rothstein's thesis confirmed and extended an earlier observation of Sellin,[33] who had come to the conclusion that the foundations of the Temple were laid not on the twenty-fourth day of the ninth month (Hag. 2:18) but on the date mentioned in Haggai 1:15. Sellin writes:[34]

> I have come to the only possible conclusion . . . , that 1:15 originally told about a laying of foundations by Zerubbabel on the 24th day of the 6th month, but that the report about this was eliminated later because it contradicted the presentation of the Chronicler who knew only of a foundation laying in the second year of Cyrus (Ezra 3:8 ff.).[35]

Now Rothstein claimed to have found the lost piece in Haggai 2:15-19.[36] It is not surprising then that Sellin would appreciate his colleague's thesis and endorse not only the relocation of Haggai 2:15-19 but also his interpretation of 2:10-14 and other aspects of his argumentation:

> Earlier interpretation considered this little dialogue to be the first section of the complete speech vv 10-19, which Haggai would have given on the

24th of the 9th month, two months after his previous proclamation. . . .
We have already seen that the second part, vv 15-19, does not relate to
the first part at all. Hence also the first part has lost its common basis of
interpretation.

With a lucky strike Rothstein *(Juden und Samaritaner,* pp. 5-11) has uncovered the original meaning and the content of verses 10-14. It is Haggai's decision to the question whether the "people of the land," the Samaritans and the Jews who had remained in the land, would be allowed
to participate in the construction of the Temple. It is impossible that the
term "the people" in v 14 refers to the returnees from exile. Without
doubt the dialogue belongs in the context of Ezra 4:1-5 and signifies the
real birthday of postexilic Judaism. This is a moment of world-historic
importance.[37]

A theory that Rothstein himself had considered as frequently based on
assumptions, guesses, and opinion now had become classified as a discovery beyond any doubt. Hence it is not surprising to find in *Biblia Hebraica,*
beginning with the third edition (1937), the critical note: "v 15-19 post
1,15a trsp" (place vv. 15-19 after 1:15a).

Consequently A. Jepsen in his scholarly and yet popular commentary no
longer mentions Rothstein when he repeats his interpretation: "The words
in chap. 2:15-19 belong to the date in chap. 1:15, as has been made very
probable."[38] Again following Rothstein without mentioning him, he maintains that the questions in 2:10-14 are not to be taken literally as in Leviticus, but present an image: "If you have dealings with tribes which are unclean, estranged from God, then they will defile you. Therefore separate
yourselves from them."[39]

At about the same time on the Catholic side, H. Junker interprets Haggai without any major changes to the text.[40] He sharply rejects both Rothstein and Sellin. After summarizing Rothstein's theory he continues:

Other reasons, however, render Rothstein's suggested solution impossible. 1. It would be extraordinary and improbable that the historic reason
for the questions would not have been mentioned, if v 14 was dealing
with the Samaritans. 2. According to Ezra 4:1ff. the attempt of the Samaritans to participate in the construction of the temple took place already in 538 B.C, not in 520 when Haggai appears. One would have to assume, as Rothstein and Sellin indeed do, that the Chronicler got the
events in Ezra 4 mixed up. This assumption would only be permissible, if

Rothstein's interpretation could definitely be ascertained. 3. There is a close connection between 2:10-14 and 15-20 through the introduction "and now" in v. 15. It is scarcely likely that a later redactor would have connected the two passages in such a way that a word spoken originally against the Samaritans would be turned against his own people.[41]

Because Protestant German scholarship provided the model for Old Testament interpretation, Junker's objections were not considered in new commentaries. Instead Rothstein's views, transmitted through Sellin's commentary, became standard.

Rudolph accepted Rothstein's views concerning Ezra 4. Hans Walter Wolff wrote a short commentary on Haggai[42] that is quoted in most following works. Without much discussion he gives a vivid description of the events after the exile. Following Rothstein he paints Haggai as the defender of a pure faith in God against the influences of the Samaritan syncretists. Wolff's commentary is followed by a series of new works in the next sixteen years taking the results of Rothstein's theories for granted.

F. Horst states in the introduction to his commentary: "It is the merit of Haggai's proclamation, that Zerubbabel, the repatriate nobility and the rest of the population became willing to begin the reconstruction of the temple without assistance by the Samaritan leaders."[43]

Gerhard von Rad no longer mentions Rothstein but claims the support of the majority of the commentators for the Samaritan hypothesis:

> The question of who are meant by "this people" in Hag. II.14 is answered by most commentators in the sense that these people who had been refused a share in the building of the temple are to be identified with the non-Israelite ruling class in Samaria. Cp. also Ezra V.1-6,15, and the more recent commentaries.[44]

That the interpretation of Haggai 2:14 influences one's evaluation of Haggai's ministry can be seen from Karl Elliger's commentary: "By taking a position against the 'Samaritans' he had a decisive influence on the religious and political life of the post-exilic community."[45]

With the general acceptance of German Protestant exegetical methods by Catholic scholars after World War 2 and especially after the Second Vatican Council, Rothstein's thesis found also entrance into Catholic commentaries. W. A. M. Beuken[46] treats Haggai 2:10-14 under the title "The Rejection of the 'Samaritans' and Their Cult."

I have already shown that before Rothstein the text was universally interpreted as referring to Jews. Sellin and others wrote about a "new discovery" when they treated the Samaritan theory. Thus it is interesting to read in Beuken's introduction to the discussion of the issue: "Since antiquity there are two questions associated with this text: 1. Which people is rejected with this priestly *Torah* and why? 2. Is there an original connection with vv 15-19?"[47] He goes on to mention many commentaries from the turn of the century that maintained that the returnees from exile were rejected here. They were considered unclean because the Temple had not been constructed yet, rendering their sacrifices on the provisional altar worthless.[48] Then Beuken concludes: "This interpretation has been ultimately disproven by Rothstein in his analysis which continues to be considered the classical commentary to this passage."[49]

English commentators are more reluctant to throw all their weight on radical new interpretations. Peter Ackroyd and Douglas Jones[50] repeat traditional interpretations and present Rothstein's thesis as one possibility among others. Then their wish to synthesize the various theories leads them to a new reconstruction, which seems logical when one considers the historical development of the Samaritan question but which turns Rothstein on his head.

After quoting William Barnes for the traditional point of view and Rothstein for his interpretation, Ackroyd continues:

> But it is not clear why the phrase "this people" and its poetic parallel "this nation" should be used in a different sense here from that in 1:2. The possibility that the passage, originally applicable to the Jewish community, has been given a later, anti-Samaritan interpretation, may be suggested as a third alternative.[51]

Inasmuch as there is no textual evidence to support this claim, it can only be understood as a forced attempt to accommodate an interpretation that was considered normative for good scholarship on the continent in 1962 when these books were written.

Some major objections against some of Rothstein's arguments have been mentioned already. Because his theory involved a reconstruction of historical events, it is interesting to note that most scholarly works about Israel's history completely ignore Rothstein's view of early postexilic times. This is true of the books by Martin Noth,[52] Charles Pfeiffer,[53] S. Herrmann,[54] W. S. McCullough[55] and G. Widengren.[56] John Bright is one of the few who follow Rothstein in an historical work: "Sternly separatist, Haggai urged the cutting of all contacts with religious syncretists in the land, which, he declared, were as contaminating as handling a corpse (ch. 2:10-14)."[57] However, the common historical viewpoint is summarized by Widengren: "Recent investigations of the Jewish-Samaritan relations by Rowley, Smith, Cross, and Coggins have tended to interpret the breach between the Judeans and Samaritans as a gradual development rather than the product of any particular event."[58]

Archaeological research provided another clue to the date of the foundation-laying of the Temple that puzzled Rothstein and others. Having in mind modern European customs of celebrating the very beginning of the work with the laying of the foundation stone,[59] Rothstein could not believe that the ceremony should have been delayed until three months after the beginning of the work (Hag. 1:15; 2:18), especially because he concluded from Haggai 2:3 on the basis of Ezra 3:12 that the construction had progressed far enough for people to make comparisons between the old Temple and the new one and to become discouraged in their efforts. K. Galling[60] points to the possibility that "foundation stone" could be used here in a collective sense, meaning a structure at the four corners of the building or a three-layered foundation of the Temple (Ezra 6:4) as has been found in several buildings excavated in the area of Syro-Palestine.[61]

Other objections to Rothstein are based on semantic studies. Two synonyms[62] for "people" appear in Haggai 2:14, evidently referring to the same group: *'am* and *gôy*. According to R. E. Clements, *'am* carries the idea of consanguinity as the basis of union into a people, whereas *gôy* emphasizes rather political and territorial affiliation.[63] Although the plural *gôyîm* frequently refers to Gentile nations, the singular form does not carry a negative implication in the Bible. Clements writes:

> At no point in the OT is the semantic development reached in which *gôy* in itself means 'heathen nation'. . . . Existence as a *gôy* was to be desired, and the term did not itself imply any adverse religious connotation. In line with this, there is no support in the OT for the usage which emerged in Talmudic Hebrew where the sing. *gôy* could denote an individual member of a non-Israelite nation.[64]

Thus Haggai could only have denounced the Samaritans in 2:14 by explicitly stating that he referred to a foreign nation.[65] Whereas special studies had eroded the evidence for Rothstein's theory, it was still the stan-

dard interpretation for Haggai 2:10-14 until Koch and May independently
of each other rejected it completely.

Based on form-critical methodology, K. Koch[66] treats "prophecies of salvation" in the book of Haggai. Each occurrence of this type of prophecy is
introduced by information about date, reception of the word, and recip-
ients. Then follow the messages, consisting of (1) a description of the situation, (2) a challenge to recognize the present time as the turning-point
from past to future, and (3) a pronouncement of salvation. This pattern repeats itself three times in the book of Haggai, the last instance being 2:10-
19. As a result of his study Koch firmly maintains the unity of 2:10-19
against Rothstein's division[67] and consequently identifies the people in
verse 14 with the same entity addressed in verses 15-19, namely, Judah.
Also in his literal interpretation of the text he differs from Rothstein's allegorical approach. In his detailed refutation of Rothstein's arguments his
considerations about uncleanness in verse 14 are especially important for
the debate. Many interpreters from ancient times until now have considered holiness identical with cleanness on the one hand and sin and profanation identical with defilement on the other.[68] Because they understood
verse 14 as a moral judgment, they theorized that neglect or discourage-
ment in the Temple construction might have caused the prophet's harsh
reaction that they found in verse 14. Rothstein, who shared this view,
rightly saw a contradiction between verse 14 thus understood and the context, which promises blessings to Judah. He concluded that the word could
not refer to the same people as referred to in the context. Koch clarifies
that the phrase "it is unclean" in verse 14 "is a fixed expression of priestly
terminology expressing a declaration about the sphere of uncleanness. It
does not refer to an ethical quality or religious confession. Uncleanness is
not guilt but a fate which comes over people like an infection."[69] Hence the
people called unclean in verse 14 is Judah. Koch continues: "The returnees
as well as those who had remained are unclean because they do not have
an unspoiled sanctuary where a complete cleaning would be possible."[70]

Whereas Koch rejected Rothstein's theories on form-critical grounds,
H. G. May, writing at about the same time, refuted Rothstein's interpretation of Haggai 2:10-19 on the basis of semantic studies.[71] After reviewing
Rothstein's theory he states: "The arguments for the transposition of vss.
15-19 lose some of their force if it can be shown that II 14 refers to the

same people as those addressed in vss. 15-19."[72] Thus May attempts to show that *gôy* ("people") in 2:14 refers to Judah with all probability. His studies are mainly comparative, examining similar texts in Zechariah and the use of the term *gôy* in general in the Old Testament. Then he concludes:

> If the Samaritan schism lies behind Haggai's oracle in II 10-14, more implicit than explicit. The burden of proof lies on those who presume it and who would therefore make a distinction between "this people" in II 14 and "this people" in I 2, which refers to the Judean community. General O. T. usage of "this people" and "this nation" makes it reasonably explicit that the Judean community is intended. Haggai uses "the nations" *(Haggóyím)* in the plural to refer to the gentile nations (II 7,22), but this has no bearing on the meaning of "this nation" *(haggóy haz-zéh)* in II 14.[73]

Even though Koch's and May's articles are relatively short, they left an impact on interpretations of Haggai published after 1967. Ackroyd's work *Exile and Restoration*[74] appeared the following year. Whereas in his earlier commentary he had mentioned Rothstein's theory as one among three possibilities, now he only presents two views, eliminating Rothstein's position and quoting Koch instead.[75]

The French Catholic commentary of T. Chary[76] does not yet know of Koch's article and therefore places 2:15-19 after 1:15. Chary repeats Rothstein's arguments for this change and finds it confirmed by the fact that a great number of exegetes accept it.[77] However, he does not share the view that 2:14 refers to the Samaritans. On the contrary, he provides some evidence that the declaration may have been part of a "day of repentance" or *yôm kippûr* ceremony.[78] Fellow French scholar S. Amsler shares Chary's two positions about the transposition of 2:15-19 and his rejection of the Samaritan hypothesis, which he calls the "classical interpretation."[79]

The latest German commentary on Haggai by W. Rudolph[80] takes opposite positions. He follows Rothstein's interpretation of 2:14[81] in agreement with the position he had taken already in his Ezra commentary but maintains the unity of verses 10-19,[82] making reference to Koch's work. By trying to accommodate Rothstein as well as Koch he left a major stumbling block for the Samaritan hypothesis in its place, which Rothstein already recognized. Given the close connection between verses 10-14 and 15-19, it is very unlikely that they would address two different groups of people without explicitly stating so.

Although German and English scholars are slowly backing away from Rothstein's theory, B. Z. Luria[83] defends it in Jewish theology, which traditionally considered the ruling of Haggai 2:10-14 a matter of ritual legislation directed to the Jews of the restoration.[84]

However, in general the discussion about Haggai 2:10-19 has now returned to the study of the biblical evidence rather than continuing to repeat a theory that for sixty years had been treated as factual because of its universal acceptance.

Considering that throughout the centuries Haggai 2:10-19 was taken to form a unit referring to the people of Judah, it is surprising how the situation could change radically because of the theory of Rothstein, which, as he himself admitted, consisted of much evidence with low probability. The decisive factor for the acceptance of the theory seems to have been its promotion by the commentary of Sellin, who endorsed it probably because it confirmed an earlier theory of his own. For a while Sellin is quoted when reference to Rothstein's interpretation is made, until a point is reached when it is no longer considered necessary to present biblical evidence or to refer to Rothstein because it has become "generally accepted" inasmuch as "most scholars support it." It is interesting to see how this general attitude prevailed even after special historical, archaeological, and semantic studies had already discredited many of the arguments used by Rothstein to support his idea. The circle of a theory being accepted because everybody accepts it was finally broken when a few well-known scholars challenged not only some of Rothstein's presuppositions but his whole theory, using a fresh examination of the biblical evidence. Since then the history of interpretation of Haggai 2:10-19 diversifies: Those who had considered Rothstein's thesis with caution before now ignore it. Those who had committed themselves before try to modify their position without contradicting some of their earlier publications. Some have just begun to promote Rothstein's point of view. Whatever position a particular scholar takes now, however, it is no longer possible to treat Rothstein's theory as generally accepted and beyond question. Consequently all works dealing with the matter after 1967 have included new examinations of the biblical evidence.

May this historical review encourage scholarship that considers evidence of the biblical texts the foremost basis of its interpretation rather than generally accepted theological theories. When is a *gôy* a "goy"? May it be determined by the scholarly study of the Hebrew Scriptures not by a poll of commentaries.

NOTES

1. Johann Wilhelm Rothstein, *Juden und Samaritaner. Die grundlegende Scheidung von Judentum und Heidentum. Eine kritische Studie zum Buche Haggai und zur Jüdischen Geschichte im Ersten Nachexilischen Jahrhundert.* Beiträge zur Wissenschaft vom Alten Testament 3, ed. R. Kittel (Leipzig: Hinrich, 1908).

2. See *b. Pesaḥ* 14a ff.

3. Julius Wellhausen, *Die Kleinen Propheten übersetzt und erklärt,* 3d ed. (Berlin: Reimer, 1898), p. 176.

4. E.g. J. P. Lange, *The Minor Prophets,* Commentary on the Holy Scripture (New York: Scribner's, 1886), p. 22.

5. T. André, *Le Prophète Aggée; Introduction critique et commentaire* (Paris: Fischbacher, 1895).

6. John Calvin, *Habbakkuk, Zephaniah, Haggai* (Edinburgh: Calvin Translation Society, 1848), p. 372.

7. Ibid., p. 373.

8. Rothstein, *Juden,* p. 15.

9. Ibid.

10. J. W. Rothstein, *Die Genealogie des Königs Jojachin und seine Nachkommen (1. Chron. 3, 17-24) in geschichtlicher Beleuchtung* (Berlin: Reuther and Reichard, 1902), pp. 68-69.

11. Rothstein, *Juden,* p. 24.

12. Ibid., p. 31.

13. Gleason L. Archer, Jr., *SOTI* (Chicago: Moody, 1964), p. 401, considers Ezra 4:5-23 "a long parenthesis dealing not with the building of the temple but rather with the erection of the walls of the city."

14. Rothstein, *Juden,* p. 7.

15. Actually he includes all the population in Palestine that had not been in exile. The Samaritans were the largest group within this general category.

16. Rothstein, *Juden,* pp. 6-23.

17. According to Rothstein, vv. 15-19 belong after 1:15.

18. By Rothstein and others assigned two years earlier than the biblical context of Zech. 7:1.

19. Rothstein, *Juden,* pp. 34-36.

20. Ibid., p. 41. (All translations of foreign language materials are my own.)

21. Ibid., p. 74.

22. Ibid., p. 73.

23. W. Bousset, "Geschichte, Literatur und Religion des Spät-Judentums," *Theologic Rundschau* 13 (1910):391.

24. C. Steuernagel, "Rothstein, Prof. D. J. W., Juden und Samaritaner," *Theologische Literaturzeitung* 34 (1909):68.

25. These verses are considered additions from the time after the chronicler.

26. Steuernagel argues on the basis of Hag. 2:4; Zech. 7:5, where the phrase definitely does not refer to enemies of Judah.

27. H. G. Mitchell et al., *Critical and Exegetical Commentary on Haggai, Zechariah, Malachi and Jonah*, ICC (New York: Scribner's, 1912).

28. Ibid., pp. 68-69.

29. P. F. Bloomhardt, "The Poems of Haggai" (Ph. D. diss., Johns Hopkins University, 1928).

30. Paul Joüon, "Notes philologiques sur le texte hébreu," *Bib* 10 (1929):418-19.

31. Ernst Sellin, *Das Zwölfprophetenbuch, Kommentar zum Alten Testament* 12 (Leipzig: Deichert, 1922).

32. Rothstein also was a co-worker of Sellin in the publication of the *Kommentar zum Alten Testament* commentary series.

33. Ernst Sellin, *Studien zur Entstehungsgeschichte der jüdischen Gemeinde nach dem Babylonischen Exil. II. Die Restauration der jüdischen Gemeinde in den Jahren 538-516—Das Schicksal Serubbabels* (Leipzig: Deichert, 1901), p. 50.

34. Sellin, *Zwölfprophetenbuch*, p. 405.

35. I.e., 537 B.C., seventeen years earlier.

36. Rothstein only had to change the number nine to six in Hag. 2:18, which was no problem for him.

37. Sellin, *Zwölfprophetenbuch*, pp. 412-13.

38. A. Jepsen, *Das Zwölfprophetenbuch* (Leipzig: Gustav Schloepmann, 1937), p. 160.

39. Ibid., p. 162.

40. H. Junker, *Die Zwölf kleinen Propheten, Die Heilige Schrift des Alten Testamentes*, part 2, vol. 13/3/2 (Bonn: Peter Hanstein, 1938).

41. Ibid., p. 104.

42. Hans Walter Wolff, *Haggai. Eine Auslegung, Biblische Studien* 1 (Neukirchen: Erziehungsverein, 1951).

43. T. H. Robinson and F. Horst, *Die Zwölf kleinen Propheten, Handbuch zum Alten Testament* 14 (Tübingen: Mohr, 1954), 202.

44. Gerhard von Rad, *Old Testament Theology*, 2 vols. (London: Oliver and Boyd, 1965), 2:383.

45. Karl Elliger, *Das Buch der zwölf kleinen Propheten*, 25, 6th ed. (Göttingen: Vandendoeck and Ruprecht, 1967), p. 84.

46. W. A. M. Beuken, *Haggai-Sacharja 1-8. Studien zur Überlieferungsgeschichte der frühnachexilischen Prophetie* (Assen: Gorcum, 1967).

47. Ibid., p. 64.

48. Ibid., p. 67.
49. Ibid.
50. Peter R. Ackroyd, "Haggai," in *Peake's Commentary on the Bible* (London: Nelson, 1962), pp. 643-44; Douglas R. Jones, *Haggai, Zechariah and Malachi* (London: SCM, 1962), p. 50.
51. Ackroyd, "Haggai," p. 644.
52. Martin Noth, *The History of Israel*, 2d ed. (New York: Harper, 1960), p. 311.
53. Charles Pfeiffer, *Old Testament History* (Grand Rapids: Baker, 1973), p. 416.
54. S. Herrmann, *A History of Israel in Old Testament Times* (London: SCM, 1975), p. 320.
55. W. S. McCullough, *The History and Literature of the Palestinian Jews from Cyrus to Herod* (Toronto: U. Press, 1975), p. 29.
56. G. Widengren, "IX: The Persian Period," in *Israelite and Judean History*, ed. J. H. Hayes and J. M. Miller (Philadelphia: Westminster, 1977), pp. 511-12.
57. John Bright, *A History of Israel*, 2d ed. (Philadelphia: Westminster, 1972), p. 371.
58. Widengren, "Persian," p. 511.
59. Similar to American groundbreaking ceremonies.
60. K. Galling, "Serubbabel und der Wiederaufbau des Tempels in Jerusalem," in *Verbannung und Heimkehr*, ed. A. Kuschke (Tübingen: Mohr, 1961), pp. 67-96.
61. Ibid., p. 72. Galling also (p. 80) points out that Hag. 2:3 speaks about the destroyed Temple, not a half-finished construction.
62. *TDNT*, s.v. *"gôy,"* by Ronald E. Clements, 2:427.
63. Ibid. See also *TWOT*, s.v. *"'am*. People, nation," by G. van Groningen, 2:1640; s.v. *"gôy*. Gentile, heathen, nation, people," by G. van Groningen, 1:327.
64. Clements, *"gôy,"* p. 432.
65. The demonstrative that occurs with these terms here probably does not carry negative implications in Haggai; cf. 1:3 ("this house-temple"); 1:2 ("this people—Judah").
66. K. Koch, "Haggais unreines Volk," *ZAW* 79 (1967):52-66.
67. Ibid., p. 60.
68. E. Feldmann, *Biblical and Post-Biblical Defilement and Mourning: Law as Theology* (New York: Ktav, 1977), p. 65.
69. Koch, "Haggais unreines Volk," p. 62.
70. Cf. recently also Joyce G. Baldwin, *Haggai, Zechariah, Malachi* (London: Tyndale, 1972), p. 51: "How could the defilement be purged away if every offering was itself defiled? . . . For Israel there was no known remedy. The only hope lay in free acceptance by God, and the promised blessing (v. 19) implies that such acceptance was granted."
71. H. G. May, "'This People' and 'This Nation' in Haggai," *VT* 18 (1968):190-97.
72. Ibid., p. 190.
73. Ibid., p. 192-93.
74. Peter R. Ackroyd, *Exile and Restoration. A Study in Hebrew Thought of the 6th Century B.C.* (Philadelphia: Westminster, 1968).
75. Ibid., p. 158 n. 23; pp. 168-69.
76. T. Chary, *Aggée-Zacharie-Malachie* (Paris: Lecoffre, 1969).
77. Ibid., p. 23.

78. Ibid., p. 29.
79. S. Amsler, A. Lacocque, R. Vuilleumier, *Aggée, Zacharie, Malachie* (Paris: Delacheux and Niestlé, 1981), pp. 29, 39.
80. W. Rudolph, *Haggai, Sacharja 1-8, Sacharja 9-14, Maleachi* (Gütersloh: G. Mohn, 1976).
81. Ibid., p. 49.
82. Ibid., p. 46.
83. B. Z. Luria, "The Beginning of the Split Between Returnees from the Exile and the Samaritans (Hag 2:10-14)," *Beth Mikra* 23 (1977):43-46 (Hebrew).
84. E. M. Meyers, "The Use of *tôrâ* in Haggai 2:11 and the Role of the Prophet in the Restoration Community," in *The Word of the Lord Shall Go Forth,* ed. C. L. Meyers and M. O'Connor (Winona Lake, Ind.: Eisenbrauns, 1983), p. 72.

JOHN H. SAILHAMER (Ph. D., University of California at Los Angeles) is associate professor of Old Testament and Semitic languages at Trinity Evangelical Divinity School.

17

Exegesis of the Old Testament as a Text

John H. Sailhamer

As a tribute to my colleague, Gleason L. Archer, I would like to offer the following reflections on exegetical and theological method in Old Testament studies. I address my remarks specifically to those who hold a view of Scripture similar to that defended by Archer in his many publications. It is hoped that this discussion will further our efforts to remain faithful to God's Word while at the same time seeking to be creative in our methods. Though the Old Testament is my speciality, I offer these remarks not so much from within that field as from within the larger concerns of Christian theology. In the end, Old Testament study must show itself to be a part of the Christian church, and its methodology will have to reflect that.

"ALL SCRIPTURE IS INSPIRED BY GOD"

A discussion of method in biblical studies must begin with the acknowledgment that the Old Testament is Scripture and that it is inspired. It must begin with Paul's statement: "All Scripture is inspired by God" (2 Tim. 3:16). We are accustomed to directing our theological attention to the second part of Paul's statement, "is inspired," by insisting either that one's method be adjusted to a certain view of inspiration or that one's view of inspiration be adjusted to a certain method. Methodologically, however, it seems to me to be equally appropriate to begin by focusing on the first part of Paul's statement, "all Scripture." In calling Scripture "inspired,"

Paul gives to it the highest claim to authority. It is specifically "Scripture" that Paul points to as the locus of God's revelation. In the words of the older theologians, Scripture *(sacra scriptura)* and God's Word *(verbum dei)* are one.[1] Although such an understanding of the nature of Scripture cannot claim any universal acceptance among modern theologians, it remains the hallmark of most theologians who call themselves evangelical. It is to this specific feature of the evangelical's commitment to Scripture that I want to draw attention in discussing its implications for the study of the Old Testament.

THE OLD TESTAMENT IS A TEXT

To say that the Old Testament is Scripture is to acknowledge that it is written. It is a book or, rather, a collection of books. Another way to put it is to say that the Old Testament is a text. As a text it has certain properties that distinguish it from nontexts. For example, texts are made of words, phrases, clauses, sentences, paragraphs, and the like, that is, texts are composed of language. They are structured utterances. They represent the work of an author.

A commitment to an understanding of the Old Testament as Scripture, then, implies an exegetical method and biblical theology that is a direct function of the meaning of a text. It means that exegesis must ask the question: How does a text have meaning? One must seek to discover the way in which the authors of Scripture have construed words, phrases, clauses, and the like into whole texts.

Several methodological implications arise out of this basic commitment to the Scriptures as a text.

TEXT THEORY AND TEXT LINGUISTICS

An important implication of approaching the Old Testament as a text is the need to be explicit about what a text actually is. One who holds to the inspiration of the text of Scripture should have a clear understanding of just what a text is and how a text has meaning. In recent years considerable attention has been focused on such questions, and much of it has already begun to make an impact on Old Testament studies.[2]

The development of the study of the nature of a text (text theory and text linguistics) is an outgrowth of the ongoing development of modern linguistics.[3] Since its inception, modern linguistics has been committed to understanding language as a coherent structure. In its formative stages linguists were successful in developing coherent linguistic systems to describe the internal structure of language at the level of the articulation of sounds (phonology) and grammatical form (morphology). As the attention of the linguists continued to move to higher levels of the language, for example, to clauses and sentences, it became increasingly difficult to explain or describe the structure of a language without making reference to even larger linguistic units. It became obvious that what happens within a linguistic unit the size of a clause (e.g., word order or verb choice) often cannot be explained or described simply on the basis of the internal structure of the clause. Very often the internal structure of a clause is determined by its larger linguistic environment. A simple example of this is the use of pronouns in a text (pronominalization). What are the conditions for the use of a pronoun within a clause? Often that use of a pronoun is determined by the use of a noun that is identical to it in the preceding clause. Thus, to explain why a pronoun is used one must look beyond the immediate clause or sentence to that which precedes it. Self-evident observations such as this led to the development of a "linguistics beyond the sentence," that is, a "text-linguistics."

The aim of text-linguistics is the formulation of rules or preferences that describe the inherent competency of those who send messages in texts (senders) and those who receive messages in texts (hearers). Just as linguistics focuses on the linguistic competency of language users, so text-linguistics focuses on the competency of text-users to assimilate and process meaning in texts. What are the factors that give texts cohesion, that make the words, phrases, clauses, sentences, paragraphs, and the like cling together to form larger units of meaning? How does a text produce a coherent whole? That is, what factors enable the reader of a text to make correlations among the parts of a text so that the sense of the whole becomes apparent when a text is read? Just as importantly, what enables the reader of a text to break a text down into units of manageable size so that the whole of the text can be processed in its parts? Text-linguistics attempts to describe and explain these processes of text structure and formation. Text-linguistics also aims to describe the processes of text-sending and text-receiving in such a way that a text-semantics (i.e., a text-based description of meaning that enables one to speak of the meaning of texts as a function of the specific shape and strategy of a text) is made possible.[4]

It is not enough, however, to merely describe and explain how texts work. If texts are to be understood as texts, a theoretical framework must be developed in which texts can be defined and distinguished from nontexts. Such is the task of a text-theory. If text-linguistics attempts to explain how a text works, a text-theory attempts to describe what a text is.[5]

It would go far beyond the purpose of this article to attempt to present a text-theory[6] or to develop a text-linguistic description of the Old Testament.[7] The point is simply that a commitment to an inspired text seems to be greatly in need of the kind of description and formulations available in this relatively new field of study. What makes the procedures of text-linguistics especially adaptable within the context of a view of Scripture as an inspired text is that its focus is text-specific and text-immanent. It seeks to explain the compositional features of real texts. As such, text-linguistics is quite different from the type of "structuralism" that recently has made inroads into biblical studies, though it has close affinities with Prague-school structuralism, an approach that so far has had only little influence in biblical studies.[8] It should also be kept distinct from studies that may fall under the general category of "discourse analysis"[9] in that the scope of such studies is often set to include ranges of discourse beyond mere texts, for example, conversations.

A blurred notion of what a text is can open one to the possibility of either missing the message of the inspired text or of mixing the message of Scripture with "messages" from many "nontextual" sources. This is especially true in those parts of Scripture that are "historical narrative" texts.

REVELATION IN SCRIPTURE (TEXT) AND IN HISTORY (EVENT)

An emphasis on Scripture as an inspired text has a direct bearing on the problem of revelation in history. To a great extent the texts of the Old Testament are historical narrative texts.[10] The texts, in other words, are about events in the real world. In speaking of historical narrative, however, important distinctions have to be made in the use of the term *history*. It is not enough to say with Hans Frei[11] that the biblical narratives are only "history-like" and to relegate them to the level of "realistic narrative." Much has yet to be investigated regarding the categories of "history" and "fictionality,"[12] but it can be said with reasonable certainty that the authors of the biblical narratives give every indication of intending their works to be taken as history rather than fiction.[13] Their aim, they imply throughout, is to record what actually happened. It can also be said today with confidence that there is reasonable evidence that the history that the narratives recount did in fact happen. The point at stake, however, is that in ordinary language the term *history* itself can have two very different senses. On the one hand *history* can refer to the kind of text we suppose the narratives to be, namely, nonfiction texts that intend to recount actual events from the past. As such the term fits the biblical narratives well. On the other hand, *history* can refer to the actual events from the past. In this sense the term refers to that which the biblical texts are about: the real world. This distinction is of some importance when attempting to develop an approach to the Old Testament that is text-oriented. We must recognize that in only one of the above senses does *history* actually refer to a text, the recording of past events. In the other sense *history* refers not to a text but to the actual event in the real world. This distinction becomes important in using the expression "revelation in history." Which of the above senses is given to *history* in such formulas? Does one mean revelation in history as a revelation in a text or revelation in an event as such?[14]

A text-oriented approach to the Old Testament would insist that the locus of God's revelation is in the Scriptures themselves, in the text. There is no reason to try to discount the fact that God has made known His will in other ways at other times. But, given the theological priority of an inspired text (2 Tim. 3:16), one must see in the text of Scripture itself the locus of God's revelation today. Thus, on the question of God's revelation in history the sense of *history* in a text-oriented approach would be that of the "record of past events." The history in which God makes known His will is the recorded history in the text of Scripture. When formulated this way, evangelical biblical theology can be seen to be based on a revelation that consists of the meaning of a text with its focus on Scripture as a written document. Even the formula "revelation in history" is then a question of the meaning of a text.

Evangelical biblical scholars have not always been clear on this point. Although holding to a view of Scripture as God's revelation, there has been a tendency to interpret the formula "revelation in history" in such a way that the term *history* refers not to the text of Scripture but rather to the past events themselves. In other words, the locus of revelation is taken to lie not in the text of Scripture but in the events witnessed to by the text. In such an approach the events lying behind the text of Scripture are then read as a salvation history within which God makes known His will to man.

Though subtle, the distinction is a real one. The effect of overlooking the text of Scripture in favor of a focus on the events of Israel's history can often be a "biblical" theology that is little more than a philosophy of history, an exegetical method that is set on expounding the meaning of the events lying behind Scripture rather than those depicted in Scripture itself. Meier Sternberg has aptly described such an approach:

> The theologian, qua theologian, dreams of piecing together a full picture of ancient Israelite religion, mutations and conflicts included. The historian wants to know what happened in Israelite history, the linguist what the language system (phonology, grammar, semantics) underlying the Bible was like. And the geneticist concentrates on the real-life processes that generated and shaped the biblical text.[15]

Even when one clearly has in view the goal to be biblical in the textual sense of the term, that is, to get at the meaning of the text of Scripture, it is all too easy to blur the boundaries between the text and the event and handle the text as if one were in fact the event represented in the text. Therein lies a fundamental threat among evangelicals to a genuine Scripturally-based theology.

Emanuel Hirsch[16] points to the influence of Sigmund Jakob Baumgarten at the University of Halle in the mid-eighteenth century as the decisive turning point from a view of Scripture as revelation to a view of Scripture as a record of a revelation in events. "All and all it may well be said that with Baumgarten German Protestant theology entered the decisive stage in its transition from a Bible-faith to that of a revelation-faith in which the Bible in reality is nothing more than a document of revelation given at a specific moment in time."[17] Baumgarten did not stand alone in his view of Scripture. He himself had been influenced by Christoph Matthaus Pfaff's separation of revelation and inspiration[18] or, rather, Pfaff's separation of the notion of inspiration into that work of the Spirit of God in giving revelation to the prophets, apostles, and evangelists and that work of the Spirit of God in giving them the "impulse to write" Scripture and in "generally leading them" in their work of authorship of Scripture.[19] In other words, both Pfaff and Baumgarten, along with the "Übergangstheologen" in general, had made a major break with the traditional (orthodox) view of inspiration, which had characteristically identified Scripture itself with God's revelation. This is not to say that the orthodox theologians did not see a distinction between revelation and inspiration as two works of God in bringing Scripture into being, which they clearly did.[20] Hirsch's point is that before Baumgarten the distinction between revelation and inspiration did not mean that Scripture itself was not revelation; however, after Baumgarten the distinction between revelation and inspiration marked the break between the essentially divine act of revelation and the essentially human act of writing Scripture. Thus it is easy to see why Baumgarten could produce such a student as Johann Salomo Semler, the "father" of the historical-critical method. With Baumgarten's view of the secondary role of Scripture in relationship to revelation, a free rein could be given to all historical-critical questions relating to the Bible without ever putting the truths of revelation in jeopardy.[21]

Baumgarten's own orthodoxy regarding the inerrancy of Scripture is, of course, not in dispute. Though for him an inerrant Scripture was not a *sine qua non* of revelation, he never doubted that the Scriptures were inerrant.[22] In fact, another of his students was the Hamburg pastor Melchior Goeze, who for many years waged a heated attack against the rationalism of Lessing.[23] Because of this, Baumgarten is regarded as a "transition theologian" *(Übergangstheolog)*, a carrier of theological views who was apparently not affected by them. Such is no doubt an accurate description of Baumgarten's view of the inerrancy of Scripture, but it misses the point of his view of revelation. In his view of revelation and Scripture Baumgarten had clearly broken with the orthodox view of Scripture. I will leave it up to the historians to decide how this particular aspect of Baumgarten's view of Scripture was received in his day. However, it is clear that Baumgarten's separation of revelation and Scripture has been heralded by later generations of biblical critics as the inevitable consequence of the emerging historical consciousness in the late eighteenth century. Henceforth any attempt to hold to an identification of Scripture as such with revelation must face the charge of "repristination" or "biblicism"[24] or, what is worse, given the context of biblical studies in the years to follow Baumgarten, it is to leave oneself open to the charge of being unhistorical.

The reasons for these charges lie perhaps in the actual responses of evangelical biblical scholarship to the threat of biblical criticism, particularly in regard to the amount of ground these biblical scholars thought they might safely concede to the critics in defense of the authority or inerrancy of Scripture. Frei has convincingly argued that in the early years of the rise of biblical criticism those who sought to defend the Bible against pure unbelief often made major concessions to the other side in an effort to save the Bible from the charge of being untrue.[25] Accepting Frei's analysis, it seems possible to say with Frei that one of the major concessions made by the defenders of the Bible was the acceptance of the critics' own replacement of the biblical historical narratives by a history that could be conceived independently of those narratives themselves.[26]

This problem is not passé for Old Testament studies. Rather, it lies at the root of the questions raised in the name of "canon criticism," which in response to the older forms of historicism wants to reassert the theological emphasis on the final shape of the text rather than on some remote and little-understood event or the fragmentary and diverse expressions of faith that paved the way to the final canonical text. There is a sense of complacency among some evangelicals today that the problem of "revelation in history" as a choice between revelation in the text of Scripture and revelation in the events of the past is somehow resolved when it is agreed that the text presents an accurate picture of the events that really happened. Thus the idea of an inerrant Scripture is taken as a hedge against the threat of diverting one's attention away from the text of Scripture to focus on events in Israel's past. Such a complacency, however, rests on a faulty perception of the real nature of the problem. Certainly from an evangelical perspective the approach of canon criticism seems to founder on its inability to correlate the statements of the text of Scripture with the results of historical criticism.[27] That which Scripture records does not match up with what the critic knows to have actually happened. To this extent the evangelical foundation of an inerrant Scripture is a hedge only against the problem of "faith and knowledge." For the evangelical, that which the biblical authors reported (faith) is taken to be an accurate account of what actually happened (knowledge). To think that this resolves the question of revelation, though, is to miss the important fact that what the biblical authors recorded comes to us in the form of a text. The biblical message has been encoded in a text. Insofar as we say that this text is inspired and thus is the locus of God's revelation, then the meaning or sense of that revelation is of the nature of the meaning of a text. To say that the text is an accurate portrayal of what actually happened is an important part of the evangelical view of Scripture, but it does not alter the fact that God's revelation has come to us through an inspired text, and thus no amount of delving into the history of Israel as an event apart from the text can take the place of the meaning of the text of Scripture. To quote Sternberg once more, our task is to understand

> the text itself as a pattern of meaning and effect. What does this piece of language—metaphor, epigram, dialogue, tale, cycle, book—signify in context? What are the rules governing the transaction between storytell-

er or poet and reader? . . . What image of a world does the narrative project? Why does it unfold the action in this particular order and from this particular viewpoint? What is the part played by the omissions, redundancies, ambiguities, alternations between scene and summary or elevated and colloquial language? How does the work hang together?[28]

It may be helpful to give an example of where it appears that evangelical biblical scholarship has failed to see clearly this aspect of its commitment to an inspired text of Scripture and has looked beyond the text of Scripture in its exegesis to expound on the events behind the text. The most obvious example is that of the salvation-history school, an approach to biblical studies that was thoroughly evangelical in its origins[29] and continues to play an important role in evangelical theology. It cannot be said that everyone taking a salvation-history approach to the Old Testament necessarily overlooks the message of Scripture itself in favor of the meaning of the event. From the very beginning, however, that tendency can be seen within their writings. In an unusually perceptive article[30] Benjamim Warfield has focused the problem on what appears to be an equivocation of the meaning of the phrase *salvation history*. At times the notion of salvation history was taken to refer to the work of God in history, specific acts of redemption by which He has brought about His promised salvation. Thus salvation history is the history of what God did to effect man's salvation and not revelatory as such. This has been a common position among mainline evangelicals and that of Warfield himself. It is because of such a position that evangelicals have rightly raised their banner in the face of the critical challenge to the importance of the historicity of the biblical record. At the same time among evangelicals, however, the notion of salvation history was increasingly understood to refer to the revelation of the will of God in history, God's making known His will to man through concrete historical events. According to one early history-of-salvation theologian, Richard Rothe,[31]

> revelation consists fundamentally in the "manifestation" of God in the series of redemptive acts, by which God enters into natural history by means of an unambiguously supernatural and peculiarly divine history, and which man is enabled to understand and rightly to interpret by virtue of an inward work of the Divine Spirit.[32]

In this sense the salvation history is revelatory. It is true that when God works in history He inevitably makes Himself known, and thus revelation in history is a natural consequence of God's working in history. But the category of revelation alone is not sufficient to deal with the problems raised by the idea of salvation history. In order to show the limits of the revelation that comes out of this salvation history, Warfield argues, one must point to the work of inspiration. The important distinction lies in the final evaluation of the status of the text of Scripture as revelation. Here Scripture, as a text, is more than a mere record of God's revelatory acts. It is itself revelation. To quote Warfield:

> Scripture records the direct revelations which God gave to men in days past, so far as those revelations were intended for permanent and universal use. But it is much more than a record of past revelations. It is itself the final revelation of God, completing the whole disclosure of his unfathomable love to lost sinners, the whole proclamation of his purposes of grace, and the whole exhibition of his gracious provisions for their salvation.[33]

Such a view of Scripture in Warfield's own day was regarded as sheer biblicism and continually faced the unjust charge of being merely a "repristination" of the outmoded dictation theory of inspiration. Warfield was, of course, fully aware of the charge and in the face of it offers his critique of the early and influential history-of-salvation theologians J. C. K. Hofmann, Richard Rothe, and A. B. Bruce. Warfield was not alone in his opposition to the views of Rothe and von Hofmann, however. At least two other noted evangelical theologians entered into the debate: F. A. Philippi[34] and W. Rohnert.[35] Both argued strenuously against the tendency to reduce Scripture to the role of witness to revelation, rather than a source of revelation, by defending the orthodox identification of "revelation" and "Scripture." Even such representative evangelical theologians as K. F. A. Kahnis,[36] Friedrich A. G. Tholuck, and C. Ernst Luthardt had moved away from the orthodox notion that revelation rests in the written words of Scripture, largely under the influence of the prevailing interest in "Heilsgeschichte."[37]

Today, however, it remains just at this point, so deftly uncovered by Warfield years ago, that confusion still lies between viewing the text of Scripture as the source of revelation and viewing the text as a witness to the revelation that lies somewhere behind the text in the events of Israel's history. The confusion is simply this: The Old Testament, which is clearly and simply a text and as such gives a representation of an event, is often treated by contemporary evangelicals as if it were the event that it represents. Such a confusion is perpetuated when, in calling for a history of salvation, evangelicals use the words of earlier theologians who, like Rothe and von Hofmann, saw a revelation in the events lying behind the text, but at the same time, wanting to remain faithful to the orthodox view of Scripture as revelation, they identify that history with the text. In what can only be described as a complete collapse of the genre-category "text," biblical revelation is made synonymous with "that which happened in the history of Israel," and revelation is posited in an event.

The "biblical theology" of Geerhardus Vos[38] is a classical evangelical work and exhibits very clearly the kind of mixture of text and event that characterizes many recent evangelical salvation-history approaches to the Old Testament. For example, in his definition of biblical theology Vos lays out its task as "to exhibit the organic growth or development of the truths of Special Revelation from the primitive preredemptive Special Revelation given in Eden to the close of the New Testament canon."[39] Inasmuch as this is his definition of "biblical theology," what else can Vos mean than that it is possible to speak of a biblical theology already in the Garden of Eden? Can the word "biblical" here be related to the sense of the word "biblical" as it is used of the Bible as Scripture (text)? When he speaks of a biblical theology in the days of Adam and Eve, Vos shows that he has simply not made a distinction between any kind of special revelation in history and God's revelation of His will in the inspired Scriptures. Indeed Vos is clear that this is exactly his understanding of the sense of "biblical theology": It is any form of special revelation from the time before the Fall to the time of Christ. The point is not to criticize Vos's approach to biblical theology or his view of revelation. The point is to show how his salvation-historical approach has blurred his distinction between the Bible as a record of revelation and the Bible as that revelation itself. For Vos, revelation may go far beyond the scope of the text of Scripture. This category of "salvation history," which he had apparently inherited from earlier evangelicals such as von Hofmann, allowed him to see revelation in events quite apart from the text. At the same time his deep roots in Protestant orthodoxy kept him from severing completely his ties to the biblical text as revelation. Thus both forms of revelation found their way into his biblical theology but with two quite different bases. The one form of biblical theology received the title "biblical" because it focuses on the revelation of God recorded in the Bible (e.g., "Ur-Offenbarung"). The other form of biblical theology received its title from the fact that it focuses on the revelation of God that is the Bible itself. For example, in his biblical theology Vos's discussion of the patriarchs is not in categories derived from the Pentateuch as a text and its author but rather reveals his fundamentally historical orientation. The section is entitled "Revelation in the Patriarchal Period." The focus of his interest is not the author's representation of Abraham but revelation during the patriarchal period. He is interested in the religion of Abraham. Ironically, his approach is fundamentally the same as that of Albrecht Alt,[40] though his conclusions vary greatly from those of Alt. Thus, when it is necessary to explain Abraham's role in God's revelation during this period, Vos is quite comfortable to call to his aid archaeological research to show that God brought Abraham to Canaan because "it was actually a land where the lines of intercourse crossed. In the fulness of time its strategic position proved of supreme importance for the spreading abroad of the Gospel unto the whole earth."[41] Vos may be correct in this assessment of God's plan for Abraham and for Israel, but it cannot be disputed that Vos did not get such information from the text of Genesis. Such ideas about Canaan's strategic position in the ancient Near East are gained from a knowledge of the geography of the ancient world. They are not mediated through the words of Scripture, and Vos seems fully aware of this. From his perspective it makes no difference whether we have gained our understanding from Scripture alone or from both Scripture and archaeology, as long as the information is compatible. Vos's approach, which I take to be characteristic of many recent evangelical approaches to Scripture, is not one that has neglected Scripture in favor of a revelation in history. Rather, it is an approach that can only be described as a curious lack of distinction between the sense in which texts have meaning and the sense in which events have meaning. At the same time that he can recall recent archaeological evidence as a means of explaining God's actions with Abraham at the end of the third millennium B.C., Vos can, in fact, appeal to the text of Genesis 15:6 to show the centrality of faith in the life of Abraham,[42] a text that Vos himself takes to be written by Moses hundreds of years later. The only way such a treatment of the patriarchs can be held together is to say that Vos's idea of revelation includes but goes far beyond what we now have as the text of Scripture.

A more recent example of the same confusion of text and event is an excellent and helpful commentary to Genesis by John J. Davis.[43] In the comments to Genesis 11, Davis begins by paying close attention to the words of the text: "According to verse 1 all men spoke 'one [*'eḥāt*] language and one [*'ăḥādîm*] speech.'"[44] Then in his comment on 11:2, Davis halts over the meaning of the phrase "from the east" (*miqqedem*)—it could mean "from the east" or "eastward." To solve the dilemma of the text's meaning Davis turns to a consideration of the ethno-geographic history of the region. "Peoples in the region of Ararat (8:4) would have migrated to the Fertile Crescent, which would be southeast and east, as our text suggests."[45] Thus, he concludes, *miqqedem* means "eastward." Only in a footnote does he point to the use of *miqqedem* elsewhere in Genesis, and that only as an aside to his evidence from migrations in the Fertile Crescent. In the next four pages, commenting on the same chapter, Davis gives an extended description of Sumerian and Babylonian culture and religious practices, including a full-page photograph of "the Great Ziggurat at Ur." In no uncertain terms the meaning of Genesis 11:1-9 (that is, the meaning of the text) is here made to conform to what we know of early Mesopotamian culture and religion. The use of ziggurats in ancient Mesopotamia as shrines of the gods becomes the basis for Moses' meaning in Genesis 11: "If the Tower of Babel was indeed the prototype of the later ziggurats, then it may well have represented highhanded rebellion against the true God."[46] Alternatively, if a more military interpretation of the "tower" is offered, though "admissible on linguistic grounds,"[47] not only must it be rejected because "it seems to find no support from the context" (an argument from the text), but furthermore it must be rejected because it cannot be supported by evidence from the history of Mesopotamia: "It has not been determined that military defenses were this sophisticated in Mesopotamia by this time."[48]

The hermeneutical consequences of such a mixture of text and event can be seen in the fact that the process of construing the meaning of an event is not the same as that of construing the meaning of a text. One obvious difference between construing the meaning of a text and that of an event concerns the question of perspective. Events stand open to multiple perspectives. The meaning or sense of an event lies in the ability of the onlooker to gather the appropriate data and evaluate it from a certain vantage point. In texts, however, the reader is given a privileged perspective. He has the advantage of the guidance of the author and his perspective on the event. Thus the world of the event "reaches us through the mediation of words, selected and combined to form their own logic. . . . More generally, the narrator's mediation offers the reader a preinterpreted image of reality," whereas those who attempt to interpret an event find only the "raw materials on their hands."[49] For the evangelical the privileged perspective of the reader does not so much rest in the fact that he has only the perspective of the author to go on. That would be only making a virtue of necessity. Rather, it lies more importantly in the theological fact that the text, which gives the privileged perspective, is inspired.

What this all amounts to is the simple fact that behind texts stand authors who have rendered their intentions in texts, inspired texts in the case of the Bible. It is this simple fact that makes a text-oriented approach to exegesis and biblical theology so important for the evangelical. Our task is not that of explaining what happened to Israel in Old Testament times. Though worthy of our efforts, archaeology and history must not be confused with the task of exegesis and biblical theology. What must not be lost is the fact that the authors of Scripture have already made it their task to tell us in their texts what happened to Israel. The task that remains for us is that of explaining and proclaiming what they have written in their texts. The goal of a text-oriented approach is not revelation in history in the sense of an event that must be given meaning. Rather, the goal is a revelation in history in the sense of the meaning of a history recounted in the text of Scripture.

THE COMPOSITION OF THE TEXT OF SCRIPTURE

An emphasis on Scripture as a text means that one must pay closer attention to the way in which the text was written. Evangelical biblical scholars have been correct in pointing to the inadequacies of the standard critical views of the authorship of the biblical books. Indeed, in our day, even from within the ranks of biblical criticism itself, objection has been raised to the older critical views of authorship, views that looked entirely beyond existing biblical books to that of the authorship of the "sources" or "cycles of tradition."[50] It is not enough, however, for evangelicals to merely point out the inadequacies of critical views. If the Scriptures are to be taken seriously as texts, we must acknowledge that texts have authors and that authors go about their work in describable ways. Texts do not put themselves together. Whether we acknowledge it or not, behind every reading of a text lies a set of assumptions that one brings to a text about how the author has gone about his work. Evangelicals have said little about this important process of text formation. Certainly the right starting point is the acknowledgment that the authors of Scripture were "holy men of God" who were "borne along by the Holy Spirit" in their work of composing texts. But one must recognize that all interpretive procedures in exegesis and theology have embedded in them assumptions that go far beyond these general statements to specific assumptions about how the biblical authors actually went about their tasks. Until those assumptions have been uncovered and examined on the basis of the evidence from Scripture itself, evangelicals cannot make the claim that their approach to the text is any more adequate than that of the critics.

The activity of the biblical authors can be described from two vantage points. On the one hand they can be understood along with their ancient Near East counterparts, the scribes of the great literary cultures of Egypt and Mesopotamia, now including the scribal practices of Ebla as well. Such a text-external approach has proven of inestimable value,[51] at least in the beginning states of the work. Even if all the work were completed, a text-external approach to biblical authorship would not be sufficient to lay an adequate foundation for biblical exegesis. There is still further need of a text-internal, or text-immanent, description. One must move from a general description of the work of authors to a specific tracking of the steps taken by the biblical authors in specific biblical books. Yet here is where evangelicals seem to lag farthest behind. Evangelicals have excelled in areas such as history and archaeology, but we have hardly begun to broach some of the most basic questions directed at the nature of the authorship of the biblical books at texts. The question of authorship that faces the evangelical can be described under three general headings. First, we must investigate the smallest segments of the texts we now have to see what they tell us of the work and intention of the biblical authors, for example, small self-contained narratives like that of the city of Babylon in Genesis 11:1-9. Then we must be able to show how the author has grouped these smallest segments into literary units, such as the primeval history in Genesis 1-11. Finally, we have to show how these literary units are combined to form books and whole texts like the book of Genesis or the Pentateuch. Insofar as we say that the texts of Scripture have authors, we must seek to describe the nature of their composition from that of the smallest segment to that of the whole.

NOTES

1. "Unicum Theologiae principium esse Verbum Dei in Scripturis sacris propositum"; Johann Gerhard, *Locorum Theologicorum cum pro adstruenda veritate, tum pro destruenda quorumuis contradicentium falsitate, per theses nervose, solide et copiose explicatorum*, 1. De Scriptura sacra (Geneva, 1639), 1:1.

2. Christof Hardmeier, *Texttheorie und biblische Exegese* (Chr. Kaiser, 1978); Robert Oberforcher, *Die Flutprologe als kompositions-schluessel der biblischen Urgeschichte* (Tyrolia, 1981); Wolfgang Richter, *Grundlagen einer althebräischen Grammatik*, VIII, X, XIII (EOS, 1978-80); Harald Schweizer, *Metaphorische Grammatik: Wege zur Integration von Grammatik und Textinterpretation in der Exegese*, XIII (EOS, 1981); Franz Schicklberger, "Biblische Literarkritik und linguistische Texttheorie, Bemerkungen zu einer Textsyntax von Hebräischen Erzähltexten," *Theologische Zeitschrift* 34 (1978):65-81.

3. See Hardmeier, *Texttheorie*, pp. 29-34; Schicklberger, "Literarkritik," p. 66 n. 9; Siegfried J. Schmidt, *Texttheorie: Probleme einer Linguistik der sprachlichen Kommunikation* (Wilhelm Fink, 1976), pp. I-XVII.

4. See Schweizer, *Metaphorische Grammatik*; T. A. van Dijk, *Some Aspects of Text Grammars: A Study in Theoretical Linguistics and Poetics* (Mouton, 1972), pp. 130-62.

5. See Robert-Alain de Beaugrande and Wolfgang Dressler, *Introduction to Text Linguistics* (Longman, 1981); Elisabeth Guelich, and Wolfgang Raible, *Linguistische Textmodelle, Grundlagen und Möglichkeiten* (Wilhelm Fink, 1977); Klaus Heger, *Nomem, Wort, Satz und Text* (Max Niemeyer, 1976); Schmidt, *Texttheorie*.

6. See Schmidt, *Texttheorie*.

7. See Hardmeier, *Texttheorie*; Oberforcher, *Flutprologe*.

8. Stanislav Segert, "Prague Structuralism in American Biblical Scholarship: Performance and Potential," in *The Word of the Lord Shall Go Forth*, ed. C. L. Meyers and M. O'Connor (Winona Lake, Ind.: Eisenbrauns, 1983), pp. 697-708.

9. For excellent introductions to discourse analysis see Gillian Brown, *Discourse Analysis* (Cambridge: Cambridge U., 1983); Robert E. Longacre, *The Grammar of Discourse* (Plenum, 1983).

10. See John Sailhamer, "Exegetical Notes, Genesis 1:1-24a," *Trinity Journal* (1984):73-82.

11. Hans W. Frei, *The Eclipse of Biblical Narrative: A Study in Eighteenth and Nineteenth Century Hermeneutics* (New Haven, Conn.: Yale U., 1974), p. 10. In my judgment,

Frei's work has not received the attention it deserves among evangelicals. No doubt a large part of the reason is his negative evaluation of the historicity of the biblical narratives. Meir Sternberg's recent critique of Frei has suggested, however, that his negative evaluation of the biblical narratives' historical worth is merely an unacceptable corollary to an otherwise "reasonable claim" (*Poetics*, p. 81).

12. Manfred Öming, "Bedeutung und Funktionen von 'Fiktionen' in der alttestamentlichen Geschichtsschreibung," *Evangelische Theologie* (1984):254-66; Siegfried J. Schmidt, "Towards a Pragmatic Interpretation of 'Fictionality,'" in *Pragmatics of Language and Literature*, ed. T. A. van Dijk (1976), pp. 161-78; Sternberg, *Poetics*, pp. 23-35; Hayden White, "The Value of Narrativity in the Representation of Reality," *Critical Inquiry* 7 (1980):5-27.

13. Sternberg, *Poetics*, pp. 32-33.

14. It should be emphasized for clarity's sake that the issue being raised here is not the question of whether a text is historically accurate. In both senses of the term *history* the accuracy of the text is without question. Fictionalized history or historical fiction, both legitimate literary categories, are not here in view. Both categories are anachronistic when applied to the biblical narratives. One cannot overemphasize the importance of the apologetic task of demonstrating the accuracy of Scripture, but that is no reason to push the hermeneutical question of the meaning of the text aside. Both questions are of utmost importance. The present article, however, wishes to focus on the second. Nor is the issue raised here that which the neo-orthodox (more precisely the "pneumatischen Schriftausleger") would call the distinction between "Historie" and "Geschichte," where two kinds of history are posited: that which actually happened, and that which Israel believed.

15. Sternberg, *Poetics*, p. 15.

16. Emanuel Hirsch, *Geschichte der Neuern Evangelischen Theologie im Zusammenhang mit den allgemeinen Bewegungen des europäischen Denkens*, 5 vols. (C. Bertelsmann, 1949).

17. Ibid., 2:378.

18. Ibid., 2:377.

19. Ibid., 2:345-46.

20. The concept of an "Ur-Offenbarung" in the early Protestant theologies is a case in point (Paul Althaus, *Die christliche Wahrheit: Lehrbuch der Dogmatik* [Gütersloher Verlagshaus, 1972], pp. 51 ff.). Already Martin Chemnitz (1565) can base his argument on the assumption that "God has from the beginning of the world, both before and after the Fall, come forth from His hidden dwelling place, which is an unapproachable light, and has revealed Himself and His will to the human race by giving His sure Word and adding manifest miracles" (*Examination of the Council of Trent* (Concordia, 1971).

21. Hirsch, *Geschichte*, 2:379.

22. Ibid., 2:378.

23. Ibid., 2:370.

24. Horst Sephan and Martin Schmidt, *Geschichte der evangelischen Theologie in Deutschland seit dem Idealismus* (Walter de Gruyter, 1973), pp. 203-8.

25. Frei, *Eclipse*, pp. 66-104.

26. "For the older conservatives the unity and *Theopneustie* of the Bible had lain *in verbis*; for the newer ones it was *in re*, and the *res* in this instance was primarily and crucially historical in a dual sense: it was the sequence of outer biblical history as well as a supposed historical connectedness of its ideas and the outlooks they embodied. The con-

junction of *Theopneustie* with the developing history of religion within the Bible simply added an element of uncertainty to this situation. For the historical *res* or reference the stricter Supernaturalists had in mind was the actual occurrence of the supernatural events which the writers reported, whereas less strict but still conservative commentators added to it the history of Hebrew religion and interpretive tradition under divine guidance" (Frei, *Eclipse*, p. 92).

27. I do not mean this as a criticism of canon criticism as a methodology. On the contrary, the evangelical emphasis on an inspired Scripture makes the question of the canon of central theological importance. Evangelicals have tended to shy away from recent canonical approaches, however, because of their frequent acceptance of historical views inimical to the concept of inerrancy. For a positive canonical approach by an evangelical see Bruce K. Waltke, "A Canonical Process Approach to the Psalms," in *Tradition and Testament*, ed. J. Feinberg and P. Feinberg (Chicago: Moody, 1981).

28. Sternberg, *Poetics*, p. 15.

29. Hans-Joachim Kraus, *Die Biblische Theologie: Ihre Geschichte und Problematik* (Neukirchener, 1970) 240 ff.

30. Benjamin B. Warfield, "The Idea of Revelation and Theories of Revelation," in *Revelation and Inspiration* (Oxford: Oxford U., 1927; Grand Rapids: Baker, 1981), pp. 41-48.

31. Richard Rothe, *Zur Dogmatik* (Gotha, 1863).

32. Warfield, "Idea," p. 43.

33. Ibid., p. 48.

34. Friedrich A. Philippi, *Kirchliche Glaubenslehre*, 5 vols. (C. Bertelsmann, 1883), pp. 282 ff.

35. W. Rohnert, *Die Dogmatik der evangelisch-lutherischen Kirche* (Hellmuth Wollermann, 1902), pp. 41 ff.

36. Karl F. A. Kahnis, *Die lutherische Dogmatik historisch-genetisch dargestellt* (Doerffling and Franke, 1874), pp. 256 ff.

37. Rohnert, *Dogmatik*, pp. 103-105; Kahnis, *Dogmatik*, p. 256.

38. G. Vos, *Biblical Theology: Old and New Testaments* (Grand Rapids: Eerdmans, 1948).

39. Ibid., p. 5.

40. Albrecht Alt, "Der Gott der Väter," *Kleine Schriften zur Geschichte des Volkes Israel* (Munich: C. H. Beck'sche Verlagsbuchhandlung, 1959), 1:1 ff.

41. Vos, *Biblical*, p. 90.

42. Ibid., p. 96.

43. John J. Davis, *Paradise to Prison* (Grand Rapids: Baker, 1975).

44. Ibid., p. 144.

45. Ibid., p. 148.

46. Ibid.

47. Ibid.

48. Ibid.

49. Sternberg, *Poetics*, p. 162.

50. Rolf Rendtorff, *Das Alte Testament: Eine Einführung* (Neukirchener, 1983), pp. 169-73.

51. Donald J. Wiseman, "Books in the Ancient Near East and in the Old Testament," in *The Cambridge History of the Bible*, ed. P. R. Ackroyd (Cambridge: Cambridge U., 1970), 1:30-48.

DENNIS R. MAGARY (Ph. D. candidate, University of Wisconsin) is instructor of Old Testament and Semitic languages at Trinity Evangelical Divinity School.

18

A Select Bibliography of the Writings
of
Gleason Leonard Archer, Jr.

Dennis R. Magary

1947

Summary of "The Reception of Pindar in Germany During the Eighteenth Century." In *Summaries of Ph.D. Theses, Harvard University 1943-1945*. Cambridge, Mass.: Harvard U., 1947. Pp. 449-53.

"Why Jesus, Being God, Became Man." *Jewish Missionary Magazine* (June 1947):127-29, 140.

1951

"In the Shadow of the Cross." *Our Hope Magazine* 57 (February 1951): 461-67.

"In the Shadow of the Cross." *Our Hope Magazine* 57 (March 1951):553-60.

"In the Shadow of the Cross." *Our Hope Magazine* 57 (April 1951):632-35.

1952

Review of Stanley Rypins, *The Book of Thirty Centuries: An Introduction to Modern Study of the Bible*. New York: Macmillan, 1951. In *WTJ* (May 1952):201-3.

1957

In the Shadow of the Cross. Grand Rapids: Zondervan, 1957.
The Epistle to the Hebrews: A Study Manual. Shield Bible Study Series. Grand Rapids: Baker, 1957.

1959

Translation of Jerome's *Commentary on Daniel*. Grand Rapids: Baker, 1958.
"Bible Book of the Month: Micah." *Christianity Today* (17 February 1958):23-24, 38.
"The Militant Coinage of Early Islam." *The Numismatist Magazine* (February 1958):141-45.
Review of Merrill F. Unger, ed. *Unger's Bible Dictionary*. Chicago: Moody, 1957. In *Christianity Today* (21 July 1958):36.
Review of E. E. Ellis, *Paul's Use of the Old Testament*. Grand Rapids: Eerdmans, 1957. In *Eternity* (October 1958):36-38.

1959

The Epistle to the Romans: A Study Manual. Shield Bible Study Series. Grand Rapids: Baker, 1959.
Translation of Psalms 135-150. In *The Berkeley Bible*. Grand Rapids: Zondervan, 1959. Pp. 633-41.
"All Things for the Good of God's People." *Park Street Spire* (September 1959):4-8.
Review of Edward J. Young, *Who Wrote Isaiah?* Grand Rapids: Eerdmans, 1958. In *Christianity Today* (2 February 1959):35-36.
Review of H. L. Ellison, *Men Spake from God*. 2d ed. Grand Rapids: Eerdmans, 1958. In *WTJ* (November 1959):84-86.

1960

"Isaiah." In *The Biblical Expositor*. Edited by Carl F. H. Henry. Philadelphia: Holman, 1960. Vol. 2:123-62.

"Abandon," "Altar," "Covenant," "Temple." In *Baker's Dictionary of Theology*. Edited by Everett F. Harrison. Grand Rapids: Baker, 1960. Pp. 15, 38, 142-44, 513-14.

"Goliath," "Ishmael," "Jacob," "Midianites," "Moloch," "Solomon." In *World Book Encyclopedia*. Edited by J. Morris. Chicago: Field Enterprises, 1960.

Review of Gustavus S. Paine, *The Learned Men*. N.p.: Crowell, 1959. In *Christianity Today* (29 February 1960):39-41.

1962

"Isaiah." In *The Wycliffe Bible Commentary*. Edited by Charles F. Pfeiffer and Everett F. Harrison. Chicago: Moody, 1962. Pp. 605-54.

"Preacher Extraordinary." (A Tribute to Harold J. Ockenga.) *Park Street Spire* (January 1962):12-13.

Review of Leon Morris, *The Biblical Doctrine of Judgment*. Grand Rapids: Eerdmans, 1960. In *Christianity Today* (20 July 1962):42-43.

Review of Charles F. Pfeiffer, *The Patriarchal Age*. Grand Rapids: Baker, 1961. In *WTJ* 25 (November 1962):60-62.

1963

"Writing." In *The Zondervan Pictorial Bible Dictionary*. Edited by M. C. Tenney. Grand Rapids: Zondervan, 1963. Pp. 900-904.

"The Biblical Doctrine of Man and His Predicament." In *Things Most Surely Believed*. Edited by C. S. Roddy. Old Tappan, N.J.: Revell, 1963. Pp. 86-98.

1964

A Survey of Old Testament Introduction. Chicago: Moody, 1964.

1965

"Is the Old Testament Reliable?" *Moody Monthly* (October 1965):24-27.

Psychology for Living, "Your Only Foundation" Series. Pasadena, Calif.: Narramore Christian Foundation, 1965.

1966

"Old Testament Literature in 1965." *Christianity Today* (4 February 1966):7-11.

"Is the Old Testament Reliable?" *Evangelical Beacon* (12 April 1966):4-5.

Review of E. R. Thiele, *The Mysterious Numbers of the Hebrew Kings*. Grand Rapids: Eerdmans, 1965. In *Christianity Today* (15 April 1966):34-36.

1967

Review of E. H. Merrill, *An Historical Survey of the Old Testament*. Nutley, N.J.: Craig, 1966. In *Christianity Today* (26 May 1967):36-37.

1968

"Peoples of Bible Times." In *Holy Bible*. Family Heritage Edition. Philadelphia: Holman, 1968.

1969

"The Linguistic Evidence for the Date of Ecclesiates." *JETS* 12 (1969):167-81.

Review of Samuel J. Schultz, *The Prophets Speak*. New York: Harper, 1968. In *Christianity Today* (6 June 1969):22-23.

"Old Testament Study: Isaiah." In *Decision* (June 1969):5.

1970

"Micah." In *New Bible Commentary: Revised*. Edited by D. Guthrie and J. A. Motyer. Downers Grove, Ill.: InterVarsity, 1970. Pp. 752-61.

"The Aramaic of the *Genesis Apocryphon* Compared with the Aramaic of Daniel." In *New Perspectives on the Old Testament*. Edited by J. Barton Payne. Waco, Tex.: Word, 1970. Pp. 160-69.

"Old Testament History and Recent Archaeology from Abraham to Moses." *BibSac* 505 (January-March 1970):3-25.

"Old Testament History and Recent Archaeology from Moses to David." *BibSac* 506 (April-June 1970):99-115.

"Old Testament History and Recent Archaeology from Solomon to Zedekiah." *BibSac* 507 (July-September 1970):195-211.

"Old Testament History and Recent Archaeology from the Exile to Malachi." *BibSac* 508 (October-December 1970):291-98.

Review of G. Ernest Wright, *The Old Testament and Theology*. New York: Harper, 1969. In *Christianity Today* (22 May 1970):16-17.

1971

"Does Pacifism Have a Scriptural Basis?" *Evangelical Beacon* (28 December 1971):4-6.
Review of Alexander Jones, ed. *The Old Testament of the Jerusalem Bible*. Garden City, N.Y.: Doubleday, 1969. In *WTJ* 33 (May 1971):191-94.
"Old Testament Study: Jonah." *Decision* (June 1971):5.
"Old Testament Study: Micah." *Decision* (August 1971):5.

1972

"Old Testament Study: Haggai." *Decision* (March 1972):5.
"Old Testament Study: Genesis." *Decision* (August-December 1972):5.
"A New Look at the Old Testament." *Lutheran Alert National* (November 1972; reprint from *Decision*):11-12.
"A New Look at the Old Testament." *Lutheran Alert National* (December 1972; reprint from *Decision*):13-14.
"Das Habräische im Buch Daniel verglichen mit Schriften der Sekte von Qumran." Basel: Verlag Freie Evangelische-Theologische Akademie Basel, 1972.

1973

"A New Look at the Old Testament." *Lutheran Alert National* (January 1973; reprint from *Decision*):7, 9.
"A New Look at the Old Testament." *Lutheran Alert National* (February 1973; reprint from *Decision*):10-11.
"Old Testament Study: Genesis." *Decision* (January-August 1973).
"Old Testament Study: Genesis." *Decision* (September 1973):5.
Introduzione all' Antico Testamento. Modena: Vocedella Biblia, 1973.
"Harvard College Class of 1938." In *Thirty-Fifth Anniversary Report*. Cambridge, Mass.: Harvard U., 1973. P. 5.
"Nuevo Enfoque del Antiguo Testamento." *Decision* (May 1973):5, 13.
"Blasphemy," "False Witness," "Gods, False," "Hosea," "Isaiah," "Jeremiah." In *Baker's Dictionary of Christian Ethics*. Edited by Carl F. H. Henry. Grand Rapids: Baker, 1973. Pp. 64-65, 237, 265-66, 298-99, 339-41, 347.

1974

"Old Testament Study: Exodus." *Decision* (February-August, October-December 1974):5.

A Survey of Old Testament Introduction. Revised ed. Chicago: Moody, 1974.

"The Hebrew of Daniel Compared with the Qumran Sectarian Documents." In *The Law and the Prophets*. Edited by John H. Skilton. Nutley, N.J.: Presbyterian and Reformed, 1974. Pp. 470-81.

"Jesus Is Coming Again: Mid-Tribulation." In *When Is Jesus Coming Again?* Edited by Hal Lindsey. Carol Stream, Ill.: Creation House, 1974. Pp. 43-52.

"An Eighteenth Dynasty Rameses." *JETS* 17 (1974):49-50.

"Jesus Is Coming Again: Mid-Tribulation." *Christian Life* (May 1974):21, 68, 69.

1975

"Coins," "Cuneiform." In *Zondervan Pictorial Encyclopedia of the Bible* Edited by Merrill C. Tenney; Grand Rapids: Zondervan, 1975. Vol. 1:902-11, 1043-44.

"Please Explain — Questions on the Old Testament." *Decision* (January-December 1975):5.

"The Victory of the Cross." *The Church Herald* (21 March 1975):14-15, 26-28.

1976

"Please Explain — Questions on the Old Testament." *Decision* (January-November 1976):5.

"Please Explain — Questions on the Old Testament." *Decision* (December 1976):6.

1977

"Please Explain — Questions on the Old Testament." *Decision* (January-July 1977):5.

"Please Explain — Questions on the Old Testament." *Decision* (August-December 1977):13.

"The Right Battle." *Faith and Fellowship* (5 March 1977):4-7, 13.

"The Right Battle." *United Evangelical Action* (Spring 1977):6, 38.

"The Right Battle." *The Evangelical Beacon* (7 June 1977):6-7.

1978

"Please Explain — Questions on the Old Testament." *Decision* (January-August 1978):13.

"Please Explain — Questions on the Old Testament." *Decision* (September-December 1978):14.

Introduction a l'Ancien Testament. St. Legier, Switzerland: Editions Emmaus, 1978.

"The Witness of the Bible to Its Own Authority." In *The Foundation of Biblical Authority*. Edited by James Montgomery Boice. Grand Rapids: Zondervan, 1978. Pp. 85-99.

"Is Ararat Known?" *Eternity* (February 1978):28-29.

1979

"Please Explain — Questions on the Old Testament." *Decision* (January-December 1979):14.

Merece Confianca o Antigo Testamento. 2d ed. Sao Paolo, Brazil: Panorama de Introducao, 1979.

"Alleged Errors and Discrepancies in the Original Manuscripts of the Bible." In *Inerrancy*. Edited by Norman L. Geisler. Grand Rapids: Zondervan, 1979. Pp. 57-82.

"Contextualization: Some Implications from Life and Witness in the Old Testament." In *New Horizons in World Mission*. Edited by David J. Hesselgrave. Grand Rapids: Baker, 1979. Pp. 199-216.

"Dionysus," "Money," "Stumbling Block," "Talent," "Testament." In *International Standard Bible Encyclopedia*. 2d ed. Edited by Geoffrey W. Bromiley. Grand Rapids: Eerdmans, 1979. Vol. 1:944-45 ("Dionysus").

"The Metallic Sky: A Travesty of Modern Pseudo-Scholarship." *Journal of the American Scientific Affiliation* 31 (December 1979):220-21.

"Modern Rationalism and the Book of Daniel." *BibSac* 136 (April-June 1979):129- 47.

1980

"Please Explain — Questions on the Old Testament." *Decision* (January-December 1980):14.

"The Crucial Issue." *The Evangelical Beacon* (1 October 1980):8-10.

1981

Resena Critica de una Introduccion al Antiguo Testamento. Editorial Libertado. A. E. Sipowicz and M. F. Llievano. Chicago: Moody, 1981. Translation of the 1974 revised edition of *SOTI.*

"A Reassessment of the Value of the Septuagint of I Samuel for Textual Emendation in the Light of the Qumran Fragments." In *Tradition and Testament: Essays in Honor of Charles Lee Feinberg.* Edited by John S. Feinberg and Paul D. Feinberg. Chicago: Moody, 1981. Pp. 223-40.

"Eight Reasons Why Evangelicals Care About the Land of Israel." *The Evangelical Beacon* (1 September 1981):8, 10.

1982

The Book of Job: God's Answer to Undeserved Suffering. Grand Rapids: Baker, 1982.

Encyclopedia of Bible Difficulties. Grand Rapids: Zondervan, 1982.

1983

Old Testament Quotations in the New Testament: A Complete Survey. Co-authored with Gregory Chirichigno. Chicago: Moody, 1983.

1984

"To Whom It May Concern." *Moody Monthly* (January 1984):15-16.

"Abaddon," "Amen," "Covenant." In *Evangelical Dictionary of Theology* Edited by Walter A. Elwell. Grand Rapids: Baker, 1984. Pp. 1, 39, 276-78.

"The Case for the Mid-Seventieth-Week Rapture Position." In *The Rapture: Pre-, Mid-, or Post-Tribulational?* Co-authored with Paul D. Feinberg, Douglas J. Moo, and Richard R. Reiter. Grand Rapids: Zondervan, 1984. Pp. 113-45, 103-12, 213-21.

1985

"No Margin for Error." *Moody Monthly* (April 1985):23-25.

Subject Index

Author Index

Scripture Index

31:12-13	201
31:19, 35	26
32	26

Joshua

1:8	26
9:7	44
10:13	26
11:1-10	81
11:19	44
21:27	214
24:25-27	26

Judges

1:16	56
2:6—3:6	59, 77
2:11	60
2:14	60
3:7—16:31	54, 59
3:8-9	60
3:12-13	60
3:31	60
4	54-78
5	26, 54
5:4-5	107
5:10	42
5:20-21	68
5:31	76
6:5	148, 164
7:12	148, 164
8:14	26
8:21, 26	148
15:18	72
20:37	63

1 Samuel

1:2	180
1:5	189

1:6-7	180
2:9	216
13:21	189
20:31	39
30:17	148

2 Samuel

1:18	26
6:7	253
8:2	156
8:3-4	156
8:6	158
8:7-8	156
8:9-10	156
8:14	26, 156
10:15-19	155
10:25	26
17:12	240
19:43 [MT 44]	188
22	16
22:8-16	107
24:16	44

1 Kings

4:1-6	154
4:1-19	155
4:20-25	156
4:22-23	154
4:27-28	155
4:28	146
5:8-10	153
5:11	155
5:13-18	155
6-7	153
8:12-13	227
8:41-43	118
8:43	201
8:63	153

Moody Press, a ministry of the Moody Bible Institute, is designed for education, evangelization, and edification. If we may assist you in knowing more about Christ and the Christian life, please write us without obligation: Moody Press, c/o MLM, Chicago, Illinois 60610.